# MCAT 45

For more Kaplan books relating to

Medical School Admissions and the MCAT please visit

http://kaplanpublishing.com

# MCAT® 45

## Advanced Prep for Advanced Students

## Ninth Edition

The Staff of Kaplan Test Prep and Admissions

KAPLAN)

PUBLISHING

New York

© 2013 by Kaplan, Inc.

Published by Kaplan Publishing, a division of Kaplan, Inc.
395 Hudson Street
New York, NY 10014

Printed in the United States of America

10 9 8 7 6 5 4 3 2 1

ISBN: 978-1-60978-927-5

Kaplan Publishing books are available at special quantity discounts to use for sales promotions, employee premiums, or educational purposes. For more information or to purchase books, please call the Simon & Schuster special sales department at 866-506-1949.

## Section Three: Verbal Reasoning

# Contents

# The Perfect Score

Ah, perfection . . .

We humans are a demanding bunch. We don't bound out of bed in the morning aspiring to mediocrity, but rather striving for perfection. The perfect mate. The perfect job. The perfect shoes to go with the perfect outfit. We head to the beach on a perfect summer day to find the perfect spot to get the perfect tan.

Webster's Dictionary defines perfection as "the quality or state of being complete and correct in every way, conforming to a standard or ideal with no omissions, errors, flaws or extraneous elements."

The MCAT test makers define perfection as a score of 45.

If MCAT perfection is what you're after, then you've come to the right place. We at Kaplan have been training test takers to ace the MCAT for over 40 years. We understand your desire for the highest possible score. For those of you shooting for the moon, we salute your quest for perfection: The perfect MCAT score. The perfect medical school. The perfect career. Do we have the perfect book for you? You bet we do. You're holding it in your hands.

## WHO SHOULD USE THIS BOOK

We should warn you up front: This book is not for the faint at heart. It is composed exclusively of examples of the toughest material that you're likely to see on the MCAT. No easy stuff, no run-of-the-mill strategies—just killer passages and questions, complete with Kaplan's proven techniques to help you transcend "above average" and enter the rarefied arena of the MCAT elite. If you're entertaining the notion of pulling off the perfect 45, then you're going to have to face down the most brutal material that the MCAT test makers have to offer. We've compiled 35 of the toughest passages, and over 200 questions, to help you do just that, with complete explanations every step of the way.

This book is unique in the Kaplan series since we presume that you already have a strong knowledge base in the premed curriculum; we're assuming you have excelled in your studies. Content review is not a major component of this book. Instead, this book focuses on strategies for success on the exam in addition to practice passages and questions.

Even if a perfect score is not your immediate goal, diligent practice with the difficult material in this book can help develop your skills and raise your score. If you're looking for a more fundamental introduction to the MCAT, or practice with questions ranging from easy to difficult, then we recommend working through Kaplan's *New MCAT Premier Program*, which covers all the necessary science for the MCAT, and provides practice sets and full-length tests.

## HOW TO USE THIS BOOK

Each chapter of the book provides detailed guidelines on how to make the most of the material. Jump right to the chapter that gives you the most trouble, or work through the chapters in the order presented—it's up to you. You may want to start with chapter 2, "General Test Taking Strategies," which presents Kaplan's latest strategies for the computer-based test. Go on to chapter 3, "Approaching the Science Sections of the MCAT," where you'll learn about the three basic types of science passages and the four basic types of questions.

## Physical Sciences

| Scaled Score | Percent Achieving Score | Percentile Rank Range |
|---|---|---|
| 15 | 0.1 | 99.9–99.9 |
| 14 | 1.7 | 98.2–99.8 |
| 13 | 2.5 | 95.7–98.1 |
| 12 | 4.9 | 90.8–95.6 |
| 11 | 7.0 | 83.8–90.7 |
| 10 | 13.1 | 70.7–83.7 |
| 9 | 12.4 | 58.3–70.6 |
| 8 | 15.8 | 42.5–58.2 |
| 7 | 16.8 | 25.7–42.4 |
| 6 | 12.8 | 12.9–25.6 |
| 5 | 7.3 | 05.6–12.8 |
| 4 | 3.8 | 01.8–05.5 |
| 3 | 1.6 | 00.2–01.7 |
| 2 | 0.1 | 00.1–00.1 |
| 1 | 0.0 | 00.0–00.0 |

## Verbal Reasoning

| Scaled Score | Percent Achieving Score | Percentile Rank Range |
|---|---|---|
| 15 | 0.1 | 99.9–99.9 |
| 14 | 1.3 | 99.6–99.8 |
| 13 | 1.5 | 98.1–99.5 |
| 12 | 3.6 | 94.5–98.0 |
| 11 | 9.6 | 84.9–94.4 |
| 10 | 14.0 | 70.9–84.8 |
| 9 | 16.5 | 54.4–70.8 |
| 8 | 14.4 | 40.0–54.3 |
| 7 | 12.4 | 27.6–39.9 |
| 6 | 11.8 | 15.8–27.5 |
| 5 | 6.4 | 09.4–15.7 |
| 4 | 4.5 | 04.9–09.3 |
| 3 | 2.9 | 02.0–04.8 |
| 2 | 1.8 | 00.1–01.9 |
| 1 | 0.1 | 00.0–00.1 |

## Biological Sciences

| Scaled Score | Percent Achieving Score | Percentile Rank Range |
|---|---|---|
| 15 | 0.1 | 99.9–99.9 |
| 14 | 1.0 | 98.9–99.8 |
| 13 | 3.2 | 95.7–98.8 |
| 12 | 6.1 | 89.6–95.6 |
| 11 | 9.9 | 79.7–89.5 |
| 10 | 16.0 | 63.7–79.6 |
| 9 | 17.9 | 45.8–63.6 |
| 8 | 14.0 | 31.8–45.7 |
| 7 | 10.2 | 21.6–31.7 |
| 6 | 8.5 | 13.1–21.5 |
| 5 | 5.8 | 07.3–13.0 |
| 4 | 4.0 | 03.3–07.2 |
| 3 | 1.9 | 01.4–03.2 |
| 2 | 1.2 | 00.1–01.3 |
| 1 | 0.1 | 00.0–00.1 |

| | Total Score | | | | |
|---|---|---|---|---|---|
| Scaled Score | Percent Achieving Score | Percentile Rank Range | Scaled Score | Percent Achieving Score | Percentile Rank Range |
| 45 | 0.0 | 99.9–99.9 | 22 | 5.3 | 30.9–36.1 |
| 44 | 0.0 | 99.9–99.9 | 21 | 4.7 | 26.2–30.8 |
| 43 | 0.0 | 99.9–99.9 | 20 | 4.2 | 22.0–26.1 |
| 42 | 0.1 | 99.9–99.9 | 19 | 3.9 | 18.1–21.9 |
| 41 | 0.1 | 99.8–99.8 | 18 | 3.4 | 14.7–18.0 |
| 40 | 0.3 | 99.5–99.7 | 17 | 3.0 | 11.7–14.6 |
| 39 | 0.4 | 99.1–99.4 | 16 | 2.4 | 09.3–11.6 |
| 38 | 0.7 | 98.4–99.0 | 15 | 2.1 | 07.2–09.2 |
| 37 | 1.0 | 97.4–98.3 | 14 | 1.8 | 05.4–07.1 |
| 36 | 1.3 | 96.1–97.3 | 13 | 1.4 | 04.0–05.3 |
| 35 | 1.8 | 94.3–96.0 | 12 | 1.1 | 02.9–03.9 |
| 34 | 2.3 | 92.0–94.2 | 11 | 0.9 | 02.0–02.8 |
| 33 | 2.9 | 89.1–91.9 | 10 | 0.7 | 01.3–01.9 |
| 32 | 3.5 | 85.6–89.0 | 9 | 0.5 | 00.8–01.2 |
| 31 | 4.0 | 81.6–85.5 | 8 | 0.4 | 00.4–00.7 |
| 30 | 4.7 | 76.9–81.5 | 7 | 0.2 | 00.2–00.3 |
| 29 | 5.3 | 71.6–76.8 | 6 | 0.1 | 00.1–00.1 |
| 28 | 5.7 | 65.9–71.5 | 5 | 0.0 | 00.0–00.0 |
| 27 | 5.9 | 60.0–65.8 | 4 | 0.0 | 00.0–00.0 |
| 26 | 6.1 | 53.9–59.9 | 3 | 0.0 | 00.0–00.0 |
| 25 | 6.0 | 47.9–53.8 | 2 | 0.0 | 00.0–00.0 |
| 24 | 6.0 | 41.9–47.8 | 1 | 0.0 | 00.0–00.0 |
| 23 | 5.7 | 36.2–41.8 | | | |

# REGISTRATION

The only way to register for the MCAT is online. The registration site is:

www.aamc.org/mcat

Go to www.aamc.org/students/mcat/start.htm and download *MCAT Essentials* for information about registration, fees, test administration, and preparation. For other questions, contact:

MCAT Care Team
Association of American Medical Colleges
Section for Applicant Assessment Services
2450 N St., NW
Washington, DC 20037
Email: mcat@aamc.org

## AAMC PUBLICATIONS

For a complete listing of MCAT product descriptions, view AAMC student publications at www.aamc.org. Online access is available for tests 3, 4, 5, 7, 8, 9, 10, and 11. Test 3 is free, and the others are available for purchase.

You can purchase these publications at most college bookstores or order them directly from AAMC by going online to www.aamc.org or by writing AAMC at:

> Association of American Medical Colleges
> Attn: Membership and Publication Orders
> 2450 N Street, NW
> Washington, DC 20037

## PREPARING FOR THE MCAT

As you can see, it's important to maximize your performance on every question. Just a few questions one way or the other can make a big difference in your scaled score.

We recommend that you take one year each of courses in biology, general chemistry, organic chemistry, and physics prior to taking the MCAT, and that you review the content in this book thoroughly and supplement it as needed from your textbooks. However, knowing these basics is just the beginning of doing well on the MCAT. You should take as many practice tests on the computer as possible. Kaplan's *MCAT Premier* is a personalized study program that integrates online practice with a comprehensive review book. In addition, its online practice tests will familiarize you with the MCAT computer interface.

Learning and applying the Kaplan methods and strategies outlined in this book will build your skills and confidence. When you're familiar with them, practice with all the materials available from the AAMC and Kaplan, working consistently throughout your preparation period. You can't be assured that your actual score will be predicted by your score on any practice test, but the score you'll get on a practice test is less important than the practice itself. Getting your best score will require lots of practice and skill building. Let's get started!

CHAPTER 2

# General Test Taking Strategies

In this chapter you will find general strategies for reading passages and answering questions. You will also find strategies for developing and maintaining a positive attitude, plus tips on how to be prepared for Test Day conditions.

It's a good idea to read this chapter closely, even if you are already scoring well on practice tests. You will find some useful nuggets of information that can help you edge your score upward.

## READING PASSAGES

Your goal from the outset of the passage is to figure out what the author is saying and how ideas are linked. Every passage contains a main idea, and when you're done reading, you should be able to state it in your own words. Answering the questions successfully depends on your ability to quickly glean the author's point and to map out the passage in your mind. Don't be afraid to take a few brief notes on scratch paper as you read—nothing lengthy. You can highlight information on the computer screen. As you read through MCAT passages, try to articulate the main idea to yourself. Read actively and critically. Consider what the author is trying to say and how the ideas are communicated. Pause between paragraphs to digest what you've read and put the ideas into your own words.

When you study for college exams, you usually commit lots of data and information to memory so that you can recite it on the test. The MCAT isn't like this at all. True, you have to master a lot of conceptual material, but you don't have to memorize complicated equations such as Bernoulli's principle, or know the value of the ideal gas constant R. When reading a passage, there is no need to commit its details to memory. You will be able to look them up in the passage when you need them. It's more important to understand why the details are there than to memorize them.

Some test takers feel more anchored as they read the passage if they've scoped out the questions first. As a general rule, it won't save you time or effort to do so.

# FACING THE QUESTIONS

Be sure that you understand the question before you move to the answer choices. Otherwise, you'll be vulnerable to persuasive but incorrect choices. One of the biggest mistakes that high-scorers make when they practice MCAT questions is carelessness. Practice makes permanence: Treat every practice question as if it were the real thing.

In general, if you need an important detail on an MCAT question, it will be provided by the question or the passage. If you've followed the advice this book has to offer on how to read passages, then you will not be wasting your time when, on Test Day, you go back to the passage to look up details that you need to answer questions.

If you don't know an answer, guess! Do this while you're still working on the passage, so you won't have to reread it later. There's no penalty for wrong answers on the MCAT. Only a very few people are able to answer every single question correctly. If you get to a question that tests specific knowledge you do not possess, skim the choices carefully to see if you can glean any clues or information from them. If not, guess quickly, don't look back, and move on.

Use the structure of a Roman numeral question to your advantage. Eliminate choices as soon as you find them to be inconsistent with the truth or falsehood of a statement in the stimulus. Similarly, consider only those choices that include a statement that you've already determined to be true. Remember that you don't have to consider the statements in order. Knowing about any one of them will get you off to a great start answering the question, so if you're unsure about the first statement, go on to the second or third. You will have plenty of opportunity to practice your Roman numeral strategy on the subject practice tests in Section 2 of this book.

# COMPUTER-BASED TESTING STRATEGIES

## Arrive at the Testing Center Early

Get to the testing center early to jump-start your brain. However, if the center allows you to begin your test early, decline.

## Use the Mouse to Your Advantage

If you are right-handed, practice using the mouse with your left hand for Test Day. This way, you'll increase speed by keeping the pencil in your right hand to write on your scratch paper. If you are left-handed, learn to use your right hand for the mouse.

## Know the Tutorial Before Test Day

You will save time on Test Day by knowing exactly how the test will work. Click through any tutorial pages and save time.

## Practice with Scratch Paper

Going forward, always practice using scratch paper when solving questions because this is how you will do it on Test Day. Never write directly on a written test.

## Get New Scratch Paper

Between sections, get a new piece of scratch paper even if you used only part of the old one. This will maximize the available space for each section and minimize the likelihood of your running out of paper to write on.

## Mark Incomplete Work

If you need to go back to a question, clearly mark the work you've done on the scratch paper with the question number. This way, you will be able to find your work easily when you come back to tackle the question.

## Look Away at Times

Taking the test on computer leads to faster eye-muscle fatigue. Use the Kaplan strategy of looking at a distant object at regular intervals. This will keep you fresher at the end of the test.

## Practice on the Computer

This is the most critical aspect of adapting to computer-based testing. Like anything else, in order to perform well on computer-based tests you must practice. Spend time reading passages and answering questions on the computer. You often will have to scroll when reading passages.

# PACING

Remember that every question is of equal value, so don't get hung up on any one of them. Think about it—if a question is so hard that it takes you a long time to answer it, chances are you may get it wrong anyway. In that case, you'd have nothing to show for your extra time but a lower score, and less time for other questions.

Don't feel that you have to understand everything in a passage before you go on to the questions. You may not need a deep understanding to answer questions, since a lot of information may be extraneous. You should overcome your perfectionism and use your time wisely.

You will see that you have about eight to nine minutes per passage on Verbal Reasoning and eight minutes per passage on Physical and Biological Sciences. On Test Day, some passages will be harder and longer, and others easier and shorter.

# BASIC PRINCIPLES OF GOOD TEST MENTALITY

Knowing the test content arms you with the weapons you need to do well on the MCAT. But you must wield those weapons with the right frame of mind and in the right spirit.

## Test Awareness

To do your best on the MCAT, you must always keep in mind that this test is like no other test you've taken before, both in terms of content and in terms of the scoring system. If you took a test in high school or college and got a number of the questions wrong, you wouldn't receive a perfect score. But on the MCAT, you can get a handful of questions wrong and still get a "perfect" score. The test is geared so that only the very best test takers are able to finish every section. But even these people rarely get every question right.

What does this mean for you? Well, just as you shouldn't let one bad passage ruin an entire section, you shouldn't let what you consider to be a subpar performance on one section ruin your performance on the entire test. If you allow that subpar performance to rattle you, it can have a cumulative negative effect, setting in motion a downward spiral. It's that kind of thing that could potentially do serious damage to your score. Losing a few extra points won't do you in, but losing your cool will.

Remember, if you feel you've done poorly on a section, don't sweat it. Chances are it's just a difficult section, and that factor will already be figured into the scoring curve. The point is, remain calm and collected. Simply do your best on each section, and once a section is over, forget about it and move on.

## Confidence

Confidence feeds on itself and, unfortunately, so does the opposite of confidence—self-doubt. Confidence in your ability leads to quick, sure answers and a sense of well-being that translates into more points. If you lack confidence, you end up reading the sentences and answer choices two, three, or four times, until you confuse yourself and get off track. This leads to timing difficulties, which only perpetuate the downward spiral, causing anxiety and a tendency to rush in order to finish sections.

If you subscribe to the MCAT mindset we've described, however, you'll gear all of your practice toward the major goal of taking control of the test. When you've achieved that goal—armed with the principles, techniques, strategies, and approaches set forth in this book—you'll be ready to face the MCAT with supreme confidence. And that's the one sure way to score your best on Test Day.

## The Right Attitude

It may sound a little dubious, but take our word for it: Attitude adjustment is a proven test taking technique. Here are a few steps you can take to make sure you develop the right MCAT attitude:

- Look at the MCAT as a challenge, but try not to obsess over it; you certainly don't want to psyche yourself out of the game.
- Remember that, yes, the MCAT is obviously important, but, contrary to what some premeds think, this one test will not single-handedly determine the outcome of your life.
- Try to have fun with the test. Learning how to match your wits against the test makers can be a very satisfying experience, and the reading and thinking skills you'll acquire will benefit you in medical school as well as in your future medical career.
- Remember that you're more prepared than most people. You've trained with Kaplan. You have the tools you need, plus the know-how to use those tools.

# THE DAY BEFORE TEST DAY

This is not the time to be working on a new full-length practice test—relax! Instead of studying, do something fun but low-key. Make sure that you know how to get to the test center; rehearse the drive, if necessary. Have a quiet, relaxing evening, and go to bed early.

# TEST DAY: THE COMFORT ZONE

Get a good night's sleep the evening before the exam. Wake up early, so that you aren't rushed. Prepare your admission ticket and one form of government-issued identification containing both a photo and a signature (such as a driver's license or passport). While eating breakfast on the day of the MCAT, jump-start your brain by reading something unrelated to the test.

Be sure to arrive at the testing center 30 minutes before your appointment time to check in. You won't be able to bring anything into the exam room. (You will be allowed to wear a watch.) A locker and lock will be provided for you to store your belongings during the test. (Cell phones must be turned off while in lockers.) You can request a noise-reducing headset from a test administrator to help you concentrate. There will be up to 16 other test takers in the exam room.

With these strategies in mind, let's now turn to the test itself for specific approaches for handling each section.

section two

# PHYSICAL SCIENCES AND BIOLOGICAL SCIENCES

CHAPTER 3

# Approaching the Science Sections of the MCAT

In Section One we took a look at the MCAT, gave some advice for coping with stress, and learned some general test taking strategies. In this section, we will focus on the science portions of the MCAT, providing specific advice for reading the passages and handling the questions associated with each of the four sciences. Each chapter contains seven practice passages that will allow you to put this advice into practice. Concluding each chapter is a list of specific concepts and skills you should have mastered before Test Day.

In this chapter we offer some general advice for tackling science passages and questions. But first, let's review the structure of the two science sections on the MCAT: Physical Sciences and Biological Sciences.

## THE SCIENCE SECTIONS

The Physical Sciences and the Biological Sciences sections last 70 minutes each. Each has 52 questions: approximately 13 discrete questions, which stand alone from passages, and 39 passage-based questions. Each section has 7 passages. The Physical Sciences section usually splits evenly between Physics questions and General Chemistry questions. However, the split between Biology questions and Organic Chemistry questions in the Biological Sciences section isn't always the same. Typically, the questions split 75–25 in favor of Biology; however, this is not always the case.

In Section One we gave some general advice on how to handle MCAT passages. On the science portions of the test, it is true that having a core knowledge in the basic concepts in the four sciences on the MCAT is very important to scoring well on Test Day. However, shrewd, sophisticated premedical students will want the extra edge needed to maximize their MCAT score. It is the purpose of the remainder of this book to provide you with that edge.

What we're talking about is test taking strategy. Not just "eat a good breakfast" and "don't burn out before Test Day" (both of which happen to be good pieces of advice), but specific pearls of wisdom organized by science (with corresponding advice for Verbal Reasoning to follow). Many people see the MCAT as purely a content-based test: know your stuff and a good score should follow. Those people are surprised to learn that, in general, they should read a Physics passage much differently than an Organic Chemistry passage.

Test taking strategy on the science portions of the MCAT can be divided into two major areas: Absorbing the passages, and handling the questions. Before diving into science-specific advice in subsequent chapters, let's build a framework around these two ideas.

# ABSORBING THE MCAT SCIENCE PASSAGE

## Passage Types

One of the first things you'll want to do when absorbing a science passage is to identify what type of passage you're reading. MCAT science passages fall into three broad categories:

*Information*

*Experiment*

*Persuasive Argument*

*Information* passages resemble a textbook. They often include diagrams, but are largely paragraphs of dry description. Information passages describe natural or manmade phenomena.

Here's an example of an Organic Chemistry information passage:

> Aspirin, also known as acetylsalicylic acid, is one of the most useful and economical drugs available. It belongs to a class of drugs known as nonsteroidal anti-inflammatory drugs, and can be used to treat pain and alleviate inflammation and fever. The mechanism of aspirin's action is not fully understood, although recent research suggests that it functions by inhibiting cyclooxygenase-2, an enzyme that creates prostaglandin precursors. Prostaglandins contribute to the body's perception of pain and its inflammatory response. Prostaglandins also aid in the formation of blood clots, so aspirin thins the blood and may consequently help prevent heart disease.

> Aspirin can be synthesized from salicylic acid via the reaction shown in Figure 1.

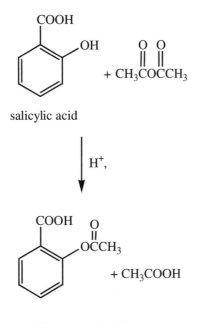

salicylic acid

**Figure 1**   Aspirin

Both salicylic acid and aspirin are aromatic carboxylic acids. Carboxylic acids are generally weak acids, although they are among the strongest organic acids, with $pK_a$'s usually in the range of 3 to 5, much lower than those of corresponding alcohols. The $pK_a$'s of some compounds are given in Table 1.

**Table 1**   $pK_a$'s of Compounds

| Compound | $pK_a$ |
|---|---|
| Acetic acid | 4.76 |
| Fluoroacetic acid | 2.66 |
| Difluoroacetic acid | 1.24 |
| Trifluoroacetic acid | 0.23 |
| 2,2-Dimethylpropanoic acid | 5.05 |
| Benzoic acid | 4.18 |
| p-Nitrobenzoic acid | 3.43 |
| 2,4,6-Trinitrobenzoic acid | 0.65 |
| p-Methoxybenzoic acid | 4.47 |
| Phenol | 9.95 |
| Ethanol | 15.9 |
| Methanol | 15.1 |
| Water | 14 |

*Experiment* passages describe one (or more) experiments, and have clear goals. Something is varied, something else is measured, and conclusions can be formed. Sometimes an experiment passage focuses on a table or a graph giving the results of the experiment, and sometimes the passage focuses on the experimental apparatus.

This is an example of a Physics experiment passage:

The mass spectrometer is a device that utilizes electric and magnetic fields to determine the masses of the elements or compounds that exist within a certain sample. The operation of the mass spectrometer relies on the fact that the path of a moving charge is affected by the presence of electric and magnetic fields.

To analyze a sample, it must first be ionized. This may be accomplished by bombarding it with a stream of electrons. The ionized particles are then accelerated through a potential difference of several thousand volts that is set up between two slits $S_1$ and $S_2$ (see Figure 1 below). For the mass spectrometer to give useful results, all the particles entering the chamber below $S_3$ must be traveling at the same velocity. This is ensured by passing the particles through a *velocity selector*, a region of a crossed magnetic field, $B$, and an electric field, $E$, located between $S_2$ and $S_3$. This electric field is produced by two charged parallel plates, $P_1$ and $P_2$. Only particles that are traveling at a velocity such that the force due to the electric field ($qE$) and that due to the magnetic field ($qvB$) cancel one another will remain undeflected and pass through the slit in $S_3$.

The stream of charged particles then passes though another magnetic field, $B'$, but this time, there is no electric field. The second magnetic field is perpendicular to the page, and deflects the particles in a circular path, toward the detector. Based on the radius of curvature of the path of the particle, its mass can be determined from the formula:

$$\frac{q}{m} = \frac{E}{rBB'}$$

where q is the charge of the particle, m is the mass of the particle, E is the electric field, and r is the radius of the circular path of the particle. In the mass spectrometer below, $E = 8 \times 10^4$ V/m, 0.4 T, and B' = 0.5 T. The fundamental unit of charge is $1.6 \times 10^{-19}$ C.

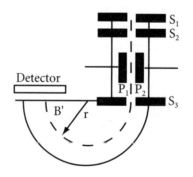

**Figure 1**   Mass Spectrometer

*Persuasive argument* passages present contrasting viewpoints on a subject. The typical format is for the passage to introduce a phenomenon, and then present the differing viewpoints or hypotheses. Answering the accompanying questions correctly will then rely on your understanding the similarities of and the differences between the hypotheses.

The following is an example of a Biology persuasive argument passage:

> *Alzheimer's disease* is a neurological condition that results in degeneration of the brain. Two forms of the disease exist: a hereditary form, which is characterized by early onset of symptoms, usually when the patients are in their forties, and a late-developing form of the disease, called senile dementia, which may not be of genetic origin. Two current hypotheses describing possible mechanisms of hereditary Alzheimer's disease are outlined below.

> *Hypothesis A*
> Alzheimer's disease is a result of a mutation in the gene encoding amyloid precursor protein (APP). APP usually gives rise to a smaller protein known as beta–amyloid, which is a major component of the abnormal plaques that are a feature of Alzheimer's pathology. The presence of these plaques is the cause of the neuronal deterioration associated with the disease.

> The mutation results in the insertion of an isoleucine residue in place of a valine residue. The mutation interferes with normal APP function, causing membrane degeneration and enhancing beta–amyloid release. The increase in beta amyloid release promotes the formation of the Alzheimer's-causing plaques.

> *Hypothesis B*
> Alzheimer's disease is a result of a mutation in the gene encoding a protein called *acetylcholinesterase*, the enzyme responsible for the breakdown of the neurotransmitter acetylcholine. A comparison of the abnormal acetylcholinesterase to the normal acetylcholinesterase reveals that the mutant enzyme is 30 amino acids shorter. The mutation inactivates acetylcholinesterase, resulting in a buildup of acetylcholine in the neurons. A high level of acetylcholine blocks impulse transmission from one neuron to another, resulting in a loss of cholinergic nerve terminals in the cerebral cortex; thus, Alzheimer's disease is promoted. The consequence of cholinergic nerve degradation is a buildup of beta–amyloid–containing plaques.

# Reading the Passage

One of the traps that many test takers fall into is spending too much time reading the passages. They waste effort trying to retain every fact and detail introduced, and to understand every aspect of the phenomenon or experiment described. This is especially true of students who have performed very well in school, who expect to master everything. However, this type of reading will *not* pay off on an MCAT science passage.

First, keep in mind that the same passage may appear on different test forms *with slightly different sets of questions*. So, something that baffles you may not even be touched on by the questions. There is certainly no point in wasting time trying to figure out something that ultimately does not win you any points on the test. Second, the data and information from the passage are always there if you need them. For example, the mass of the block sliding down an inclined plane, the melting point of an unknown compound isolated in a reaction, or the value of the gas constant $R$ can be retrieved from the passage *when you need it to answer a question.*

### Mapping the Passage

The key to efficient, critical reading of an MCAT science passage lies in creating a *passage map*. The idea of mapping a passage lies *in reading for structure*. Instead of trying to memorize everything, take a broad look at what is happening in the passage. Come out of each paragraph with a grasp on what is going on. Identify the role of each "structural component" of the passage by asking yourself: "What is this diagram/table/equation doing here?" At the beginning of your MCAT preparation, you should write down the main idea of each paragraph explicitly on scratch paper.

In subsequent chapters, the technique of mapping a passage and jotting down notes on key elements is illustrated for each of the four science areas and for each passage type.

### Identifying the Topic

In addition to mapping the passage, you should also identify the topic of the passage. However, determining the topic involves more than just coming up with a scientific term corresponding to the main subject of the passage. To identify the topic, you should answer the question, "What is the author trying to accomplish in this passage?" Being able to formulate an answer to this question means that you have read the passage critically. The answer to this question is what we mean by the topic of the passage.

The topic of a passage is related to the passage type. For an information passage, for example, the topic usually takes the following form:

> *The passage describes/discusses ...*

The topic of an experiment passage can usually be phrased as follows:

> *The passage is about an experiment, the purpose of which is to ...*

The topic of a persuasive argument passage usually has the following form:

> *The passage presents (some number of) hypotheses about ...*

## HANDLING THE QUESTIONS

Once we have made our passage map, we'll begin handling the questions. The first thing to do as we encounter a question is to classify it. This step is crucial, as it will help us answer the question in the quickest, most efficient manner. Each question will fall into one of the following four categories:

1. Discrete questions
2. Questions that require an understanding of the passage
3. Questions for which we need only data from the passage
4. Questions that can stand alone from the passage

Let's discuss these question types and look at an example of each.

1. Discrete questions are those that do not follow any passage and are always preceded by a header such as "Questions 48 through 52 are NOT based on a descriptive passage." Since they do not accompany a passage, all the information needed to answer these questions will be found in the question stem, the answer choices, and your outside knowledge. For example, to answer the following question, you need only your outside knowledge of periodic trends:

> Which of the following properties generally decreases as one goes from left to right across the periodic table?
>
> **A.** Number of neutrons
>
> **B.** Electronegativity
>
> **C.** Atomic weight
>
> **D.** Atomic radius

The final three question types will always follow a passage:

2. Questions that require an understanding of the passage cannot be answered without having read the passage. These questions usually follow experiment or persuasive argument passages, though they may follow information passages. A question may ask us to evaluate experiments or hypotheses presented in the passage and will require us to have a conceptual understanding of topics discussed in the passage. For example, it would be virtually impossible to answer the following question correctly if we had not closely read the passage about Alzheimer's disease:

> In which of the following ways does Hypothesis A differ from Hypothesis B?
>
> **A.** Hypothesis A describes the mechanism of hereditary Alzheimer's; Hypothesis B describes the mechanism of senile dementia.
>
> **B.** Hypothesis A argues for the formation of beta–amyloid–containing plaques; Hypothesis B argues against the formation of beta–amyloid–containing plaques.
>
> **C.** Hypothesis A assumes beta–amyloid–containing plaques are the cause of Alzheimer's; Hypothesis B assumes beta–amyloid–containing plaques are the result of Alzheimer's.
>
> **D.** Hypothesis A claims that neuronal cells deteriorate in Alzheimer's; Hypothesis B claims that neuronal cells are only rendered dysfunctional.

We may have some outside knowledge of Alzheimer's disease, but reading the passage is still the best way to answer this question, since our outside knowledge may or may not be applicable to the specific hypotheses presented in this passage. For questions that require knowledge of the passage, we must adhere to the logic of the passage, even if it contradicts our outside knowledge.

3. Questions for which we need only data from the passage are similar to understanding questions in that the passage provides necessary information, but in this case, we need only refer to the passage for a piece of data. We are not required to have read the surrounding prose in order to answer these questions correctly. We will usually be referring to a table or an equation. One example of this type of "data question" could follow the physics passage we read about the mass spectrometer:

What is the force on a singly charged ion due to the electric field between plates $P_1$ and $P_2$?

**A.** $6.4 \times 10^{-20}$ N

**B.** $8.0 \times 10^{-20}$ N

**C.** $8.0 \times 10^{-15}$ N

**D.** $1.3 \times 10^{-14}$ N

In order to answer this question, we need to refer to the data in the passage, but we don't need to have read or understood the prose in the passage. Once we have found the piece of data we need, we can just plug it in to whatever equations and formulas we are using to get the correct answer.

4. Questions that can stand alone from the passage ("pseudodiscretes") are those that follow a passage but are in all other ways discrete questions. They require absolutely no knowledge of information from the passage, and are only related to the passage by their subject. The following question, for example, could follow the passage we read earlier about aspirin:

Which of the following best accounts for the higher acidity of phenol compared to ethanol?

**A.** Phenol is hydrophobic.

**B.** Phenol has a higher molecular weight.

**C.** The benzene ring of phenol stabilizes negative charge.

**D.** The oxygen atom in phenol is $sp^2$-hybridized.

Even though this question follows the aspirin passage, it is basically a discrete question about the acidity of organic compounds. No knowledge of the passage is necessary to answer it correctly.

## Answering the Questions

When answering the questions, go through the following steps:

- Understand what you are being asked.
- Figure out where to go to get any information that you need.
- Integrating your science knowledge with any necessary passage research, determine the correct answer.

### Understand what you are being asked.

The first thing to do is read the entire question, including the answer choices. Reading the answer choices can help you focus your thoughts if the question stem by itself doesn't look particularly manageable. Using your reading comprehension skills, simplify the question to its bare essentials. Translate the question into your own words if necessary. Use the answer choices to help you. Does the question ask for a numerical answer (e.g., "What is the tension in the rope?"), a distinct piece of information (e.g., "What type of reaction is illustrated in the figure below?"), or a sentence (e.g., "Why did the scientist add liver extract to the sample in Experiment 2?")?

Let's look at one of the sample questions presented earlier.

> What is the force on a singly charged ion due to the electric field between plates $P_1$ and $P_2$?
>
> A. $6.4 \times 10^{-20}$ N
> B. $8.0 \times 10^{-20}$ N
> C. $8.0 \times 10^{-15}$ N
> D. $1.3 \times 10^{-14}$ N

Simplify/translate the question: what is it asking? Here you are asked to calculate the force due to an electric field on a particle.

### Figure out where to go to get any information that you need.

Do you have enough information to answer the question? Do you need information from the passage? If so, where in the passage can you find it? From your map of the passage, you should be able to quickly locate any information that you may need.

> What is the force on a singly charged ion due to the electric field between plates $P_1$ and $P_2$?
>
> A. $6.4 \times 10^{-20}$ N
> B. $8.0 \times 10^{-20}$ N
> C. $8.0 \times 10^{-15}$ N
> D. $1.3 \times 10^{-14}$ N

To calculate the force due to an electric field on a particle, you need to know the formula for the force on an electric charge in an electric field (outside knowledge). You also need to know the electric field strength and the charge on a singly charged ion—both provided by the passage. From your passage map, you should know where to get this information.

### Integrating your science knowledge with any necessary passage research, determine the correct answer.

This is the step where you bring together all the previous steps along with your science knowledge to determine the correct answer. Prior to arriving at this step, you need to understand what you are being asked and gather any information you may need from the passage. Once these tasks are accomplished, use your reasoning and/or calculation skills together with your science knowledge to arrive at the answer.

Try to formulate your own explanation before going through the answer choices.

What is the force on a singly charged ion due to the electric field between plates $P_1$ and $P_2$?

A.   $6.4 \times 10^{-20}$ N

B.   $8.0 \times 10^{-20}$ N

C.   $8.0 \times 10^{-15}$ N

D.   $1.3 \times 10^{-14}$ N

From your outside knowledge of physics, recall that the formula needed in this case is $F = qE$, where q is the charge on a singly charged ion and $E$ is the electric field strength. From the passage, q is $1.6 \times 10^{-19}$ C and the electric field strength is $E = 8 \times 10^4$ V/m. Carrying through the calculation, we get $1.28 \times 10^{-14}$ N, which is closest to choice **D**.

CHAPTER 4

# Physics

The one thing that you want to keep in mind as you tackle the Physics passages is that the MCAT is only asking you to apply a basic set of physics principles. The test certainly isn't asking you to push the boundaries of known science. As a result, your success on the Physics questions on the MCAT will depend in large part on your *mastery* of the concepts of physics. At the end of this chapter is a list of the physics skills and concepts you should have in your arsenal by Test Day.

But although mastery of physics is an important ingredient to MCAT success, it isn't the only ingredient. You will want to be familiar with the test, with how the physics is tested. The better prepared you are for what you are going to see, the more confident you will feel on Test Day. The purposes of this chapter are to show you how the MCAT sets up Physics passages, to show you what kinds of Physics questions to expect, and to describe an efficient, time-saving method for tackling both Physics passages and Physics questions on Test Day.

## READING THE PASSAGE

One of the worst things you can do as a test taker is to approach a Physics passage with an attitude such as, "I'm going to read this entire passage, memorizing all the details and data points as I go along, so that I won't need to waste time referring to the passage while I answer the questions." You don't want to spend most of your time reading the passage; you'd be much better off spending the bulk of your time thinking about the questions. You won't get any points for knowing the passage. Remember that the MCAT is asking you to apply what you know to the topic at hand. For some questions, the topic of the passage won't even be important; you'll simply need to apply what you know.

### Passage Types

One of the first things you'll want to do is to identify what type of passage you're reading. Physics *information* passages describe natural (fission of uranium nuclei, supernovae) or manmade (sledding down a hill, standing waves in a laser cavity) physical phenomena. Look out for definitions of new terms. Roughly half of Physics passages on the MCAT are information passages.

The other half of Physics passages are *experiment* passages. Physics passages that carry out an experiment (or multiple experiments) have clear goals. Something is varied, something else is measured, and conclusions can be formed. Sometimes these passages focus on a table or a graph giving the results of the experiment, and sometimes the passage focuses on the experimental apparatus. When multiple experiments are performed, be aware of the similarities and differences between the experiments: If making a small change to an experiment creates a radically different result, you can bet that there will be a question whose solution will require you to understand what the causes are. You saw an example of a Physics experiment passage in the previous chapter.

Physics *persuasive information* passages are very rare. When physicists disagree about the nature of a phenomenon, the argument pertains to those laws of physics that are too advanced to be tested on the MCAT. You won't see two scientists arguing about whether or not Newton's Second Law applies to a scenario.

As you prepare for the MCAT, remember that your skill at absorbing what needs absorbing and skimming over what can be skimmed over will directly translate into time saved and more points on Test Day. With that in mind, here are two things to always do when reading a Physics passage: map the passage and identify the topic.

## Map the Passage

As previously mentioned, you shouldn't try to memorize everything as you read a passage. Instead, you should employ your critical reading skills. You want to come out of each paragraph knowing its gist. One way of thinking about this is to ask yourself, after every paragraph, "What is this paragraph doing? Why is it here?"

The degree of detail you need to absorb depends on the type of passage. Since it isn't always immediately obvious what type of passage you are reading, you should quickly attempt to determine the passage type as you start reading any passage. Since there are only two major types of Physics passage, with practice you should be able to quickly figure this out. Once you know the passage type, then you'll know how to read it, as we discuss presently.

In an *information* passage, all you need to know from each paragraph is a general idea of what's being discussed. Since each paragraph will be a dry recounting of information, simply learning what's being talked about will be sufficient.

In an *experiment* passage, you will want to pay close attention to the manner in which an experiment is carried out. This is in contrast to Organic Chemistry passages, in which the laboratory details of complicated chemical syntheses are unimportant. After Physics experiment passages, there will be at least one question asked which depends on your detailed understanding of how the experiment is done. What is the goal of the experiment(s)? What is being tested? Which variables are held constant, and which variables are changing? It's not necessary for you to memorize data points, or data from tables or graphs. If you happen to notice any general trends, so much the better, but don't worry about it too much at this stage. You can come back for data points later, if a question calls for it.

In a *persuasive argument* passage, you'll want to pay close attention to two things: the phenomenon being discussed, and the contrasting arguments cited. Questions can focus on the subtle difference between hypotheses, or can be tightly focused on one hypothesis.

Another common way for the MCAT to present information in a Physics passage (of any type) is to devote a paragraph to defining something. Many times a new equation will be introduced.

In circumstances like this, the test makers are announcing their intention to make you use this information in a question. What you don't want to do is focus on the equation or term; instead, make a note of or highlight on your screen the phrase or sentence that describes what the equation or term *means* or *does*. For example, imagine this paragraph thrown in at the end of a passage:

> The magnetic force per unit length on two current carrying wires is $\frac{\mu_0 I_1 I_2}{2\pi a}$, where $a$ is the distance between the two wires, $I_1$ and $I_2$ are the currents in each wire, and $\mu_0 = 4\pi \times 10^{-7}\ \frac{N}{A^2}$ is the permeability of free space.

The information that describes the equation is what you want to make note of, instead of committing the equation to memory.

Whether or not you take written notes as you read a passage depends on your comfort level. We recommend that you take notes as you begin to practice reading passages, and then wean yourself off note-taking as you feel comfortable keeping all the needed information in your head. Maybe you'll discover that note-taking is a great help to you, and you'll decide to keep doing it right up through Test Day. Either way, it's up to you. As you take notes, be sure to summarize each paragraph, including the meanings of new terms or equations, as discussed above. Your notes for each paragraph usually don't need to be much more than a few words to a sentence.

## Identify the Topic

Once you have finished reading a passage, you'll want to be able to answer the question, "What is the author trying to accomplish in this passage?" Being able to answer this question means that you have read the passage critically—and critical reading is the most important skill for reading MCAT passages. The answer to this question provides the *topic* of the passage.

While determining the topic, you will also want to identify what Physics *concepts* are involved in the passage. It stands to reason that if the MCAT chooses a passage in which a mass oscillates on the end of a spring, there will be at least a few questions covering periodic motion. It is worth your time to take a few seconds to review in your mind what science the questions might cover. This exercise will help you focus and understand what you just read, and will prepare you for at least a good number of the questions to follow.

This is not good advice to follow for the other sciences. Physics passages are unique, because by connecting what was discussed to the concepts you learned in class, you can predict the nature of some of the questions that follow.

This step will be particularly helpful for experiment passages; the physics concepts involved will dictate the results of the experiment. For example, suppose the goal of the experiment in a passage is to measure the current in a simple circuit as different resistors are inserted. The concept behind this is Ohm's Law, $V = IR$. You'd expect the voltage, different resistances, and the circuits to follow Ohm's Law every time. Perhaps there will be a question about power ($P = IV$); maybe different groups of resistors will be hooked up in series or parallel.

Don't take more than a few seconds to think about concepts, however. The concepts you're going to be tested on are already in front of you, in the questions themselves. The odds are good that the MCAT is going to ask you at least one question about something you couldn't have anticipated—so don't spend more than a few seconds trying!

Over the next two pages are examples of how to read the two major passages types in Physics, the information passage and the experiment passage. Starting with the following information passage, read the passage, and think carefully about the passage map as you read the comments that follow them.

> Progress in the field of cellular and subcellular systems is made possible by compound microscopes. These multiple-lens instruments magnify objects that would otherwise be undetectable to the human eye. A compound microscope is composed of two converging lenses, the objective and the eyepiece. The objective forms a real image of the object. This image is then magnified by the eyepiece, which functions as a simple magnifier. The image formed by a simple magnifier is virtual, erect, and farther from the magnifier than the object. The overall magnification of the microscope is the product of the magnifications of the eyepiece and the objective.

Your notes may read as follows: Information passage—lenses in microscopes. This paragraph describes the two lenses in a microscope.

> The specimen to be magnified by the microscope is set on a support known as the stage. The stage is located just beyond the focal length of the objective lens. Light from a lamp and mirror arrangement illuminates the specimen from below. The light that passes through the specimen enters the objective lens, and the image produced is an enlarged, inverted image of the specimen. The image produced by the objective serves as the object for the next lens, the eyepiece. This second lens further enlarges the image, but does not invert it.

Second paragraph: Describes how a microscope works—not important to learn the details now.

> A specific example of the use of microscopes occurs in cellular biology, where scientists often use fluorescently labeled proteins to highlight different regions of a cell. In a special microscope equipped with a fluorescent lamp (which radiates light in the ultraviolet region of the spectrum), the areas of interest can be identified by observing the brightly colored areas where the proteins have attached themselves to specific components of the cell.

Third paragraph: cites an example—fluorescently labeled proteins.

**Topic:** This is an information passage on lenses in microscopes. You can certainly expect questions on lenses and maybe on fluorescence.

Now let's look at another example.

> The mass spectrometer is a device that utilizes electric and magnetic fields to determine the masses of the elements or compounds that exist within a certain sample. The operation of the mass spectrometer relies on the fact that the path of a moving charge is affected by the presence of electric and magnetic fields.

Coupling this paragraph with the included figure, you can tell that this is an experiment passage about a mass spectrometer. You'll need to read the experimental details carefully.

To analyze a sample, it must first be ionized. This may be accomplished by bombarding it with a stream of electrons. The ionized particles are then accelerated through a potential difference of several thousand volts that is set up between two slits $S_1$ and $S_2$ (see Figure 1 below). For the mass spectrometer to give useful results, all the particles entering the chamber below $S_3$ must be traveling at the same velocity. This is assured by passing the particles through a *velocity selector*, a region of a crossed magnetic field, B, and an electric field, E, located between $S_2$ and $S_3$. This electric field is produced by two charged parallel plates, $P_1$ and $P_2$. Only particles that are traveling at a velocity such that the force due to the electric field (qE) and that due to the magnetic field (qvB) cancel one another will remain undeflected and pass through the slit in $S_3$.

This paragraph provides the details of the experiment. The underlining indicates key information. Only charged particles of a certain velocity pass through. Remember that you will not be able to underline information on the computer, but you will be able to highlight material on screen.

The stream of charged particles then pass though another magnetic field, B', but this time, there is no electric field. The second magnetic field is perpendicular to the page, and deflects the particles in a circular path, toward the detector. Based on the radius of curvature of the path of the particle, its mass can be determined from the formula:

$$\frac{q}{m} = \frac{E}{rBB'}$$

where $q$ is the charge of the particle, $m$ is the mass of the particle, $E$ is the electric field, and $r$ is the radius of the circular path of the particle. In the mass spectrometer below, $E = 8 \times 10^4$ V/m, $B = 0.4$ T, and $B' = 0.5$ T. The fundamental unit of charge is $1.6 \times 10^{-19}$ C.

Second paragraph: What happens to the charges as they leave the velocity selector—mass is measured based on how curved their paths are in another magnetic field.

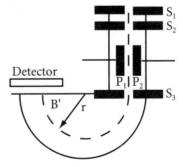

**Figure 1**   Mass Spectrometer

The figure—can you see how the components of the setup contribute to the experiment?

**Topic:** An experiment passage, in which the masses of charged particles are measured using electric and magnetic fields. Expect questions on E-fields and on magnetism.

Could you, without looking back to the last passage, describe how the experiment is carried out? Unlike in an Organic Chemistry passage, it's important in a Physics passage to read these portions carefully.

# HANDLING THE QUESTIONS

There is certainly more than one method for handling questions, but at the foundation of each is the idea that the test taker's grounding in basic physics must be good. There are few "plug-and-chug" or graph interpretation–like questions in MCAT Physics. As you read in chapter 3, four types of questions appear in the science sections of the MCAT:

*Discrete questions:* These are the questions that don't accompany a passage; blocks of discrete questions are always preceded by a warning, such as "Questions 12 through 15 are NOT based on a descriptive passage." If you don't know the relevant science, you don't have much hope of getting these questions right. There isn't a passage to fall back on. All the information you'll need will be in the question stem, the answer choices, and your outside knowledge.

*Questions that stand alone from the passage:* These are questions that follow a passage, but for all practical purposes are discrete questions. Usually they are thematically related to the passage (for example, an unrelated question on photon energies might follow a passage about laser standing waves), but require no information from the passage. In Physics, you'll get a lot of questions of this type following an information passage.

*Questions where you need only data from the passage:* These questions can't be answered without the passage—but you don't need to understand the passage to do so. At best, all you'll need is data from the passage. You'll need only outside knowledge to figure out how to answer the question.

*Questions that require an understanding of the passage:* In Physics, you'll mostly find this type of question following experiment passages. This type of question can't be answered solely by applying outside knowledge; you'll need to understand at least a portion of the passage. Once you have read the passages the Kaplan way, you'll either have already absorbed from the passage the information you'll need, or know exactly where in the passage to go back and get it.

## Answering the Questions

Following the steps outlined in chapter 3 on every question will help you develop habits that lead you to a higher score on Test Day.

### Understand what you are being asked.

The first thing you want to do is to read the entire question, including the answer choices. Some MCAT science questions can seem very confusing as you read them. Reading the answer choices right after reading the question stem will help you focus on how to go about solving the problem. You can waste a lot of time trying to come up with the answer to a question you don't really understand.

Sometimes, the question will ask for something very directly. Consider this discrete question:

$$^{228}_{89}\text{Ac} \rightarrow {}^{228}_{90}\text{Th} + \text{X}$$

What decay particle does X represent?

- **A.** Alpha particle
- **B.** Gamma ray
- **C.** Positive beta particle (positron)
- **D.** Negative beta particle (electron)

You are asked to figure out what type of particle X is, given the parent and daughter nuclei.

There are times when you may read the question stem and still not quite understand what you need to do to get the right answer. This is why you should read the answer choices along with the question stem. The next example follows the mass spectrometer passage:

If the voltage at $S_1$ is 10,000 V, and at $S_2$ is zero V, how much work is done by the electric force on a doubly ionized particle between $S_1$ and $S_2$?

- **A.** 0 eV
- **B.** 5,000 eV
- **C.** 10,000 eV
- **D.** 20,000 eV

Since the answer choices are numbers, a *calculation* is required for the work due to an electric field.

A close relative of this question type is the question that asks you to remember the relevant formula but doesn't require you to carry out the calculation. Always be careful to use the right units on questions like this. This example follows the microscope passage:

The objective has a focal length of 6.0 mm and is located at a distance of 6.2 mm from the specimen under consideration. How far away from the objective will the image be?

- **A.** $\dfrac{(6.0)(6.2)}{6.2 - 6.0}$ mm
- **B.** $\dfrac{6.2 - 6.0}{(6.0)(6.2)}$ mm
- **C.** $\dfrac{6.0 - 6.2}{(6.0)(6.2)}$ mm
- **D.** $\dfrac{(6.0)(6.0)}{6.2 - 6.0}$ mm

The answer choices are formulas, so no calculations are required, but you'll need to know the formula that gives you the image distance.

There will be times when the answer choices won't hint directly at what you need to do, but will instead put a limit on the number of things you'll have to think about. Consider the following question, which follows the microscope passage:

> Which of the following accurately describes the image formed by placing the object farther from the objective than the objective's focal point?
>
> **A.** The image is inverted and enlarged.
>
> **B.** The image is inverted and shrunk.
>
> **C.** The image is upright and enlarged.
>
> **D.** The image is upright and shrunk.

Even if you can't figure out whether the image is inverted or upright, but can determine whether it's enlarged or shrunk, you can at least eliminate two answer choices as wrong—and you've got a 50-50 shot at getting this question right.

It is not always so easy to decipher what the question is looking for. On many questions, you will need to translate or paraphrase the question stem. Rephrase the question, in your own words, paring it down to its essentials. To do this, you have to ask yourself, "What am I really being asked?" Perhaps you've heard the expression about "not being able to see the forest for the trees." The questions on the MCAT can seem very daunting, so it's essential to take a step back and connect what you see in the question to both the passage and the science concepts that might be involved in answering the question.

Answering the question, "What am I being asked?" can be particularly important for Physics questions. Difficult Physics questions are made difficult by obscuring the fact that you are being asked only to apply basic concepts from physics.

Consider this example, from the microscope passage:

> A bacterium is studied by using a microscope whose lens magnifies the specimen $100\times$ and whose eyepiece magnifies the specimen $10\times$. If the bacterium appears to be 2 mm long, what is the actual size of the bacterium?
>
> **A.** $2 \, \mu m$
>
> **B.** $20 \, \mu m$
>
> **C.** $0.5 \, \mu m$
>
> **D.** $50 \, \mu m$

The question that must be answered before you can calculate the actual size of the bacterium is: Given the magnification of each lens individually, what is the total magnification when both are used together? In this question, notice that it's the middle stage that the MCAT is really testing. If you were asked, "A 2-mm object has been magnified $1,000\times$. What is its actual size?" it wouldn't take you long to divide 2 mm by 1,000 and get the correct answer. What the MCAT wants to know is, "If we give the test taker the magnification of both lenses separately, will she or he know how to combine them and then calculate the correct answer?" You will be ready for these "questions behind the question" when you have mastered the Physics you've learned in class, and had lots of practice with MCAT-style passages.

One important note: *There is no a magic wand that you can wave that makes all MCAT questions easy to answer.* The good news is that the concepts that the MCAT tests are finite in number. As you practice Physics passages, you will see that some passages and questions are harder than others, requiring you to step back and determine what basic concepts the questions are *really* asking you to use.

### Figure out where to go to get any information that you need.

Now that you understand what the question is asking for, you'll want to figure out what you are going to do to get to the correct answer. Normally, once you understand the question, your knowledge of the sciences will tell you exactly what's going on and the path to the correct answer will be clear.

Where you will need to go to find any information you'll need will largely depend on the type of question. If you are tackling a discrete question, independent of any passages, the only place for you to look besides the question stem and the answer choices is to your brain—discrete questions always call upon outside science knowledge.

For questions that can stand alone from the passage, you'll need neither information from nor understanding of the passage. You'll have to rely on your outside knowledge again. Most of the questions following information passages will be of this variety. But how do you know whether or not a question relies on the passage? If you read the information passage for structure, to understand the gist of what was going on, then you'll probably be able to recognize when a question presents a new situation, a scenario that falls outside the discussion in the passage. For example, imagine this question following the microscope passage:

A converging lens has a focal length of 4 cm. What is the magnification of an image due to an object placed 3 cm away from the lens?

A. −12

B. −4

C. 1

D. 4

The topic of the passage was lenses in microscopes. This question gives information about a specific lens, and makes no reference whatsoever to the passage. This question calls upon your ability to remember how the object distance, image distance, and focal length of a converging lens relate to each other—you need nothing from the passage.

Some questions will require you to go back to the passage for information, but not for understanding. Usually, this means that to answer the question, you need to use data given in the passage. Consider this example from the mass spectrometer passage:

What is the force on a singly charged ion due to the electric field between plates $P_1$ and $P_2$?

**A.** $6.4 \times 10^{-20}$ N

**B.** $8.0 \times 10^{-20}$ N

**C.** $8.0 \times 10^{-15}$ N

**D.** $1.3 \times 10^{-14}$ N

The question asks you to calculate the force due to an electric field on a particle. You'll need to come up with the formula for the force on an electric charge in an electric field by yourself. You'll need the electric field strength and the charge on a singly charged ion—both provided by the passage.

Experiment passages will be followed mostly by questions requiring that you understand the passage in detail. This is why you need to read the passage so closely the first time. Look at this question from the mass spectrometer passage:

What is the velocity of particles entering the mass spectrometer?

**A.** q/m

**B.** E/B'

**C.** B'/E

**D.** E/B

This question requires that you understand how the mass spectrometer works—not a surprise, coming from an experiment passage. Indeed, the passage has something very detailed to say about the velocity of particles in the spectrometer: The velocity selector ensures that only particles with speeds such that the electric and magnetic forces on them are in balance will pass through.

If you hadn't read for the details of how the experiment was carried out, you would now have to spend a lot of time rereading the passage, to try to figure out how to calculate the velocity of the particles. Realistically, if you read the experimental details carefully, but didn't remember how the velocity selector works, then at least you'd know where exactly to go back and reread.

***Integrating science knowledge with any necessary passage research, determine the correct answer.***

This is where you pull it all together and come up with the answer. If you've managed to avoid needing any outside science knowledge, you'll probably need it now. This is when it's important to remember two things:

- If you are doing a calculation, always be sure that your units are correct and consistent.
- The MCAT isn't asking you to reinvent the field of physics. If you get stuck on a spring question, ask yourself, "What are all the things I know about springs?" You might surprise yourself with all the things you can come up with.

Let's have a look at how some of the problems you've seen in the past few pages finish up.

If the voltage at $S_1$ is 10,000 V, and at $S_2$ is zero V, how much work is done by the electric force on a doubly ionized particle between $S_1$ and $S_2$?

**A.** 0 eV

**B.** 5,000 eV

**C.** 10,000 eV

**D.** 20,000 eV

Since the answer choices are numbers, a calculation is required for the work due to an electric field.

The reason the electron-volt (eV) is convenient as a unit is because one eV is the energy a singly ionized particle (q=e) loses as it travels across a one-volt potential. So, remembering that the work done on charge q in traveling through a potential difference V is $W = qV$, you can calculate as follows:

$W = (2e)(10000\ V) = 20,000\ eV$, choice **D**.

What is the velocity of particles entering the mass spectrometer?

**A.** q/m

**B.** E/B'

**C.** B'/E

**D.** E/B

As we've seen before, this question requires that you understand how the mass spectrometer described in this experiment passage works. The passage tells us that the velocity selector ensures that only particles with speeds such that the electric and magnetic forces on them are in balance will pass through.

From your outside knowledge, you know that the force on a charge due to an electric field is qE, and the force by a magnetic field on a charge q moving at speed v is qvB. Since the velocity selector acts between $S_2$ and $S_3$, the correct magnetic field to use is B, not B' (eliminate choices **B** and **C**). So, since these two forces balance for particles that traverse the spectrometer: $qE = qvB$, $v = E/B$, choice **D**.

Here's a completely new question, from the spectrometer passage.

The electric field points from the positive to the negative plate, or in other words, toward the right. What is the direction of the magnetic field B?

**A.** To the left

**B.** Into the page

**C.** Out of the page

**D.** It is unrelated to the direction of the electric field

The question asks for the direction of the magnetic field B, given that the electric field points from left to right. The real question here is: Is there a relationship between the direction of E and the direction of B, or is choice **D** correct?

To answer that question, you need to understand how and why the spectrometer works. According to the second paragraph, the region of interest is called the velocity selector; in it, the E and B fields are crossed in such a way that the magnetic force on the charges traveling down the page tends to cancel the force due to the electric field. Since the field points to the right, the electric force on the charges is to the right. So the magnetic force must be to the left. Now you understand the real question: In what direction should B point so that the magnetic force on the charges is to the left?

You can use the right-hand rule to work it out. The fingers point in the direction of the velocity, to the right, and the thumb points toward the force, to the left. So the fingers, which point in the direction of the field, must curl upward, out of the page. Choice **C** is correct.

What follows is a list of the physics skills and concepts that you should have mastered before taking the MCAT. If you find that you are weak in any of these areas, incorporate these concepts into your study schedule.

# IN PREPARING FOR THE MCAT, I SHOULD UNDERSTAND...

## 1. Kinematics

- The four fundamental physical dimensions and their SI units
- The difference between displacement and distance traveled
- The difference between velocity and speed
- The difference between instantaneous velocity and average velocity
- The difference between instantaneous acceleration and average acceleration
- How graphs of position, velocity, and acceleration versus time relate to physical motion
- The equations for motion under constant acceleration, and when each is useful
- The types of initial conditions which occur in free fall, and how to use the equations for motion under constant acceleration appropriately

## 2. Newtonian Mechanics

- What a force is and how it affects the object to which it is applied
- Newton's First Law and what it implies
- Newton's Second Law and what it implies
- How to construct free–body diagrams for objects experiencing external forces, and how to apply Newton's Second Law to those diagrams
- Newton's Third Law and what it implies
- The two types of friction and how each is applied
- Newton's Law of Gravitation and how it is applied
- How Newton's Second Law is affected by uniform circular motion
- What torque is and how it affects the object to which it is applied
- Translational equilibrium and rotational equilibrium, and the circumstances that cause each to occur

## 3. Energy and Momentum

- The definition of work and how doing work affects the energy of an object
- The definition of kinetic energy
- The relationship between the net work done on an object and the object's kinetic energy
- The formulas for gravitational potential energy, in general and near the earth
- Under which circumstances the total mechanical energy of a system is conserved, and how to use the conservation of energy to solve problems
- The difference between conservative forces and nonconservative forces
- The concept of the average power applied to a system by having work done on it
- The definitions of the momentum of an object and the momentum of a system
- The conditions under which the total momentum of a system is conserved
- The differences among elastic, inelastic, and totally inelastic collisions, and what each implies about the system
- The definition of impulse, and the consequences of applying an average force to an object over a short period of time

## 4. Thermodynamics

- What *temperature* means and the different temperature scales
- What *heat* is, and how it is different from temperature
- How materials expand and contract as their temperature changes
- All three parts of the first law of thermodynamics, and how the law is applied
- The definition of entropy
- How the second law of thermodynamics is applied, and the difference between the entropy of an object and the entropy of a system of objects

## 5. Fluids and Solids

- The definition of density
- The definition of pressure
- The difference between gauge pressure and total pressure
- Pascal's principle and how it is applied
- The formula for hydrostatic pressure and how it is applied
- The formula for the buoyant force and how it is applied to Newton's Second Law
- The density rule and the definition of specific gravity
- How the continuity equation applies to a fluid
- How Bernoulli's equation applies to nonviscous fluids, and its common applications
- The definition of viscosity and how it affects other fluid concepts
- The definitions of stress and strain, and how they relate to Young's modulus and shear modulus; have a basic understanding of what Young's modulus means

## 6. Electrostatics

- The definition of electric charge
- Coulomb's law and how different charges exert a force on one another

- What an electric field is and under what conditions it arises
- Electric field due to charge, and the difference between a test charge and a source charge
- The properties of electric field lines
- How to calculate the total electric field at one point due to multiple sources
- The effects on a conductor due to an external electric field
- The definition of electric potential energy and how it applies to systems of point charges
- The definition of electric potential, how electric potential is different than electric potential energy, and how electric potential is applied to point charges and parallel plates of opposite charge

## 7. DC/AC Circuits

- The definition of *current*, and *conventional current*
- The definition of *direct current* (DC)
- How an electromotive force (emf) isn't a force but a potential difference, and how an emf generates current in a wire
- The definition of *resistance*
- Ohm's Law, and how it applies not only to circuits as a whole, but also to individual circuit elements (resistors, charged capacitors, batteries)
- How resistors operate in series and in parallel in a circuit
- How the internal resistance of a battery can influence a circuit
- The definition of resistivity and how it is applied
- The function and properties of capacitors
- The definition of capacitance and how much energy can be stored in a capacitor
- How capacitors operate in series and in parallel in a circuit
- What a dielectric is, and how inserting a dielectric into a capacitor influences its properties
- How systems with current use power, and how much power is given off by a resistor due to heat
- What alternating current (AC) is, and why we measure root-mean-square (rms) voltages and currents

## 8. Magnetism

- What magnetic fields are, and how they are generated
- The formula for the magnetic field generated due to a current-carrying straight wire
- The formula for the magnetic field generated due to a current-carrying loop of wire
- The magnetic force law, and when an object experiences a force due to a magnetic field
- How to calculate the force on a charge in a magnetic field
- How to calculate the force on a current-carrying wire in an external magnetic field

## 9. Periodic Motion

- What simple harmonic motion is
- Hooke's law, and how to apply it using Newton's Second Law

- How to calculate the frequency, angular frequency, and period of a system undergoing simple harmonic oscillation
- How simple harmonic motion applies to springs
- How simple harmonic motion applies to pendula, as opposed to springs

## 10. Waves

- The properties of waves: speed, amplitude, intensity, and transverse or longitudinal oscillation
- Under what conditions two waves with the same frequency experience constructive and destructive interference, and what it means for two waves of the same frequency to be in phase, 90° out of phase, and 180° out of phase
- How the general properties of waves apply to sound waves, including the decibel scale, pitch, beat frequency, and the Doppler effect
- How standing waves are generated in oscillating systems of fixed length

## 11. Light and Optics

- The speed of light, and how it relates to frequency and wavelength
- What photons are
- How photons oscillate, what linear polarization is, and the effects of placing a polarizer in the path of a light wave
- The law of reflection
- The definition of *the index of refraction, Snell's law of refraction* and how to apply it
- The circumstances under which total internal reflection occurs
- The lens-makers equation, the sign conventions for object distance, image distance, and focal length, what magnification is and how to apply it, and how to treat light traveling through multiple lenses

## 12. Atomic Phenomena

- The phenomena of atomic electron energy levels, and how the binding energy depends on principal quantum number
- How electrons can transition between energy levels by emitting or absorbing photons

## 13. Nuclear Phenomena

- What the atomic number and mass number of a nucleus mean in terms of what's inside
- The relationship between rest mass and its equivalent energy
- Why the mass of a nucleus doesn't equal the sum of the masses of its parts
- That not all isotopes are stable, and that unstable nuclei undergo radioactive decay into other nuclei, the four common types of radioactive decay, and what the half-life of an unstable isotope is

# PHYSICS PRACTICE SET

## Answer Sheet

| 1 | Ⓐ Ⓑ Ⓒ Ⓓ | 16 | Ⓐ Ⓑ Ⓒ Ⓓ | 31 | Ⓐ Ⓑ Ⓒ Ⓓ |
|---|---|---|---|---|---|
| 2 | Ⓐ Ⓑ Ⓒ Ⓓ | 17 | Ⓐ Ⓑ Ⓒ Ⓓ | 32 | Ⓐ Ⓑ Ⓒ Ⓓ |
| 3 | Ⓐ Ⓑ Ⓒ Ⓓ | 18 | Ⓐ Ⓑ Ⓒ Ⓓ | 33 | Ⓐ Ⓑ Ⓒ Ⓓ |
| 4 | Ⓐ Ⓑ Ⓒ Ⓓ | 19 | Ⓐ Ⓑ Ⓒ Ⓓ | 34 | Ⓐ Ⓑ Ⓒ Ⓓ |
| 5 | Ⓐ Ⓑ Ⓒ Ⓓ | 20 | Ⓐ Ⓑ Ⓒ Ⓓ | 35 | Ⓐ Ⓑ Ⓒ Ⓓ |
| 6 | Ⓐ Ⓑ Ⓒ Ⓓ | 21 | Ⓐ Ⓑ Ⓒ Ⓓ | 36 | Ⓐ Ⓑ Ⓒ Ⓓ |
| 7 | Ⓐ Ⓑ Ⓒ Ⓓ | 22 | Ⓐ Ⓑ Ⓒ Ⓓ | 37 | Ⓐ Ⓑ Ⓒ Ⓓ |
| 8 | Ⓐ Ⓑ Ⓒ Ⓓ | 23 | Ⓐ Ⓑ Ⓒ Ⓓ | 38 | Ⓐ Ⓑ Ⓒ Ⓓ |
| 9 | Ⓐ Ⓑ Ⓒ Ⓓ | 24 | Ⓐ Ⓑ Ⓒ Ⓓ | 39 | Ⓐ Ⓑ Ⓒ Ⓓ |
| 10 | Ⓐ Ⓑ Ⓒ Ⓓ | 25 | Ⓐ Ⓑ Ⓒ Ⓓ | 40 | Ⓐ Ⓑ Ⓒ Ⓓ |
| 11 | Ⓐ Ⓑ Ⓒ Ⓓ | 26 | Ⓐ Ⓑ Ⓒ Ⓓ | 41 | Ⓐ Ⓑ Ⓒ Ⓓ |
| 12 | Ⓐ Ⓑ Ⓒ Ⓓ | 27 | Ⓐ Ⓑ Ⓒ Ⓓ | 42 | Ⓐ Ⓑ Ⓒ Ⓓ |
| 13 | Ⓐ Ⓑ Ⓒ Ⓓ | 28 | Ⓐ Ⓑ Ⓒ Ⓓ | 43 | Ⓐ Ⓑ Ⓒ Ⓓ |
| 14 | Ⓐ Ⓑ Ⓒ Ⓓ | 29 | Ⓐ Ⓑ Ⓒ Ⓓ | 44 | Ⓐ Ⓑ Ⓒ Ⓓ |
| 15 | Ⓐ Ⓑ Ⓒ Ⓓ | 30 | Ⓐ Ⓑ Ⓒ Ⓓ | 45 | Ⓐ Ⓑ Ⓒ Ⓓ |

# PHYSICS PRACTICE SET

## Time: 60 Minutes—45 Questions

**DIRECTIONS:** There are seven passages and ten discrete questions in this physics test. Each passage is followed by five questions of above-average difficulty. After reading a passage, select the one best answer to each question. If you are not certain of an answer, eliminate the alternatives that you know to be incorrect and then select an answer from the remaining alternatives. (Note that although the passages and questions are test-like, this exercise is NOT meant to be an actual MCAT test section. For full-length MCAT practice, please see Kaplan *MCAT Practice Tests*).

## Passage I (Questions 1–5)

The Hubble Space Telescope (HST) is an astronomical satellite in low orbit above Earth's atmosphere. The telescope provides the best photometric measurements ever to be achieved from any astronomical image.

Light enters the telescope and is focused by the primary mirror onto the secondary mirror. The secondary mirror then reflects light through a small hole in the primary mirror to the focal plane, which is shared by redirecting mirrors and electromagnetic measuring instruments. The redirecting mirrors send light to the guidance center and wide-field/planetary camera (Wiff-Pick). The rays of light that are not intercepted by the redirecting mirrors pass on to the instruments: the faint-object camera (FOC), the high-resolution spectrograph (HRS) and the faint-object spectrograph (FOS).

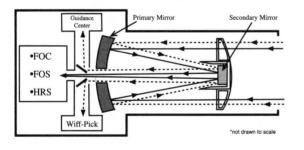

**Figure 1**

The primary mirror is approximately spherical and has a focal length of 58 m and a diameter of 2.4 m. The secondary mirror is flat and 0.3 m in diameter. The primary and secondary mirrors cooperatively focus the light at the focal plane. The mirrors are coated with aluminum and magnesium fluoride, giving them the capability to reflect light with wavelengths between 110 nm and 1 mm.

The HST enables astronomers to capture light from distant galaxies. Light emitted from the distant edges of the rapidly expanding universe is shifted to greater wavelengths by a quantity called the red shift ($z$):

$$z = \frac{\lambda_{obs} - \lambda_{emit}}{\lambda_{emit}}$$

**Equation 1**

where $\lambda_{obs}$ is the wavelength of the light measured by the HST and $\lambda_{emit}$ is the wavelength of the light emitted by the object.

The red shift is converted into $R$, the scale factor of the universe, using the formula:

$$R = \frac{1}{1 + z}$$

**Equation 2**

The value of $R$ determines how large the universe was when it emitted the light. For example, if a galaxy is observed with a $z = 1$, then $R = 1/2$; the universe was one-half its present size when the light was emitted.

[Note: $c = 3.00 \times 10^8$ m/s; $h = 6.626 \times 10^{-34}$ J·s]

1. Which of the following phenomena is responsible for the red shift?

   **A.** Ionization
   **B.** Reflection
   **C.** Refraction
   **D.** Doppler effect

**GO ON TO THE NEXT PAGE.**

2. Based on composition analysis, a certain star is expected to emit light with a wavelength of 250 nm. The FOS indicates that the star is emitting light with a wavelength of 750 nm. What was the relative size of the universe when the light was emitted?

    A.  1/3
    B.  1/2
    C.  2
    D.  3

3. The primary mirror can be described as

    A.  Convex, converging
    B.  Convex, diverging
    C.  Concave, converging
    D.  Concave, diverging

4. What are the radii of curvature of the primary and secondary mirrors, respectively?

    A.  1.2 m; 0.15 m
    B.  29 m; 0.15 m
    C.  29 m; infinity
    D.  116 m; infinity

5. If incoming parallel rays, when reflected by the mirrors, converge 2 m to the left of the reflective side of the primary mirror, what is the approximate distance between the two mirrors?

    A.  14 m
    B.  28 m
    C.  58 m
    D.  116 m

# Passage II (Questions 6–10)

The Michelson interferometer exploits the phenomenon of interference between light waves. A simplified schematic of such a device is shown below:

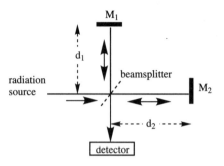

**Figure 1**

A beam of electromagnetic radiation (usually in either the visible or infrared region) falls upon a beamsplitter. The beamsplitter, which is essentially a mirror that is semitransparent to the radiation used, causes the beam of radiation to be split such that half of the intensity is transmitted while the other half is reflected. These two beams then strike mirrors $M_1$ and $M_2$, one of which is fixed and the other movable. The beams are reflected back toward the beamsplitter, where they interfere and are then directed toward the detector. In the diagram shown above, $d_1$ is the distance between the beamsplitter and $M_1$, and $d_2$ is the distance between the beamsplitter and $M_2$. Depending on the difference between $d_1$ and $d_2$, the two beams may interfere either constructively or destructively.

Consider the case in which the radiation is monochromatic. If $d_1$ is equal to $d_2$, the distance traveled by the two beams of radiation will be identical, and thus the waves will interfere constructively. However, if the two distances differ by an amount $x$, the lengths of the paths traveled by the two beams will differ by $2x$. Destructive interference occurs when this difference of $2x$, known as the retardation, causes the two beams to be 180° out of phase.

As the movable mirror is translated, its distance from the beamsplitter increases smoothly, and so does the retardation. The intensity of the radiation reaching the detector will vary as the interference goes from constructive to destructive and back. The interferogram, a plot of the intensity versus retardation, will exhibit a sinusoidal shape: It will show a series of maxima and minima (bright and dark fringes) corresponding to constructive and destructive interferences, respectively

**GO ON TO THE NEXT PAGE.**

*KAPLAN*

(Figure 2). The condition for constructive interference for the Michelson interferometer is:

$$|d_1 - d_2| = m\lambda/2$$

where m = 0, 1, 2, … and $\lambda$ is the wavelength of the radiation source.

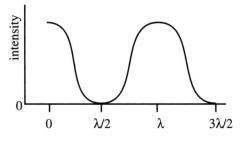

**Figure 2**

6. If a helium-neon laser is used as the light source ($\lambda$ = 6328 Å), how far should the movable mirror be displaced to move from one bright fringe to the next one?

A. 3164 Å

B. 6328 Å

C. 9492 Å

D. 12,660 Å

7. If the frequency of the monochromatic radiation is increased (all else being the same), which of the following would result?

   I. The maximum intensity registered by the detector would be lower.

   II. The minimum intensity registered by the detector would be lower.

   III. More maxima and minima will be encountered for a given distance.

A. I only

B. II only

C. III only

D. II and III only

8. If the source radiation consists of light of two distinct wavelengths $\lambda_1$ and $\lambda_2$ that are relatively close in value, which of the following characterizes the appearance of the interferogram?

A. A beat wavelength of $|\lambda_1 - \lambda_2|$

B. A beat wavelength of $|\lambda_1 + \lambda_2|$

C. A beat frequency of $\left|\frac{c}{\lambda_1} - \frac{c}{\lambda_2}\right|$

D. A beat frequency of $\left|\frac{c}{\lambda_1} + \frac{c}{\lambda_2}\right|$

9. One application of the interferometer is the determination of the index of refraction of a gas sample. If the wavelength of light in vacuum is $\lambda_0$, then how many wavelengths will fit in a distance $d$ in a medium with an index of refraction of $n$?

A. $n\lambda_0/d$

B. $nd/\lambda_0$

C. $\lambda_0/nd$

D. $d/n\lambda_0$

10. If the source radiation consists of a continuous range of wavelengths, the resulting interferogram

A. exhibits maximum constructive interference only when the retardation equals zero.

B. exhibits the same periodicity as the lowest wavelength component of the source radiation.

C. exhibits the same periodicity as the highest wavelength component of the source radiation.

D. exhibits no constructive interference.

**GO ON TO THE NEXT PAGE.**

## Passage III (Questions 11–15)

A ship is engineered with the ability to right itself under severe environmental conditions. When waves and wind cause a ship to tilt, a torque is generated that restores the ship to equilibrium. However, if the angle of tilt is too great, a ship will overturn and sink.

On calm water, a ship is in rotational equilibrium. The forces of gravity and buoyancy act along the centerline of the ship and are equal in magnitude and opposite in direction. Figure 1 contains the major physical features of this system: The buoyant force ($F_b$) acts at the hydrostatic center ($H$), which is the center of gravity of the fluid displaced by the ship. The gravitational force ($F_g$) operates at the center of gravity of the ship ($C$). When a ship tilts, $H$ shifts to the leaning side (the center of gravity does not shift) and the forces no longer operate along the same axis. The point at which the buoyant force vector intersects the centerline is called the metacenter ($M$). The displacement from $C$ to $M$ is called the metacentric height ($m$).

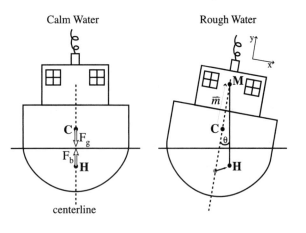

**Figure 1**

The buoyant force exerts a torque ($\tau$) about the center of gravity according to the equation:

$$\tau = F_b m \sin \theta$$

**Equation 1**

where $F_b$ is the buoyant force, $m$ is the metacentric height, and $\theta$ is the angle between the buoyant force vector and the metacentric height. The torque exerted by the buoyant force is referred to as the restoring torque.

The stability of the ship depends on the magnitude of the restoring torque. The restoring torque is proportional to the width of the ship, because the hydrostatic center gets displaced farther away from the center line the farther the ship tilts. The restoring torque is inversely proportional to the height of the ship because the higher center of gravity decreases the metacentric height.

11. Which of the following is true as the ship tilts over?

    I. H is displaced further from the centerline.

    II. A greater θ is created.

    III. The buoyant force increases.

  **A.** I only

  **B.** II only

  **C.** I and II only

  **D.** I, II, and III

12. A ship will overturn when

  **A.** the force of gravity exceeds the buoyant force.

  **B.** the metacentric height becomes negative.

  **C.** the hydrostatic center and center of gravity do not lie in a vertical line.

  **D.** the restoring torque reaches a minimum.

13. Which of the following correctly represents the mass of the water displaced by a tilting boat?

  **A.** $\dfrac{\tau}{F_b \sin \theta}$

  **B.** $\dfrac{\tau}{gm \sin \theta}$

  **C.** $\dfrac{F_b}{gV}$

  **D.** $\rho g V$

14. According to Newton's Third Law, for every action there is an equal and opposite reaction. Which of the following is the reactive force to gravity on the ship?

  **A.** The restoring torque

  **B.** The buoyant force

  **C.** The gravitational force on the earth due to the ship

  **D.** The gravitational force on the fluid due to the ship

**GO ON TO THE NEXT PAGE.**

**15.** Which of the following represents the component of the buoyant force vector that generates the restoring torque?

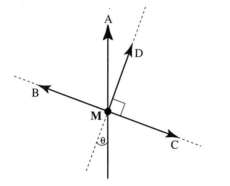

**A.** A

**B.** B

**C.** C

**D.** D

## Passage IV (Questions 16–20)

A long plastic tube is partially filled with water as shown in Figure 1. A spigot at the bottom of the tube allows water to be drained away, lowering the water level.

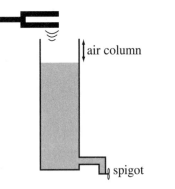

air column

spigot

**Figure 1**

A tuning fork of known frequency is struck with a rubber mallet and then placed near the open end of the tube, initiating vibrations of the air in the tube. The surface of the water always corresponds to a wave node and the mouth of the tube corresponds to an antinode.

While the tuning fork rings near the opening, the spigot is opened to lower the water level. This causes the length of the air column to increase, and occasionally it will reach a value at which the frequency of the fundamental, or one of its overtones, is the same as the frequency of the tuning fork (Figure 2). When this happens, resonance occurs and a loud ringing response is heard.

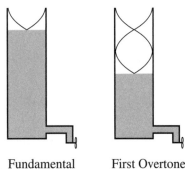

Fundamental      First Overtone

**Figure 2**

The values of the air-column lengths corresponding to resonance are recorded below:

| Frequency of tuning fork (Hz) | Length of air column at resonance (cm) |
|---|---|
| 256 | $31.9 \pm 0.5$ |
| | $96.0 \pm 0.5$ |
| 426.7 | $20.0 \pm 0.5$ |
| | $59.8 \pm 0.5$ |
| 384 | $21.5 \pm 0.5$ |
| | $66.3 \pm 0.5$ |

**Table 1**

16. In the experiment, which of the following could be the next resonance value of the length of the air column, using the tuning fork of 426.7 Hz?

   A.   80 cm

   B.   100 cm

   C.   120 cm

   D.   160 cm

17. The speed of sound in air decreases as the temperature decreases. If the experiment were conducted at a lower temperature,

   A.   the air column lengths at resonance would decrease.

   B.   the air column lengths at resonance would increase.

   C.   the frequency of the standing waves would decrease.

   D.   the frequency of the standing waves would increase.

18. The experiment is performed again using a liquid other than water to partially fill the tube. The results of the experiment turn out to be the same as those recorded in Table 1. What can we conclude about that liquid?

   A.   It has the same density as water.

   B.   It has the same index of refraction as water.

   C.   It has the same molecular weight as water.

   D.   Its properties relative to water cannot be determined.

**GO ON TO THE NEXT PAGE.**

KAPLAN

19. When using the tuning fork of frequency 256 Hz, the spigot is closed at the first resonance so that the length of the air column remains at 31.9 cm. What is the next frequency that will resonate at this length?

    A.  384 Hz
    B.  512 Hz
    C.  768 Hz
    D.  896 Hz

20. What is the speed of the sound wave emanating from the 384-Hz tuning fork?

    A.  17.9 m/s
    B.  82.6 m/s
    C.  254.6 m/s
    D.  330.2 m/s

**GO ON TO THE NEXT PAGE.**

## Passage V (Questions 21–25)

A sharpshooter standing in an open field performs two stunts, firing 5.00-gram bullets at circular targets, each with a diameter of 1 meter. (Air resistance is negligible in both stunts.)

*Stunt 1:*

A stationary target is mounted on a frictionless pivot, which constrains the target's motion so that it is only allowed to rotate. The target is at the same height as the gun. The sharpshooter fires and the bullet strikes directly to the right of the center, grazing the edge of the target and causing the target to rotate with constant angular velocity. The sharpshooter then fires again, timing the shot perfectly so that the second bullet strikes when the target is facing the shooter. The second bullet strikes a distance 0.25 m directly to the left of the center, causing the target to stop rotating.

*Stunt 2:*

Two guns, separated by 5 meters and pointed at each other, are tilted so that each gun points at an angle $\theta$ above the horizontal. Both guns are fired simultaneously, with each bullet leaving its gun at a speed of 250 m/s. The bullets collide inelastically in midair, falling to the ground together.

21. In Stunt 2, how much momentum does each bullet have when leaving its gun?

    A.  1.25 kg · m/s
    B.  2.50 kg · m/s
    C.  250 kg · m/s
    D.  $1.25 \times 10^3$ kg · m/s

22. Which of the following is true regarding the two bullets in Stunt 2?

    A.  Only the total momentum of the system is conserved.
    B.  Only the kinetic energy of the system is conserved.
    C.  Both the total momentum and the kinetic energy of the system are conserved.
    D.  Neither the total momentum nor the kinetic energy of the system are conserved.

23. As the target rotates in Stunt 1, which of following must have zero value?

        I. The target's potential energy
       II. The target's translational kinetic energy
      III. The target's rotational kinetic energy

    A.  I and III only
    B.  II only
    C.  I and II only
    D.  I, II, and III

24. If the first bullet fired in Stunt 1 impacts the target with force $F_0$, with what force will the second bullet need to strike in order to stop the target's rotation?

    A.  $0.5F_0$
    B.  $F_0$
    C.  $2F_0$
    D.  $4F_0$

25. While performing another stunt, the sharpshooter faces east and shoots toward a stationary target that is very far away. The wind is blowing to the northeast. How should the shooter alter her aim so as to strike the center of the target?

    A.  Aim a little north of the target to account for the wind.
    B.  Aim a little south of the target to account for the wind.
    C.  Aim a little north of the target to account for the wind, and a little above the target to account for gravity.
    D.  Aim a little south of the target to account for the wind, and a little above the target to account for gravity.

**GO ON TO THE NEXT PAGE.**

## Passage VI (Questions 26–30)

Semiconductor lasers typically produce light with a wavelength on the order of 1 μm. The active region of the laser consists of a thin, narrow semiconductor crystal about 200 μm long with partially reflecting facets at the ends through which light can enter or exit.

In a semiconductor crystal, electron energies are confined to bands (collections of energy levels very close together in energy) rather than to the discrete energy levels found in a single atom. All semiconductors have a valence band, which is almost completely filled with electrons, and a higher energy conduction band. The smallest energy difference between these two bands is called the band gap $E_g$. Figure 1 shows the energy of the bands, $E$, as a function of the electron wave momentum for a typical semiconductor. ($k$ is the magnitude of the wave vector of the electron and plays a role analogous to that of a quantum number: The larger its value, the greater the momentum of the electron.) In the semiconductor laser, electrons are optically pumped from the valence band to the conduction band with a light source that produces photons of frequency $\nu_p$.

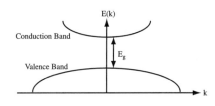

**Figure 1**

A second light source, having energy $E_s$ near the band gap, can now be amplified by the process of stimulated emission. In this process, a photon interacts with a conduction band electron, causing it to drop to the valence band. This induces the emission of another photon of the same frequency, which then stimulates another conduction band electron to drop to the valence band. The number of photons increases, and the light is amplified as it travels back and forth through the active region. Figure 2 shows a graph of the natural log of the output intensity $I_{out}$ divided by the input intensity $I_{in}$ as a function of $E_s$ for a typical semiconductor laser. (Note: $hc = 1.24 \times 10^{-6}$ eV·m, where $c$ is the speed of light in a vacuum.)

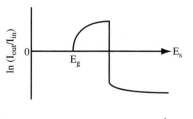

**Figure 2**

26. Semiconductor lasers are often used as light sources for optical fiber communications. As a photon travels from the laser (index of refraction 3.5) into a glass fiber (index of refraction 1.4), which of the following changes?

    I. Its energy

    II. Its frequency

    III. Its wavelength

**A.** I only

**B.** III only

**C.** I and II only

**D.** I, II, and III

27. Which of the following is true of the energy $E_p$ of the photons produced by the optical pump?

**A.** $E_p$ must be smaller than the band gap $E_g$.

**B.** $E_p$ must equal the band gap $E_g$.

**C.** $E_p$ must be greater than or equal to the band gap $E_g$.

**D.** $E_p$ can be chosen independently of the band gap $E_g$.

28. A photon emitted by a semiconductor laser is incident on a hydrogen atom. Assuming no ionization takes place, the photon will be absorbed by the atom

**A.** only if its energy equals the difference between two electron energy levels.

**B.** only if its energy is an integer multiple of Planck's constant $h$.

**C.** only if its energy is greater than 13.6 eV.

**D.** independent of the value of its frequency.

## GO ON TO THE NEXT PAGE.

29. A particular semiconductor has a band gap of 2.48 eV. What is the wavelength of the photon that is emitted when an electron drops from the lowest energy state of the conduction band to the highest energy state of the valence band?

    A. 4.0 μm
    B. 2.0 μm
    C. 1.0 μm
    D. 0.5 μm

30. Examination of Figure 2 reveals that above a certain energy, $\ln(I_{out}/I_{in})$ becomes less than zero. This implies that

    A. $E_p = E_g$.
    B. $E_g = 0$.
    C. the input light is being absorbed instead of amplified.
    D. the process of stimulated emission is amplifying the input light.

**GO ON TO THE NEXT PAGE.**

## Passage VII (Questions 31–35)

RC circuits are used in many applications in which time-dependent currents are involved. The circuit shown in Figure 1 consists of a resistor, having resistance $R$, connected in series with a capacitor, having capacitance $C$, and an emf $\varepsilon$. A short circuit is included that makes it possible to exclude the voltage source $\varepsilon$ from the circuit by throwing the switch S to Position B. In this position, the capacitor completely discharges through the resistor.

When the switch is thrown to Position A, the emf produces a current $i$ that passes through the resistor and deposits positive charge on one plate of the capacitor. An equal amount of positive charge leaves the other plate and flows back to the voltage source. It can be shown that the charge $q$ on the positive plate of the capacitor as a function of time satisfies the equation $q = C\varepsilon(1 - e^{-t/RC})$, where $t = 0$ corresponds to the instant that the switch is thrown to Position A. Once the capacitor is sufficiently charged, the switch can be thrown to Position B and it will discharge through the resistor. As the capacitor discharges, $q$ satisfies the equation $q = C\varepsilon e^{-t/RC}$ where $t = 0$ now corresponds to the instant that the switch is thrown to Position B.

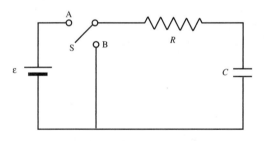

**Figure 1**

A simple model of a time-dependent current can be produced by switching S between Positions A and B at regular time intervals. Figure 2a shows a cathode-ray oscilloscope display of the voltage $V_C$ across the capacitor as a function of time; Figure 2b shows the voltage $V_R$ across the resistor as a function of time; and Figure 2c shows the sum $V_C + V_R$ as a function of time. On the displays shown in Figure 2, the time $t = 0$ corresponds to the instant that the switch is thrown to position A. Each horizontal division on the oscilloscope screen equals 0.1 s, and each vertical division equals 1.0 V. The internal resistance of the emf $\varepsilon$ is negligible.

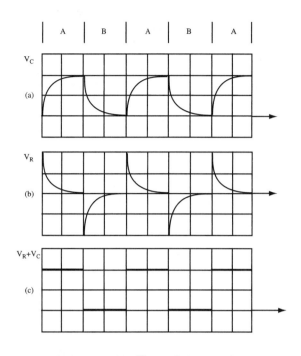

**Figure 2**

31. When the switch S is in Position A, at what value of time $t$ does the charge $q$ on the capacitor reach its maximum value?

    **A.** $t = 0$

    **B.** $t = 1/RC$

    **C.** $t = RC$

    **D.** $t = \infty$

32. How would the graph of $V_c$ versus time change if another resistor were added in series to the original resistor?

    **A.** The upper limit of the voltage would decrease.

    **B.** The upper limit of the voltage would increase.

    **C.** It would take less time for the voltage to plateau.

    **D.** It would take longer for the voltage to plateau.

**GO ON TO THE NEXT PAGE.**

33. Another capacitor, having capacitance $C$, is added in series with the original capacitor and resistor such that the two capacitors are adjacent. If the switch is thrown to Position A and remains there indefinitely, then as $t \to \infty$, the charge on each capacitor approaches

    A. $C\varepsilon/2$.
    B. $2C\varepsilon$.
    C. $2\varepsilon/C$.
    D. $\varepsilon/(2C)$.

34. What is the magnitude of the emf $\varepsilon$?

    A. 0.5 V
    B. 1.0 V
    C. 1.5 V
    D. 2.0 V

35. Why does the capacitor discharge through the resistor when the switch S is in Position B?

    A. Because the charge on the positive plate of the capacitor is at a higher potential than the charge on the negative plate
    B. Because the charge on the negative plate of the capacitor is at a higher potential than the charge on the positive plate
    C. Because the emf draws a current that has to pass through the resistor
    D. Because the voltage $V_C$ across the capacitor equals zero

## Discrete Questions (Questions 36–45)

36. Suppose an $\alpha$-particle starting from rest is accelerated through a 5-megavolt potential difference. What is the final kinetic energy of the $\alpha$-particle? (Note: Assume that $e = 1.6 \times 10^{-19}$ C.)

    A. $1.6 \times 10^{-12}$ J
    B. $8.0 \times 10^{-13}$ J
    C. $6.4 \times 10^{-26}$ J
    D. $3.2 \times 10^{-26}$ J

37. If a spring is 64 cm long when it is unstretched and is 8% longer when a 0.5-kg mass hangs from it, how long will it be with a 0.4-kg mass suspended from it?

    A. 66 cm
    B. 68 cm
    C. 70 cm
    D. 74 cm

38. A clown stands with her toes touching a fun-house mirror with a convex bottom and a concave top. Which of the following best describes the distortion of the clown's image as she walks away from the mirror?

    A. Her head will shrink; her feet will grow, then shrink.
    B. Her head will shrink, then grow; her feet will shrink, then grow.
    C. Her head will grow; her feet will grow.
    D. Her head will grow, then shrink; her feet will shrink.

**GO ON TO THE NEXT PAGE.**

**39.** Consider the static pulley system illustrated below. Which of the following would be sufficient information to determine the mass B? (Assume a frictionless system, g = 10 m/s².)

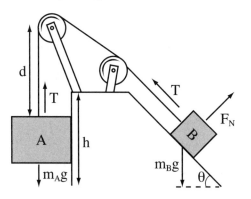

A. Mass of A and angle θ

B. Tension T, height h, and distance d

C. Height h and angle θ

D. Angle θ and distance d

**40.** In which of the following situations will the normal force on a box be the greatest?

A. When the box is placed in a stationary elevator

B. When the box is placed in an elevator moving upward at a constant velocity

C. When the box is placed in an elevator accelerating downward

D. When the box is placed in an elevator accelerating upward

**41.** An engineer designs an underground tunnel with two ventilation pipes as shown below. Pipe A opens to the air at ground level, while Pipe B extends above ground level and is exposed to air moving at a higher velocity. Which of the following is true?

(Assume constant air density, $P + \frac{1}{2}\rho v^2 + \rho gy = $ constant.)

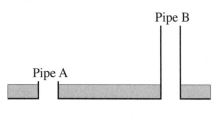

A. Air will flow from left to right in the tunnel.

B. Air will flow from right to left in the tunnel.

C. The direction of air flow in the tunnel depends on the direction of air flow (wind) in the environment.

D. Air will flow into the tunnel more rapidly via Pipe B than via Pipe A.

**42.** A crane lifts a 1000-kg steel beam off the ground, and sets it down on scaffolding 100 meters off the ground. All of the following are true EXCEPT:

A. The net work done on the steel beam is $9.8 \times 10^5$ J.

B. The net work done on the steel beam is 0 J.

C. The magnitude of the work done on the steel beam by gravity is $9.8 \times 10^5$ J.

D. The magnitude of the work done on the steel beam by the crane is $9.8 \times 10^5$ J.

**43.** An 8-kg object traveling at 5 m/s has a perfectly inelastic collision with a stationary 13-kg object. What is the ratio of the initial speed of the 8-kg object to its final speed?

A. 8:21

B. 21:40

C. 13:8

D. 21:8

**GO ON TO THE NEXT PAGE.**

**44.** In the diagram below, a stream of electrons leaves the electron gun at G and strikes the fluorescent screen at P. When the current is switched on at S, it flows through the wire coils in an anticlockwise direction as seen by the observer at O; the observer sees the spot of light at P

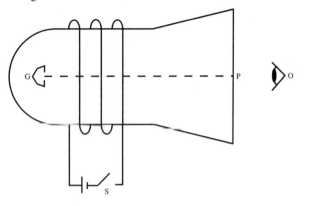

  **A.**   move downward.

  **B.**   move to the left.

  **C.**   move to the right.

  **D.**   remain still.

**45.** Eight positively charged spheres (+1 C each) are distributed at equally spaced intervals around a circular hoop whose radius is 1 m as shown below. What is the electrostatic potential at the center of the hoop? (Note: $k$ is the Boltzmann constant.)

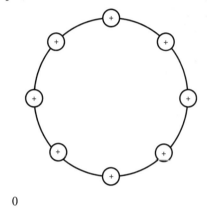

  **A.**   0

  **B.**   $4k$

  **C.**   $4\sqrt{2}\,k$

  **D.**   $8k$

---

**STOP.** IF YOU FINISH BEFORE TIME HAS EXPIRED, CHECK YOUR WORK. YOU MAY GO BACK TO ANY QUESTION IN THIS PART ONLY.

---

ANSWERS AND EXPLANATIONS BEGIN ON NEXT PAGE →

# PHYSICS PRACTICE SET

## Answer Key

**Passage I (Questions 1–5)**
1. D
2. A
3. C
4. D
5. B

**Passage II (Questions 6–10)**
6. A
7. C
8. C
9. B
10. A

**Passage III (Questions 11–15)**
11. C
12. B
13. B
14. C
15. B

**Passage IV (Questions 16–20)**
16. B
17. A
18. D
19. C
20. D

**Passage V (Questions 21–25)**
21. A
22. D
23. B
24. C
25. D

**Passage VI (Questions 26–30)**
26. B
27. C
28. A
29. D
30. C

**Passage VII (Questions 31–35)**
31. D
32. D
33. A
34. D
35. A

**Discrete Questions (Questions 36–45)**
36. A
37. B
38. D
39. A
40. D
41. A
42. A
43. D
44. D
45. D

# PHYSICS PRACTICE SET

## Answers and Explanations

## Passage I (Questions 1–5)

### 1.  D

In this question, we are asked to determine what caused light to red shift between galaxies. If we didn't pick up on the answer while reading the passage, then we can go back to the portion of the passage that discusses the red shift. The fourth paragraph informed us that light emitted from a galaxy moving away from us is shifted to greater wavelengths, and therefore lower frequencies ($\lambda f = c$). From our knowledge of the physics tested on the MCAT, we know that the Doppler effect involves frequencies (or wavelengths) that shift between emitter and observer. Choice **D** is correct.

But what if we didn't latch onto the Doppler effect right away? We can take advantage of the fact that this question, like the majority of Physics questions on the MCAT (indeed, like most MCAT questions in general) doesn't require a calculation and doesn't have numerical answer choices. In this situation, we can usually eliminate at least one or two clearly wrong answer choices.

Ionization is the stripping away of electrons from atoms and molecules. This has nothing to do with the changing frequencies of photons. Choice **A** is incorrect. Both reflection (choice **B**) and refraction (choice **C**) involve light waves (or photons) that strike boundaries between media. The reflected photons bounce back, remaining in their original medium, while refracted photons enter the new medium, changing speed, wavelength, and direction. Refraction might be a tempting answer choice, until we realize that the galactic red shift isn't a problem of light crossing between media.

### 2.  A

When you are given numbers in a problem on MCAT Physics, it is usually a sign that some sort of calculation will be required. The fact that the answer choices are all numbers only reinforces this point. We need to establish what is being asked for, what we are given, and how we are going to get from one to the other. In this case, we are given the emitted wavelength of a star (250 nm) and the wavelength of the same light as observed by the telescope (750 nm). We are asked for the relative size of the universe when the light was emitted.

The formula for the relative size of the universe is given in the passage. When a passage introduces new formulas, be sure to take note of what information is contained within

each one. In this case, we are told the relative size of the universe R (with respect to today) as a function of $z$, the red shift. We are also given the formula for the red shift, in terms of the emitted and observed wavelength. We have exactly what we need to solve for R:

$$z = \frac{\lambda_{obs} - \lambda_{emit}}{\lambda_{emit}}$$

$$z = \frac{750 - 250}{250} = \frac{500}{250} = 2$$

Plugging our value for $z$ into Equation 2 yields:

$$R = \frac{1}{1 + z} = \frac{1}{1 + 2} = \frac{1}{3}$$

The correct answer is choice **A**. The wrong answer choices represent results achieved after making common math mistakes. This is common practice on the MCAT, so always do your math carefully; miss questions by making science mistakes, not simple math mistakes.

### 3. C

The answer choices in this question are presented in a pattern often seen on the MCAT. Notice the true choices we are asked to make. Is the primary mirror convex, or concave? And is the primary mirror converging, or diverging? If we are able to answer the question straight away, perfect. If not, then we have to answer only one of the two "subquestions" in order to eliminate half the answer choices. One-in-two odds are much better than one-in-four odds.

Merely examining Figure 1 allows us to deduce that the primary mirror is focusing rays toward the secondary mirror. That makes the primary mirror a converging mirror, which eliminates answer choices **B** and **D**.

A useful mnemonic device is to pretend that we are the light ray. Does the lens or mirror bulge out, or does it *cave* in? If it caves in, then it's *concave*. The other case (bulging out) is convex. The primary mirror caves in (look at Figure 1), and so it is a concave mirror; answer choice **C** is correct. On the other hand, had the telescope utilized a converging *lens*, its shape would be convex.

### 4. D

The radius of curvature is a piece of vocabulary not defined in the passage, so we are expected to come up with the definition. Let's pretend that we don't know what radius of curvature means. We can at least deduce that it has something to do with curvature. Well, the primary mirror curves, but according to the passage, the secondary mirror is flat; it has no curvature. Which answer choice might represent no curvature for the secondary mirror? Choices **A** and **B** give a finite radius of curvature for the secondary mirror, so they are probably wrong. The lesson here is: Many times on the MCAT, there is a chance to make some headway on a question using common sense and reasoning, even if our science fails us.

Spherical mirrors can be thought of as a segment of a sphere. Looking at the cross section below, the radius of curvature of the parent sphere is equal to twice the focal length of the mirror (this applies to lenses as well). We are given the focal length of the primary mirror as 58 m. The radius of curvature is therefore $58 \times 2 = 116$ m. The radius of curvature is NOT half the diameter of the mirror. Looking at the head-on view, the diameter of the mirror describes the width of the mirror, and determines how much light the mirror can gather (the greater the diameter, the more light will be reflected by the mirror).

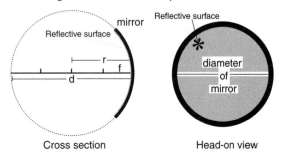

Cross section          Head-on view

A flat mirror can be considered an infinitely large sphere, so it has an infinite radius of curvature. Therefore, choice **D**, 116 m for the primary mirror and infinity for the secondary mirror, contains the correct respective values for the radii of curvature.

5. **B**

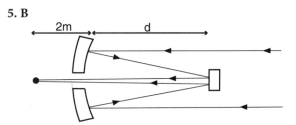

This question doesn't yield to a quick answer; we'll have to understand the workings of the mirror system in detail to answer this one correctly.

The first thing we know is that the incoming rays are parallel. This is a common approximation to use when the object is much, much farther away from the mirror (or lens) than the focal length, as is usually the case with telescopes. The incoming light strikes the primary mirror first. When parallel rays strike a converging spherical mirror, we know that they are all deflected toward the focal point of the mirror.

However, they meet the secondary mirror along the way. The fact that the secondary mirror is a plane mirror means that the incoming rays bounce off at the same angle at which they came in. So the rays will still converge; but instead of converging behind the secondary mirror, they will converge in front of it. But since the mirror isn't spherical, the rays aren't bent any further. In other words, they will still travel the same distance until they converge: the focal distance of the primary mirror, 58 m.

If we let $d$ equal the distance between the two mirrors, then $2d + 2 = 58$, and $d = 28$ m. This is the hardest type of MCAT Physics question, one that requires us to remember multiple facts from physics, and calls on calculation, and (most important) calls on your ability to reason logically based on what we're told and the science knowledge in our minds. We can take some solace from this, however, by remembering that the MCAT will never ask us to stretch the boundaries of science: all the questions are answerable using basic physics.

# Passage II (Questions 6–10)

6.   **A**

When we read an MCAT physics passage that describes an experimental apparatus, we should pay very close attention to exactly how that apparatus works. In this case, a beam of light is split, and the two resulting beams travel different paths. If each path length is the same, then the two waves will meet up again in phase, and constructive interference will occur. In fact, if one path length differs from the other but is a multiple of the light's wavelength, when they meet again, peak will still meet peak and trough will still meet trough, and constructive interference will continue to occur. The formula in the passage bears out this fact, taking careful notice of the fact that the difference in path length isn't merely the difference in mirror distances $|d_1 - d_2|$, but in fact double that difference, since each beam travels toward a mirror, bounces off, and then treads the same path again in reverse.

As can be gathered from inspection of Figure 2 or from the passage text, to go from one maximum to another would entail a one-wavelength increase in the retardation. Since the wavelength of the radiation is 6328 Å, this must also be the increase in retardation. Before leaping to choice **B** as the answer, however, we need to keep in mind the relation between the distance the mirror has traveled and the retardation. As mentioned in the passage, the distance between the beamsplitter and each mirror is traversed twice, once in each direction. Therefore, the retardation is twice $|d_1 - d_2|$. If the retardation has been increased by 6328 Å, then the movable mirror has only been moved by half this distance, or 3164 Å. Answer choice **A** is correct.

**7. C**

Roman numeral questions on the MCAT should always be handled systematically. If we consider first the statement that appears most often in the answer choices, then we raise our chances of being able to quickly eliminate wrong answers.

We can start with either statement II or III. Start with statement III: If the frequency of the radiation were increased, its wavelength would be shorter because the two are related by $c = f\lambda$, where c is the speed of light, f is the frequency, and $\lambda$ is the wavelength. We know that a mirror being moved a certain distance would thus encounter more maxima and minima, since more wavelengths could now fit into the same distance. In other words, since the wavelength is shorter, we don't have to move the mirror as far to go from maxima to maxima. Statement III is correct; choices **A** and **B** can be dismissed.

Looking at the remaining choices, we find that we need only evaluate whether statement II is correct, without having to worry about statement I.

Statement II is incorrect. The minimum intensity cannot be lowered: If total destructive interference occurs, the intensity is zero. This would be the case regardless of the frequency of the radiation. Intensity cannot be negative and so cannot possibly be lower than this. Since statement II is incorrect, choice **C** is the correct answer.

For completeness, let us see why statement I is also incorrect: The number of photons is constant, while the energy carried by each photon increases. The intensity of a beam of light isn't a function of the energy of each photon, but merely of the number of photons present; more photons, higher intensity.

**8. C**

Consulting the answer choices in this problem, we see that this question isn't about the phenomena discussed in the passage but is instead about something completely different: beats. Usually, the more difficult the passage is, the easier these "off the beaten path" questions are.

If the source radiation consists of two wavelengths, the interferogram is the sum of the two sinusoids caused by each wavelength separately. This results in a pattern similar to that of a beat pattern encountered when sound waves of close but distinct frequencies interfere. The sound intensity heard fluctuates with a frequency of $|f_1 - f_2|$, where $f_1$ and $f_2$ are the frequencies of the original sound waves. We have a similar scenario here: The intensity of the light will exhibit a beat frequency equal to the difference between the two radiation frequencies. In the question, however, only the wavelengths are given. We need to convert them into frequencies via the equation $c = f\lambda$. The light of wavelength $\lambda_1$ has a frequency of $c/\lambda_1$, and the light of wavelength $\lambda_2$ has a frequency of $c/\lambda_2$. The beat frequency is therefore $|c/\lambda_1 - c/\lambda_2|$, choice **C**.

Notice that, although dressed in the vocabulary of the passage, this question was actually a direct and straightforward application of the formula for the beat frequency.

Choices **A** and **B** are incorrect, because it is the frequencies that subtract, not the wavelengths.

**9. B**

This is actually a question that can be answered without reference to the passage. Even though the question starts by making reference to the interferometer, the scenario presented has little to do with the apparatus; the context is light traveling in a general medium n.

First, in a vacuum, the number of wavelengths $\lambda_0$ that would fit in a distance d is simply $d/\lambda_0$. When the medium has an index of refraction different from 1, however, the wavelength will change. The speed of light in a medium of index of refraction n is given by $v = c/n$, where c, the speed of light in a vacuum, has a constant value of $3.0 \times 10^8$ m/s. Since the index of refraction of a nonvacuum is going to be greater than 1, the speed of light in the medium is less than that in a vacuum. Since the speed of light can also be expressed as $v = f\lambda$, where f is the frequency, the wavelength will also be affected. (The frequency remains unchanged.) The new wavelength can be determined as follows:

$$f\lambda = v = c/n = (f\lambda_0)/n$$

Dividing both sides by f gives $\lambda = \lambda_0/n$. The number of wavelengths that would fit in a distance d of the medium is therefore $d/\lambda = d/(\lambda_0/n) = dn/\lambda_0$, answer choice **B**.

If we were having trouble working out the exact formula, we could have reasoned as follows: We know that since the wavelength is dropping, more of them will fit in a distance d. So we need a fraction that is larger than $d/\lambda_0$. Since the value of n is now larger than 1, we can eliminate choices **C** and **D**, and guess between choices **A** and **B**.

**10. A**

Again, since this is purely a reasoning question, if you have any trouble working out what the answer should be, you can at least eliminate wrong answer choices as you go.

If the source radiation is no longer monochromatic, but consists of a continuous range of wavelengths, then constructive interference will occur at different path lengths for each different wavelength of light. As can be gathered from the equation given, different values of $\lambda$ will require different values of $|d_1 - d_2|$ for constructive interference. For any one value of retardation, some components of light will interfere constructively (if the retardation is an integral multiple of the wavelength), while others will interfere destructively (if the retardation is a half-integral multiple of the wavelength). The only exception is when $|d_1 - d_2| = 0$ (each path length is the same), which constitutes a maximum ($m = 0$) regardless of $\lambda$. When this is the case, all the components of light interfere constructively. Regardless of the wavelength, the two split beams are in phase since they travel the exact same distance. The correct answer is choice **A**.

Choices **B** and **C** make little sense; why would the interferogram for a range of wavelengths take on the properties of only the wavelengths present?

## Passage III (Questions 11–15)

**11. C**
Roman numeral questions on the MCAT are much like "which of the following" questions, in the sense that it is usually impossible for us to predict the correct answer without evaluating each of the answer choices. On Test Day, don't waste time trying.

The entire passage is a discussion of what happens when the ship tilts. Statement I appears three times in the answer choices; let's start there. When a ship tilts, H shifts to the leaning side (stated midway through paragraph two). This is because as a ship tilts, it will displace a greater proportion of fluid toward the tilting side, resulting in a shift of the center of gravity of the fluid displaced. Statement I is therefore correct; eliminate answer choice **B**. (It's always a good idea to eliminate wrong answer choices by striking them out as you go along to save time.)

Statement II is also correct. Looking at the tilting ship in Figure 1, notice that the angle θ is measured between line MH (which represents the buoyant force vector) and m. As H shifts, line MH will shift with it, creating a greater angle θ. Statements I and II are saying the same thing, and both are correct. As θ increases, sin θ increases, and so does the torque. Eliminate answer choice **A**.

Statement III is incorrect. As stated in the second paragraph, the buoyant force is equal in magnitude to the force of gravity on the ship. The mass (and therefore the weight) of the ship does not change during a tilt, so the buoyant force does not change. Another way to see this is to remember the density rule: The fraction of an object's volume that is submerged in a liquid is the ratio of its density to the density of the fluid. Since the densities of the fluid and ship are unchanging, the fraction of the volume submerged is unchanging as well. So as the boat tilts, the volume of water displaced is the same—which means the buoyant force is constant, too. The correct answer is choice **C**.

**12. B**
Intuitively, we know that the ship will overturn when the waves and wind tilt the ship too far. The first paragraph of the passage backs us up on that. However, that isn't one of the answer choices. Since it's probably too difficult to work out what the precise conditions are when the ship overturns, let's use the process of elimination instead.

Answer choice **A** can be eliminated. The buoyant force is equal to the weight of the fluid displaced. Since it is the weight of the ship that is responsible for displacing the fluid, the buoyant force must equal the weight of the ship at all times. (This assumes that the ship isn't taking on water, but such a scenario is outside the scope of this passage.) Answer choice **C** is an example of a faulty use of detail. If the hydrostatic center and center of gravity are not along the same vertical line, this is simply a consequence of the ship being tilted. The buoyant force generates a restoring torque. A ship will overturn only if the angle of tilt exceeds the ships ability to restore itself. Answer choice **D** is incorrect, because the restoring torque is zero when the ship is in equilibrium, which is when it has no angle of tilt. In this position, it is in no danger of overturning.

Choice **B** is correct, but is never stated outright in the passage. The first paragraph of the passage states that a boat will overturn when the angle of tilt is too great. Imagine a boat that tilts from equilibrium until it overturns. Looking at Figure 1, in equilibrium $m$ is zero, so the torque is zero. As the ship tilts, $m$ goes from zero to a maximum, but as the angle of tilt continues to increase, the metacentric height $m$ will then decrease and then become negative (that is it will be directed downward with respect to C), because the hydrostatic center of the ship will keep moving away from the centerline. Incorporating this into the torque equation, the torque will increase (serving to right the ship) then will decrease until finally it reverses direction and contributes to overturning the ship.

**13. B**
Usually when a fluids question on MCAT Physics discusses displaced fluid, the first thing you should think to apply is the buoyant force. The buoyant force is equal in magnitude to the weight of the water displaced:

$$F_b = W_{water} = m_{water}g$$

Rearranging the equation for the mass of water and applying Equation 1 from the passage yields:

$$m_{water} = \frac{F_b}{g} \text{ and } \tau = F_b m \sin\theta \rightarrow$$
$$m_{water} = \frac{\tau}{gm \sin\theta}$$

Answer choice **B** is correct. There are a few familiar terms in some of the wrong answer choices. What if we couldn't solve for the correct answer on a question whose answer choices were all algebraic expressions? One good way to eliminate wrong answers is to determine the dimensions of each of the choices. In this case, all the other answer choices have the wrong dimensions! Choice **A** is a distance, choice **C** is a density, and choice **D** is a force.

## 14. C

A more succinct way of stating Newton's Third Law is that the force on object A due to object B is equal in magnitude and opposite in direction to the force of A on B. The force of gravity on the ship is exerted by the mass of the earth, which means that the reactive force is the gravitational force on the earth due to the mass of the ship; answer choice **C** is correct.

The buoyant force, answer choice **B**, is tempting because it is the force that balances out the weight of the ship when it is upright. But nonetheless it is incorrect. According to the above paragraph, the two forces ("the action and the equal and opposite reaction") have to be between the same two objects. Gravity operates between the earth and the ship; and so must the reactive force. Buoyancy acts between the ship and the water, so it cannot be the reactive force to gravity. The reactive force to buoyancy would be a normal force exerted by the ship's hull on the water (if that normal force were not present, the buoyant force would crush the hull).

## 15. B

Let's try to predict the answer based on our physics know-how. The formula for torque is $\tau = F_b \, m \sin \theta$. The presence of the sin θ factor means that only the vector component of the force that is perpendicular to the moment arm (the vector from the axis of rotation to the point of application of the force represented by the distance m) contributes to the torque. When the ship is tilted (as in Figure 1 of the passage), the buoyant force (at H) acts along a vertical line that passes through the metacenter, M. If we were to redraw the buoyant force vector centered at M, it would look like vector A on the diagram in the question. The moment arm of the torque, which points along the line HM, would be represented by vector D (so at this point we know that **A** and **D** are incorrect). Which of the four vectors drawn represent the component of vector A perpendicular to vector D? That's vector B. Vector C points in the opposite direction.

One of the ways the MCAT can make questions very hard is to require us to think in terms of vector quantities. Make sure to know which quantities in physics are represented by vectors, and know the basics of how to deal with them.

## Passage IV (Questions 16–20)

### 16. B

In Table 1, for each value of frequency we have two data points, corresponding to the first two occurrences of resonance. The first occurrence arises when the fundamental of the air-column vibrations matches the frequency of the tuning fork; the second occurrence arises when the first overtone of the air-column vibrations matches the frequency of the tuning fork. The next occurrence of resonance must therefore correspond to the second overtone of some air-column length. The condition that we always have to satisfy, according to the passage, is that there is a node at one end (the water–air interface) and an antinode at the other (the open end of the tube). We can thus picture that the second overtone must look like the following:

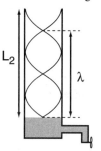

The length of the air column can therefore be seen to be $5\lambda/4$. How is this related to the other values, the ones corresponding to the lower modes? We observe that in the fundamental mode, for example, only 1/4 of the wavelength fits into the air column:

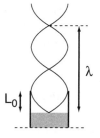

In other words, $L_0 = \lambda/4$, while $L_2$, the quantity we are trying to determine, is $5\lambda/4$. The next occurrence of resonance thus happens when the air column is five times as long as the first recorded resonance column length. For the 426.7-Hz tuning fork, this is $5 \times 20.0 \text{ cm} = 100 \text{ cm}$.

Incidentally, we have assumed that the two data points for each tuning fork recorded in Table 1 do indeed correspond to the two lowest modes—i.e., that no resonance was skipped. This can be verified by noticing the relationship between the values in each pair: One is always roughly three times the other. This relation is satisfied only with the fundamental and the first overtone, since the first overtone has an $L_1$ that is $3\lambda/4$—i.e., three times that of $L_0$:

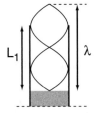

**17. A**

This point may be obvious, but it bears repeating. When an MCAT question presents a scenario that is not discussed in the passage (such as the temperature dependence of the speed of sound in air), the question is always asking you to draw on your outside knowledge of basic physics.

If the experiment were conducted at a lower temperature, the sound waves would be traveling at a slower speed, according to the question stem. Since the frequency is the same as that of the tuning fork being used, the frequency remains constant. Choices **C** and **D** can therefore be eliminated. The wavelength must decrease, since $v = f\lambda$. Therefore, the resonance air column lengths must also decrease.

**18. D**

This type of question is fairly common in experiment passages on the science sections of the MCAT. Slightly alter the experiment, and figure out how the results change. Answering this type of question correctly will always require an in-depth understanding of how the experiment is carried out, which is why it is good advice to read carefully the part of an experiment passage that describes how the experiment is performed.

The only purpose of the water is to provide a surface for a node of the standing air wave to form, and hence to offer a means of adjusting the length of the air column. If another liquid is used in its place, regardless of its density (choice **A**), index of refraction (choice **B**), or molecular weight (choice **C**), it serves the same purpose and the resonance lengths would be observed to be the same. Nothing conclusive can be deduced about the liquid. In fact, since the lengths of the air columns are used to determine the speed of sound, it would be quite disturbing indeed if a different liquid would lead to different results, as that would imply that the identity of the liquid used affects the speed of sound in air! Choice **D** is the correct answer.

**19. C**

This is another classic example of the MCAT making a question difficult by tweaking the experiment and asking us to work out the consequences.

The value of 31.9 cm corresponds to the fundamental vibration of the 256-Hz tuning fork. We know from the passage that the next highest frequency that will lead to resonance at this length is one that matches the first overtone.

The standing wave of the fundamental corresponds to the situation where $L = \lambda/4$, while the standing wave of the first overtone corresponds to the situation where $L = 3\lambda/4$. If we are keeping L constant (at 31.9 cm), the wavelength must therefore decrease by a factor of three upon going from the fundamental to the first overtone. Since the wavelength is inversely proportional to the frequency, the frequency must increase by a factor of three: $3(256\text{ Hz}) = 768\text{ Hz}$, answer choice **C**.

Note the difference between the experiment described in the question stem and the one in the passage. In the passage, the wavelength is constant for each tuning fork, and we vary the value of L to attain resonance; here, we are keeping L constant and asking what value of $\lambda$, or f, is needed for each condition for resonance.

**20. D**

Since there is no data given in the table on the speed of the sound waves, we are left to our own devices. This question does what most MCAT calculation questions do: It asks us to calculate something, but makes us figure out what raw data is appropriate to use, and makes us remember the correct equation to use. Fortunately, calculation questions rarely appear outside of Physics, and there are usually no more than two (there is usually only one) per passage.

In this case, we must use the formula for the speed of a mechanical wave: $v = f\lambda$. We are told which frequency to use by the question stem: 384 Hz. All we need now is the wavelength. Having read the table carefully, we know that we can't just read the wavelength right off the table. The length of the fundamental air column is about 21.5 cm. But, according to Figure 2, this represents only a quarter of the wavelength. Multiplying by 4 (if we divide by accident, we will arrive at answer choice **A**), the wavelength of the sound wave is 86 cm = 0.86 m. Remember to convert to standard units!

Now, we calculate the approximate speed:

$$v = (384\text{ Hz})(0.86)\text{m} \approx (400\text{ Hz})(0.9) = 360\text{ m/s},$$

which is closest to answer choice **D**. Since we overestimated both the frequency and the wavelength, we expect our approximation to come in above the true value.

Approximating, like we did in this question, is a good habit to get into on calculation questions. The MCAT will never group the answer choices so closely together that you won't be able to choose between two of them.

## Passage V (Questions 21–25)

**21. A**

This is a calculation question, calling upon us to remember the definition of momentum. The trap being laid here is that we will attempt to take *too much* information into account in working out the answer. We might mistakenly calculate the momentum of both bullets, or, worse yet, try to cancel both momenta because the horizontal components of the bullets' velocities are in opposition. Another trap is that since the mass of a bullet isn't given in the paragraph describing Stunt 2, we might forget to multiply the bullet speed by it, and arrive at answer choice **C**.

This question is asking us to apply the definition of momentum, $p = mv$. Since each bullet has a mass $m = 5 \times 10^{-3}$ kg (remember to convert to kilograms; another trap!) and leaves its gun at 250 m/s, its momentum is $p = (5 \times 10^{-3}$ kg$)(250$ m/s$) = 1.25$ kg $\cdot$ m/s. The correct answer is choice **A**.

**22. D**

Like all "which of the following" questions, we'll have to consider each of the answer choices, eliminating as we go. Fortunately for us, the answer choices focus on two questions: Is the total momentum of the system conserved? Is the kinetic energy of the system conserved?

In Stunt 2, the passage tells us that the collision is inelastic. The total momentum of the system is not conserved, since gravity acts on both bullets. The total momentum of a system of objects is conserved only when there is no net force on the system. Eliminate answer choices **A** and **C**. The kinetic energy of the system is also *not* conserved, since the collision is inelastic. Remember that the kinetic energy of a system is conserved only in a collision that is perfectly elastic. The correct answer is choice **D**.

**23. B**

Let's apply Roman numeral strategy by evaluating the statement that appears in the most answer choices: Statement II. The target's translational kinetic energy is zero throughout; the target's motion is all rotation, it never changes position. Statement II must appear in the correct answer; eliminate answer choice **A**.

What about statement I? The target's potential energy is a function of how high it sits above the ground. In fact, the zero level of gravitational potential energy is arbitrary. We usually set the potential energy at ground level equal to zero; but we could give it any number at all. So the potential energy of the target doesn't have to be zero; any answer containing statement I is wrong. Only answer choice **B** remains.

We don't have to consider statement III, but let's check it just in case. The target's rotational kinetic energy is not

zero; according to the passage, the target rotates at constant angular velocity between the two shots.

**24. C**

One of the insidious aspects of MCAT passages and questions is that they can be worded in such a way as to cause the reader to make false assumptions and draw false conclusions. In this case, it would be easy for us to not think too hard about what has to be true if firing the second bullet so that it strikes the target halfway in will cause it to stop rotating. After all, if we fire consecutive bullets out of a gun, the speed and force of impact of each bullet is going to be roughly the same, right? In this case, no! Since a bullet with identical mass strikes the target further in from where the first bullet struck, it must strike with a greater force to create a torque that overcomes the torque provided by the first bullet. Remember to be thinking about the physical consequences of all manmade phenomena described in an MCAT Physics passage.

The first bullet causes the target to rotate because it applies a torque. The second bullet will stop the target's rotation by applying an equal torque in the opposite direction. Since the bullets strike on opposite sides of the center of the target, we know the torques will be in opposite directions. We need to know the magnitude of the torque from the first bullet. Applying the definition of torque ($\tau = rF \sin \theta$, but $\theta = 90°$, so $\tau = rF$), we see that this torque is $\tau_1 = (0.5$ m$)(F_0) = 0.5F_0$ using the fact that the radius of the target is 0.5 m. The second bullet strikes the target 0.25 m away from the center with a force we'll call F. Setting the two torques equal, we see that $0.5F_0 = 0.25F$; $F = 2F_0$.

**25. D**

How should the shooter compensate for the wind? The wind blows to the northeast. The easterly part of the wind will act to speed up the bullet a little bit, but won't affect its aim. However, the northerly component of the wind will blow the bullet off course. To compensate for that, the shooter will have to aim a bit south of the target. This eliminates answer choices **A** and **C**. Answer choice **D** offers a different wrinkle: Does the shooter have to aim high to compensate for gravity? Yes, she does. The acceleration due to gravity will start pulling the bullet downward once it leaves the gun. Over a long distance, the bullet could fall far enough to pass under the target, so the shooter should also aim a bit high, so that the bullet will arc upward, and strike the target on the way down.

This question demonstrates why you should read the answer choices along with the question stem. It would be easy for us to waste time worrying simply about compensating for the wind, and then, as we check the answer choices, realize that we have to compensate for gravity as well.

## Passage VI (Questions 26–30)

**26. B**

Be sure to apply Roman numeral strategy to this problem. Statement I appears most frequently. The photon, being a quantum of light, exhibits also the wave behavior of light (and of waves in general) as it crosses the boundary from one medium to another. The frequency remains the same, and so does the energy since it is related to the frequency by the equation $E = hf$. So statements I and II are both false, which automatically makes choice **B** the correct answer.

The wavelength and the speed of the photons, on the other hand, do change. The speed of light in a medium with an index of refraction $n \geq 1$ is given by $v = c/n$, where c is the speed in vacuum. This accounts for the refraction of light, as described by Snell's law. Since the speed changes while the frequency remains constant, the wavelength will have to change to maintain the equality $v = \lambda f$.

**27. C**

Remember that "which of the following" questions require you to eliminate answer choices one by one. Let's figure out what's true of the energy of photons produced by optically pumped electrons before we jump into the answers. In the passage we are told that electrons are pumped from the valence band to the higher energy conduction band. The band gap $E_g$ is the smallest difference in energy between these two bands. When an electron is optically pumped, it absorbs a photon of a particular energy and makes a transition to a higher energy state. By conservation of energy, the difference between the final and initial energy states of the electron equals the energy of the photon absorbed. Within the band gap there are no states that the electron can occupy, so the electron must absorb enough energy to make a transition across the gap. The smallest energy that can bring about this transition is equal to the band gap. In this case, an electron in the highest energy level of the valence band is excited to the lowest energy level of the conduction band. In general, an electron may start at a lower level in the valence band and/or end up at a higher energy level in the conduction band. The photon energy then will need to be greater than the gap energy, $E_g$. The photon absorbed by an electron must therefore have an energy at least as big as the band gap energy, answer choice **C**.

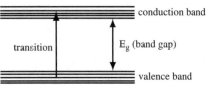

Remember that, as always, you should read the answer choices along with the question stem. In this case, we

gained an important clue that could help us figure out what was happening in this question: that there is a good chance that the photon energy $E_p$ is related in some way to the band gap energy $E_g$.

**28. A**

We can tell from the question stem that this question has absolutely nothing to do with the inner workings of the semiconductor in the passage. This question stands alone from the passage—something that happens frequently on the MCAT. When you learn to recognize these questions, you'll have a leg up on Test Day.

So this question is really about the atomic energy levels of hydrogen. When a hydrogen atom absorbs a photon, its electron makes a transition to a higher energy state. This can occur only if the difference in energy between the initial and final states equals the energy of the photon; answer choice **A** is correct.

Choice **B** states that the photon has to have an energy that is an integer multiple of h. We know that the energy of a photon is $E = hf$, where f is the frequency. Choice **B** then suggests that the photon's frequency has to be an integer in order for it to be absorbed. This is a gross distortion of the concept of quantization. There is no restriction on the value of f itself. Besides, this requirement tells us nothing about the absorption of the photon. Choice **C** is the condition for ionization: A photon above this value will eject the electron from the atom, and the residual energy will be the kinetic energy of the electron. We are told, however, that ionization does not occur and besides, a photon can be absorbed without causing ionization. So choice **C** is incorrect. Choice **D** is also clearly wrong in that the energy of a photon is proportional to its frequency, and the energy of the photon is crucial in determining whether or not it is absorbed.

**29. D**

The energy of the photon emitted is equal to the energy difference between the final and initial states of the electron. The final state of the electron in this case is the highest energy state of the valence band, while the initial state is the lowest energy state of the conduction band. The energy difference is exactly the band gap. The photon energy must therefore be 2.48 eV. To determine its wavelength, we use the relationship:

$$E = hf = hc/\lambda$$
$$\lambda = \frac{hc}{E} = \frac{1.24 \times 10^{-6} \text{ eV} \cdot \text{m}}{2.48 \text{ eV}}$$
$$= 0.5 \times 10^{-6} \text{ m} = 0.5 \ \mu\text{m}$$

**30. C**

Let's see if we can work out what it means for the natural logarithm of the ratio of output intensity to the input intensity of photons to be less than zero. When the logarithm of a number is less than zero, that means that the number lies between zero and 1. The output intensity is therefore less than the input intensity. Some of the input light has been absorbed.

Choice **A** states that the energy $E_p$ of the photon that "pumps" electrons from the valence to the conduction band is equal to the band gap $E_g$. This cannot be deduced: Pumping is needed to populate the conduction band with electrons so they can relax. As long as this is accomplished, the actual energy of photons used in pumping plays no role in the subsequent processes of stimulated emission and/or absorption. Choice **B** states that the band gap is zero. This need not be the case either. Choice **D** describes the region of the plot where $\ln (I_{out}/I_{in})$ is greater than zero.

Remember that when a question asks you to work out a consequence of a scenario presented in the passage, you should try to work out what the answer should be on your own, before eliminating answer choices. Better to do the work on your own when you can, and know you've found the correct answer, than to jump straight to the answer choices and face two or more "good-looking" potential answer choices.

## Passage VII (Questions 31–35)

**31. D**

This question requires you to analyze the formula in the passage that gives the charge on the capacitor as a function of time. Since there are two formulas, though, we have to make sure we use the correct one. When the switch is in position A the capacitor is being charged by the emf, and when the switch is in position B the capacitor discharges across the resistor. This question asks about the case where the switch is in position A; the applicable formula is therefore $q = C\varepsilon(1 - e^{-t/RC})$, where q is the charge, C is the capacitance, $\varepsilon$ is the emf, t is the time, and R is the resistance of the resistor. The time t = 0 corresponds to the instant that the switch is thrown to position A. Physically, since the capacitor is being charged by the emf, we would expect that the charge on the capacitor increases as time passes. Therefore, the maximum charge will occur as t approaches infinity. Let us verify that the mathematical formula is consistent with this rather intuitive approach.

At t = 0, the exponential term is $e^0$, which is 1. The charge q is therefore $C\varepsilon(1 - 1) = 0$. This makes sense as the capacitor is uncharged at t = 0. Let us examine closer the exponential term for t > 0. Since t, R and C are all positive quantities, the exponential term is e to a negative number. As t increases, e is being raised to a number that is increasingly negative, which means that the entire exponential term is becoming smaller and smaller, approaching zero. This term, however, is being subtracted from a constant 1; so as the exponential term gets closer and closer to zero, $(1 - e^{-t/RC})$ is increasing and getting closer and closer to 1. (Mathematically, we say that the quantity $(1 - e^{-t/RC})$ is asymptotically approaching 1, since it can never increase beyond 1 as the value of the exponential term never gets below zero.)

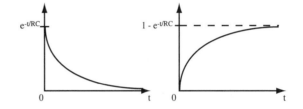

The above graphs illustrate the behavior of the exponential term itself and of the quantity $(1 - e^{-t/RC})$. There is also a multiplicative factor of $C\varepsilon$. As t approaches infinity, then, the charge approaches the value of $C\varepsilon(1) = C\varepsilon$. The capacitor becomes fully charged and the potential difference (or voltage drop) across the capacitor plates is equal to the emf. There is no potential drop across the resistor because no current flows through the circuit anymore at that point, so according to Ohm's law, the voltage drop is V = iR = (0)R = 0.

**32. D**

Remember that when an experimental apparatus is given in an MCAT physics passage, you should be sure to devote most of the 60 to 90 seconds spent reading the passage to understand how the apparatus works.

By adding another resistor in series we have increased the overall resistance of the circuit. Qualitatively, the current through the circuit at any time t would be smaller because of the higher resistance. The flow of charge to the capacitor is therefore slowed, and so it will take longer for the capacitor to charge up to a particular level. This eliminates choice **C**. Choices **A** and **B** are incorrect, because given enough time (as $t \rightarrow \infty$), the charge on a plate of the capacitor will reach $C\varepsilon$; the current will fall to zero, and the potential difference across the capacitor will be the same magnitude as the potential difference across the battery, $\varepsilon$.

**33. A**

First of all, we should recognize that the charge on each capacitor is the same. We could have inferred this from the answer choices that make no distinction between the capacitors, or we could have reasoned it out from conservation of charge. Consider two capacitors that are connected in series as shown below, with the plates labeled A, B, E, and F:

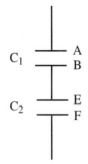

As the charge flows, let us say that the voltage source deposits positive charge on plate A and absorbs positive charge from plate F. This connects the circuit, and leaves net negative charge on plate F. Note that the negative plate of $C_1$, plate B, is connected to the positive plate of $C_2$, plate E. Since there can be no creation of net charge, the charges on these two plates have to be equal in magnitude (but opposite in sign). From the workings of a capacitor, we know that this equality of charge magnitude is manifested in the other plates as well (A and F):

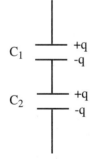

We can think of this charge as being stored on an effective capacitor that has the same capacitance as this series arrangement. Capacitors in series add in the same way as resistors in parallel do

$$\frac{1}{C_{eff}} = \frac{1}{C} + \frac{1}{C} = \frac{2}{C}, \; C_{eff} = \frac{C}{2}.$$

As t goes to infinity, the capacitors will be fully charged. Using the equation $q = C\varepsilon(1 - e^{-t/RC})$ given in the passage, the charge approaches

$$q = C_{eff}\varepsilon = \frac{C\varepsilon}{2}$$

where we have used the effective capacitance. In other words, the same amount of charge that was originally on one capacitor is now spread over two capacitors. Answer choice **A** is correct.

As with all questions containing algebraic expressions for answer choices, if we run into trouble with the reasoning, we can use dimensional analysis to eliminate wrong answer choices. In this case, answer choices **C** and **D** have dimensions of inverse charge.

**34. D**

The information needed for the answer is not found directly in the text of the passage but is contained in Figure 2. Each of the three plots that make up Figure 2 is a graph of voltage as a function of time, but none gives the emf e directly. Consider the circuit in Figure 1 when the switch is in position A. Using Kirchhoff's law, we know that the emf e must be equal to the sum of the voltage drops across the resistor and the capacitor ($V_R$ and $V_C$, respectively). So we do have exactly what we need after all: The sum ($V_R + V_C$) is plotted as a function of time in (c), and its value when the switch is in position A must be equal to the magnitude of the emf. Looking at the section of the graph that corresponds to position A, we see that the emf equals two divisions in the vertical direction. We are told in the passage that each vertical division equals 1.0 V. Therefore, the emf must be 2(1.0 V) = 2.0 V, answer choice **D**.

When graphs or tables are presented as part of an MCAT Physics passage, you can usually expect a question that will call for you to interpret the data in some way.

**35. A**

When the switch is at position B, the circuit consists only of a capacitor in series with a resistor. The emf is no longer a part of the circuit and has no effect. The charge that is initially stored in the capacitor at high potential will flow to a lower potential. This is analogous to water flowing downhill until it reaches a point of minimum gravitational potential energy.

The positive terminal of a battery is at a higher potential than the negative terminal: Positive charge flows from the positive to the negative terminal around the circuit. This applies to capacitor plates as well: The plate with positive charge is at a higher potential than the plate with the negative charge. Without an emf to provide the potential energy to separate the charges, charge will flow from the positive to the negative plate if a path exists. In this case, the path is through the resistor:

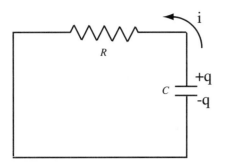

As the charge flows, the positive and negative charges cancel each other until each plate is neutral (no more separation of charge). The capacitor is then completely discharged, and the two plates are at the same potential. Choice **A** is consistent with this analysis.

Here's another way to think about it. The positive charge will flow toward the negative charge because, like a mass dropped from a height above the ground, it's always trying to lower its potential energy. The formula for the change in electrical potential energy is $\Delta U = q\Delta V$. Since $\Delta U$ is negative (charges travel from a region of high potential energy to a region of lower potential energy), and q is positive (we are discussing the flow of positive charges), the sign of $\Delta V$ must be negative as well: the charges move from high to low potential.

Choice **B** is incorrect, because, as just described, the reverse is true. Choice **C** is incorrect, because the emf is no longer part of the circuit when the switch is at position B. A current does flow through the resistor, but it has nothing to do with the emf. Choice **D** is also incorrect: The voltage across the capacitor is not zero since the plates are at different potentials. (The voltage across the capacitor is just the potential difference across the plates.) This quantity is zero only after the capacitor is fully discharged.

## Discrete Questions (Questions 36–45)

### 36. A

This question is an application of the conservation of energy. The absolute value of the change in kinetic energy equals the absolute value of the change in potential energy: $\Delta KE = \Delta PE$. Since the particle starts from rest, the change in kinetic energy is just the final kinetic energy. An $\alpha$-particle is a helium-4 nucleus consisting of 2 protons and 2 neutrons. The change in potential energy is equal to the charge times the potential difference: $\Delta U = q\Delta V$. The charge of an $\alpha$-particle is twice the charge of a proton, or +2e. So the final kinetic energy is therefore equal to the potential difference of $5 \times 10^6$ volts times the alpha particle charge of $2 \times 1.6 \times 10^{-19}$ coulombs, which equals $1.6 \times 10^{-12}$ joules, choice **A**.

### 37. B

To solve this problem, apply Hooke's law, $F = kx$, where $F$ is the force applied to the spring, $x$ is the distance the spring stretches, and k is the spring constant. The force applied in this case is the weight of the hanging mass. Since weight is proportional to mass, the distance the spring stretches is also proportional to the mass of the object attached to the spring: kx = mg. We are solving for x when m = 0.4 kg. We know m and g, but not k; we'll need to use the m = 0.5 kg example to determine k.

The spring starts out with a length of 64 cm. When the 0.5-kg mass is attached, it stretches 8%, or an extra (64 cm)(0.08) = 5.12 cm. Since the spring force balances the weight of the mass:

$$kx = mg$$
$$k = mg/x = \frac{(0.5 \text{ kg})(9.8 \text{ m/s}^2)}{0.0512 \text{ m}} \cong 100 \text{ N/m}$$

Now we can solve for the displacement of the spring when m = 0.4 kg:

$$x = \frac{mg}{k} \cong \frac{(0.4 \text{ kg})(9.8 \text{ m/s}^2)}{100 \text{ N/m}} \cong 0.04 \text{ m} = 4 \text{ cm}$$

Therefore, the new length of the spring is 64 cm + 4 cm = 68 cm, answer choice **B**.

### 38. D

Note from the answer choices that we can determine either the convex or concave mirror distortion to answer the question; we do not need to determine both.

Consider the convex bottom: We first note that the focal length of a convex mirror must be some negative value. Let's draw a diagram and examine the distortion of the clown's feet in the convex bottom of the mirror as she walks away from it. Recall that we can draw three kinds of rays in a ray tracing diagram:

1. Rays that pass through the focal point will be reflected parallel. For a convex mirror, rays directed toward the focal point will be reflected parallel (because the focal point is in the virtual space behind the mirror).
2. Rays that hit the axis of the mirror will be reflected with the same angle on the other side of the axis (like a plane mirror).
3. Parallel rays will be reflected through the focal point. For a convex mirror, parallels rays will appear to pass through the focal point (because the focal point is in the virtual space behind the mirror).

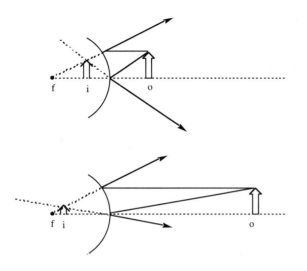

From the diagram above, it is clear that the image in a convex mirror shrinks as the object moves away. Thus, the image of the clown's feet will shrink in the convex bottom of the mirror as she walks away; answer choice **D** is correct.

**39. A**

This problem asks us to work backward from the condition of static equilibrium to find what information is required to determine the mass of B. In equilibrium, there is no net force (and no net torque) acting on mass A or mass B. Let's consider mass B first.

The forces acting on mass B are the tension of the rope, the force of gravity, and the normal force from the inclined plane. This is indicated in the free-body diagram below:

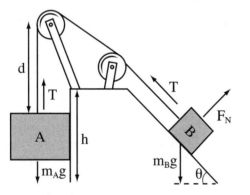

Because there is no net force acting on mass A, we can see that the tension (T) is equal to the force of gravity on mass A. $T = m_Ag$. The force of gravity on mass B is given by $m_Bg$ and the normal force is related to the force of gravity and the angle of the slope. Therefore, if we know the mass of A and the angle of the slope, the only unknown is the mass of B. Note that we must know the value of g, which is given in the question stem.

The other answer choices do not provide sufficient information for solving the problem. If we knew the

tension (T) and the angle, this would be sufficient. We get the same information from the mass of A as we would from knowing the tension T.

**40. D**

Looking at the answer choices, we know that we want to find out how the normal force varies with the motion of the box. In all cases listed in the answer choices, there are two forces acting on the box: the normal force and the force of gravity. These two act in opposite directions: The normal force, N, in the upward direction; and gravity, mg, in the downward direction. Taking the upward direction to be positive, we can express the net force on the box as N – mg.

From Newton's second law, this is also equal to ma, where a is the acceleration of the box (again with the upward direction being positive). For answer choices **A** and **B**, the net acceleration on the box is zero, so N = mg. We can see how the acceleration of the elevator (and, hence, of the box) affects the normal force. The larger the acceleration (in the positive—i.e., upward—direction), the larger the normal force is to preserve the equality: N – mg = ma, N = ma + mg. Answer choice **D**, in which the elevator is accelerating upward, results in the greatest normal force, since in that case the magnitude of the normal force is greater than gravity by the amount ma.

Choice **C** is incorrect, because with a downward acceleration, N – mg = –ma; N = ma – mg is less than the normal force when the elevator accelerates upward.

**41. A**

When we see a question involving the movement of a fluid, we first think of Bernoulli's equation. Bernoulli's equation, shown below, allows us to relate air pressures, velocities and altitudes in moving fluids along a stream line.

$$P + \frac{1}{2}\rho v^2 + \rho g y = constant$$

where P is the pressure, $\rho$ is the density of the fluid, $v$ is the speed of the fluid, and $y$ is the height of the fluid.

We can use Bernoulli's equation to solve this problem. But first, let's try to solve it more simply. Fluid will flow from a region of high pressure to a region of low pressure. In order to determine the direction air will flow in the tunnel, we must consider where the pressure is high and where the pressure is low.

Pipe A opens up to the stagnant air at ground level while Pipe B opens up to the rapidly moving air higher above the ground. Knowing that (thanks to Bernoulli's equation), a higher velocity fluid has a lower pressure, we can determine that Pipe B is exposed to a lower pressure than Pipe A. Therefore, air in the tunnel will flow from the entrance to Pipe A to the entrance of Pipe B (from a high pressure to a low pressure). Thus, air will flow from left to right in the tunnel; answer choice **A** is correct.

We can use Bernoulli's equation to solve this problem and prove that faster moving air has a lower pressure:

$$P_A + \frac{1}{2}\rho v_A^2 + \rho g y_A = P_B + \frac{1}{2}\rho v_B^2 + \rho g y_B$$

First, we know that $v_A < v_B$. We also know that $y_A$ is less than $y_B$. Consequently

$$P_A - P_B = \frac{1}{2}\rho(v_B^2 - v_A^2) + \rho g(y_B - y_A)$$

implies that $P_A$ is greater than $P_B$; the fluid flows from left to right.

Notice that the direction of the wind doesn't matter. We are only concerned with the magnitude of the velocity of the wind, and not its direction.

**42. A**

All of the answer choices have to do with the work done on the steel beam as it is lifted 100 m off the ground. Let's evaluate each answer choice:

**A:** What is the net work done on the steel beam? Since the change in kinetic energy of the beam is zero, the work-energy theorem tells us that the net work done on the beam must be zero as well. So this statement is false, making choice **A** the correct answer. Let's check the other answers.

**B:** The net work done on the beam is zero, as we discovered above.

**C:** The work done on the beam by gravity is negative (the beam does work on the Earth), because the direction of the force (downward) is opposite to the direction of displacement (upward). The magnitude of the work is:

mgh = (1000 kg)(9.8 m/s2)(100 m) = 9.8 × 10⁵ J.

**D:** The work done on the beam by the crane is positive (force and displacement both point up) and is also mgh = 9.8 × 10⁵ J. Notice that the work done by gravity cancels the work done by the crane; confirmation that the net work done on the beam is 0 J.

**43. D**

In a perfectly inelastic collision, the two objects move together after the collision. The momentum of the system is conserved; the kinetic energy of the system is not. Let's apply conservation of momentum to the system. Initially:

p$_i$ = (8 kg)(5 m/s) + (13 kg)(0 m/s) = 40 kg · m/s

After the collision, the combined mass moves off at unknown speed v:

p$_f$ = (21 kg)v

Conserving momentum, we can solve for v:

p$_i$ = p$_f$

40 kg · m/s = (21 kg)v

v = 40/21 m/s

The initial speed of the 8-kg mass is 5 m/s, and the final speed is $\frac{40}{21}$ m/s. The ratio of the initial to final speeds is

$$\frac{5 \text{ m/s}}{40/21 \text{ m/s}} = \frac{21 \times 5}{40} = \frac{21}{8}.$$

The correct answer is choice **D**. Always take special care on discrete questions to determine *exactly* what the question is asking for.

**44. D**

This question asks us to determine how an electron beam is deflected when current flows in the wire coils. When current flows in the wire coils, it creates a magnetic field. This magnetic field can exert a force on the electron beam, causing the beam to be deflected. In order to find the direction of the magnetic force, we first need to know the direction of the magnetic field. To find the direction of the field, we curl the fingers of our right hand along the wire in the direction of the current. Our thumb then points in the direction of the resulting magnetic field. We are told that the current travels counterclockwise with respect to the observer. So if you imagine yourself at O looking at the tube, the current travels from your right to your left at the top of the tube. As we apply the right-hand rule, we see that our thumb points along the path of the electrons: The magnetic field direction is the same as the direction of travel of the electrons. Now whenever the magnetic field is in the same direction or in the opposite direction to the motion of the charged particle, the magnetic force on the particle is zero. This can be seen from the equation F = qvB sin $\theta$. If the magnetic field is in the same or opposite direction, then $\theta$ is either 0° or 180°. Therefore the sine of $\theta$ is 0, so the magnetic force is also zero. When no magnetic force is present, there is no deflection of the beam. The correct answer is choice **D**.

**45. D**

We are asked to find the electrostatic potential at a specific point given a distribution of charged spheres. We have eight spheres charged to +1 C. These spheres are arranged in a circle with a radius of 1 meter. What is the electrostatic potential? In the case of point charges, the relevant formula is V = kq/r. The potential at the center of the circle due to any one of the charges is V = k(1 C)/(1 m) = + k volts.

Now since electrostatic potential is scalar, we can add the effect from each charge directly. In other words, there is no directional component to worry about. So, V$_{total}$ = 8(+k) = 8k volts, answer choice **D**.

The trap in this case is the temptation to cancel the potential contributions from charges that are directly across the circle from one another; this would lead us to erroneously cancel all of the potential, yielding answer choice **A**. Remember that electrical potential isn't a vector quantity, it's a scalar quantity. The only way for the potential from charges to cancel out is if you have some positive charges and some negative charges.

# CHAPTER 5

# General Chemistry

We have already developed a repertoire of general strategies and methods to use with MCAT passages and questions. Now let's concentrate on the specifics of General Chemistry. General Chemistry passages and discrete questions appear as part of the Physical Sciences section of the MCAT, but they are not distinguished in any way from the Physics passages and questions. Therefore, it is up to you to determine which portions are General Chemistry–based, and apply our strategies accordingly.

One of the most difficult aspects of the MCAT is in reading the passages. Test takers tend to waste a lot of time reading passages the same way they read a textbook or a newspaper; they attempt to understand completely every argument made and every detail given. Although this is useful for a history or biology test, this type of reading will not pay off on Test Day. The MCAT science passages are full of data that will always be there if you need it. When you read a passage, take a broad look at what is happening and think about what basic science concepts are being applied in the situations described in the passage. Allow yourself a maximum of 90 seconds to absorb what you need from the passage. In this chapter, you will practice reading General Chemistry passages quickly, going into the questions having a good sense of the passage and being prepared for what may arise. Included in your arsenal of General Chemistry skills for Test Day should be those listed later on in this chapter. Excelling in General Chemistry on the MCAT depends in part on mastery of this skill set.

## READING THE PASSAGE

### Passage Types

General Chemistry passages fall into the three categories described in chapter 3, but are also unique in many ways.

*Information* passages read very much like textbooks or scientific review journals and usually explain the chemistry behind some natural phenomenon. In General Chemistry, these passages are very graphics-intensive, so you should expect to see reactions, equations, tables, or graphs.

The text functions primarily to explain the graphics and put them in some sort of context.

*Experiment* passages typically consist of brief background information about some compound, reaction, or chemical process, followed by a series of experiments and a presentation of results. These passages read very much like laboratory manuals or reports. The purpose of the experiments is usually stated in the first sentence of the passage. Numerical results may be presented in a table or graph.

*Persuasive argument* passages present contrasting views on a subject. The typical format is for the passage to introduce a chemical phenomenon, and then present the differing viewpoints as hypotheses. Many of the questions will then rely on understanding the similarities and the differences of the hypotheses. Since persuasive argument passages are rare in the General Chemistry portion of the MCAT, you can focus primarily upon information and experiment passages.

## Mapping the Passage

As you learned in chapter 3, passage mapping is the process by which you create a "map" of the main ideas and critical concepts. Mapping is the best way to grasp the structure of a passage without getting bogged down or confused by detail. In General Chemistry, mapping a passage consists of two steps: Mapping graphics and mapping text.

### Mapping Graphics

A surprisingly high percentage of General Chemistry questions can actually be answered using only the graphics found in a passage. In General Chemistry passages, you will encounter five types of graphics: graphs, tables, reactions, equations, and figures. If a graphic exists in a passage, you are likely to be asked about it.

*Graphs and Tables*: Graphs typically present the results of some experiment or series of measurements. Tables may often do the same, but can also show you the physical or chemical properties of some element or compound. When mapping a graph or table, you should primarily be noting the following:

- The subject of the graphic
- Any obvious trends or similarities

Frequently, the subject of the graphic will be explicitly stated in the caption—it is simply what the graphic presents to you (e.g., the dissociation constants for several compounds). You should make some quick and obvious deductions from the graphic. If a table displays the results of some experiment, you may want to figure out what the results show you. Below you will find an example of a table that you might find on the MCAT. The types of observations recorded beside the table are similar to those you should be making as you map the passage.

**Table 1    Electron Affinities of Several Elements**

| Element | Electron Affinity (eV) |
|---------|------------------------|
| Li | 0.618 |
| H | 0.754 |
| C | 1.26 |
| O | 1.46 |
| Br | 3.36 |
| F | 3.40 |

Subject: electron affinities of several elements. There's nothing new here—just specific values that reflect trends you should already know.

You should be sure to note the subject of the table/graph in the margins. This will help you find information when you refer back to the passage to answer questions. Other observations and deductions should probably be made only in your head, since they may take longer to write down. If a graph or table does not demand obvious interpretation, then don't waste time looking for one. Remember that the MCAT only rewards you for correctly answering questions, not understanding passages.

*Reactions*: Mapping an equation or reaction should be done with a more focused approach than with a graph, table, or figure, since you know the range of General Chemistry reaction types possible on the MCAT. Questions you should be asking yourself when you see an equation include the following:

- What is the reaction type: acid–base, redox, or other?
- What are the species involved?
- Are there phases or phase changes?
- Is the reaction in equilibrium, or does it run to completion?

This list is neither exhaustive nor rigid. With practice you will see that these kinds of observations will help you better understand passages without wasting time on unnecessary detail.

When you are shown a series of reactions, you should also pay attention to how they are most obviously related—again, looking for trends and similarities. For example, if you are given three equations and ammonia shows up in all three, it is likely that the text of the passage talks about different reactions of ammonia. Similarly, if you are given four acid–base reactions you should expect to see some acid–base questions. However, you should NOT sit and brainstorm possible question types on Test Day. The questions are right there on the screen—go ahead and answer them!

Let's look at the example below and see what we can learn from the equations given:

Step 1:   $Cl_2 \rightarrow 2\ Cl\cdot$
Step 2:   $Cl\cdot + CH_4 \rightarrow CH_3 + HCl$
Step 3:   $CH_3 + Cl_2 \rightarrow CH_3Cl + Cl\cdot$
Step 4:   $Cl\cdot + CH_3\cdot \rightarrow CH_3Cl$

Your notes might read:

4-step radical chain rxn
$Cl_2 + CH_4 \rightarrow CH_3Cl$

### Mapping the Text

After you have mapped the graphics found within the passage, your next step is to map the text. As previously stated, you shouldn't read a passage trying to memorize every detail. Instead, you should employ your critical reasoning skills. You want to come out of each paragraph having gotten the gist of what's going on. As you finish each paragraph, ask, "What is this paragraph doing?" Make note of the main ideas and major concepts of the text on scratch paper so that you can find the details later, if needed. The extent to which you take notes as you read a passage depends upon your individual comfort level. Wean yourself off written notes as you become more and more comfortable keeping the necessary information in your head. As you take notes, be sure to summarize each paragraph, including the meanings of new terms or equations.

The degree of detail you need to absorb from the text depends on the type of passage. Information passages are filled with text that is primarily complementary to the equations/tables presented. The important information in these passages can be almost entirely discerned from the graphics, so skim the text very quickly. You need to know only what the text is about, not what it actually says. Experiment passages, on the other hand, are more conceptually difficult and require you to follow the logical progression of some experiment. After an experiment passage, there is likely to be at least one question asked that depends upon a detailed understanding of how the experiment works and what is being tested. You will want to read these passages with a much more critical mind than you would with an information passage. The same is true for persuasive argument passages, which can often be followed by a question or two that is tightly focused on one or more of the hypotheses.

### Identifying the Topic

In addition to mapping the passage, you should also aim to *identify the topic* of the passage. This means more than simply coming up with a scientific term corresponding to the main subject of the passage. Rather, identifying the topic means answering the question, "What is the author trying to do in the passage?" Being able to answer this question means that you have read the passage critically—and critical reading is the most important skill for reading MCAT passages.

Now that you've broken down the components of your passage-reading strategy, put them together and see how you might read a passage on Test Day. Look at the following information passage. It has been mapped using the techniques described on the previous pages. Although there is no one correct way to map a passage, the notes and observations written below the passage are similar to those you should be making on Test Day.

> The concentration of nitrogen oxides in our atmosphere has greatly increased during the past century, having significant negative impact on the environment. Nitrous oxide ($N_2O$), which is released into the air by fertilizers and from newly cleared soil, is thought to contribute to the greenhouse effect by absorbing infrared radiation given off by the earth. Nitric oxide (NO) and nitrogen dioxide ($NO_2$) produced by the burning of organic material contribute to the phenomenon known as photochemical smog. Although smog is generally thought of as resulting from the burning of fossil fuels, the burning of vegetation in the tropics is also a source of air pollution.

prose about $NO_x$ sources

On a smoggy day, the nitric oxide concentration in the air peaks early in the morning. This NO later combines with oxygen to form $NO_2$, which in turn combines with oxygen in a light-catalyzed reaction to form ozone ($O_3$).

**Reaction 1:** $2NO(g) + O_2(g) \rightarrow 2NO_2(g)$
$H° = -113$ kJ/mol $\qquad G° = -69.8$ kJ/mol

**Reaction 2:** $2NO_2(g) + O_2(g) \xrightarrow{hv} NO(g) + O_3(g)$
$H° = -199$ kJ/mol $\qquad G° = 298.3$ kJ/mol

rxns. and thermo. data for ozone formation

Photochemical smog attacks living matter such as plants and lung tissue; it also reacts with organic materials such as rubber and various atmospheric hydrocarbons. It reacts with moisture to form nitric acid, which corrodes metals and contributes to acid rain.

prose about effects of photochem. smog

To decrease smog levels, cars are equipped with catalytic converters, in which the following reactions take place:

**Reaction 3:** $2NO_2(g) \rightarrow 2O_2(g)$
$H° = -68$ kJ/mol $\qquad G° = -104$ kJ/mol

**Reaction 4:** $2NO(g) \rightarrow N_2 + O_2(g)$
$H° = -181$ kJ/mol $\qquad G° = -173$ kJ/mol

**Reaction 5:** $2NO + 2CO(g) \rightarrow 2CO_2(g) + N_2(g)$
$H° = -747$ kJ/mol $\qquad G° = -688$ kJ/mol

**Reaction 6:** $2NO(g) + 2H_2(g) \rightarrow 2H_2O(g) + N_2(g)$
$H° = -752$ kJ/mol $\qquad G° = -648$ kJ/mol

rxns. and thermo. data for breakdown of $NO_x$ in catalytic converter

**topic:** discusses rxns. that break down atmospheric nitrogen oxides

This passage should not take you very long to map. The critical points are the two series of reactions and the thermodynamic data. From inspection, Reactions 1 and 2 show the formation of ozone ($O_3$). Reactions 3–6 involve nitrogen oxides, so the passage is about smog formation and decomposition. You should expect to answer questions about the thermodynamics of these processes.

Now let's see how a map for an experiment passage might look.

A chemist studies the thermodynamics of the equilibrium between $SO_2$, $O_2$, and $SO_3$. $SO_2$ and $O_2$ react to form $SO_3$ by the stoichiometric relationship given in Reaction 1.

$$2SO_2(g) + O_2(g) \rightleftarrows 2SO_3(g)$$
**Reaction 1**

rxn. being studied: gas-phase equilibrium

Sulfur dioxide and oxygen gas, at 298 K and 1 atm, are injected into an evacuated metal cylinder in a 2:1 molar ratio. The cylinder is then sealed so that the gases cannot escape. The chemist proceeds to heat the cylinder, pausing every 100 K. At each pause, the chemist measures the internal pressure after it has stabilized for at least 20 minutes. The table below shows the pressures recorded for a series of temperatures, as well as the pressures expected were the gases not to react.

experiment: measure pressure inside canister as function of temperature

**Table 1    Total Internal Pressure at Various Temperatures**

| T (K) | $P_r$ (P recorded after reaction, in atm.) | $P_e$ (P expected without reaction, in atm.) |
|-------|------------------------------------|-------------------------------------|
| 600   | 1.3 | 2.0 |
| 700   | 1.6 | 2.3 |
| 800   | 1.9 | 2.7 |
| 900   | 2.3 | 3.0 |
| 1000  | 2.8 | 3.3 |
| 1100  | 3.3 | 3.7 |
| 1200  | 3.8 | 4.0 |
| 1300  | 4.2 | 4.3 |

results: actual pressure gets closer to predicted pressure as temperature increases

**topic:** experiment about effect of temperature on reaction equilibrium

Again, you should not take more than 90 seconds to map a passage like this. This passage basically consists of one experiment studying the thermochemistry of one reaction. Though you should read the second paragraph closely enough that you understand how the experiment studies the thermodynamics of the reaction, the key elements of the passage are the reaction and the data table.

# HANDLING THE QUESTIONS

Now that we've discussed how to read General Chemistry passages, let's move on to handling questions—the part of the test where you actually earn your points.

As you learned in chapter 3, you will encounter four types of MCAT science questions:

- Discrete questions
- Questions that require an understanding of the passage
- Questions where you need only data from the passage
- Questions that can stand alone from the passage

*Discrete questions*: These questions do not follow any passage and are always preceded by a warning such as "Questions 31 through 35 are NOT based on a descriptive passage." Consequently, all the information needed to answer these questions will be found in the question stem, the answer choices, and your outside knowledge.

*Questions that require an understanding of the passage*: As opposed to discrete questions, these questions follow a passage and cannot be answered without having read the passage. These questions typically follow experiment or persuasive argument passages and, less frequently, information passages (another reason why information passages should be read quickly). A question might ask you to interpret an experiment or a chemical process, and require that you have a conceptual understanding of topics discussed in the passage. For example, it would be difficult to answer the following question if you had not closely read the corresponding passage.

The gas that evolved when the chemist tried to dissolve element X
was most likely

    **A.**   water vapor produced from the heat of reaction.

    **B.**   oxygen produced by chemical reaction.

    **C.**   hydrogen produced by chemical reaction.

    **D.**   nitrogen that had been dissolved in the water from air.

*Questions where you need only data from the passage*: These questions are similar to the previous question type in that they cannot be answered without the passage. However, these questions do not demand a thorough understanding of the passage. Rather, they ask you to return to the passage to look at a table or equation—information that can be extracted from the passage without an understanding of their context or relevance. For example, a question might ask you to apply Le Chatelier's principle to an equilibrium reaction found in the passage. In this case you do not need to know the relevance of that reaction; you just need to know what the reaction is so that you can apply your outside knowledge of Le Chatelier's principle. Now let's take a look at the following question:

What is the rate law for Reaction 1?

    **A.**   Rate = $k[NO_2]^2$

    **B.**   Rate = $k[NO_2]^2[O_2]$

    **C.**   Rate = $k[NO_2]^2[O_2][NO_2]^2$

    **D.**   The rate of the reaction cannot be determined without more information.

All you need to answer this question is the stoichiometry of the reaction and/or some rate measurements. You don't need to understand the relevance of the reaction in context of the rest of the passage; in a case like this, you would just need to flip back to the passage to see what the reaction was.

Indeed, most General Chemistry questions on the MCAT can be answered using only pieces of information from the passage—an equation, a number, etc. Many, however, lead you to believe that you need a greater understanding of the passage than you actually do. These questions refer to compounds or reactions that are specific to the passage, tempting you to lean heavily on the passage for support. Still, the only information you need to retrieve from the passage for these questions is a number or a reaction—combing the passage for "the answer" will only waste time better spent thinking or checking answers. Most MCAT passages are filled with extraneous information that won't help you answer the questions. So when you refer back to a passage, do so with a very focused eye, looking only for the information specified by the questions.

*Questions that can stand alone from the passage*: These questions follow passages, but are in all other ways discrete questions. They require absolutely no knowledge or information from the passage, because they are related to the passage only in subject. The following question, for example, could follow the information passage that you read earlier about nitrogen oxide gases in our atmosphere.

What is the relationship between $\Delta G$, $\Delta S$, $\Delta H$, and $T$?

**A.**  $\Delta G = \Delta S - T\Delta H$

**B.**  $\Delta G = T(\Delta H - \Delta S)$

**C.**  $\Delta G = \Delta H + T\Delta S$

**D.**  $\Delta G = \Delta H - T\Delta S$

Though linked to the passage by the subject of thermochemistry, the question can be solved using only your previous outside knowledge.

Determining the passage type will allow you to predict the types of questions you will see. Rarely will you need to return to an information passage to learn some logical sequence: You will usually return just to target specific kernels of information. Experiment and persuasive argument passages, on the other hand, are commonly followed by questions asking you to interpret experiments or hypotheses.

## Answering the Questions

Correctly answering MCAT questions is highly correlated to efficiently identifying the essential underlying question and relevant science. The MCAT is designed to test our scientific thinking: Our ability to identify specific chemistry topics and apply them in new situations. So to become a better test taker, you need to look past the distraction of unfamiliar subjects and language, and look toward the core science of the question.

### Understand what you are being asked.

The first thing to do is to read the question stem and the answer choices. Often, MCAT science questions can be confusing. Reading the answer choices after you read the question stem will help focus your thinking and provide useful clues. In this step, your goal is to boil down the question down to its essence and determine as precisely as possible what science concepts you're being asked about. You're not going to look back to the passage with a hazy notion of the question, hoping that something in the passage will suddenly crystallize your thinking. You need to know as precisely as possible the question being asked and the major chemistry concepts being tested, as illustrated by the following questions:

What factors directly contribute to the average velocity of gas particles?

    I. Molecular mass

    II. Temperature

    III. Pressure

**A.** I and II only

**B.** I and III only

**C.** II and III only

**D.** I, II, and III

You are asked to identify those physical properties that directly affect gas particle velocity. Consider only molecular mass, temperature, and pressure.

Let's look at our next question:

What is the rate law for Reaction 1?

**A.** Rate $= k[NO_2]^2$

**B.** Rate $= k[NO_2]^2[O_2]$

**C.** Rate $= k[NO_2]^2[O_2][NO_2]^2$

**D.** The rate of the reaction cannot be determined without more information.

You are asked to determine the rate law for a reaction given in the passage. Reaction stoichiometry and rate measurements would be helpful.

Often, the question stem presents the science problem in a straightforward manner, in which case there is not much to do for this step.

What is the relationship between $\Delta G$, $\Delta S$, $\Delta H$, and $T$?

**A.** $\Delta G = \Delta S - T\Delta H$

**B.** $\Delta G = T(\Delta H - \Delta S)$

**C.** $\Delta G = \Delta H + T\Delta S$

**D.** $\Delta G = \Delta H - T\Delta S$

You are asked to identify the mathematical relationship between four thermodynamic values.

However, sometimes the question stem may include unfamiliar language or bulky clauses. If this is the case, you'll paraphrase or translate the question stem in your mind, then look to the answer choices for additional hints.

If the KHP had been exposed to moisture prior to the titration, the calculated concentration of the KOH(*aq*) would be:

Question: How does water affect the calculated titration measurement?

**A.** Greater than the actual concentration, since the quantity of KHP actually titrated would be greater than the quantity used in calculations

**B.** Greater than the actual concentration, since the quantity of KHP actually titrated would be less than the quantity used in calculations

**C.** Less than the actual concentration, since the quantity of KHP actually titrated would be greater than the quantity used in calculations

**D.** Equal to the actual concentration, since the titration calculation depends on moles of KHP, not concentration

You are asked to determine the effect of contaminants on titration points. You need to know what a titration measures and how it does that. Hint: Would you have to use more or less KHP to reach endpoint of titration, if KHP contains water?

If the question requires conceptual understanding of the passage, try to figure out what sorts of properties, relationships, or concepts you will be looking for.

### Figure out where to go to get any information you may need.

Having a grasp of the problem at hand, use your passage map and science skill set to determine what information—both factual and conceptual—you may need to answer the question. Is the question topic something you should know? Does the question test a concept you should understand (e.g., Le Chatelier's principle, galvanic cells, etc.)? Will concepts introduced in the passage help you? Do you need to retrieve facts from the passage (e.g., a value from a table or a compound from a reaction)? Using your passage map, figure out where this information is located. Below you will see how this step can be applied to the questions just covered.

What factors directly contribute to the average velocity of gas particles?

I. Molecular mass

II. Temperature

III. Pressure

**A.** I and II only

**B.** I and III only

**C.** II and III only

**D.** I, II, and III

Pure outside knowledge: nothing is needed from the passage.

What is the rate law for Reaction 1?

A.   Rate = $k[NO_2]^2$

B.   Rate = $k[NO_2]^2[O_2]$

C.   Rate = $k[NO_2]^2[O_2][NO_2]^2$

D.   The rate of the reaction cannot be determined without more information.

Look at Reaction 1 and observe the stoichiometry. If reaction rate tables exist, look at them. If reaction rate is discussed in the passage, look at that text as well.

What is the relationship between $\Delta G$, $\Delta S$, $\Delta H$, and $T$?

A.   $\Delta G = \Delta S - T\Delta H$

B.   $\Delta G = T(\Delta H - \Delta S)$

C.   $\Delta G = \Delta H + T\Delta S$

D.   $\Delta G = \Delta H - T\Delta S$

Pure outside knowledge: nothing is needed from the passage.

In the second example above, the question stem does a pretty good job of telling you what information you need and where to find it. In the first and third examples, you recognized that the questions could be answered without returning to the passage. Being able to make such a determination requires a solid foundation in the science content, as well as a good passage map, which will give you a good sense of whether or not the passage will be of any help to you. A key part of learning science skills is not just being able to apply them when asked, but being able to identify when you need to use them. In the KHP question you saw earlier, you need to raise your level of critical thinking a bit to target what information will be useful.

If the KHP had been exposed to moisture prior to the titration, the calculated concentration of the KOH($aq$) would be

A.   greater than the actual concentration, since the quantity of KHP actually titrated would be greater than the quantity used in calculations.

B.   greater than the actual concentration, since the quantity of KHP actually titrated would be less than the quantity used in calculations.

C.   less than the actual concentration, since the quantity of KHP actually titrated would be greater than the quantity used in calculations.

D.   equal to the actual concentration, since the titration calculation depends on moles of KHP, not concentration.

You would want to refer back to the passage to find the titration reaction, as well as information on how the titration was performed.

*Integrating science knowledge with any necessary passage research, determine the correct answer.*

This last step is easier said than done. Here you will bring all components together: Outside knowledge, information from the passage, and reasoning/calculation. The exercises outlined in the previous three steps should lead you to the content wall, the point at which getting the correct answer depends on scientific knowledge and reasoning skills.

Remember, test strategy is designed to complement, not replace your knowledge of MCAT General Chemistry. If you don't know the science, then there is little else you can do to improve your score. However, if you do have a grasp on the science, then adhering to solid test strategy will lead to points on Test Day.

Now let's take a look at our question strategy in action. The following questions, which pertain to the information passage about atmospheric nitrogen oxides you read earlier, have already been attacked using the method described above. Note how this method allows you to address the basic science more directly.

> What reactions would occur spontaneously under standard conditions?
>
> **A.** All except 2
> **B.** Only 2
> **C.** All except 5 and 6
> **D.** Only 1, 3, and 4

Q: How can you tell whether a reaction proceeds spontaneously? Look back to specific reactions (1–6) in the passage.

From the passage map you know you have six reactions, all with given values of H° and G°. If you remember that reaction spontaneity is related to some thermodynamic values, but don't know how, you could at least improve your chances of guessing correctly by noticing that Reaction 2 has thermodynamic values of opposite sign than the others. This reasoning would eliminate choices **C** and **D**. However, to answer correctly you must be able to recall that reactions proceed spontaneously when the Gibbs free energy has a negative value; the answer is therefore choice **A**.

> What values are commonly used to estimate enthalpies?
>
> **A.** Heat capacities
> **B.** Bond dissociation energies
> **C.** Oxidation states
> **D.** Activation energies

Q: What does enthalpy measure? How does enthalpy relate to what each value in the answer choices measures?

This question requires absolutely no information from the passage and is asked in a very straightforward manner. Without the passage, you should already know what enthalpy is and what the four answer choices measure. If you lack this knowledge, all you can do strategically is to eliminate those answers you know to be incorrect. The enthalpy of reaction is related to changes in energy associated with bond breaking and forming. The correct answer is therefore choice **B**.

Now, as an additional exercise, let's see how far we can progress with a series of questions given only the map of the passage upon which they are based.

Topic: discusses antacids and the regulation of stomach pH
- Prose regarding stomach biology
- Prose regarding antacids

Reaction: $Al(OH)_3 + 3HCl \rightarrow AlCl_3 + 3H_2O$

This passage is then followed by the following four questions:

1. How many grams of $AlCl_3$ are produced when 3 grams of $Al(OH)_3$ react completely with excess HCl?

    A. 2.36 g

    B. 3.00 g

    C. 5.05 g

    D. 9.07 g

How to handle this question: You are asked to calculate mass of reaction product; use stoichiometry skills. Your notes might read:

Q: 3g $Al(OH)_3$ + excess HCl → ? $AlCl_3$

How do you convert between mass and moles?

Reaction equation given in map includes all three species.

The basic question here is, "What is the stoichiometric relationship between $AlCl_3$ and $Al(OH)_3$?" Though this relationship is not something you would know off the top of your head, it can be found in the balanced equation given in the passage summary. You don't need to understand stomach acid, antacids, or anything else from the passage: All the information you need can be extracted from the passage map, the periodic table (access via a button, labeled "exhibit," on the bottom of your screen), and your outside knowledge.

2. If HCl is the only substance present in the stomach, what is the pH?

    A. $-\log (0.15)$

    B. $-\log (0.2)$

    C. $\log (0.15)$

    D. $\log (0.2)$

How to handle this question: You are asked to calculate the pH using acid concentration.

What is the relationship between pH and concentration?

How much HCl is there in the stomach? The prose about stomach biology may provide this info.

This question asks for the stomach pH, limiting your consideration to the effects of HCl. What do you know about HCl? Well, it's a strong acid, so it will dissociate completely in solution. Okay, so how much of it is in the stomach? This you probably don't know, so you look to the passage summary, which tells you that there is prose in the passage describing stomach biology. If indeed you were to refer to the passage, you could very quickly find that the concentration of HCl in the stomach is 0.15 $N$. With this little kernel of knowledge, you can now answer the question. 0.15 $N$ HCl corresponds to a proton concentration of 0.15 $M$, since HCl is a strong monoprotic acid that will completely dissociate in solution. From our studies of acids and bases, you should recall that pH is related to the concentration of protons by pH = $-\log [H^+]$. Therefore the pH in the stomach is equal to $-\log (0.15)$, choice **A**.

3. While the active ingredients in most antacids are soluble in the acidic environment of the stomach, their solubility is significantly reduced in pure water. If a finely divided powder of one such compound, say $CaCO_3$, is mixed with deionized water, which of the following will be true?

Solubility of antacids significantly reduced in pure water

You are asked to apply your knowledge of solution chemistry. Q: What happens when $CaCO_3$ is mixed with deionized water?

    I. The mixture will be homogeneous.

    II. A colloidal mixture will be formed.

    III. Separation of the mixture will produce a nonelectrolytic aqueous phase.

    **A.** I only

    **B.** III only

    **C.** I and II only

    **D.** II only

What is a colloidal mixture? What will the aqueous phase consist of?

The question stem here is very lengthy, but it provides you with all the information you need to answer the question. You are first told that antacids are not very soluble in pure water. You are then told that $CaCO_3$, an antacid, is mixed with deionized water. So what do you expect to happen? You should expect $CaCO_3$ will not dissolve in the water. With this expectation in mind, you are now ready to evaluate the three statements given to you.

- Statement I: Is the mixture of water and undissolved $CaCO_3$ homogeneous? No—there's a solid phase and a liquid phase. Eliminate choices **A** and **C**.

- Statement II: Is the mixture of water and undissolved $CaCO_3$ a colloid? Yes. Being able to recognize this depends on two sources of information: your outside knowledge of what a colloid is and the statement in the question stem that the $CaCO_3$ is divided into a fine powder. Fine powders of insoluble substances become suspended in the liquid, forming a colloid. Choice **D** is correct.

- Statement III is false, since the aqueous phase contains no electrolytes; the only possible source of ions, $CaCO_3$, never entered the aqueous phase.

4. Strong, soluble bases such as alkaline earth metal hydroxides are not used as antacids, but are often used in laboratory titrations. What volume of an aqueous 1.5 $M$ $Ba(OH)_2$ solution would be required to neutralize 10 mL of stomach acid?

You are asked to calculate the volume of base necessary to neutralize acid.

    **A.** 0.5 mL

    **B.** 1.5 mL

    **C.** 10.0 mL

    **D.** 15.0 mL

How many equivalents of protons are there in 10 mL of stomach acid? This is yet another question that can be answered using only tiny bits of information from the passage. Here, the task is relatively straightforward: You are to calculate the volume of a base of known strength that is sufficient to neutralize a known volume of an acid of known strength. The acid is again stomach acid, 0.15 $N$ HCl. In 10 mL of stomach acid, there are 10 mL $\times$ (1 L/1000 mL) $\times$ (0.15 mol $H^+$/1 L) = $1.5 \times 10^{-3}$ mol $H^+$. To neutralize the acid, you need equal quantities of $H^+$ and $OH^-$. Each mole of the base, $Ba(OH)_2$, can give up two moles of hydroxide ions upon dissociation, and so a 1.5 $M$ solution of the base has a normality of 3.0 $N$. The volume of the base you need to add is then ($1.5 \times 10^{-3}$ mol $OH^-$)/(3.0 mol $OH^-$/L) = $0.5 \times 10^{-3}$ L = 0.5 mL, choice **A**.

A list of chemistry skills and concepts that you will need to have in your arsenal before taking the MCAT follows.

# IN PREPARING FOR THE MCAT, I SHOULD UNDERSTAND...

## 1.    Atomic Structure/Periodic Table

- How to determine the electronic configurations of atoms/ions
- Periodic trends: atomic radii, ionization energy, electronegativity, electron affinity
- The four quantum numbers: how they are related and what each defines
- The chemical properties of groups
- Atomic absorption/emission and how to calculate photon energies

## 2.    Bonding

- Intermolecular forces: dipole-dipole, dispersion, and H-bonding
- Molecular/electronic geometry
- Resonance structures
- How to calculate formal charges
- Lewis structures
- Dipole moment, polarity, and their effects on reactivity
- The relation between bond length and bond energy

## 3.    Stoichiometry

- How to calculate the molecular weight of a compound
- How to balance a chemical equation
- How to calculate molecular composition by percent mass
- How molecular and empirical formulas are related
- Basic reaction types: single/double displacement, combustion, decomposition
- Limiting reagents and how to calculate percent yields

## 4. Kinetics/Rate Processes/Equilibrium

- Rate laws and reaction rate order
- Le Chatelier's principle
- Energy profiles of reactions
- Chemical equilibrium, equilibrium constants, and law of mass action
- Catalysts

## 5. Thermochemistry

- Enthalpy: exothermic/endothermic
- State functions and thermodynamic terms (e.g., adiabatic, isobaric, etc.)
- How to calculate enthalpy changes of chemical processes (e.g., heat of vaporization, heat of reaction, etc.)
- Heat transfer and specific heat (calorimetry)
- Reaction profiles
- $\Delta G = \Delta H - T\Delta S$
- First law of thermodynamics: $\Delta E = Q - W$
- Gibbs' free energy and spontaneity

## 6. Gases

- Kinetic molecular theory and its assumptions
- How to calculate average and root-mean-square molecular speeds, and rates of effusion and diffusion
- The ideal gas law, including Boyle's and Charles' laws
- How to calculate density and molar mass
- Van der Waals' equation of state

## 7. Phase Changes/Phase Equilibria

- Single- and multiple-component phase diagrams
- How to calculate colligative properties: vapor pressure lowering, boiling point elevation, freezing point depression, and osmotic pressure
- Phase equilibria and phase properties

## 8. Solutions

- Common ions by name, formula, and charge
- How to calculate ion concentration using $K_{sp}$, or vice versa
- How to calculate solution concentration: mole fraction, molarity, molality, normality, solution composition by percent mass
- The common ion effect

## 9. Acids and Bases

- How to identify Arrhenius/Bronsted/Lewis acids and bases
- How to identify conjugate acid–base pairs
- The conversion between p-scale and concentration/equilibrium constant
- How to interpret titration curves
- Strong acids/bases and weak acids/bases
- How to calculate pH of weak acid/base solutions
- Neutralization reactions and hydrolysis
- Amphoteric species and polyprotic acids
- Henderson–Hasselbalch equation

## 10. Electrochemistry

- The difference between electrolytic and galvanic cells and how it affects the designation of the cathode, anode, reduction electrode, oxidation electrode, electrode charge, electron flow, and ion flow in electrochemical cells
- How to calculate cell potential using reduction potentials
- How to balance redox reactions using half-reactions
- Oxidation numbers
- Common oxidizing and reducing agents
- How to convert between EMF, Gibbs' free energy, and equilibrium constant

# GENERAL CHEMISTRY PRACTICE SET

## Answer Sheet

1 Ⓐ Ⓑ Ⓒ Ⓓ     16 Ⓐ Ⓑ Ⓒ Ⓓ     31 Ⓐ Ⓑ Ⓒ Ⓓ

2 Ⓐ Ⓑ Ⓒ Ⓓ     17 Ⓐ Ⓑ Ⓒ Ⓓ     32 Ⓐ Ⓑ Ⓒ Ⓓ

3 Ⓐ Ⓑ Ⓒ Ⓓ     18 Ⓐ Ⓑ Ⓒ Ⓓ     33 Ⓐ Ⓑ Ⓒ Ⓓ

4 Ⓐ Ⓑ Ⓒ Ⓓ     19 Ⓐ Ⓑ Ⓒ Ⓓ     34 Ⓐ Ⓑ Ⓒ Ⓓ

5 Ⓐ Ⓑ Ⓒ Ⓓ     20 Ⓐ Ⓑ Ⓒ Ⓓ     35 Ⓐ Ⓑ Ⓒ Ⓓ

6 Ⓐ Ⓑ Ⓒ Ⓓ     21 Ⓐ Ⓑ Ⓒ Ⓓ     36 Ⓐ Ⓑ Ⓒ Ⓓ

7 Ⓐ Ⓑ Ⓒ Ⓓ     22 Ⓐ Ⓑ Ⓒ Ⓓ     37 Ⓐ Ⓑ Ⓒ Ⓓ

8 Ⓐ Ⓑ Ⓒ Ⓓ     23 Ⓐ Ⓑ Ⓒ Ⓓ     38 Ⓐ Ⓑ Ⓒ Ⓓ

9 Ⓐ Ⓑ Ⓒ Ⓓ     24 Ⓐ Ⓑ Ⓒ Ⓓ     39 Ⓐ Ⓑ Ⓒ Ⓓ

10 Ⓐ Ⓑ Ⓒ Ⓓ     25 Ⓐ Ⓑ Ⓒ Ⓓ     40 Ⓐ Ⓑ Ⓒ Ⓓ

11 Ⓐ Ⓑ Ⓒ Ⓓ     26 Ⓐ Ⓑ Ⓒ Ⓓ     41 Ⓐ Ⓑ Ⓒ Ⓓ

12 Ⓐ Ⓑ Ⓒ Ⓓ     27 Ⓐ Ⓑ Ⓒ Ⓓ     42 Ⓐ Ⓑ Ⓒ Ⓓ

13 Ⓐ Ⓑ Ⓒ Ⓓ     28 Ⓐ Ⓑ Ⓒ Ⓓ     43 Ⓐ Ⓑ Ⓒ Ⓓ

14 Ⓐ Ⓑ Ⓒ Ⓓ     29 Ⓐ Ⓑ Ⓒ Ⓓ     44 Ⓐ Ⓑ Ⓒ Ⓓ

15 Ⓐ Ⓑ Ⓒ Ⓓ     30 Ⓐ Ⓑ Ⓒ Ⓓ     45 Ⓐ Ⓑ Ⓒ Ⓓ

# GENERAL CHEMISTRY PRACTICE SET

## Time: 60 Minutes—45 Questions

**DIRECTIONS**: There are seven passages and ten discrete questions in this General Chemistry test. Each passage is followed by five questions of above-average difficulty. After reading a passage, select the one best answer to each question. If you are not certain of an answer, eliminate the alternatives that you know to be incorrect and then select an answer from the remaining alternatives. (Note that although the passages and questions are test-like, this exercise is NOT meant to be an actual MCAT test section. For full-length MCAT practice, please see Kaplan *MCAT Practice Tests*).

## Passage I (Questions 1–5)

In 1965, Boris Deryagin reported the discovery of an unusual substance formed during the condensation of water vapor in quartz capillaries. The material, called polywater, appeared to be a polymer of water monomers and differed from normal water in a number of ways. It had a freezing point of –40°C and solidified into a glass-like solid with substantially less volumetric expansion than that of ordinary water upon freezing. It had a density 40% greater than water and a refractive index of 1.48.

An intricate apparatus was used to produce the polywater. Ordinary distilled water was placed in a chamber held at 160° C with pressure below atmospheric pressure. This chamber was connected to a second chamber by a tube held at 500°C in order to prevent the passage of liquid water. The second chamber was held at 0°C and contained a drawn quartz capillary in which the water vapor condensed, forming polywater.

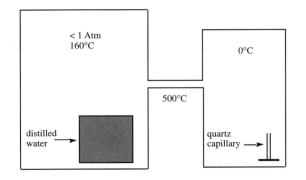

**Figure 1**　Polywater Apparatus

*Hypothesis 1*

Deryagin proposed that polywater was a polymer of water monomers arranged in a network of hexagonal units. The polymerization was catalyzed by the silicate surface of the quartz capillary.

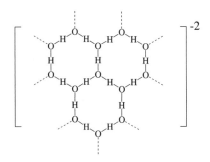

**Figure 2**　Proposed Structure of Polywater

*Hypothesis 2*

Analysis indicated that polywater was merely a solution of water and dissolved particles including silicon, carbon dioxide, and substantial concentrations of ions ($Na^+$ and $Cl^-$). These contaminants dissolved from the quartz capillary and from materials used in the apparatus. (Note: constants for normal water: density = 1 $g/cm^3$, index of refraction = 1.33, freezing point depression constant $K_f = 1.86°C \cdot m^{-1}$)

1. Hypothesis 1 proposes that polywater is a repeating structure of $H_2O$ monomers. What is the formal charge on any given hydrogen atom in this structure?

    A. –1
    B. +1
    C. –2
    D. +2

**GO ON TO THE NEXT PAGE.**

2. Which of the following statements is NOT supported by the passage?

   A. Light entering polywater from air will bend more toward the normal than light entering regular water.

   B. Polywater can be produced in a variety of conditions.

   C. 1 $\mu$g of water has a larger volume than 1 $\mu$g of polywater, at room temperature.

   D. Polywater exists in the liquid state at 0°C.

3. Assume that Hypothesis 2 is correct. Compared to normal water, polywater would have a

   A. lower vapor pressure and higher boiling point.

   B. lower vapor pressure and lower boiling point.

   C. higher vapor pressure and lower boiling point.

   D. similar vapor pressure and boiling point.

4. The pressure ($P_i$) in the first chamber is decreased by raising a piston and increasing the volume of the chamber from $V_i$ to $V_f$. If the temperature is kept at 160°C, which of the following values expresses the new pressure ($P_f$) in the chamber?

   A. $\dfrac{P_i V_i}{V_f}$

   B. $P_i - \dfrac{P_i V_i}{V_f}$

   C. $\dfrac{nRT}{V_i}$

   D. $V_i T_i - V_f T_f$

5. Which of the following pieces of evidence would best support Hypothesis 1 over Hypothesis 2?

   A. The mass of the quartz capillary did not change throughout the experiment.

   B. Filtration of the polywater increased its freezing temperature.

   C. The polywater and normal water had different boiling points.

   D. The second chamber could be kept at 50°C with similar results.

## Passage II (Questions 6–10)

A student conducts an experiment comparing different techniques for drying coffee. A liter of dilute coffee is brewed by grinding Sumatra beans, adding 1 L of water at 100°C, then passing the mixture through filter paper to remove the coffee bean solids. The student divides the coffee into two 0.48-L samples and uses different techniques to remove water from each of the samples.

*Experiment 1*

Following brewing, sample 1 is quickly placed in a 105°C chamber whose temperature and pressure can be carefully controlled. The 5-L chamber can be considered an open system that allows the transfer of mass and energy. With the temperature and pressure (1 atm) of the chamber held constant, the temperature of the coffee rises and the water evaporates. When all of the water has evaporated, the dry powder left in the flask is removed. It has a mass of 2.11 g.

*Experiment 2*

Sample 2 undergoes a process known as freeze drying. The sample is frozen and placed at –20°C in a chamber identical to the one in Experiment 1. The pressure in the chamber is then reduced to 0.005 atm. With chamber pressure held constant, the chamber temperature is raised to –5°C. The sample is allowed to sublime until only a granular solid remains.

The phase diagram for water is shown below:

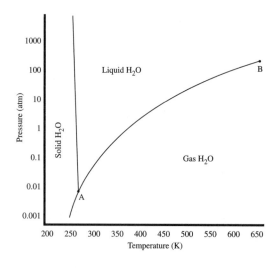

**Figure 1**   Phase Diagram for Water

**GO ON TO THE NEXT PAGE.**

6. Consider the frozen sample in Experiment 2. When this sample is placed in the chamber at an initial pressure of 1 atm, which of the following phases of water is the most thermodynamically stable?

   A. Gas

   B. Liquid

   C. Solid

   D. Plasma

7. Which of the following could be the boiling point and freezing point of coffee, respectively (273 K = 0°C)?

   A. 373 K, 273 K

   B. 398 K, 298 K

   C. 374 K, 270 K

   D. 370 K, 276 K

8. Freeze drying produces a more aromatic and flavorful coffee because the process provides a slower oxidation rate, decreased protein denaturation, and reduced transport of volatile flavor and aroma species. Which of the following would be expected to improve the quality of coffee over that produced by Experiment 2?

   A. Replacing the air in the chamber with helium gas at 0.005 atm

   B. Changing the final temperature of the chamber to 0°C

   C. Providing a larger interface area between the surface of the frozen coffee and the air in the chamber

   D. Compressing the frozen sample using a piston mechanism

9. Regulation of the chamber temperature is achieved by increasing or decreasing the flow of liquid nitrogen (−200°C) or steam (150°C) through pipes about the chamber's metal walls. Which of the following could describe the flow of heat from the sample in Experiment 2?

   A. Conduction, then radiation

   B. Radiation, then conduction

   C. Radiation, then conduction, then convection

   D. Convection, then radiation, then conduction

10. A glass of pure water at room temperature is placed in the chamber and the pressure is decreased to 0.05 atm. A "heat sink" is used to extract heat from the chamber at a constant rate and the temperature of the water is measured at intervals. Which of the following plots best indicates the temperature of the water over time?

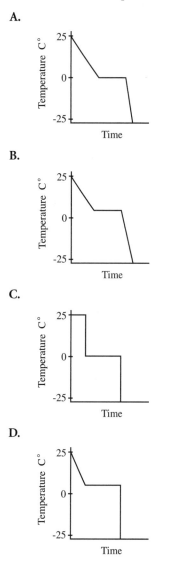

A.

B.

C.

D.

**GO ON TO THE NEXT PAGE.**

## Passage III (Questions 11–15)

Chemiluminescence occurs when a chemical reaction produces an electronically excited species, which then emits a photon in the visible range as it relaxes to the ground electronic state. The following is an example of a reaction scheme exhibiting chemiluminescence:

$$NO + O_3 \rightarrow NO_2{}^* + O_2$$
$$NO_2{}^* \rightarrow NO_2 + h\nu$$

**Equation 1**

where the asterisk denotes an excited state. Monitoring the intensity of the luminescence produced in this reaction sequence, for example, offers an accurate and very sensitive way of determining the concentration of NO in a sample of air.

Chemiluminescence can also be useful as an analytical method in the liquid phase; the chemiluminescent compound luminol is often used in this capacity. Upon oxidation, luminol forms the 3-aminophthalate anion which then luminesces in the blue region of the electromagnetic spectrum.

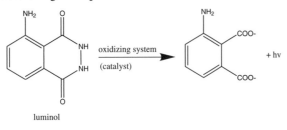

luminol

**Equation 2**

The oxidation reaction of luminol by hydrogen peroxide requires a catalyst such as peroxidase or $Fe^{2+}$ ions. The intensity of the luminescence increases linearly with the concentration of the catalyst (at least over a certain range of concentrations).

The luminol reaction can also be used as the basis for an analytic technique to determine the concentration of species that cause suppression of chemiluminescence. Many organic molecules, for example, form complexes with metal ions. In the luminol reaction, the presence of these molecules will make the $Fe^{2+}$ ions unavailable as catalysts; as part of a complex, the ions are effectively removed from the system. To determine the concentration of the organic species, the intensity of the chemiluminescence is first recorded when none of the organic molecules is present. This establishes a "baseline" signal. Then the reaction is carried out again in the presence of the organic species, and the intensity is again recorded. The decrease in intensity is an indication of the concentration of the organic species.

11. Chemiluminescence of which of the following colors corresponds to electromagnetic radiation with the highest frequency?

    A. Red
    B. Yellow
    C. Green
    D. Violet

12. Upon oxidation to the 3-aminophthalate anion, the number of $sp^2$-hybridized carbon atoms in luminol

    A. increases by 2.
    B. remains unchanged.
    C. decreases by 2.
    D. decreases by 4.

13. Not all of the energy of the excited-state molecule is necessarily emitted during luminescence. Molecules can also undergo "nonradiative relaxation," in which part of the energy is dissipated through collisions with other molecules. One consequence of this "collisional deactivation" channel is that

    A. increasing the total pressure of the system would lead to higher frequency luminescence for a gas-phase reaction.
    B. increasing the total pressure of the system would lead to higher intensity luminescence for a gas-phase reaction.
    C. molecules may luminesce over a range of wavelengths rather than at a single discrete one.
    D. molecules may remain in the excited state and never luminesce.

**GO ON TO THE NEXT PAGE.**

14. Which of the following is NOT an acceptable Lewis structure for NO?

    A. $\overset{\oplus}{\ddot{N}}-\overset{\ominus}{\ddot{O}}:$

    B. $\cdot\ddot{N}=\ddot{O}\cdot$

    C. $\ominus\cdot\ddot{N}=\ddot{O}\cdot\oplus$

    D. $:N\equiv O:$

15. In order to carry out the analysis described in the last paragraph of the passage, which of the following conditions need to be true?

    A. The $Fe^{2+}$ ions should encounter the organic species before being introduced into the luminol–peroxide mixture, and the concentration of the organic species should be lower than the concentration of $Fe^{2+}$.

    B. The $Fe^{2+}$ ions should encounter the organic species before being introduced into the luminol–peroxide mixture, and the concentration of the organic species should be higher than the concentration of $Fe^{2+}$.

    C. The $Fe^{2+}$ ions should encounter the organic species after being introduced into the luminol–peroxide mixture, and the concentration of the organic species should be lower than the concentration of $Fe^{2+}$.

    D. The $Fe^{2+}$ ions should encounter the organic species after being introduced into the luminol–peroxide mixture, and the concentration of the organic species should be higher than the concentration of $Fe^{2+}$.

**GO ON TO THE NEXT PAGE.**

## Passage IV (Questions 16–20)

A chemist determined the amount of chloride ion in a solid unknown sample by gravimetric precipitation with silver ions. A 0.2020-g sample of the unknown was dissolved completely in 100 mL of dilute, aqueous nitric acid. The subsequent addition of 20 mL of 0.20 $M$ aqueous silver nitrate solution resulted in the immediate formation of a white precipitate.

The solution containing the precipitate was swirled and cooled, then filtered through a sintered glass crucible. The precipitate was then washed with cold, dilute nitric acid and dried. The mass of silver chloride recovered was determined to be 0.3485 g.

Reaction 1 describes the solubility of silver chloride in water at the temperature at which the analysis was done.

$$AgCl(s) \rightleftarrows Ag+(aq) + Cl^-(aq)$$

$$K_{sp} = 1.56 \times 10^{-10}$$

**Reaction 1**

Until it is dried, a silver chloride precipitate is susceptible to photodecomposition (Reaction 2):

$$AgCl(s) \xrightarrow{h\nu} Ag(s) + \frac{1}{2} Cl_2(g)$$

**Reaction 2**

The further reaction of excess silver ion with dissolved chlorine gas (Reaction 3) is also a possibility.

$$3Cl_2(aq) + 5Ag^+(aq) + 3H_2O(l) \rightarrow$$

$$5AgCl(s) + ClO_3^-(aq) + 6H^+(aq)$$

**Reaction 3**

**16.** What is the approximate mass percent of chloride ion in the original sample?

    **A.**   34%

    **B.**   43%

    **C.**   58%

    **D.**   85%

**17.** Which of the following would have the least effect on the accuracy of the results obtained from the analysis described in the passage?

    **A.**   Prolonged exposure of the precipitate to sunlight

    **B.**   Filtration and recovery of the precipitate at elevated temperatures

    **C.**   $NaNO_3$ impurities in the $AgNO_3$ solution

    **D.**   Washing the precipitate with dilute HCl instead of $HNO_3$

**18.** What is the minimum concentration of chloride ion necessary to induce precipitation upon addition of the silver nitrate solution in the procedure outlined in the passage?

    **A.**   $4.68 \times 10^{-9}\ M$

    **B.**   $3.12 \times 10^{-11}\ M$

    **C.**   $5.20 \times 10^{-12}\ M$

    **D.**   $6.24 \times 10^{-12}\ M$

**19.** The precipitate obtained in another experiment following the described procedure was a light violet-gray. A possible explanation for the color is that

    **A.**   the precipitate was contaminated by nitrate ion due to excessive washing with nitric acid.

    **B.**   higher temperatures led to an excess of silver ions trapped within the crystal lattice of the precipitate.

    **C.**   finely divided silver produced by photodecomposition contaminated the precipitate.

    **D.**   silver chloride precipitates are violet in color.

**20.** If the solution containing the silver chloride precipitate is to be stored overnight before filtration, which of the following would be true?

    **A.**   The sample must be protected from light to avoid photodecomposition of the precipitate.

    **B.**   The extra time will allow for an increase in the mass of precipitate formed.

    **C.**   Evaporation of the solvent will lead to a decrease in the mass of precipitate recovered.

    **D.**   Exposure of the solution to chlorine vapors in the air will lead to artificially low results.

**GO ON TO THE NEXT PAGE.**

## Passage V (Questions 21–25)

The apparatus for the Joule-Thomson experiment is shown below in Figure 1. Two chambers of gas are separated by a porous plug. A piston is used to force the gas in chamber 1 at constant pressure $P_1$ through the plug into chamber 2 at constant pressure $P_2$, where $P_1 > P_2$. The entire system is thermally insulated and the plug is also made of thermally insulating material. As a result, the process takes place adiabatically, and each chamber is maintained at its own constant temperature.

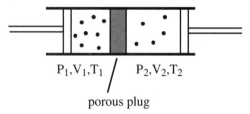

$$P_1, V_1, T_1 \quad\quad P_2, V_2, T_2$$

porous plug

**Figure 1**

An ideal gas undergoes no temperature change as it moves into the second chamber. For a real gas, however, internal work is done against the intermolecular forces and so the temperature changes as the gas expands into the other chamber.

In general, the expansion of the real gas into the second chamber may either raise or lower the temperature. Every real gas has a characteristic inversion temperature, $T_{inv}$. When the temperature is below this inversion temperature, the Joule-Thomson effect causes cooling; when the temperature is above the inversion temperature, heating results.

If the real gas is adequately described by the van der Waals equation of state, its $T_{inv}$ can be expressed as

$$T_{inv} = \frac{2a}{Rb}$$

**Equation 1**

where R is the universal gas constant, and $a$ and $b$ are the van der Waals constants that appear in the van der Waals equation of state, which offers a semi-empirical model for the behavior of real gases:

$$\left(P + \frac{an^2}{V^2}\right)(V - nb) = nRT$$

**Equation 2**

The van der Waals constants for some gases are given in Table 1:

**Table 1    A and B Values for Various Gases**

| Gas | $A$ (atm·L²/mol²) | $B$ (L/mol) |
|-----|-----|-----|
| He | 0.0341 | 0.0237 |
| $H_2$ | 0.244 | 0.0266 |
| $O_2$ | 1.36 | 0.0318 |
| $N_2$ | 1.39 | 0.0391 |
| $CH_4$ | 2.25 | 0.0428 |
| $CO_2$ | 3.59 | 0.0427 |
| HCl | 3.67 | 0.0408 |

21. Which of the following gases has the highest inversion temperature?

   A.  He
   B.  $H_2$
   C.  $N_2$
   D.  $CH_4$

22. If the amount of gas that is transferred from chamber 1 to chamber 2 does net work upon expansion, which of the following must be true?

   A.  $T_1 > T_2$
   B.  $T_1 < T_2$
   C.  $|P_1 \Delta V_1| > |P_2 \Delta V_2|$
   D.  $|P_1 \Delta V_1| < |P_2 \Delta V_2|$

23. A real gas is compressed at constant temperature from an initial pressure of $P_0$ and an initial volume of $V_0$ to a final volume of $\frac{1}{2}V_0$ Its final pressure is

   A.  more than $2P_0$.
   B.  $2P_0$.
   C.  less than $2P_0$.
   D.  indeterminate, depending on the precise initial conditions.

**GO ON TO THE NEXT PAGE.**

24. Which of the following diagrams best illustrates the potential energy of interaction between two real gas molecules as a function of their separation r?

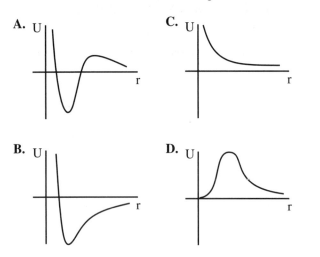

25. Two separate vessels of equal volume are filled with gas at the same temperature and pressure. One vessel contains neon, while the other contains argon. If the same amount of heat is added to both vessels at constant volume, which of the following is true? (Assume that both gases are ideal.)

    A. The two gases will be at the same final temperature, but the neon atoms will be moving faster on average.

    B. The two gases will be at the same final temperature, and the neon atoms and the argon atoms will be moving at the same average speed.

    C. The vessel containing neon will be at a higher final temperature.

    D. The vessel containing argon will be at a higher final temperature.

## Passage VI (Questions 26–30)

As Figure 1 illustrates, the reaction of *tert*-butyl bromide with aqueous sodium hydroxide results in a substitution product (Reaction I) and an elimination product (Reaction II).

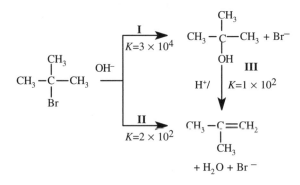

**Figure 1**

A student investigated the reaction kinetics for the conversion of *tert*-butyl bromide to *tert*-butyl alcohol (Reaction I) by varying the concentrations of the reactants and recording the reaction rate. The results are shown in Table 1.

**Table 1.   Initial Rates vs. Initial Concentrations**

| Exp. # | Initial concentration of *tert*-butyl bromide (mmol/L) | Initial concentration of OH– (mmol/L) | Initial rate of reaction (mmol/[L·sec]) |
|--------|------|------|------|
| 1 | 0.02 | 0.05 | 6.0 |
| 2 | 0.02 | 0.10 | 6.0 |
| 3 | 0.04 | 0.05 | 12.0 |

In reaction III, *tert*-butyl alcohol is converted to 2-methylpropene by the addition of aqueous acid followed by heating. This reaction involves the formation of a protonated intermediate that loses water to form a carbocation. The alkene is then generated by the loss of a proton. This mechanism is illustrated in Figure 2.

**GO ON TO THE NEXT PAGE.**

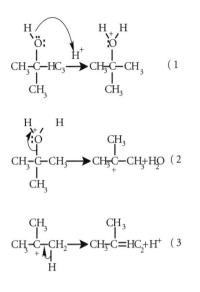

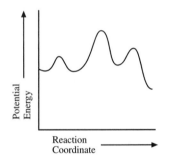

**Figure 2**

The energy profile for Reaction III is shown in Figure 3.

**Figure 3**

26. Which reaction has proceeded the farthest toward completion once equilibrium has been established?

    A. Reaction I

    B. Reaction II

    C. Reaction III

    D. It cannot be determined without more information.

27. Which of the following is the rate equation for Reaction I?

    A. Rate = $k$[*tert*-butyl bromide][OH−]

    B. Rate = $k$[OH⁻]

    C. Rate = $k$[*tert*-butyl bromide]

    D. Rate = $k$[*tert*-butyl bromide][OH⁻]²

28. If Reaction I were carried out at a higher temperature, which of the following would be observed?

    A. Both the equilibrium constant and the rate constant would change.

    B. The equilibrium constant would change, but the rate constant would remain the same.

    C. The rate constant would change, but the equilibrium constant would remain the same.

    D. Neither the equilibrium constant nor the rate constant would change.

29. For Reaction II, what could be done to shift the equilibrium to the right, favoring the formation of the alkene?

    A. Add excess water to the reaction mixture.

    B. Use *tert*-butyl chloride as the starting reagent instead of *tert*-butyl bromide.

    C. Use a lower concentration of hydroxide ions.

    D. Add $AgNO_3$ to precipitate out the bromide ions.

30. If Reactions I, II, and III were run with an appropriate catalyst, which of the equilibrium constants would change?

    A. Only the equilibrium constant for Reaction I would change.

    B. Only the equilibrium constant for Reaction II would change.

    C. The equilibrium constants for Reactions I, II, and III would change.

    D. None of the equilibrium constants would change.

**GO ON TO THE NEXT PAGE.**

## Passage VII (Questions 31–35)

Corrosivity is a chemical property that reflects a liquid's ability to dissolve other materials. The Environmental Protection Agency (EPA) defines a corrosive liquid as one that will dissolve steel at a rate of at least 6.35 mm per year at 55°C and has a pH either below 2.0 or above 12.5. The concept of pH is fundamental to corrosion because it is the hydronium and hydroxide ions in aqueous solutions that react with metals to dissolve them.

The corrosive power of a substance is twice dependent on temperature. First, the rate of a corrosion reaction is positively correlated to increases in temperature. Second, the pH of a strongly alkaline solution changes with temperature. Table 1 lists the changes in pH between 0 and 30, around the regulatory limit of pH = 12.5, for an aqueous solution with a large $OH^-$ concentration. The table shows that as temperature decreases, the pH increases past the 12.5 limit, but the pOH stays the same. Hence, while the power of a solution to dissolve another substance decreases when the temperature is decreasing, the eventual increase in pH beyond the 12.5 mark would make a so-called "noncorrosive" substance become "corrosive" at a lower temperature—contrary to the chemistry involved.

**Table 1    Data for Acid–Base Changes with Temperature**

| Temp (°C) | pH | pOH | [$OH^-$] (M) | $pK_w$ |
|---|---|---|---|---|
| 0 | 13.44 | 1.50 | 0.032 | 14.9 |
| 5 | 13.23 | 1.50 | 0.032 | 14.7 |
| 15 | 12.85 | 1.50 | 0.032 | 14.3 |
| 20 | 12.67 | 1.50 | 0.032 | 14.1 |
| 25 | 12.50 | 1.50 | 0.032 | 14.0 |
| 30 | 12.33 | 1.50 | 0.032 | 13.8 |

The corrosion process involves a spontaneous redox reaction at the surface of a substance, such as a metal exposed to a liquid. For corrosion to occur, all that is necessary is an electric potential difference between two points on the surface of the metal (due to naturally occurring imperfections in the crystal lattice) and some charge carriers in the liquid in contact with the metal. Elements such as gold and platinum resist corrosion very well while others like magnesium corrode very easily. For a solid metal immersed in a solution of its own ions, a higher relative concentration of ions will create a higher relative potential at the point of contact with the metal.

31. The standard hydrogen electrode, with a half-reaction of $2H^+ (aq) + 2e^- \rightarrow H_2(g)$ and standard reduction potential defined as 0.0 V, is the reference from which the cell potential, E, is measured for all other standard reduction reactions. Relative to this hydrogen electrode, Au and Mg should have standard half-reactions with

    A. a relatively large positive value of E for Au and a relatively large negative value of E for Mg.

    B. a relatively large negative value of E for Au and a relatively large positive value of E for Mg.

    C. a relatively large positive value of E for Au and a relatively small positive value of E for Mg.

    D. relative E values cannot be predicted from the given information and must be determined by experiment.

32. Which of the following best explains why the pH changes significantly from 30°C to 0°C in Table 1 while the pOH does not?

    A. The small concentration of $H^+$ ions from water self-ionization changes significantly with temperature, while the large $OH^-$ concentration is unaffected by a small change in the amount of from water.

    B. The excess concentration of $OH^-$ reacts more readily with available $H^+$ at higher temperatures, reducing the $H^+$ level.

    C. The pH of any aqueous solution will change with temperature at any concentration of $OH^-$; this effect is not confined to the conditions shown in Table 1.

    D. The pH measures only the amount of $H^+$ and is unaffected by the presence or absence of $OH^-$ in solution.

**GO ON TO THE NEXT PAGE.**

33. A metal surface in contact with water undergoes corrosion at pH = 2.0. One possible set of reactions at the cathode and anode, respectively, would be

   A.   $Fe(s) \rightarrow Fe^{2+}(aq) + 2e^-$;
        $4OH^-_{(aq)} + 4e^- \rightarrow O_{2(g)} + H_2O_{(1)}$
   B.   $Fe^{2+}(aq) + 2e^- \rightarrow Fe(s); \frac{1}{2}H_2(g) \rightarrow H^+(aq) + e^-$
   C.   $H^+(aq) + e^- \rightarrow \frac{1}{2}H_2(g); Fe(s) \rightarrow Fe^{2+}(aq) + 2e^-$
   D.   $Fe^{2+}(aq) + 2e^- \rightarrow Fe(s); Fe(s) \rightarrow Fe^{2+}(aq) + 2e^-$

34. Which of the following statements is NOT consistent with the passage?

   A.   The corrosivity of a given solution depends on the amount of dissolved acid or base in that solution.
   B.   In strongly basic solutions the pH decreases with increasing temperature while the pOH does not.
   C.   The corrosivity of a solution increases with increasing temperature and depends on the kinetic energies of dissolved acid or base in the solution.
   D.   The corrosivity of a solution increases with increasing temperature, while in strongly basic solutions the corrosivity decreases as the pH decreases.

35. If the solution in Table 1 were instead set at the regulatory limit of pH = 2.0 for corrosive acid solutions, which of the following statements would describe the solution as temperature increases?

   A.   pOH increases, and $pK_w$ increases
   B.   pOH decreases, and $pK_w$ decreases
   C.   pOH decreases, and $pK_w$ increases
   D.   pOH increases, and $pK_w$ decreases

## Discrete Questions

36. The Claus process reduces industrial sulfur dioxide emissions through the following high-temperature, catalytic reaction:

   $$2H_2S(g) + SO_2(g) \rightarrow 3S(s) + 2H_2O(l)$$

   If 204 kg of hydrogen sulfide reacts with 256 kg of sulfur dioxide to produce 224 kg of solid sulfur, what is the percentage yield of sulfur?

   A.   55%
   B.   66%
   C.   77%
   D.   88%

37. For the general reaction of an acid with water,

   $$HA + H_2O \rightleftharpoons A^- + H_3O^+$$

   an equilibrium constant of K = 0.05 means that

   A.   there is one mole of hydronium ion for each mole of HA at equilibrium.
   B.   there are more products than reactants in number at equilibrium.
   C.   there are 5 moles of hydronium ion per 100 moles of HA at equilibrium.
   D.   the majority of acid molecules remain undissociated at equilibrium.

38. Which of the following compounds can act as a Lewis base?

   A.   $HClO_2$
   B.   $NH_2NH_2$
   C.   $NH_4^+$
   D.   $BF_3$

39. An oxide of arsenic contains 65.2% arsenic by weight. What is its simplest formula?

   A.   AsO
   B.   $As_2O_3$
   C.   $AsO_2$
   D.   $As_2O_5$

**GO ON TO THE NEXT PAGE.**

40. Which of the following species has the same molecular (or ionic) geometry as $SO_2$?

    A. $CO_2$

    B. $NO_2^-$

    C. $XeF_2$

    D. $NH_3$

41. Solution X boils at 100.26°C and solution Y boils at 101.04°C. Both solutions are at atmospheric pressure and contain the same solute concentration. Which of the following conclusions can be drawn?

    A. The freezing point of solution X is lower than that of solution Y.

    B. The vapor pressure of solution X is higher than that of solution Y at 100.26°C.

    C. Solution X and solution Y are immiscible.

    D. The vapor pressure of solution X is lower than that of solution Y at 100.26°C.

42. Based on the table below, what is the cell voltage for the following reaction?

    $$Fe_2O_3 + 2\,Al \rightarrow 2\,Fe + Al_2O_3$$

    | Half-Reaction | Std. Potential (V) |
    |---|---|
    | $Fe^{2+} + 2e^- \rightarrow Fe$ | −0.44 |
    | $Fe^{3+} + 3e^- \rightarrow Fe$ | −0.037 |
    | $2H_2O + 2e^- \rightarrow H_2 + 2OH^-$ | −0.83 |
    | $Al^{3+} + 3e^- \rightarrow Al$ | −1.66 |

    A. −1.33 V

    B. 1.99 V

    C. 1.33 V

    D. 1.62 V

43. Given the following ΔH° values, calculate the ΔH° of formation of $Fe_2O_3$ (s).

    $6Fe_2O_3\,(s) \rightarrow 4Fe_3O_4\,(s) + O_2\,(g)$ +472.0 kJ · mol$^{-1}$

    $3Fe\,(s) + 2O_2\,(g) \rightarrow Fe_3O_4\,(s)$ −1118.4 kJ · mol$^{-1}$

    A. +667 kJ · mol$^{-1}$

    B. −1559 kJ · mol$^{-1}$

    C. −824 kJ · mol$^{-1}$

    D. −667 kJ · mol$^{-1}$

44. Which factors would you need to determine the density of oxygen in a vessel containing a mixture of gases, using the formula $PV = nRT$?

    A. The partial pressure of oxygen and the number of moles of oxygen in the container

    B. The partial pressure of oxygen and the total number of moles of gas in the container

    C. The total pressure of gas in the container and the number of moles of oxygen in the container

    D. The total pressure of gas in the container and the total number of moles of gas in the container

45. When an electron falls from $n = 3$ to $n = 2$ in a hydrogen atom, what is the value of the energy released, given that $A$ is the energy needed to remove an electron from the ground state of a hydrogen atom to an infinite distance from the atom?

    A. $0.14A$

    B. $0.17A$

    C. $1.00A$

    D. $5.00A$

**STOP.** IF YOU FINISH BEFORE TIME HAS EXPIRED, CHECK YOUR WORK. YOU MAY GO BACK TO ANY QUESTION IN THIS PART ONLY.

ANSWERS AND EXPLANATIONS BEGIN ON NEXT PAGE

# GENERAL CHEMISTRY PRACTICE SET

## Answer Key

**Passage I (Questions 1–5)**

1. A
2. B
3. A
4. A
5. A

**Passage II (Questions 6–10)**

6. C
7. C
8. A
9. C
10. B

**Passage III (Questions 11–15)**

11. D
12. B
13. C
14. D
15. A

**Passage IV (Questions 16–20)**

16. B
17. C
18. A
19. C
20. A

**Passage V (Questions 21–25)**

21. D
22. D
23. D
24. B
25. A

**Passage VI (Questions 26–30)**

26. A
27. C
28. A
29. D
30. D

**Passage VII (Questions 31–35)**

31. A
32. A
33. C
34. D
35. B

**Discrete Questions (Questions 36–45)**

36. C
37. D
38. B
39. D
40. B
41. B
42. D
43. C
44. A
45. A

# GENERAL CHEMISTRY PRACTICE SET

## Answers and Explanations

## Passage I (Questions 1–5)

**1. A**

This question requires you to recall and apply the formula for formal charge on an atom. The formal charge on an atom is given by the following equation:

*Formal charge = valence electrons in neutral atom − non-bonding electrons − 1/2 bonding electrons*

Neutral hydrogen has one valence electron. A hydrogen atom in polywater has no nonbonding electrons and four bonding electrons. Therefore, the formal charge on a given H atom in polywater is $1 - 0 - 2 = -1$, answer choice **A**. Usually hydrogen would have a formal charge of zero since it would only be involved in one bond, but in this case we see a negative formal charge for hydrogen because it is involved in more than one bond.

**2. B**

In this question, you're going to need to combine your critical reading skills with your knowledge of general chemistry. The passage describes a very intricate mechanism for producing polywater and does not support the fact that polywater can be produced in a variety of conditions, so choice **B** is ideal.

Choice **A** is incorrect, because polywater has a higher index of refraction than normal water and so would bend light more toward the normal (recall from Snell's Law that the angle of refraction will be smaller than the angle of incidence).

$$n_1 \sin\theta_1 = n_2 \sin\theta_2$$

So, if $n_{poly} > n_{water}$ then $\theta_{poly} < \theta_{water}$. Choice **C** is incorrect, because polywater is 40% more dense than water. So, an equal mass of polywater will have a smaller volume. Choice **D** is incorrect, because the passage states that polywater has a freezing point of −40°C.

**3. A**

Focus on Hypothesis 2. We already know that vapor pressure and boiling point are colligative properties that depend on the number of particles in a solution, so assuming that Hypothesis 2 is correct and that polywater is merely an aqueous solution with dissolved materials, its vapor pressure would be lower than that of normal water, and its boiling point would be higher.

**4. A**

Many MCAT students choose the wrong answer not because they don't know the science, but because they end up getting bogged down by algebra. This is one example of a time when a question hinges not only on our conceptual understanding, but also on our ability to perform algebraic operations fastidiously. Because the temperature is kept constant during the expansion process, we may use Boyle's Law to find the final pressure in the chamber. Boyle's Law states that $P_i V_i = P_f V_f$. Now, simply solve for $P_f = \dfrac{P_i V_i}{V_f}$.

Answer choice **C** might seem tempting as it uses the ideal gas law form, solved for pressure, but the question stem asks for the final pressure, and the volume in **C** is an initial volume.

**5. A**

In this question, we must take care to consider the ramifications of each answer choice in relation to both hypotheses if we are to distinguish the individual validity of each. If the mass of the capillary remained unchanged (answer choice **A**), this would weaken Hypothesis 2, which states that the contaminants in polywater dissolved from the quartz capillary. Weakening Hypothesis 2 would support Hypothesis 1.

Choice **B** is incorrect. If deionization of polywater increased its freezing temperature, this would indicate that polywater contained dissolved solids and would provide support for Hypothesis 2. Choice **C** is incorrect. If Hypothesis 2 is correct, we expect polywater to have a higher boiling point than normal water because dissolved solids increase the boiling point of solvents. Choice **D** is incorrect, because the temperature of the second chamber is irrelevant as long as it is below the boiling point of water—keeping it at 50°C and seeing similar results would neither support nor weaken Hypothesis 1.

## Passage II (Questions 6–10)

**6. C**

This question basically requires you to consult the phase diagram at the given values for temperature and pressure. The phase that exists at a particular temperature and pressure is the most thermodynamically favored phase. Thus, when the solid, frozen sample is placed in the chamber, it must be the solid frozen phase that is most stable. By the same reasoning, the most thermodynamically favorable phase of water at atmospheric pressure and room temperature (25°C) is the liquid phase.

We can look at the phase diagram for pure water provided in the passage to give us a hint about the most stable phase of dilute coffee at –20°C and 1 atm. Recall that –20°C is 273 K – 20 K = 253 K. At 250 K and 1 atm, water is in the solid phase. We cannot rely solely on the information in the phase diagram because the properties of a solution (like coffee) can differ from those of a pure substance (like water), but in this case, the division between solid and the other two phases is far enough from the point we're examining that we can qualitatively predict the solid phase for dilute coffee and arrive at answer choice **C**.

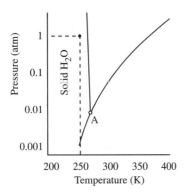

Choice **D** is incorrect. Plasma is sometimes considered the fourth phase of matter. It is a very high-temperature, ionized gas that behaves like a gas in many ways but that has additional properties, like conduction of electricity, which differentiate it from the gas phase.

**7. C**

What is the best approach to this question? Focus on the fact that the question stem says "could be." In other words, you don't have to do calculations, just recognize that the values given in the answer choices are going to fall into a few different categories, and choose the pair of values that best fits the information you gleaned from the passage. The passage describes the brewing of coffee and indicates that some amount of solid, 2.11 g, is dissolved or suspended in a 0.48-L sample of the beverage. The boiling point and freezing point of a liquid are colligative properties. That is, they are affected by the concentration of dissolved solutes in the solution. The boiling point of a liquid is raised by the presence of solutes (boiling point elevation), while the freezing point is decreased (freezing point depression). Therefore, while we do not have sufficient information to calculate the numerical values, we can predict, qualitatively, that coffee will have a higher boiling point and a lower freezing point than does pure water. The question stem states that 0°C is equivalent to 273 K. Therefore, we expect coffee to have a boiling point higher than 373 K (100°C) and lower than 273 K (0°C). Only choice **C** has the expected values.

**8. A**

Before answering the question, it is important to consider what factors can affect reaction rates. Temperature, concentration of reactants, catalysts, and the medium in which the reaction takes place can all have an effect on the rate of the reaction.

The question stem discusses the factors that make freeze-drying a better means of producing dehydrated coffee. It is up to us to determine why freeze-drying promotes these factors:

1. The oxidation rate is lower (due to low partial pressure of oxygen in the vacuum chamber).
2. The rate of protein denaturation is lower (due to lower temperatures).
3. There is reduced transport of volatile soluble flavor and aroma species (because the coffee is frozen solid).

Any changes that improve these properties would tend to produce a higher quality coffee. Filling the chamber with helium gas reduces the rate of oxidation in the coffee by decreasing (to zero) the partial pressure of oxygen in the chamber (answer choice **A**).

Choice **B** is incorrect, because raising the final temperature from –5°C to 0°C would tend to increase the reaction rates, including the rate of oxidation, thereby lowering the coffee quality. Choice **C** is incorrect, because increasing the surface area between the oxygen in the chamber and the frozen coffee would increase the oxidation reaction rate. This is similar to providing a larger catalytic surface on which the reaction (oxidation) can take place. Choice **D** is incorrect, because compressing the sample of frozen coffee with a piston would not have a significant effect on the important reaction rates. Recall that solids are generally incompressible. While this may increase the pressure on the frozen coffee, it doesn't affect the concentration of oxygen, the flow of materials in the coffee, or the rate of protein denaturation. In an extreme case, it is possible that the increased pressure on the frozen coffee would cause it to melt. You can see in the phase diagram that increased pressure (be it pressure applied by the atmosphere or by a piston) can cause water to undergo a phase change from solid to liquid.

**9. C**

Heat transfer is the transfer of thermal energy from a hot body to a cooler one. Radiation is the transfer of heat by electromagnetic (infrared) waves. This kind of heat transfer can occur even through a vacuum and is the means by which heat flows from the sun to the earth. Conduction is the transfer of heat between two physically touching bodies. Convection is the transport of heat by the movement of a fluid, like steam or liquid nitrogen. For example, a radiator radiates heat into a room, but the heat is transferred to the metal radiator by the flow of steam through its pipes (convection).

In Experiment 2, heat flows from the sample by radiation to the chamber walls, conduction from the metal wall to

General Chemistry

the pipes containing the liquid nitrogen, then convection by the movement of the liquid nitrogen away from the chamber (answer **C**).

Note that in Experiment 1, the heat flows in the opposite direction. The steam carries the heat to the chamber by convection; the heat is transferred from the pipes to the chamber walls by conduction and then radiated to the sample.

What if the sample were in direct contact with the chamber walls? In this case, heat would be conducted from the sample to the walls, then conducted from the walls to the pipes, then carried away by convection. However, conduction then convection is not an option among the answer choices and choice **C** is the only possibility.

**10. B**

Since the question stem finishes by asking about the temperature of the water *over time*, we should approach it by considering each element of the process separately in order to come up with a plot. The question states that first the pressure is reduced to 0.05 atm. This is our cue not to confuse the plot at 1 atm with that at 0.05 atm when we start examining the answer choices. During this time, the temperature will decrease since pressure is decreasing and volume remains constant. (The size of the chamber hasn't been altered.) So let's consider the phase diagram of water at 0.05 atm:

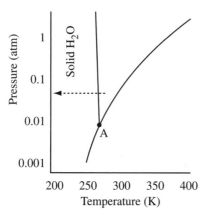

As heat is extracted, the water will cool to its freezing point at 0.05 atm. At the freezing point it will begin to freeze. Once all the water has frozen, the ice will begin to cool below its freezing point as more heat is extracted. From the phase diagram we can see that the freezing point of water at 0.05 atm is a little higher than the freezing point at 1 atm. This is because water, unlike most liquids, expands as it freezes.

Freezing is an exothermic process and the heat released is extracted by the heat sink at a constant rate. All of the heat that is extracted during the freezing process comes from the $\Delta H_{freezing}$ and the temperature of the $H_2O$ remains constant

until it is completely frozen. This is the part of the plot where the line is essentially horizontal. At this point, the temperature of the ice begins to fall from the freezing point.

In the graph, we expect to see a downward slope until the freezing point is reached. We expect a horizontal plateau of temperature, or isotherm, as the water freezes, then another downward slope as the ice cools.

Only choices **A** and **B** have this kind of profile. Choice **A** represents the temperature profile for water at 1 atm, while choice **B** is correct for the given pressure of 0.05 atm.

Choices **C** and **D** can be ruled out because they indicate instantaneous changes in temperature (the vertical portions of the plot.) Temperature changes can occur rapidly, but not instantaneously, because heat flow cannot be infinite, so vertical lines in a temperature versus time plot will never be observed.

## Passage III (Questions 11–15)

**11. D**

This is one of those times when we just have to commit certain pieces of information to memory. The colors of visible light, in the order of increasing energy and frequency, are ROYGBIV: red, orange, yellow, green, blue, indigo, violet. The way we can remember that red is on the low-frequency, low-energy end and that violet is on the high-frequency, high-energy end is to recall the types of radiation adjacent to visible light in the electromagnetic spectrum: infra*red* and ultra*violet*.

**12. B**

The best strategy here is to count the number of $sp^2$-hybridized carbon atoms in the 3-aminophthalate anion and in the luminol molecule. There are eight carbon atoms in luminol: the six that form the benzene ring, and the two carbonyl carbons. They all form a double bond and two single bonds and are hence $sp^2$-hybridized. In the 3-aminophthalate anion, none of the carbon atoms was removed and all of the atoms remain $sp^2$-hybridized; the only difference is that the amide functionalities have been converted into carboxylates. The two carbon atoms, however, are still carbonyl carbons, so the number of $sp^2$-hybridized carbon atoms remains unchanged.

**13. C**

The first thing to recognize when considering the question stem here is the phrase *not all of the energy*, indicating that most of the excited-state energy is emitted during luminescence, but that some is dissipated through the collisions. From this we can assume that whatever phenomenon we observe will exhibit a bit of blurriness. The amount of energy dissipated through collisions will obviously depend on such factors as the number of collisions and their efficiencies. Hence, the energy that will ultimately be radiated is indeterminate: It can be as high as the difference in energy between A* and A, but more likely it is less than this amount because part of the difference is dissipated through collisions. We know that the energy of a photon is related to its frequency by $E = hf$, where E is the energy, h is Planck's constant, and f is the frequency. The photon emitted during chemiluminescence carries with it the excess energy that the chemical species possesses. In other words, the energy carried by the photon is, in the simplest case, the difference in energy between A* and A, where A stands for some generic chemical species that is formed in the reaction producing the luminescence. In short, a range of energy values can be carried by the photons, resulting in a range of frequencies (and hence wavelengths). Therefore, choice **C** is correct.

Choice **A** is incorrect. If the total pressure were increased, the frequency of collisions would also increase. More energy would then be dissipated via collisions than by luminescence. Choice **B** is also incorrect, because the exact reverse should be the result of collisional deactivation. As described above, a higher pressure would increase the probability that energy is dissipated by collisions rather than radiated in the form of luminescence. In fact, gas-phase chemiluminescent reactions are often carried out under conditions of low total pressure to enhance the intensity. (One may argue that if the pressure were increased by increasing the concentration of the gas-phase reactants, this would increase the rate of reaction and hence the intensity. This, however, would not be a direct effect of collisional deactivation, which is what we are asked for.) Choice **D** is incorrect, because when the energy is dissipated through collisions, the species moves toward the ground state. It may not luminesce (if all of its energy is dissipated through collisions), but it will not remain in the excited state.

**14.  D**

The key to quickly answering this question is to recognize that three of the four choices have 11 electrons in their Lewis dot structures, while the fourth has only 10. Even without knowing anything about the compound, the fact that one is drastically different from the others means that it will probably be the answer to the question. Still, let's consider exactly what is going on in this question: Nitrogen has five valence electrons while oxygen has six. NO thus has a total of 11 valence electrons. The structure shown in choice D has only 10 valence electrons: three pairs of bonding electrons gives six electrons, plus two lone pairs which provides another four electrons. It does not have the correct number of electrons and thus cannot be a correct Lewis structure. All of the other structures have a total of 11 valence electrons.

**15.  A**

This is a complicated and involved question, so the best approach is to map out exactly what is being asked, compare that with what we know from the passage, and go from there. The answer choices have two parts each: the order in which $Fe^{2+}$ ions encounter the organic species and are introduced into the luminol–peroxide mixture, and the concentration of the organic species relative to the concentration of $Fe^{2+}$. So, the thing to do here is to sketch out which combination of conditions will produce the results we want, then match this to our answer choices. In order for the intensity to be suppressed, the $Fe^{2+}$ ions must be complexed with the organic species whose concentration we are trying to determine. This complexing must occur before the $Fe^{2+}$ can react with the luminol–peroxidase solution; otherwise luminescence will be generated at its full intensity before there is a chance for the complexing to occur. Furthermore, the concentration of $Fe^{2+}$ must be higher than that of the organic species. If this were not the case, we would not observe any luminescent signal at all, and we would not get any quantitative information about the concentration of the organic species, other than the fact that it is greater than that of $Fe^{2+}$.

## Passage IV (Questions 16–20)

**16.  B**

The question stem asks for the approximate mass percent of chloride ion in the original sample, so we should proceed to calculate it using any approximations necessary to lighten the workload. As with the majority of MCAT questions, the answer choices provided are far enough apart in magnitude that we can make reasonable approximations and still arrive at the correct answer. The mass percent of chloride ions is defined as:

$$\frac{\text{mass of chloride ions}}{\text{mass of sample}} \times 100\%$$

The passage states that the unknown sample had a mass of 0.2020 g. We need to calculate the mass of the chloride ions. The mass of AgCl formed was 0.3485 g, and for each mole AgCl formed, one mole of chloride ions was present in the original sample. The dimensional setup for the stoichiometry is as follows:

$$0.3485 \text{ g AgCl} \times \frac{1 \text{ mol AgCl}}{(107.9 + 35.5) \text{ g AgCl}}$$

$$\times \frac{1 \text{ mol Cl}^-}{1 \text{ mol AgCl}} \times \frac{35.5 \text{ g Cl}^-}{1 \text{ mol Cl}^-}$$

After canceling units and approximating, we obtain:

$$(0.35 \times \frac{1}{140} \times 35 \text{ g})\text{Cl}^- = \frac{0.35}{4} \text{ g Cl}^- = 0.09 \text{ g Cl}^-$$

The percent by mass is therefore approximately

$$\frac{0.09 \text{ g Cl}}{0.20 \text{ g sample}} \times 100\%$$

which is a bit less than 50%. Choice **B** is therefore the correct answer.

**17. C**

Since the question stem asks which of the choices would have the least effect on the accuracy of the results, we should examine the consequences of each answer choice before making our selection. The gist of the procedure is that chloride ion is precipitated, as AgCl, by reaction with excess silver ion. The precipitate is then washed to remove unreacted silver ion, and filtered and dried quickly enough to avoid unwanted side reactions. Choice **C** is correct, because the presence of sodium ions, and additional nitrate ions, will not result in the formation of any additional product. Nor will they prevent precipitation of AgCl in any way. Nitrate is a spectator ion in the procedure described; sodium would be another spectator ion if it were present.

Choice **A** can be eliminated because, according to Reaction 2, exposure to light will cause the reduction of silver ions to metallic silver with the concurrent release of chlorine gas. This reaction, if it occurs appreciably, will result in a decrease in the mass of AgCl recovered and, consequently, an artificially low chloride determination. Answer choice **B** can be eliminated because $K_{sp}$, as an equilibrium constant, will be affected by a change in temperature. Since the calculations are, at least partially, based on the assumption that precipitation is nearly complete, any increase in the temperature will put this assumption in doubt, and therefore affect the accuracy of the analysis. Recall that an increase in temperature usually leads to an increase in solubility. Choice **D** can be eliminated, since hydrochloric acid, which is dissociated into $H^+$ and $Cl^-$, will react with any remaining silver ions on the surface of the precipitate to form additional AgCl.

**18. A**

Since we're asked about precipitation in the question stem, we know our calculations will involve dilution, the common ion effect, and $K_{sp}$ calculations as well as a general understanding of the meaning of $K_{sp}$. Chloride ions precipitate out to form solid AgCl upon encountering the silver ions from the silver nitrate ($AgNO_3$). Precipitation will occur if the ion product, $[Ag^+][Cl^-]$ is greater than $K_{sp}$. Hence, the concentration of chloride ions in solution (unprecipitated) is also dependent on the concentration of silver ions present (as well as on the solubility of AgCl). The concentration of the silver nitrate solution, before it is added to the sample to be analyzed, is $0.2\ M$. From the stoichiometry of the compound, we see that there is a 1:1 ratio between $AgNO_3$ and $Ag^+$, and so the concentration of

silver ions is also originally $0.2\ M$. This is, however, diluted as it is added to the 100 mL of the other solution, giving a final volume of about 120 mL. The new concentration is calculated as:

$$M_1V_1 = M_2V_2$$

$$(0.2\ M)(20 \text{ mL}) = M_2(120 \text{ mL})$$

$$M_2 = 4/120\ M = 1/30\ M\ Ag^+$$

The necessary concentration of $Cl^-$ can then be determined from the silver ion concentration and the $K_{sp}$ of AgCl:

$$K_{sp} = [Ag^+][Cl^-] =>$$

$$[Cl^-] = K_{sp}/[Ag^+] = 1.56 \times 10^{-10}/(1/30), \text{ or}$$

$$[Cl^-] = 1.5 \times 10^{-10} \times 30 = 4.5 \times 10^{-9}\ M$$

Note that it is not necessary to carry out this last multiplication, as only choice **A** is larger than $1.56 \times 10^{-10}$.

**19. C**

In this question we're going to use our analysis of the passage in tandem with our general knowledge of common substances. We know that the precipitate described in the passage was white, so the precipitate obtained in the other experiment must be contaminated with something else. Choice **A** is incorrect since nitrate ions, like those in the silver nitrate solution, are colorless; we know this because the nitric acid solution was colorless. Choice **B** is incorrect, because, as described in an earlier question, elevated temperatures would decrease the yield of AgCl but would not affect its color. In fact, since crystallization is slower at higher temperatures, it would be less likely that extra silver ions become trapped in the crystal lattice as it forms. Choice **D** is incorrect, because the passage specifically describes the formation of a "fine, white" silver chloride precipitate. Therefore, Choice **C** is correct; since silver metal has a gray color, when it is mixed in with a white precipitate, the resulting solid will have a faint violet color.

**20. A**

The key to answering this question quickly and correctly is recognizing that in the passage we learned that a wet silver chloride precipitate is susceptible to photodecomposition. Therefore, if the silver chloride solution must be stored overnight before filtration, we must guard against the photodecomposition side reaction by protecting the sample from light. Therefore, choice **A** is correct. Choice **B** is incorrect, because the passage tells us that the silver chloride precipitate formed immediately, so extra time will not result in a higher mass of precipitate. Choice **C** is incorrect, because solvent evaporation does not affect the mass of recovered precipitate—the precipitate would be left behind if the solvent were to evaporate. Choice **D** is incorrect, because exposure to chlorine vapors could only increase the mass of the precipitate using stray silver ions in solution, resulting in a higher (not lower) result.

## Passage V (Questions 21–25)

**21. D**

The question stem asks about the inversion temperature of various gases. Since the inversion temperature is given in the passage as $2a/Rb$, a high inversion temperature results from a large $a$ and/or a small $b$. With questions of this type, it is important to know how to make prudent approximations. We will try to come up with estimates of the quantity $a/b$ for each gas, but note first of all that helium can be easily eliminated since its $a$ and $b$ are of the same magnitude, whereas for the other gases $a$ is bigger than $b$ by a factor of 10 or more.

$$H_2: \frac{0.244}{0.0266} = \sim 10$$

$$N_2: \frac{1.39}{0.0391} = \sim \frac{1.4}{0.04} = \sim \frac{140}{4} = 35$$

$$(>10; \text{ eliminate choice } \mathbf{B})$$

$$CH_4: \frac{2.25}{0.0428} = \sim \frac{2.25}{0.04} \left(> \frac{1.4}{0.04}, \text{ which is the value for } N_2\right)$$

Hence $CH_4$ has the highest $a/b$ value, and should thus be expected to have the highest inversion temperature.

**22. D**

The magnitude of work associated with the volume change of a gas at constant pressure is given by $|W| = |P\Delta V|$, where P is the pressure and $\Delta V$ is the change in volume. If the gas expands, it does work on the environment; whereas if it contracts, work is done on the gas. If net work is done, then the magnitude of the work done by the gas upon expansion must be greater than the magnitude of the work done on the gas in contraction. Let us apply this to the Joule–Thomson experiment.

Let us focus our attention on the particular amount of gas that is transferred from chamber 1 to chamber 2. This gas is compressed against pressure $P_1$. The change in volume associated with this compression is its entire volume, since all of it is removed from chamber 1. In other words, its volume change upon compression is the volume change of chamber 1 as a whole, i.e. $\Delta V_1$. The amount of work done on the transferred gas therefore has a magnitude of $|P_1\Delta V_1|$.

This gas enters chamber 2, where it expands against a pressure $P_2$. The volume change of this expansion is the volume change of chamber 2 as a whole, i.e., $\Delta V_2$. So the gas does work of magnitude $|P_2\Delta V_2|$. As mentioned at the beginning, if net work is done, then $|W|_{expansion} > |W|_{compression}$. Hence $|P_2\Delta V_2| > |P_1\Delta V_1|$.

**23. D**

Although it may be tempting to answer this question using the Ideal Gas Law, this is in fact a qualitative question on the behavior of real gases. When an ideal gas is compressed to half its initial volume at constant temperature, we know from Boyle's Law (or the ideal gas law) that its pressure doubles. When a real gas is compressed, however, there are two competing factors that come into play. The attractive forces become stronger as the average distance between the gas molecules decreases. This has the effect of lowering the pressure from the expected doubling. At the same time, however, the excluded volume taken up by the gas particles now constitutes a more significant fraction of the total volume. The effective volume available to the gas molecules, therefore, is less than half of the initial effective volume. The pressure is therefore expected to be more than doubled from this factor. Which factor dominates depends on the actual numerical values of such parameters as $a$, $b$, initial pressure, etc.

**24. B**

When answering this question, it's worthwhile to notice that we don't need to have read the passage to answer correctly. We have three options. The first is to recall what the plot looks like from our chemistry studies. The second option is to think through the behavior of real gases in order to generate our own plot and compare it with the answer choices. Our third option is to examine the repercussions of each answer choice and decide which is the best. This backsolving approach is going to be quickest if we can't immediately remember how the plot should look. When the separation between two neutral particles is relatively large, there is a weak attractive force between them because of van der Waals forces. These forces tend to draw the particles closer together, and hence the potential energy is lowered as the two approach each other from far away. This by itself is sufficient to enable us to pick **B** as the correct answer. For completeness, let us continue with the analysis. The lowering of the potential energy does not continue indefinitely, as eventually the particles get so close together that their electron clouds start to repel. Beyond a certain point, then, the potential energy starts to increase as the separation keeps decreasing. This is illustrated in the curve shown in choice **B**.

**25. A**

This is another one of those questions that follow a passage but don't really require you to have read the passage to answer correctly. We're told that we have two vessels, one with argon, one with neon. If the same amount of heat is added to both samples of gases and no volume change occurs (hence W = 0), then all the heat is used to increase the internal energies of the gases. For ideal gases, the internal energy, U, is proportional to the temperature. Since the two gases have the same initial temperature and experience the same amount of kinetic energy increase (same temperature change), they will also have the same final temperature. Choices **C** and **D** can thus be eliminated. To decide between choices **A** and **B**, we need to recognize that neon and argon have different atomic masses. Since

kinetic energy is $\frac{1}{2}mv^2$, and the two have the same average kinetic energy, the less massive of the two gases will be moving more quickly. Neon is lighter than argon, which is enough for us to conclude that choice **A** must be correct.

## Passage VI (Questions 26–30)

**26. A**

The key to answering this question correctly is recognizing which part of the passage is relevant. The energy profile, reaction mechanisms, and rates-concentrations table might throw us off, so we need to stay focused on the K values given in the reaction scheme in Figure 1. K represents the ratio of products to reactants at equilibrium, so the reaction with the largest K value will proceed the farthest toward completion at equilibrium. The equilibrium constants for the three reactions are given in Figure 1. Reaction I, with a K = $3 \times 10^4$, will have proceeded the farthest toward completion once equilibrium has been established. Answer choice **A** is correct.

**27. C**

For this question, begin by noting that the generic rate expression for this process is

$$\text{Rate} = k[tert\text{-butyl bromide}]^x[\text{OH}^-]^y$$

Then use the experimental data given in Table 1 to determine the values of $x$ and $y$. First, examine the changes observed between experiments 1 and 2. The concentration of hydroxide was doubled, but the initial rate remained unchanged. Therefore, rate does not depend on hydroxide concentration, so $y = 0$. Now focus on experiments 1 and 3. When the concentration of *tert*-butyl bromide is doubled, the initial rate also doubles, so $x = 1$. Therefore, the rate expression is:

$$\text{Rate} = k[tert\text{-butyl bromide}]$$

**28. A**

Although the question specifically refers to Reaction I, it is really asking us to consider the consequences of running any reaction at a higher temperature. Rate constants and equilibrium constants are both affected by temperature. Let's consider how. The temperature dependence of the rate constant is explained by the Arrhenius equation:

$$\ln k = \ln A - \frac{E_a}{RT}$$

In order for a collision between two species to result in a chemical reaction, the two species must have sufficient kinetic energy to overcome the activation energy barrier for that reaction. As temperature increases, so does kinetic energy. With a higher proportion of molecules having a kinetic energy greater than the activation energy for a reaction, more collisions will result in a reaction and the rate will increase. Therefore, the important thing to recognize is that as the temperature increases, so does the rate constant. You can now eliminate answer choices **B** and **D**. Now let's consider the equilibrium constant. The temperature dependence of the equilibrium constant is described by the equation $\Delta G = -RT \ln K$, where $\Delta G$ is the standard free energy change of the reaction. If we solve for ln K, we find an inverse relationship between K and temperature. This means that as temperature changes, so will the rate constant. Since both the equilibrium and the rate constant change with temperature, the correct answer choice is **A**.

**29. D**

Whenever a question asks about shifting an equilibrium, we should immediately think of Le Chatelier's principle. Le Chatelier's principle states if a system is subjected to a stress, it will adjust itself in order to alleviate that stress. One of the stresses a system can experience relates to the concentrations of reactants and products. For Reaction II, the alkene will be favored if bromide can be removed from the product side of the equilibrium. This could be accomplished by precipitating the bromide ion through addition of silver nitrate.

**30. D**

In order to answer this question correctly, we must consider the functions of a catalyst. Adding a catalyst causes the rate of the forward reaction to increase because the activation energy for the forward process with a catalyst is lower than the activation energy without the catalyst. We know this from the Boltzmann distribution. However, the activation energy for the reverse reaction is also lowered by addition of a catalyst, so the equilibrium constant will remain the same. Addition of a catalyst affects the forward and reverse reactions equally, so none of the equilibrium constants will change.

## Passage VII (Questions 31–35)

**31. A**

Although the last phrase in the question stem does not explicitly say "standard reduction half-reactions" but rather "standard half-reactions," the question does state that E values are for reduction half-reactions. You must be aware of this in order to master this type of question. This means that from left to right, we have "oxidized form, reduced form" as the half-reaction to which E refers. A metal such as gold—which, according to the passage, does not corrode under normal circumstances—is resistant to oxidation. You should therefore predict that a reduction reaction like $Au^+(aq) + e^- \rightarrow Au(s)$ would have a positive E relative to the hydrogen reference electrode, since the passage told us that Au is not easily corroded. At the opposite end of the spectrum, metals like Mg, as well as Group IA and IIA metals in general, are easily corroded—*oxidized*—meaning that they should have a negative E relative to hydrogen so that a spontaneous cell reaction can occur in solution. Choice **A** is correct.

**32. A**

Based on the wording of the question stem, we already know that we need to compare the pH with the pOH to determine why one changes and the other does not. As Table 1 shows, in strongly basic solution [OH$^-$] remains constant with increasing temperature because the extreme pH comes from having such a large number of basic ions present—in this case, 0.032 M base. This number is much, much greater than the amount of OH$^-$ (or H$_3$O$^+$) that comes from water—only $10^{-7}$ M at 25°C. The change in pK$_w$ values from 0 to 30 yields a change in [OH$^-$] or [H$_3$O$^+$] contributed from water of less than a factor of ten, so we can see how little the temperature will affect the makeup of strongly basic or acidic solutions through changes in water self-ionization. Choice **B** is misleading in that it does contain a kernel of truth: At higher temperatures, reactants have more energy and reaction rates can go faster, and the excess base will (by Le Chatelier's principle) shift the position of the water equilibrium. But the excess [OH$^-$] will not change the value of K$_w$—only the change in temperature does that. Choice **C**, though a true statement, does not correctly explain the behavior described in the question. That is, it does explain why the pH changes; however, it does not explain why pOH remains essentially fixed. Finally, choice **D** begins with a true statement, but then makes a false statement. Yes, pH does measure [H$^+$]. However, [H$^+$] and [OH$^-$] are interrelated by the autoionization of water. The point of the question is that although they *are* interrelated, the magnitude of the concentration overwhelms this relation.

**33. C**

To answer this question, let's first remember that reduction takes place at the cathode (mnemonic: RED CAT), while oxidation takes place at the anode (mnemonic: AN OX). Then let's focus on the crucial fact that solid metal is being dissolved (not formed), so the metal half-reaction will need to go from the neutral atom state to the ionized state. This leads us to choice **C**. Choice **A** is wrong because it shows an oxidation followed by a reduction. The question

stem, however, asks for reduction followed by an oxidation (look back: cathode first, anode second). Choice **B** is reduction and then oxidation, which could be cathodic and anodic reactions, but not for corrosion: Fe(s) in this choice is being formed, not dissolved. Finally, choice **D** is incorrect, since there is no redox potential to drive this reaction.

**34. D**

This type of question cannot be answered by prediction—we must go through the answer choices and evaluate each one. The passage clearly states that choice **A** is true—hydronium and hydroxide ions in water determine the corrosiveness of a solution. Table 1 indicates that choice **B** is true as well. The pH changes with temperature because of the change in water's contribution to the proton concentration. However, the high concentration of hydroxide is unaffected by the small contribution from water. The first phrase in choice **C** was stated in the passage, and the second choice is really saying the same thing as the first—temperature is representative of kinetic energies of solution particles, and more kinetic energy means a greater chance of reaction, or in this case corrosion. So by process of elimination, this leaves choice **D** as the answer. Table 1 indicates that pH decreases with increasing temperature—therefore corrosivity decreases.

**35. B**

This question challenges us to draw conclusions from what we read in the passage and observed in Table 1, using our knowledge of acid–base equilibria and pH trends. This is an ideal time to *predict* the answer before reading all the answer choices. If in strongly basic solutions the pOH stays fixed, then in strongly acidic solutions the pH should stay fixed. The pK$_w$ will do exactly the same thing whether you are in acid or base solution, so Table 1 shows that it will decrease (more products at equilibrium) at higher temperature. Likewise, water will produce more OH$^-$ ions at higher temperature and so the pOH will decrease to show this behavior, just as the pH decreased in highly basic solutions. Remember that in both cases—strong acid or base—the water autoionization reaction is producing more H$^+$ and more OH$^-$ with increasing temperature. We only see a change in the amount of the more dilute component. Choice **B** reflects these predictions.

**36. C**

The first step in solving a percentage yield question is to determine the limiting reagent. The balanced chemical equation shows H$_2$S reacting with SO$_2$ in a 2:1 molar ratio. 204 kg of H$_2$S corresponds to:

$$\frac{204 \times 10^3 \text{ g}}{(2 \times 1.0 + 32.0) \text{ g/mol}} = 6 \times 10^3 \text{ mol H}_2\text{S}$$

256 kg of $SO_2$ corresponds to:

$$\frac{256 \times 10^3 \, g}{(32.0 + 2 \times 16.0) \, g/mol} = 4 \times 10^3 \, mol \, SO_2$$

The molar ratio of $H_2S$ to $SO_2$ is $6 \times 10^3 : 4 \times 10^3 = 6:4 = 1.5:1$. Since there are only 1.5 moles of $H_2S$ for every mole of $SO_2$ (instead of 2:1), $H_2S$ is the limiting reagent.

The chemical equation shows that the Claus process produces 3 moles of $S_2$ for every 2 moles of $H_2S$. Hence, if we start with $6 \times 10^3$ mol of $H_2S$, the theoretical yield of the reaction would be:

$$\text{theoretical yield} = \frac{3 \text{ moles S}}{2 \text{ moles } H_2S} \times (6 \times 10^3 \text{ moles } H_2S)$$
$$= 9 \times 10^3 \text{ moles S}$$

However, the question stem tells us that we only end up with 224 kg of S. This corresponds to $7 \times 10^3$ moles S:

$$\text{actual yield} = \frac{224 \times 10^3 \, gS}{32 g/mol \, S} = 7 \times 10^3 \text{ moles S}$$

Therefore the percentage yield of sulfur is

$$\text{percentage yield} = \frac{\text{actual yield}}{\text{theoretical yield}} \times 100\%$$
$$= \frac{7 \times 10^3 \text{ moles S}}{9 \times 10^3 \text{ moles S}} \times 100\% = 77\%, \text{ choice } C.$$

**37. D**

An equilibrium constant of 0.05 means that at equilibrium the ratio of product $[A^-][H_3O^+]$ to the amount [HA] is 5:100. This eliminates choices **A** and **B**. If we forget that there are *two* products in the formula for K,

$$K = \frac{[H_3O^+][A^-]}{[HA]}, \text{ not } K = \frac{[A-]}{[HA]}$$

then choice **C** would appear to be correct. With an equilibrium constant K << 1, the reactant HA undergoes little ionization (also called hydrolysis or dissociation) in water. Choice **D** is therefore the correct answer. Choice **A** could appear to be correct if we were looking at the balanced equation (a 1:1 mole ratio) and ignoring the value of K. Balanced equations tell us only how many individual product species will be present at equilibrium relative to one reactant species, not how many of those reactants are actually converted to products by the time the equilibrium is established.

**38. B**

A Lewis base is a compound that can donate an electron pair. Choice **A**, chlorous acid, will not act as a Lewis base. Rather, it is an Arrhenius acid, capable of donating a hydrogen ion in solution. Choice **B**, hydrazine, consists of two nitrogens bonded to each other and to two hydrogen atoms each. A nitrogen atom has a valence of 5, and when it is bonded to another nitrogen and two hydrogens, it is only using three of its five valence electrons. Therefore, each nitrogen will have a pair of unbonded electrons. This makes hydrazine able to act as an electron-pair donor, or Lewis base, so choice **B** is the correct answer. Looking at the other choices, choice **C**, an ammonium ion, is not a Lewis base. In fact, it's the conjugate acid of ammonia. Choice **D** is boron trifluoride. The boron atom has three valence electrons, each of which is involved in a covalent bond with a fluorine atom, and thus has no electron pairs to donate. Once again, choice **B** is the correct answer.

**39. D**

Perhaps the easiest way to solve a problem such as this is to imagine a particular sample mass of the compound. We shall choose a mass of 100 grams for convenience, though any mass we use will lead us to the correct answer. Because the oxide of arsenic contains only arsenic and oxygen, a 100-gram sample would contain 65.2 grams of arsenic and the remainder, 34.8 grams, must be oxygen. To find the ratio between these two elements in the compound we divide the mass of arsenic by the atomic weight of arsenic, 74.7 grams per mole, and the mass of oxygen by the atomic weight of oxygen, 16 grams per mole. This will give the mole ratio between arsenic and oxygen in the compound. To convert to a more easily useful ratio, we divide both by the lowest number of the two, here arsenic. This gives us a ratio of 1 mole arsenic to 2.5 moles oxygen. Multiply both of these to get 2 moles arsenic per 5 moles of oxygen. This corresponds to $As_2O_5$, the formula in choice **D**.

**40. B**

This question tests your understanding of VSEPR, the Valence Shell Electron Pair Repulsion theory of molecular geometry. First, we must determine the molecular geometry of $SO_2$ and then compare this to the answer choices. Using Lewis dot structures, we can get an idea of the number of bonds and lone electron pairs. Use the periodic table in your test booklet to determine the number of electrons in the valence shells of different elements. Sulfur (S) has six electrons in its valence shell, as does each oxygen (O) in its valence shell.

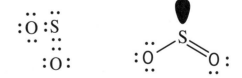

VSEPR proposes that the repulsion between electron pairs makes molecules adopt shapes that have the greatest separation between the electron pairs. The lone pair of electrons in $SO_2$ push the atoms into a bent configuration. Note that when we discuss molecular geometry, we are concerned with the arrangements of the bonds, not the arrangements of the electron pairs. Note also that the diagram above only shows one of the resonance structures of $SO_2$. In reality, the double bond is shared equally between the two NO bonds.

Now let's consider the answer choices.

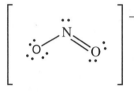

Answer choice **A**, $CO_2$, has a linear configuration. It has two double bonds of carbon to oxygen. $CO_2$ does not have a bent structure.

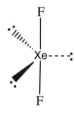

Answer choice **B** is the correct answer. $NO_2^-$ has a bent molecular structure. Again, the diagram above only shows one of the resonance structures of $NO_2^-$. These bonds are bent by the influence of the lone pair of electrons. Note that this is a negative ion, which explains the extra electron. We will consider the other answer choices for completeness.

Answer choice **C**, $XeF_2$, has a linear molecular structure. Note that the electron pairs are arranged in a trigonal bipyramidal geometry. However, when we consider just the bonds to other nuclei, the geometry is linear.

Answer choice **D**, $NH_3$, has three hydrogens bonded to the central nitrogen, so we can already determine that it will not have the bent structure. The bent structure requires that there be two atoms bonded to a central atom. $NH_3$ has a trigonal pyramidal structure. The three hydrogens are pushed out of the plane by the lone pair.

**41. B**

This question deals with the colligative properties of solutions. The first is that the presence of a solute in a solution always raises the boiling point and lowers the freezing point, relative to the boiling and freezing points of the pure solvent. A higher concentration of solute in the solution leads to a greater boiling-point elevation and freezing-point depression. Thus it is clear that choice **A** is incorrect; since Solution Y's boiling point is higher than Solution X's, its freezing point must be lower as well. The second important concept is that of vapor pressure, which is the topic of both answers **B** and **D**. A solution boils when its vapor pressure is equal to the atmospheric pressure. Since solution Y is not boiling at 100.26°C and solution X is boiling, we know the vapor pressure of solution Y must be below that of solution X. Choice **B** is therefore correct, and choice **D** incorrect. Choice **C** concerns the miscibility of solutions X and Y, i.e., the solubility of the two solutions in each other. We don't have enough information to say that this answer is correct. We are not given any information about the solubilities of solutions X and Y, so Choice **C** is irrelevant.

**42. D**

The standard potential of a reaction is a measure of the driving force behind the reaction. When the potential is positive, as it is in this case, the reaction will take place spontaneously.

To answer this question, we must first express the balanced equation given in terms of separate oxidation and reduction equations. Once we do this, the equations you get are, for oxidation,

$$2\, Al \rightarrow 2\, Al^{3+} + 6e^-$$

and, for reduction,

$$2\, Fe^{3+} + 6e^- \rightarrow 2\, Fe$$

The oxidation state of the oxide ions does not change, and therefore these are not taken into account when determining the voltage. Next, we determine and add up the standard potentials for these half-reactions. The table indicates that the standard potential for the reduction of aluminum is –1.66 volts. Since in this case the aluminum is being oxidized instead of reduced, we subtract the –1.66 volts, changing its sign from minus to plus. *We do not multiply the 1.66 by 2 for the two moles of aluminum in the balanced equation.*

Next, we determine the reduction potential for iron from the +3 valence to 0. This is given in the table as –0.037 V. Finally, we add together the –0.037 volts from the reduction of iron with the 1.66 volts from the oxidation of aluminum. This gives us a total of 1.62 volts for the total reaction, choice **D**.

**43. C**

The $\Delta H°$ for a reaction can be calculated as the difference between the heat of formation of the products and that of the reactants.

$$\Delta H°_{reaction} = \Delta H°_{f(products)} - \Delta H°_{f(reactants)}$$

Recall that heat of formation is the heat of the reaction that produces 1 mol of the material in question from pure elements in their standard states. The heat of formation of elements in their standard states is zero. The question stem provides the reaction for formation of $Fe_3O_4$:

$$3\,Fe(s) + 2\,O_2(g) \rightarrow Fe_3O_4(s)\,\Delta H - 1118.4\,kJ \cdot mol^{-1}$$

So we can determine the heat of formation of $Fe_2O_3$ from the first equation and the $\Delta H°_f$ of $Fe_3O_4$ given by the equation above.

$$\Delta H°_{reaction} = 4(\Delta H°_f Fe_3O_4) + \Delta H°_f O_2 - 6(\Delta H°_f Fe_2O_3)$$
$$+472 = 4(-1118.4) + 0 - 6(\Delta H°_f Fe_2O_3)$$
$$4944 = -6(\Delta H°_f Fe_2O_3)$$
$$\Delta H°_f Fe_2O_3 = -824\,kJ \cdot mol^{-1}$$

which is answer choice **C**. We should, of course, use approximations judiciously to save time.

**44. A**

The key to answering this question correctly is remembering the definition of density. Remember that we can manipulate the equation into a more useful form and then think over what else we would need to know to answer the question. Recall that density is mass divided by volume. If we want to know the density of oxygen in a container, we need to know the mass of the oxygen divided by the volume of the oxygen. This is true regardless of the fact that there may also be other gases present in the container. Since we are required to use the formula $PV = nRT$, we'll rearrange this formula so that we have mass over volume on the left and what it is equal to, in all those other terms, on the right. First, remember that $P$ equals pressure, $V$ equals volume, $n$ equals number of moles, $T$ is temperature and $R$ is the gas constant. How do we get mass into this equation? The number of moles of oxygen, $n$, is equal to the actual mass of oxygen, m, divided by the molar mass of oxygen, M. Substituting into the $PV = nRT$ equation we get $PV = m/MRT$. Next we have to rearrange the formula to

solve for density—that is, mass, m, over volume, $V$. The final formula is $m/V = MP/RT$. Now to figure out what values to plug into the equation we need to answer two questions. First, should we use the number of moles of oxygen in the container, or the total number of moles of gas in the container? And second, should we use the partial pressure of oxygen in the container, or the total pressure of all the gases in the container? First let's consider the number of moles. We are using the number of moles times the molecular weight of oxygen to equal the total mass of oxygen in the container. If we multiplied the molecular weight of oxygen by the total number of moles of all of the gases in the container, that would give us a value much greater than the mass of the oxygen alone. Thus we must use only the number of moles of oxygen. If we use the total pressure of all the gases, then the value on the right of our density equation could be changed by adding or subtracting other gases, even though the amount of oxygen remained constant. In order for the value on the right to be equal to the value on the left, which we just calculated based on the actual amount of oxygen present, the ratio of the pressure on the right to the number of moles of oxygen on the left must be constant. Therefore we have to use the partial pressure of oxygen together with the number of moles of oxygen, and the answer choice is **A**.

**45. A**

The equation needed to answer this question, which was derived by Bohr, predicts the frequency of light produced when an electron falls from one quantum level to another in a hydrogen atom, though it doesn't work for other kinds of atoms, since those have interelectronic interactions that complicate the energetics. The equation states that

$$E = -A\left(\frac{1}{n_i^2} - \frac{1}{n_f^2}\right)$$

where $n_i$ is the first quantum number of the electron in its initial state and $n_f$ is the first quantum number of the electron in its final state. A, which is a constant, is the amount of energy needed to remove an electron from the lowest energy level of a hydrogen atom to a point at an infinite distance away. The negative sign in front of the A is there because the electron in the question is falling *toward* the nucleus of the atom, and therefore is giving off energy. So, to get back to this question here, we have to multiply $-A$ by $1/3^2 - 1/2^2$. This comes to $-A\,\alpha\,-5/36$, which is equal to 0.14 A, choice **A**.

CHAPTER 6

# Organic Chemistry

## READING THE PASSAGE

### Organic Chemistry Passage Types

Recall from our earlier discussion that MCAT science passages fall into one of three categories: information, experiment, and persuasive argument.

For *information* passages in Organic Chemistry, the paragraphs are often relatively short and are often accompanied by diagrams illustrating reactions or mechanisms. If the passage describes a specific laboratory technique or setup, it may contain lengthier text with a graphic of the relevant apparatuses. In chapter 3 of this section you saw an example of an Organic Chemistry information passage.

An information passage in Organic Chemistry may:

- Present a new reaction: its mechanism, its stereochemistry, factors affecting its rate, other factors.
- Present a series of related reactions, for example, different ways to synthesize a class of compounds, typical reactions that a class of compounds undergoes, etc.
- Describe the characteristics of a class of compounds.
- Describe an experimental technique.

*Experiment* passages often include a presentation of the results of one or more experiments. In Organic Chemistry, the data may be presented in a variety of forms: the percentage yield of a synthesis, a verbal summary of whether the reaction or isolation procedure is successful, a description of the appearance or spectroscopic properties of the product, etc. As a result, an experiment passage may not immediately be as easily recognizable from the visual layout of the passage. An information passage describing a synthesis, for example, would technically be categorized as an experiment passage if the reaction were framed within the context of "A student carried out the following synthesis...." In other words, identifying the passage type is not as easy for Organic Chemistry passages as it may be for the other science areas.

One subcategory of Organic Chemistry experiment passages, however, does merit a special mention. These are the passages detailing an extraction or purification procedure. Often the passage is accompanied by a flowchart depicting the steps; however, there may be instances when the entire procedure is only described verbally. The following is an example of such an experiment passage.

Soil contains organic matter called humus. Humus is classified into humic and nonhumic materials. Humic materials are operationally divided into three main fractions: Humic acid, fulvic acid, and humin. Because soil is heterogeneous and its composition varies from one locale to another, the actual composition of each fraction is elusive. Figure 1 shows the proposed structure for one possible component of fulvic acid.

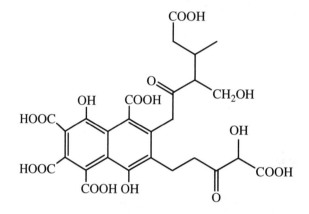

**Figure 1**

The traditional procedure for the separation of the three fractions from humic materials is shown in Figure 2.

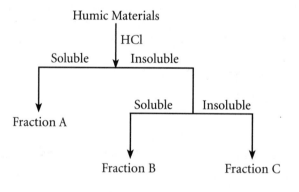

**Figure 2**

Some important properties of the three fractions of humic materials are listed in Table 1.

Table 1   Properties of Humic Materials

|  | Humic acid | Fulvic acid | Humin |
|---|---|---|---|
| **Solubility in water** | soluble in alkaline pHs | soluble at all pHs | insoluble at all pHs |
| **Carboxylic acid content** | some | high | low |
| **Phenolic content** | some | some | some |
| **Molecular weight range (Daltons)** | 5000–10,000 | 800–4000 | >100,000 |

Note that the previous passage again illustrates how the information/experiment distinction in Organic Chemistry is quite artificial at times. No actual experiment is carried out in the passage, so it could technically qualify as an information passage. However, the flowchart illustrating the separation procedure lends a very heavy experiment "flavor" to the passage.

*Persuasive argument* passages are relatively rare in Organic Chemistry. When they do occur, they usually appear in the form of passages presenting different proposed mechanisms for a reaction. However, it is sometimes difficult to draw the distinction between such a passage and an information passage presenting several mechanisms that are not conflicting hypotheses but are instead different mechanisms thought to operate under different conditions (acidic vs. basic, etc.). Persuasive argument passages can also resemble experiment passages in which different explanations are presented to account for a piece of data, or in which experimental data are included to support each hypothesis.

As the previous discussion suggests, categorization of passage types in Organic Chemistry is not quite as meaningful as it may be in other sciences. Nor is it especially effective in helping you answer the questions, as we shall see later. The distinction between passage types can be very fluid. In fact, regardless of what the passage deals with (and to what category it would technically belong), it will generally consist of combinations of elements, some of which are listed below:

- Diagram/chemical equation illustrating a reaction or mechanism
- Table presenting data on related compounds
- Flowchart presenting extraction series and other experimental procedures
- Prose summarizing what is already presented in a diagram
- Prose presenting new information on some aspect of the reaction(s) or on the compounds involved
- Prose detailing the experimental procedure for a reaction shown in a diagram
- Description of a proposed mechanism

Often the emphasis on one of these elements over the others is what determines the passage type.

Despite the problematic issue of categorizing Organic Chemistry passages, the technique on reading a passage still holds. You should always aim to perform two tasks on each passage: *map the passage* and *identify the topic*.

### Mapping the Passage and Identifying the Topic

For Organic Chemistry passages, you need to evaluate the nature of individual blocks of text to determine what amount of attention you need to pay to the prose. Text introducing a reaction presented in a diagram often serves only to provide a context for the reaction and can be skimmed quickly for any new terms introduced; you may want to highlight these terms or their definitions. Text detailing experimental protocol tends to be extraneous in Organic Chemistry (in contrast to Physics passages, for example). Description of a serial extraction procedure, on the other hand, merits closer attention, especially if no accompanying flowchart is included as a graphic. But again, keep in mind that you can always go back to the passage if you need to.

On the following pages, you will see the technique of mapping and identifying the topic applied to the sample passages you encountered in chapter 5 and earlier in this chapter.

> Aspirin, also known as acetylsalicylic acid, is one of the most useful and economical drugs available. It belongs to a class of drugs known as nonsteroidal anti-inflammatory drugs, and can be used to treat pain and alleviate inflammation and fever. The mechanism of aspirin's action is not fully understood, although recent research suggests that it functions by inhibiting cyclooxygenase-2, an enzyme that creates prostaglandin precursors. Prostaglandins contribute to the body's perception of pain and its inflammatory response. Prostaglandins also aid in the formation of blood clots, so aspirin thins the blood and may consequently help prevent heart disease.

Background information on aspirin. (This kind of prose, heavy on physiology and general observations, is usually not very important. Do NOT let yourself be bogged down by the details.)

> Aspirin can be synthesized from salicylic acid via the reaction shown in Figure 1.

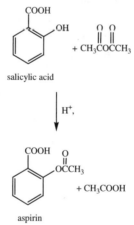

**Figure 1**

Reaction illustrating how aspirin can be synthesized.

> Both salicylic acid and aspirin are aromatic carboxylic acids. Carboxylic acids are generally weak acids, although they are among the strongest organic acids, with $pK_a$'s usually in the range of 3 to 5, much lower than those of corresponding alcohols. The $pK_a$'s of some compounds are given in Table 1.

A broadening in scope: discussion of organic acids.

**Table 1    pKa's of Compounds**

| Compound | pKa |
|---|---|
| Acetic acid | 4.76 |
| Fluoroacetic acid | 2.66 |
| Difluoroacetic acid | 1.24 |
| Trifluoroacetic acid | 0.23 |
| 2,2-Dimethylpropanoic acid | 5.05 |
| Benzoic acid | 4.18 |
| p-Nitrobenzoic acid | 3.43 |
| 2,4,6-Trinitrobenzoic acid | 0.65 |
| p-Methoxybenzoic acid | 4.47 |
| Phenol | 9.95 |
| Ethanol | 15.9 |
| Methanol | 15.1 |
| Water | 14 |

Table presenting pK$_a$'s of different compounds.

**Topic:** The passage deals with aspirin (esp. its synthesis) and then generalizes into the topic of organic acids.

Let's map the passage we looked at before.

Soil contains organic matter called humus. Humus is classified into humic and nonhumic materials. Humic materials are operationally divided into three main fractions: humic acid, fulvic acid, and humin. Because soil is heterogeneous and its composition varies from one locale to another, the actual composition of each fraction is elusive. Figure 1 shows the proposed structure for one possible component of fulvic acid.

Composition of soil: some new terms introduced—humic acid, fulvic acid, humin.

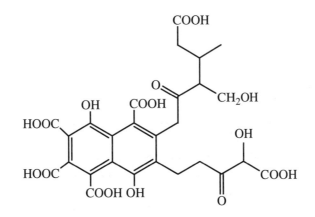

**Figure 1**

Structure of something that may be found in fulvic acid.

The traditional procedure for the separation of the three fractions from humic materials is shown in Figure 2.

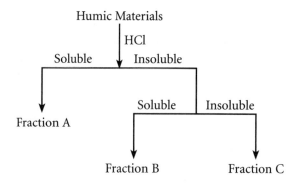

**Figure 2**

Some important properties of the three fractions of humic materials are listed in Table 1.

Scheme for separating the three fractions of humic materials in soil.

**Table 1  Properties of Humic Materials**

|  | **Humic acid** | **Fulvic acid** | **Humin** |
|---|---|---|---|
| **Solubility in water** | soluble in alkaline pHs | soluble at all pHs | insoluble at all pHs |
| **Carboxylic acid content** | some | high | low |
| **Phenolic content** | some | some | some |
| **Molecular weight range (Daltons)** | 5000–10,000 | 800–4000 | >100,000 |

Characteristics of the different fractions. (Again, do NOT get bogged down with the content. At this point, a look at the categories should suffice.)

**Topic:** The passage discusses the different components of soil and offers a scheme of separating them.

# HANDLING THE QUESTIONS

For Organic Chemistry questions, wording is often straightforward and easy to grasp, which makes applying the first step of our question-answering strategy (*Understand what you are being asked*) fairly simple. This is true of most questions dealing with nomenclature, isomerism, molecular structure, etc. The following are two typical MCAT Organic Chemistry questions, together with the concepts they test:

The two organomercurial compounds in Equation 3 are

A.  constitutional isomers.

B.  diastereomers.

C.  enantiomers.

D.  optical antipoles.

You are asked to identify the isomeric relationship between two compounds.

A surprisingly large number of Organic Chemistry questions on the MCAT are conceptually independent of the passages they accompany. They either stand alone from the passage completely, or require only very specific data from the passage, not an in-depth understanding of it. For example, the questions may test you on outside knowledge of certain characteristics of one or more compounds mentioned in the passage.

The following question pertaining to the aspirin passage we read earlier is an example of a question that can stand alone from the passage.

> Which of the following best accounts for the higher acidity of phenol compared to ethanol?
>
> A.  Phenol is hydrophobic.
> B.  Phenol has a higher molecular weight.
> C.  The benzene ring of phenol stabilizes negative charge.
> D.  The oxygen atom in phenol is $sp^2$-hybridized.

You are asked to identify the one statement from among the answer choices that explains why phenol is a stronger acid than ethanol. Nothing is needed from the passage. It is based on pure outside knowledge of acidity.

The relationship of the question to the aspirin passage is tenuous: it lies in the appearance of phenol and ethanol (and their $pK_a$'s) in Table 1 of the passage. But the wording of the question is self-contained, and it could easily have appeared as a discrete question not accompanying any passage.

More frequently, however, you will need to go back to the passage, but only to retrieve a very specific piece of information. Consider the following questions that could accompany the passage on soil composition.

> How many stereogenic centers does the structure shown in Figure 1 contain?
>
> A.  3
> B.  6
> C.  9
> D.  12

Translate the question and figure out what you need to do: Identify the number of stereogenic centers (or chiral centers) contained in the molecule. (Or: Identify the number of atoms bonded to four different groups arranged in a tetrahedral geometry.)

All of the following functional groups are present in the structure shown in Figure 1 EXCEPT

A.  alcohol.

B.  carboxylic acid.

C.  ester.

D.  ketone.

Take each answer choice and match it against the structure to see if it appears.

Translation: Need to examine Figure 1 in the passage.

For either question you need to examine the structure shown in Figure 1 (the proposed structure for a component of fulvic acid). However, for the purpose of the questions, you do not need to know what role the diagram is playing in the passage. The fact that the structure comes up during a discussion on soil composition is irrelevant to answering the question. With a slight change in wording, the structure could be included as part of the question stem and the question would be completely independent of the passage. To answer these questions you need only specific *data* from the passage.

Almost every Organic Chemistry passage on the MCAT will contain questions of this nature. Whether you need to go back to the passage or not, the important component is outside knowledge.

In Organic Chemistry, questions calling for an understanding of the passage often involve applying a reaction presented in the passage to a new set of compounds, identifying trends in data, or interpreting the result of an experiment. Success with these questions depends on critical reading of the passage and on the application of scientific reasoning in unfamiliar situations. However, even these questions usually call for outside knowledge. Consider the following question accompanying the aspirin passage:

Based on the data in Table 1, what is the expected $pK_a$ of the following compound?

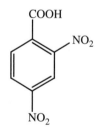

A.  $pK_a < 0.65$

B.  $0.65 < pK_a < 3.43$

C.  $3.43 < pK_a < 4.18$

D.  $pK_a > 4.18$

Determine how the structure shown is related to the ones appearing in Table 1 (using outside knowledge of nomenclature), and determine how its $pK_a$ compares to that of other relevant compounds. Use the answer choices to decide what's demanded of you (you don't need to come up with a specific value!). Look at the relevant compounds in Table 1 to establish a trend. Use their $pK_a$ values as benchmarks to establish the range.

In some instances the purpose of the passage can reveal a likely line of questioning when it comes to questions calling for an understanding of the passage. For example, with a passage dealing with a multistep synthesis, you are likely to be called upon to perform one or more of the following:

- Determine what the product would be if the starting compound were a similar but distinct molecule; conversely, determine what the starting compound must have been to synthesize a similar but distinct product using the same method.
- Rationalize why each step is necessary (what it accomplishes), and predict what would have been the result if the step were modified or omitted.
- Predict where an isotopic label in one of the reactants ends up as a result of the reaction.

An experiment passage presenting an extraction procedure, such as the passage on soil composition, may very likely be followed by questions testing your understanding of the rationale behind the scheme and the nature of the compound isolated at specific steps:

> In Figure 2, Fraction B is most likely
>
> **A.** humic acid.
>
> **B.** fulvic acid.
>
> **C.** humin.
>
> **D.** Cannot be determined from the information given

Apply the solubility data in Figure 2 and, combining it with knowledge of the properties of the different fractions from Table 1, determine the identity of Fraction B.

This last example illustrates one point: Your evaluation of what you are being asked may undergo some refinement after you have determined exactly what in the passage is going to help you answer the question. For example, after having studied Figure 2, a more efficient characterization of your task may be: "Which of the three fractions is most likely to be insoluble in HCl but soluble in NaOH?" This, in turn, helps you narrow down what data is relevant in Table 1. As you gain experience in reading MCAT passages effectively and tackling Organic Chemistry questions, you'll learn to figure out where to find what you need and to apply your science knowledge in parallel.

A list of topics most frequently tested on the MCAT Organic Chemistry section follows. If you find you need brushing up in any of these areas, add them to your study schedule.

# IN PREPARING FOR THE MCAT, I SHOULD UNDERSTAND ...

### 1. Molecular Structure: Hybridization, Bonding, Polarity, Resonance, Physical Properties

- Be able to identify the hybridization of carbon atoms in different molecules
- Know the implications of hybridization on molecular geometry, bond order, etc.
- Be familiar with the characteristics of sigma versus pi bonds
- Be able to assign formal charges to atoms in a molecule
- Be able to identify polar bonds and polar molecules
- Be able to draw resonance structures and assess their stability (and hence contribution)
- Know how inductive effects and resonance stabilize charge
- Be able to identify conjugated systems, and know how conjugation affects the stability of a compound
- Know the implications of resonance on hybridization and geometry
- Be able to identify compounds capable of hydrogen bonding
- Know the trend of physical properties in hydrocarbons
- Know the common reactions of hydrocarbons, and how structural factors affect them (strain, stability of radicals, etc.)
- Be able to classify a carbon atom as methyl, primary, secondary, tertiary, or quaternary, and know the implications on reactivity
- Know how the stability of a molecule can be quantified in terms of heat of combustion, heat of hydrogenation, etc.
- Know how polarity, hydrogen bonding, molecular weight, etc., affect physical properties of compounds

### 2. Functional Groups

- Be able to identify the functional groups present in a molecule
- Know how to interpret condensed structural formulas
- Be aware of major characteristics of functional groups (hydrogen bonding, acidity, solubility, etc.)
- Know the fundamental rules of nomenclature for each family of compounds

### 3. Acidity and Basicity

- Be able to identify the most acidic proton in an organic molecule
- Know the factors affecting acidity and basicity
- Be able to account for the acidity of carboxylic acids, phenols, etc.
- Be able to predict (or rationalize) trends in acidity and basicity

### 4. Isomerism

- Know the definitions of the different isomers
- Be able to identify the isomeric relationship between two compounds
- Be able to identify the number of stereogenic centers in an organic molecule

- Be able to classify a compound as chiral or achiral
- Know the origins of optical activity (specific rotation)
- Be able to identify meso compounds
- Be able to assign the absolute configuration of a chiral center
- Be able to interpret different representations of compounds: Fischer and Newman projections, etc.
- Know the conformational dynamics of ethane, butane, substituted cyclohexanes, etc.
- Know the differences/similarities in chemical and physical properties between two isomers
- Be able to identify means of separating different isomer types

## 5. Reactions and Syntheses: General Principles

- Be able to apply a reaction scheme given in a passage to a new set of reactants
- Be able to keep track of how bonds are formed and broken in a given mechanism by "pushing electrons," be able to apply a given, but previously unknown, mechanism to specific compounds
- Be able to visualize the mechanism in three-dimensional space to deduce the stereochemistry of the product
- Be able to deduce the structure of transition states and intermediates in a given reaction
- For a multistep synthesis, be able to recognize what happens at each step (what the step accomplishes)
- Be able to predict where an isotopic label ends up if one is employed in the reaction

## 6. $S_N1$, $S_N2$, E1, E2

- Know the mechanism of each reaction
- Know the rate law of each reaction
- Be able to identify reaction profiles of single-step vs. multistep reactions
- Be able to predict (in simple situations) which reaction is likely to predominate
- Be aware of the synthetic uses of the reactions
- Know the factors affecting the rate of each reaction
- Be able to predict the relative stability of carbocation intermediates
- Be able to identify good nucleophiles and good leaving groups
- Know the stereochemical implications of $S_N1$ versus $S_N2$
- Be aware of some specific examples: dehydration, solvolysis, Williamson ether synthesis, etc.
- Be able to apply Zaitsev's rule to determine the most stable elimination product

## 7. Addition Reactions

- Know the difference between Markovnikov and anti-Markovnikov addition; be able to predict the addition product of each
- Know the fundamental concepts of radical chemistry
- Know the mechanism of anti addition via a cyclic ion intermediate; be able to predict the product (and its most stable conformation)
- Know the stereochemistry of catalytic hydrogenation

## 8. Carbonyl Chemistry

- Be able to identify different families of compounds containing the carbonyl group
- Be aware of the characteristics of the carbonyl group and how they affect its chemical reactivity
- Know the nomenclature of simple carbonyl compounds
- Know the relative position of different carbonyl compounds in the oxidation-reduction scheme
- Know the common oxidizing and reducing agents used on (or used to synthesize) carbonyl compounds
- Know the mechanism of addition reactions of aldehydes and ketones: (hemi)acetal formation
- Know the mechanism of nucleophilic acyl substitution reactions in both acidic and basic conditions, and how these reactions can be used to synthesize carboxylic acid derivatives
- Know the terms for specific examples: esterification, hydrolysis, saponification
- Know the relative reactivity of different carboxylic acid derivatives
- Know how long-chain carboxylic acids form micelles in aqueous solution
- Be able to recognize the principles of carbonyl chemistry in the context of the reactions of fatty acids and triacylglycerols
- Know the relative order of reactivity of different carboxylic acid derivatives
- Be aware of the acidity of alpha protons, and how abstraction of an alpha proton generates a carbonyl-containing nucleophile (leading to aldol condensation)
- Be aware of keto-enol tautomerism

## 9. Amines

- Know the rules for naming simple amines
- Be able to classify an amine as primary, secondary, or tertiary
- Know the stereochemical and physical properties of amines
- Know how amines can form quaternary salts
- Know the factors affecting the basicity of amines, including aromatic amines
- Know the key ways to synthesize amines
- Know how amines act as nucleophiles in carbonyl reactions

## 10. Carbohydrate Chemistry

- Be able to classify monosaccharides as aldoses or ketoses
- Be able to identify stereogenic centers in (straight-chain) monosaccharides
- Be able to classify a monosaccharide as a D- or L-sugar
- Be able to characterize the isomeric relationship between monosaccharides
- Be aware of the cyclic form of hexoses in aqueous solution
- Be able to apply the principles of conformational dynamics to the cyclic form of hexoses
- Know what epimers and anomers are
- Be aware of some of the common reactions of monosaccharides
- Know how monosaccharides form disaccharides, and how the linkage can be broken

## 11. Protein Chemistry

- Be aware of the amphoteric nature of amino acids
- Be aware of the presence of a chiral center in an amino acid
- Be able to predict the predominant form of an amino acid in acidic and basic environments
- Be able to classify amino acids according to their side chains
- Know the characteristics of a peptide bond
- Know the different levels of protein structure
- Know the special role played by certain amino acids (proline, cystine) in the structure of a protein
- Know the importance of the isoelectric point of an amino acid or a protein

## 12. Separation and Purification Techniques

- Be aware that the presence of impurities is often revealed by broadening and depression of melting point
- Know the principles at work in common techniques used to separate and purify compounds
- Be able to select the most efficient technique in separating two given compounds
- Be able to apply acid–base principles to extraction based on solubility
- Be able to apply principles of intermolecular forces to chromatographic techniques

## 13. Spectroscopy

- Know the principles at work in different types of spectroscopy
- Be able to identify the spectroscopic technique that would be most effective in distinguishing between given compounds
- Know the IR frequency of common functional groups
- Know how to interpret a proton NMR spectrum: splitting, chemical shift, etc.
- Know the chemical shift of common proton types
- Be able to predict general features of the proton NMR spectrum of an organic compound
- Be able to identify a compound based on a combination of IR and NMR (and perhaps UV-vis) data

# ORGANIC CHEMISTRY PRACTICE SET

## Answer Sheet

1 Ⓐ Ⓑ Ⓒ Ⓓ

2 Ⓐ Ⓑ Ⓒ Ⓓ

3 Ⓐ Ⓑ Ⓒ Ⓓ

4 Ⓐ Ⓑ Ⓒ Ⓓ

5 Ⓐ Ⓑ Ⓒ Ⓓ

6 Ⓐ Ⓑ Ⓒ Ⓓ

7 Ⓐ Ⓑ Ⓒ Ⓓ

8 Ⓐ Ⓑ Ⓒ Ⓓ

9 Ⓐ Ⓑ Ⓒ Ⓓ

10 Ⓐ Ⓑ Ⓒ Ⓓ

11 Ⓐ Ⓑ Ⓒ Ⓓ

12 Ⓐ Ⓑ Ⓒ Ⓓ

13 Ⓐ Ⓑ Ⓒ Ⓓ

14 Ⓐ Ⓑ Ⓒ Ⓓ

15 Ⓐ Ⓑ Ⓒ Ⓓ

16 Ⓐ Ⓑ Ⓒ Ⓓ

17 Ⓐ Ⓑ Ⓒ Ⓓ

18 Ⓐ Ⓑ Ⓒ Ⓓ

19 Ⓐ Ⓑ Ⓒ Ⓓ

20 Ⓐ Ⓑ Ⓒ Ⓓ

21 Ⓐ Ⓑ Ⓒ Ⓓ

22 Ⓐ Ⓑ Ⓒ Ⓓ

23 Ⓐ Ⓑ Ⓒ Ⓓ

24 Ⓐ Ⓑ Ⓒ Ⓓ

25 Ⓐ Ⓑ Ⓒ Ⓓ

26 Ⓐ Ⓑ Ⓒ Ⓓ

27 Ⓐ Ⓑ Ⓒ Ⓓ

28 Ⓐ Ⓑ Ⓒ Ⓓ

29 Ⓐ Ⓑ Ⓒ Ⓓ

30 Ⓐ Ⓑ Ⓒ Ⓓ

31 Ⓐ Ⓑ Ⓒ Ⓓ

32 Ⓐ Ⓑ Ⓒ Ⓓ

33 Ⓐ Ⓑ Ⓒ Ⓓ

34 Ⓐ Ⓑ Ⓒ Ⓓ

35 Ⓐ Ⓑ Ⓒ Ⓓ

36 Ⓐ Ⓑ Ⓒ Ⓓ

37 Ⓐ Ⓑ Ⓒ Ⓓ

38 Ⓐ Ⓑ Ⓒ Ⓓ

39 Ⓐ Ⓑ Ⓒ Ⓓ

40 Ⓐ Ⓑ Ⓒ Ⓓ

41 Ⓐ Ⓑ Ⓒ Ⓓ

42 Ⓐ Ⓑ Ⓒ Ⓓ

43 Ⓐ Ⓑ Ⓒ Ⓓ

44 Ⓐ Ⓑ Ⓒ Ⓓ

45 Ⓐ Ⓑ Ⓒ Ⓓ

# ORGANIC CHEMISTRY PRACTICE SET

## Time: 60 Minutes—45 Questions

DIRECTIONS: There are seven passages and ten discrete questions in this Organic Chemistry test. Each passage is followed by five questions of above-average difficulty. After reading a passage, select the one best answer to each question. If you are not certain of an answer, eliminate the alternatives that you know to be incorrect and then select an answer from the remaining alternatives. (Note that although the passages and questions are test-like, this exercise is NOT meant to be an actual MCAT test section. For full-length MCAT practice, please see Kaplan *MCAT Practice Tests*).

## Passage I (Questions 1–5)

Much of the chemical reactivity of substituted cyclohexane derivatives is controlled by their conformation. In particular, bimolecular elimination reactions require an antiperiplanar geometry in which the abstracted hydrogen and the leaving group are *trans*-diaxial to each other. Because of this requirement, the alkene product thus obtained may be the less thermodynamically stable Hofmann elimination product. Unimolecular elimination reactions, on the other hand, do not require a specific conformation because the mechanism proceeds through a carbocation intermediate. Therefore, one might expect the more stable Zaitsev product to be obtained more often from E1 reactions.

A student attempting to carry out the microscale elimination reaction of 2-methylcyclohexanol performed the following experiment. After placing 2-methylcyclohexanol in a conical vial, approximately 0.25 mL of concentrated (85%) phosphoric acid was added dropwise. After thoroughly mixing the liquids, the solution was heated under gentle reflux at 100°C and the product was distilled. A Pasteur pipette was used to remove the distillate as it formed. The distillate was then washed with 1.0 mL of saturated sodium chloride solution and the aqueous layer was removed. Anhydrous sodium sulfate was used to complete the drying process. The infrared spectrum of the product displayed relatively sharp peaks at approximately 1660 cm$^{-1}$, 2910 cm$^{-1}$, and 3090 cm$^{-1}$. Proton-NMR displayed multiple peaks in the vinylic region, indicating that more than one product was formed.

1. According to Zaitsev's rule, which of the following structures is the most likely product of the reaction carried out by the student?

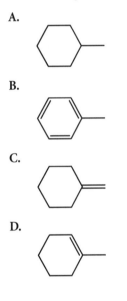

A.

B.

C.

D.

2. Which of the following statements is at least partly responsible for the formation of multiple products in the reaction?

A. The positive charge in the intermediate is delocalized.

B. The intermediate may undergo a hydride shift.

C. A base may only abstract a proton antiperiplanar to the leaving group.

D. The methyl group withdraws electron density to stabilize the transition state.

**GO ON TO THE NEXT PAGE.**

3. What is the E2 product of the following molecule?

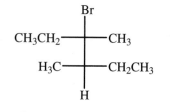

A.

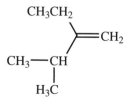

B.

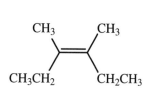

C.

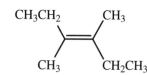

D.

CH₃CH₂          CH₃

CH₃          CH₂CH₃

4. Which of the following compounds is expected to be most stable in its favored conformation?

A. *cis*-2-methylcyclohexanol
B. *trans*-2-methylcyclohexanol
C. *cis*-3-methylcyclohexanol
D. *trans*-3-methylcyclohexanol

5. Which of the following statements is true about the E2 reactions of Compounds I and II shown below?

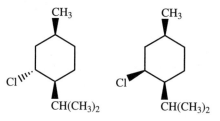

A. The E2 reaction of Compound I proceeds more rapidly, and leads to one single product.
B. The E2 reaction of Compound I proceeds more rapidly, and leads to more than one product.
C. The E2 reaction of Compound II proceeds more rapidly, and leads to one single product.
D. The E2 reaction of Compound II proceeds more rapidly, and leads to more than one product.

**GO ON TO THE NEXT PAGE.**

# Passage II (Questions 6–10)

Esters and amides can undergo hydrolysis in both acidic and basic conditions. In living systems, the process can be catalyzed by enzymes.

*Acid-catalyzed hydrolysis*

In the acid-catalyzed hydrolysis of esters or amides, the acid protonates the carbonyl oxygen, facilitating the nucleophilic attack by water on the compound. A tetrahedral addition intermediate is formed. The leaving group is released after the oxygen or nitrogen is protonated. Deprotonation of the carbonyl oxygen regenerates the acid catalyst, and the product is a carboxylic acid.

*Base-promoted hydrolysis*

In base-promoted hydrolysis, a hydroxide ion, rather than a water molecule, is the nucleophile that attacks the carbonyl compound. The leaving group is an alkoxide ion, or, in the case of amide hydrolysis, an amide ion ($NH_2^-$) that abstracts a proton from water in a concerted step. The resulting carboxylic acid rapidly deprotonates to yield the carboxylate ion.

*Enzyme-catalyzed hydrolysis*

Serine proteases are enzymes that catalyze the hydrolysis of peptide bonds. They also allow hydrolysis of ester linkages. Figure 1 shows the active site of a serine protease catalyzing the peptide bond hydrolysis.

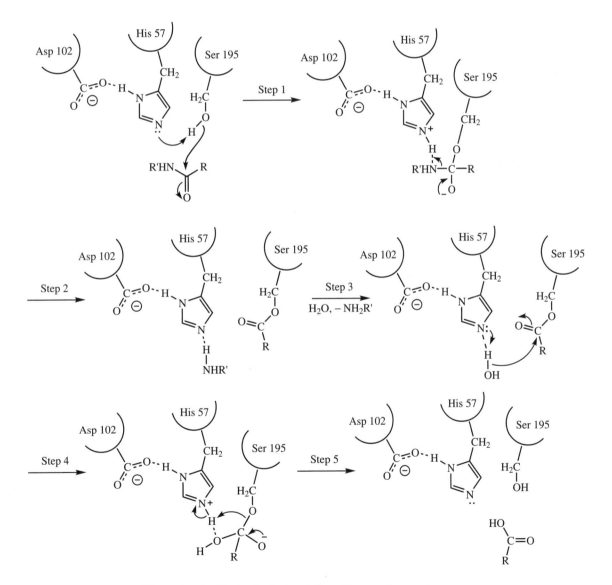

**Figure 1   Amide hydrolysis catalyzed by a serine protease**

**GO ON TO THE NEXT PAGE.**

6. Which of the following statements about the reversibility of ester hydrolysis is accurate?

   A.   Ester hydrolysis is reversible in acidic conditions, but irreversible in basic conditions.

   B.   Ester hydrolysis is reversible in basic conditions, but irreversible in acidic conditions.

   C.   Ester hydrolysis is reversible in both acidic and basic conditions.

   D.   Ester hydrolysis is irreversible in both acidic and basic conditions.

7. If the following isotopically labeled ester undergoes hydrolysis catalyzed by a serine protease, where will the isotopic label end up?

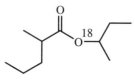

   A.   In the carboxylic acid molecule

   B.   In an alcohol molecule

   C.   In a water molecule

   D.   At serine 195

8. What are the products of the base-promoted hydrolysis of N-propylbutanamide?

   A.   Propanoic acid and 1-butanamine

   B.   Propanoate ion and 1-butanamine

   C.   Butanoic acid and 1-propanamine

   D.   Butanoate ion and 1-propanamine

9. Which of the following CANNOT be partially responsible for the fact that amide hydrolysis is irreversible in both acidic and basic conditions?

   A.   At low pH, the amine product becomes protonated.

   B.   At low pH, the nitrogen atom in the tetrahedral intermediate favors being protonated.

   C.   At high pH, amide hydrolysis involves the elimination of the strongly basic $NH_2^-$ as leaving group.

   D.   At high pH, the hydrolysis product is the carboxylate ion.

10. In Figure 1, in which step is an acyl-enzyme intermediate formed?

   A.   Step 1

   B.   Step 2

   C.   Step 3

   D.   Step 4

**GO ON TO THE NEXT PAGE.**

## Passage III (Questions 11–15)

A student was given four or five organic compounds in a vial. The compounds are naphthalene, 4-methyaniline, *p*-cresol, 2-methylbenzoic acid, and possibly one more unknown compound. The structures of the four known compounds are shown below.

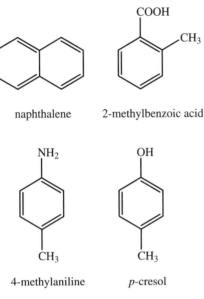

naphthalene            2-methylbenzoic acid

4-methylaniline            *p*-cresol

The student performed the following extraction sequence:

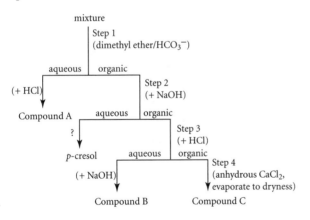

**11.** In the aqueous phase after Step 2 but before the addition of HCl, the predominant form of Compound A is

A.   an amine salt.

B.   an amine.

C.   a phenoxide ion.

D.   a carboxylate ion.

**12.** In which step would the student need to take special care to properly avoid pressure buildup in the separatory funnel?

A.   Step 1

B.   Step 2

C.   Step 3

D.   Step 4

**13.** Which of the following is the most appropriate technique to determine if Compound C contains the unknown fifth compound?

A.   NMR

B.   IR

C.   TLC

D.   Mass spectrometry

**14.** If the fifth, unknown compound were benzylamine, from which step would it be isolated?

A.   Step 1

B.   Step 2

C.   Step 3

D.   Step 4

**15.** In which chemical shift region do the four unknown compounds all have signals in their proton NMR spectra?

A.   0.5–0.9 ppm

B.   2–3 ppm

C.   4.5–6 ppm

D.   6–8.5 ppm

**GO ON TO THE NEXT PAGE.**

## Passage IV (Questions 16–20)

Aldohexoses have four stereogenic centers with a total of 16 possible stereoisomers, eight of which are shown in Figure 1.

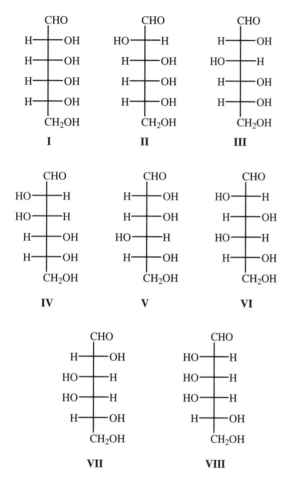

**Figure 1** Eight stereoisomers of aldohexoses

The aldohexoses shown are all in the D-configuration, in which the hydroxy group of the highest-numbered stereogenic center is drawn to the right. The remaining eight possible stereoisomers are the enantiomers of these structures. They are considered to be in the L-configuration.

In the late 1800s, Emil Fischer conducted a series of experiments to deduce the structure of (+)-glucose. (+)-Glucose is expected to be one of the 16 possible structures, but because of the inherent difficulties in distinguishing between enantiomers, Fischer (arbitrarily) decided to limit his possibilities to only those structures with the D-configuration, with the understanding that the actual structure may be the enantiomer of the one he would decide is the correct structure.

Some of the reactions that monosaccharides can undergo are described below, together with the results Fischer obtained when he carried them out on (+)-glucose and related compounds.

*Nitric acid oxidation*

Nitric acid oxidizes the aldehyde and primary alcohol functional groups of monosaccharides to the carboxyl group. The resulting compound is a dicarboxylic acid known as an aldaric acid. When Fischer carried out the oxidation of (+)-glucose with nitric acid, the resulting aldaric acid was optically active.

*Kiliani-Fischer synthesis*

The Kiliani-Fischer synthesis reaction lengthens the chain of an aldose by one carbon at the aldehyde group. This creates a new stereogenic center in the monosaccharide. Both configurations would be obtained in the product mixture. When Fischer carried out the reaction on (−)-arabinose, an aldopentose, he obtained a mixture of (+)-glucose and (+)-mannose.

16. Based on the results of the nitric acid oxidation reaction, which of the structures shown in Figure 1 CANNOT be (+)-glucose?

   **A.** Compound IV
   **B.** Compound V
   **C.** Compound VI
   **D.** Compound VII

17. The structure of L-gulose is shown below. Which compound shown in Figure 1 is D-gulose?

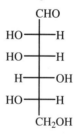

   **A.** Compound III
   **B.** Compound IV
   **C.** Compound V
   **D.** Compound VI

**GO ON TO THE NEXT PAGE.**

18. Which of the following compounds is a ketohexose?

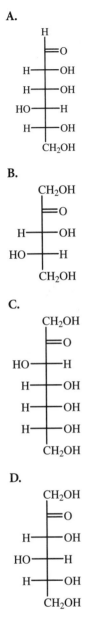

A.

B.

C.

D.

19. Based on the results of the Kiliani-Fischer synthesis reaction, which of the following pairs of compounds could be (+)-glucose and (+)-mannose, not necessarily respectively?

A.  Compounds II and III

B.  Compounds III and IV

C.  Compounds V and VII

D.  Compounds VI and VII

20. Which of the following is a correct representation of the cyclic form of compound VII?

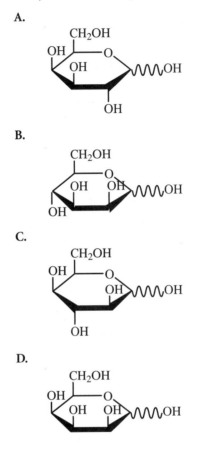

A.

B.

C.

D.

**GO ON TO THE NEXT PAGE.**

## Passage V (Questions 21–25)

An enantioselective aldol reaction catalyzed by the amino acid proline is proposed to occur via an enamine mechanism. The reaction, which can be carried out at room temperature, is inexpensive and leads to good yield and high enantioselectivity. The catalyst proline is water-soluble and is easily removed from the product by aqueous extraction. It functions as a "micro-aldolase," providing both the nucleophilic group and an acid/base co-catalyst. The proposed mechanism for the aldol reaction between acetone and an aldehyde with proline as the catalyst is shown below.

In Step 1, the nitrogen on proline acts as a nucleophile and attacks the carbonyl carbon of acetone. The product, a carbinolamine, yields an iminium ion in Step 2. Carbon-

carbon bond formation occurs in Step 4 as the compound reacts with an aldehyde. The transition state of this process involves a tricyclic, hydrogen-bonded framework, which provides for enantiofacial selectivity during the attack of the alkene functional group on the aldehyde. The product, a β-hydroxyketone, is obtained and the proline catalyst is regenerated in the last step.

21. The product of Step 3 is the conjugate acid of an

    A.  imine.

    B.  enamine.

    C.  imide.

    D.  amide.

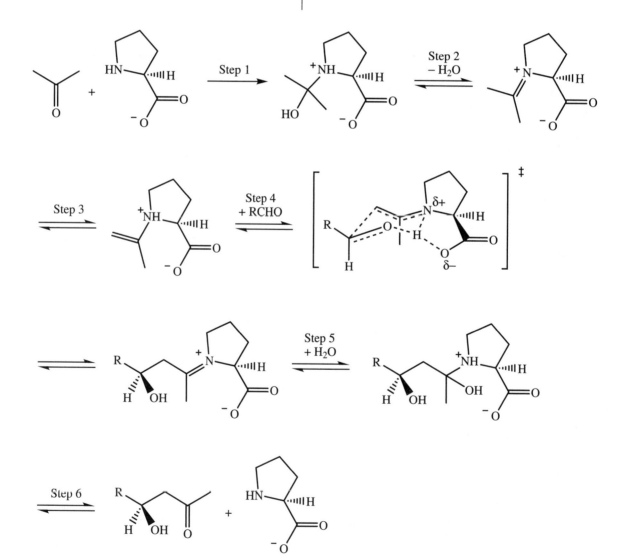

**GO ON TO THE NEXT PAGE.**

**22.** If the final product of the reaction (formed in Step 6) were heated, what compound would be obtained?

A.

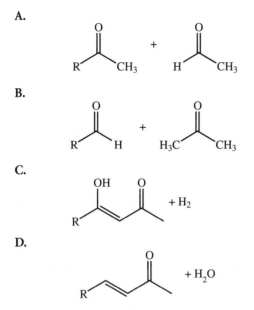

B.

C.

D.

**23.** What must be true about the medium in Step 1?

A. It must be acidic to make the acetone more susceptible to nucleophilic attack.

B. It must be neutral or slightly basic to deprotonate the carboxyl group.

C. It must initially be acidic, then neutral.

D. It must initially be neutral or slightly basic, then acidic.

**24.** Which of the following best explains why the stereogenic center created in Step 4 predominantly exists in only one configuration?

A. In order to create the stereogenic center with the opposite configuration, the addition to the alkene would have to take place in the anti-Markovnikov fashion.

B. In order to create the stereogenic center with the opposite configuration, the reaction would have to proceed through a more strained transition state.

C. In order to create the stereogenic center with the opposite configuration, the reaction would need to be carried out with a racemic mixture of L- and D-proline.

D. In order to create the stereogenic center with the opposite configuration, the reaction would need to be carried out with the enantiomer of the aldehyde.

**25.** All of the following occur during the course of the proline-catalyzed reaction EXCEPT

A. nucleophilic acyl substitution.

B. nucleophilic addition.

C. addition to an alkene.

D. hydrolysis.

**GO ON TO THE NEXT PAGE.**

## Passage VI (Questions 26–30)

Spectroscopic determination of the structure of long-chain polyunsaturated carboxylic acids is often difficult because of the relatively large number of functionally similar isomers possible for a given molecular formula. While standard wet analytical techniques—e.g., bromination or hydrogenation—are generally employed to elucidate such facets of an unknown acid's identity as its degree of unsaturation, a combination of chemical and spectral analysis is usually necessary to determine the exact structure of the carboxylic acid.

A researcher attempting to determine the structure of an unknown carboxylic acid with molecular formula $C_{18}H_{26}O_2$ took a mass spectrum of a small sample of the unknown, then performed a series of chemical tests:

*Test 1*: Catalytic hydrogenation of the unknown over palladium on charcoal (Pd/C) yielded stearic acid, $CH_3(CH_2)_{16}COOH$.

*Test 2*: Hydrogenation of the unknown over Lindlar's catalyst resulted in the absorption of exactly two equivalents of $H_2$.

*Test 3*: Oxidation of the unknown with $KMnO_4$ followed by acidification produced four distinct, nonisomeric compounds, three of which were dicarboxylic acids.

*Test 4*: Ozonolysis of the unknown produced four compounds, one of which was formaldehyde.

*Test 5*: Titration with KHP indicated that the unknown had only one carboxylic acid functionality.

Product mixtures resulting from Tests 3 and 4 were separated by HPLC. Spectral analysis was employed to determine the structures of the various reaction products. Based on the results of the five chemical tests and the interpretation of the spectral data, the researcher concluded that the unknown compound was one of the compounds shown below:

$$H_2C{=}CH(CH_2)_4C{\equiv}CC{\equiv}C(CH_2)_7COOH$$

$$H_2C{=}CH(CH_2)_4C{\equiv}C(CH_2)_7C{\equiv}CCOOH$$

26. The major difference between hydrogenation over Pd/C and hydrogenation over Lindlar's catalyst is that

    A. the use of Lindlar's catalyst results in the hydogenation of only one pi bond in each triple bond, while Pd/C catalyzes the hydrogenation of all the carbon–carbon pi bonds in the compound.

    B. the use of Lindlar's catalyst results in the hydrogenation of carbon–oxygen double bonds, while the use of Pd/C does not.

    C. quantitative measurement of the hydrogen absorbed during catalytic hydrogenation is possible only when Lindlar's catalyst is used.

    D. hydrogenation over Pd/C is an oxidative process, while that over Lindlar's catalyst is reductive.

27. One of the products of Test 3 is not a dicarboxylic acid. Its most likely identity is

    A. $CO_2$.
    B. $CH_3COOH$.
    C. $CH_3OH$.
    D. $CH_4$.

28. Which of the following can be inferred from the results of Test 1 but NOT from the results of Test 5?

    A. The unknown contains unsaturated carbon atoms.

    B. The unknown is not capable of *cis/trans* isomerism.

    C. The unknown contains an acidic hydrogen.

    D. The unknown is unbranched.

**GO ON TO THE NEXT PAGE.**

29. Which of the following observations would be most helpful in distinguishing stearic acid from the unknown compound?

   A. The existence of a $^1$H-NMR singlet between 10 and 12 ppm

   B. A strong, broad IR absorption from 2500 to 3400 cm$^{-1}$

   C. The absence of an IR stretch around 2200 cm$^{-1}$

   D. A boiling point lower than that of $CH_3(CH_2)_{17}OH$

30. What is the relationship between the two proposed structures for the unknown?

   A. They are geometric isomers.

   B. They are diastereomers.

   C. They are constitutional isomers.

   D. They are not isomers of each other.

**GO ON TO THE NEXT PAGE.**

## Passage VII (Questions 31–35)

In a Diels-Alder reaction, a conjugated diene and an alkene (known as the dienophile) react to form a new cyclic compound as shown in Equation 1.

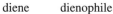
diene       dienophile

**Equation 1**

Recently, scientists have isolated and studied several enzymes that appear to catalyze Diels–Alder reactions. Lovastatin nonaketide synthase (LNKS) has been found to catalyze a step in the biosynthesis of lovastatin, a cholesterol-lowering drug, by the fungus *Aspergillus terreus*. This step and the end product are illustrated in Equation 2.

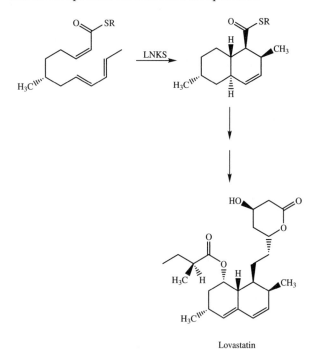

Lovastatin

**Equation 2**

Another enzyme-catalyzed Diels-Alder reaction is the conversion of 2-pyrones into benzoates. The enzyme, macrophomate synthase (MPS), produced by the fungus *Macrophoma commelinae*, catalyzes the addition of a pyruvate enolate to a 2-pyrone to form a bicyclic intermediate in the biosynthesis of macrophomic acid, as illustrated in Equation 3.

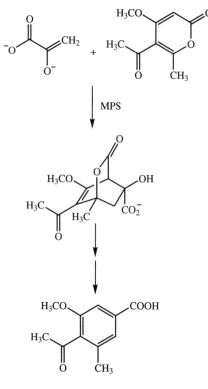

Macrophomic acid

**Equation 3**

31. How many stereogenic centers does the compound lovastatin contain?

   A.  6
   B.  7
   C.  8
   D.  9

**GO ON TO THE NEXT PAGE.**

**32.** What is the Diels-Alder product between two molecules of cyclopentadiene?

**A.**

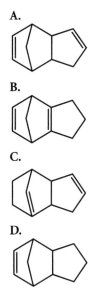

**B.**

**C.**

**D.**

**33.** What is the product of the first step of Equation 3 if the pyruvate enolate ion is radiolabeled with an $^{18}O$ isotope as shown below?

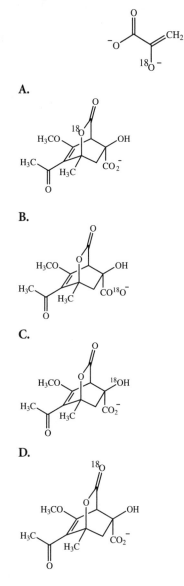

**A.**

**B.**

**C.**

**D.**

**GO ON TO THE NEXT PAGE.**

34. In order to determine whether the enzyme-catalyzed reactions are truly Diels–Alder reactions in the classical sense, kinetic studies determining the rates of reaction with different analogs must be conducted. Which of the following compounds cannot be converted into a Diels–Alder adduct by the enzyme in the kinetic study of MPS?

A.

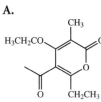

B.

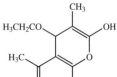

C.

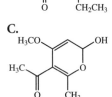

D.

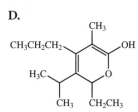

35. The active form of lovastatin is actually not the structure shown in Equation 2, but instead the open chain form shown below. What process will create the active form from the structure shown in Equation 2?

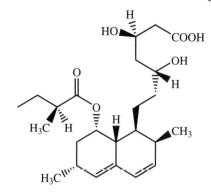

A. Oxidation

B. Reduction

C. Ozonolysis

D. Hydrolysis

## Discrete Questions

36. The compound $CH_3COCH_2COOC_2H_5$ contains which of the following functional groups?

A. Ether

B. Ester

C. Acid anhydride

D. Carboxylic acid

37. How many constitutional isomers exist for the formula $C_5H_{12}$?

A. 3

B. 4

C. 5

D. 6

38. Which of the following compounds has the highest boiling point?

A. 3-Pentanone

B. 3-Hexanone

C. Heptanoic acid

D. Octanoic acid

**GO ON TO THE NEXT PAGE.**

39. Which of the following would form the most stable carbocation?

    A.   $(CH_3)_2CHBr$ dissolved in toluene

    B.   $(CH_3CH_2)_3COH$ dissolved in acetone

    C.   $(CH_3)_3COH$ dissolved in $H_2SO_4$

    D.   $CH_3CH_2I$ dissolved in diethyl ether

40. Which of the following compounds contains the least basic nitrogen atom?

    A.   $NH_3$

    B.   $H_2C=NH$

    C.

    D.

41. When 1-chloropropane reacts with sodium hydroxide in dimethyl sulfoxide (DMSO) to form an alcohol, all of the following statements are true EXCEPT:

    A.   The product mixture will include an alkene.

    B.   The rate of reaction is dependent upon the concentration of both the alkyl halide and the hydroxide ion.

    C.   2-Chloropropane will react more rapidly under the same conditions.

    D.   The reaction proceeds via a concerted mechanism.

42. Which of the following families of compounds will lead to the decoloration of bromine in carbon tetrachloride?

    A.   Alkenes

    B.   Alcohols

    C.   Ethers

    D.   Ketones

43. If a researcher needed to distinguish between catechol and 2-hydroxymuconic semialdehyde, which of the following types of spectroscopy would be useful?

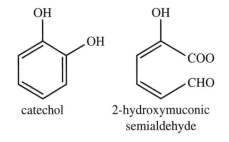

catechol        2-hydroxymuconic semialdehyde

    I.     Mass spectroscopy

    II.    NMR spectroscopy

    III.   Infrared spectroscopy

    A.   I only

    B.   I and II only

    C.   II and III only

    D.   I, II, and III

**GO ON TO THE NEXT PAGE.**

44. The $^1$H-NMR spectrum of 2-bromopropane contains which of the following signals?

    A.  A septet and two doublets

    B.  A septet and a doublet

    C.  Two quartets and a doublet

    D.  Two quartets and a triplet

45. The amino acid tyrosine has the following side group:

    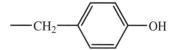

    The residue's approximate pK values are as follows: 2.2 for the carboxyl group, 9.2 for the amino group, and 10.1 for the side chain. At a pH of 11, what is the net charge on the amino acid?

    A.  −2

    B.  −1

    C.  +1

    D.  +2

**STOP.** IF YOU FINISH BEFORE TIME HAS EXPIRED, CHECK YOUR WORK. YOU MAY GO BACK TO ANY QUESTION IN THIS PART ONLY.

**GO ON TO THE NEXT PAGE.**

ANSWERS AND EXPLANATIONS BEGIN ON NEXT PAGE ⇒

# ORGANIC CHEMISTRY PRACTICE SET

## Answer Key

**Passage I (Questions 1–5)**
1. D
2. B
3. C
4. C
5. B

**Passage II (Questions 6–10)**
6. A
7. B
8. C
9. C
10. B

**Passage III (Questions 11–15)**
11. D
12. A
13. C
14. C
15. D

**Passage IV (Questions 16–20)**
16. D
17. C
18. D
19. B
20. A

**Passage V (Questions 21–25)**
21. B
22. D
23. D
24. B
25. A

**Passage VI (Questions 26–30)**
26. A
27. A
28. D
29. C
30. C

**Passage VII (Questions 31–35)**
31. C
32. A
33. C
34. B
35. D

**Discrete Questions (Questions 36–45)**
36. B
37. A
38. D
39. C
40. D
41. C
42. A
43. D
44. B
45. A

# ORGANIC CHEMISTRY PRACTICE SET

## Answers and Explanations

**1. D**

This question calls for outside knowledge of elimination reactions. When an elimination reaction can lead to the production of more than one alkene, Zaitsev's rule predicts that the major product is the most thermodynamically stable alkene—in other words, the most highly substituted one. For example, when 2-bromo-2-methylbutane undergoes elimination, the double bond can be formed either between C1 and C2, or between C2 and C3, depending on which hydrogen is abstracted:

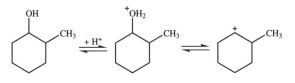

Zaitsev's rule predicts that the alkene with the double bond between C2 and C3 will be the more dominant product, because there are more alkyl groups (three methyl groups) bonded to the $sp^2$-hybridized carbons and it is thus more thermodynamically stable. The other alkene, with the double bond between C1 and C2, only has two alkyl groups (one methyl and one ethyl) attached to the $sp^2$-hybridized carbons. It is less thermodynamically stable and forms in the lower proportion. It is known as the Hofmann (as opposed to the Zaitsev) product.

To predict the product in this particular case, we need to determine what the possibilities are given the starting compound, 2-methylcyclohexanol, which has the following structure:

Because the reaction employs acid and heat, we know that it is an E1 reaction. (The MCAT expects students to deduce from reaction conditions whether an E1 or an E2 reaction is more likely.) It progresses via a carbocation intermediate. An acid catalyst is needed because the compound does not contain a good leaving group, so the first step is the conversion of the hydroxy group into a water molecule by protonation:

A proton is then abstracted from the carbocation intermediate, regenerating the acid catalyst and also leading to the formation of a pi bond. The proton can be abstracted from either of the two carbon atoms adjacent to the positive charge:

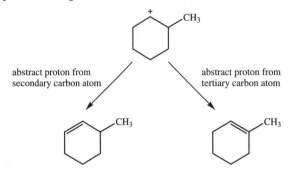

The two alkene products are not equally thermodynamically stable. The structure shown on the right, formed by the abstraction of the proton from the tertiary carbon atom, is more substituted and thus more stable: The double bond is attached to a total of three alkyl groups, while the other alkene product has a double bond attached to only two alkyl groups. The structure shown in choice **D** is therefore the most likely product of the reaction.

**2. B**

The intermediate formed with the leaving of the water molecule can lead to one of two possible alkene products, as illustrated above. This arises from the structure of the compound and the nature of the reaction. However, yet another possibility exists because the carbocation intermediate can undergo rearrangement via a hydride shift:

The driving force behind this rearrangement is the additional stability of the carbocation: Prior to the hydride shift, the carbocation is secondary, but the hydride shift leads to a tertiary carbocation, which is more stable because of the electron-donating ability of alkyl groups. With this new intermediate, a new alkene product is possible:

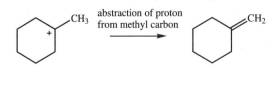

(Notice that a proton can also be abstracted from an adjacent carbon atom that is part of the ring. However, that leads to the same Zaitsev product.) The percentage yield of this product depends on the rate of the hydride shift versus the rate of proton abstraction leading to the alkene product, among other factors. Not all intermediates undergo rearrangement. The fact that hydride shift may occur is hence at least partly responsible for the formation of multiple products.

Choice **A** is incorrect, because the positive charge is not delocalized. It resides on only one carbon atom at a time. (Do not confuse the moving of the charge from rearrangement with charge delocalization! The movement of the charge arises from an actual modification of the skeleton of the molecule. In other words, the structures for the intermediate before and after rearrangement are NOT resonance structures.) Choice **C** is incorrect, because the reaction is an E1 reaction, not an E2 reaction, so considerations of conformation are not relevant. An antiperiplanar configuration is not required. Choice **D** is incorrect, because the methyl group, compared to hydrogen, is actually electron-donating, not electron-withdrawing.

**3. C**
In order to arrive at the answer, we must be able to interpret the Fischer structure shown in the question stem correctly and visualize how the antiperiplanar requirement for E2 reactions applies to the molecule. In a Fischer projection, the vertical bonds are going into the plane of the paper while the horizontal bonds are projecting out of the plane:

An antiperiplanar configuration means that Br, H, and the two central carbon atoms lie in the same plane and that the Br and the H are pointing in opposite directions. The molecule therefore needs to adopt the following staggered conformation for E2 to occur:

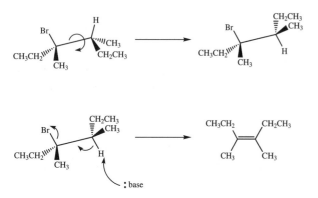

This is the structure shown in choice **C**. Notice that choices **A** and **B** can be eliminated, because they do not have the right number of carbons. The starting material contains eight carbon atoms, and the E2 reaction does not lead to a change in the number of carbons.

**4. C**
Cyclohexanes, in their most favorable state, adopt a chair conformation minimizing strain arising from repulsion between electrons. However, there are two possible chair conformations, interconvertible by a "ring flip" via a boat conformation transition state:

If the cyclohexane is unsubstituted, the two chair conformations are completely equivalent. However, the ring flip causes axial groups to occupy the equatorial position, and vice versa. If one of the hydrogen atoms were replaced by an alkyl group, for example, then in one chair conformation the alkyl group would be in the axial position, and in the other chair conformation it would be in the equatorial position. The conformation in which it is in the equatorial position is more favorable:

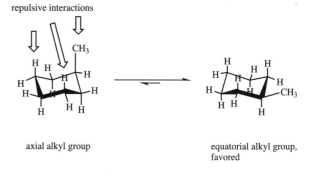

In general, a cyclohexane derivative (a substituted cyclohexane) prefers to adopt a conformation in which its substituents all occupy the equatorial position. However, this is not always possible depending on the *cis/trans* relationship of the substituents, as can be demonstrated using the compounds listed in the answer choices. Our first step is to determine the most stable conformation of each compound.

*cis*-2-methylcyclohexanol:

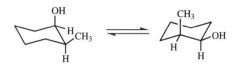

*trans*-2-methylcyclohexanol:

*cis*-3-methylcyclohexanol:

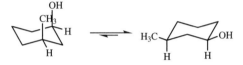

*trans*-3-methylcyclohexanol:

Choices **A** and **D** can only have one of its substituents occupy the equatorial position. Only choices **B** and **C** can adopt a conformation in which both substituents are equatorial, and this is the favored conformation for the compound. Choice **B** is therefore more stable than choice **A**, and choice **C** is more stable than choice **D**. We next need to decide which of the two diequatorial compounds is more stable: *trans*-2-methylcyclohexanol or *cis*-3-methylcyclohexanol. In *trans*-2-methylcyclohexanol, the substituents are on adjacent carbon atoms. When they both occupy the equatorial position, gauche interactions arise between the two. This is not as stable as in the case of *cis*-3-methylcyclohexanol, in which the two substituents are farther apart and hence no gauche interactions exist between them. Choice **C** is therefore the correct answer.

**5.   B**

For the two compounds shown in the question stem, the antiperiplanar requirement for E2 to take place means that the chlorine (leaving group) needs to be in the axial position. We need to be careful in deducing the position of the alkyl substituents from the *cis/trans* relationship.

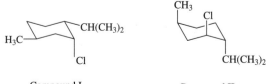

Compound I                    Compound II

The conformation for each compound shown above is not necessarily the favored one. Rather, it is the conformation that the molecule must adopt if E2 were to occur—i.e., the one in which the chlorine is in the axial position. For example, in Compound I the isopropyl group is *trans* to the chlorine. When the chlorine is in the axial position, it *has* to occupy the equatorial position. Similarly, the methyl group two carbon atoms away from the chlorine has to be in the equatorial position based on its *cis/trans* relationship with chlorine.

The question stem asks us to determine two things: Which compound would undergo E2 more rapidly, and whether it leads to one or more products. As mentioned above, the conformation required for E2 is not necessarily the favored one. If, in order to undergo E2, the molecule must first adopt a conformation that is highly unfavorable, the reaction will be slow. This is the case for Compound II. With a "ring flip," the molecule can adopt another chair conformation in which the axial/equatorial positions of all substituents are reversed, leading to the following favored conformation in which all substituents are equatorial:

In other words, a molecule of Compound II must first adopt an unfavorable (strained) conformation before E2 can occur. This is expected to cause the reaction rate to decrease. In contrast, in its most stable conformation, Compound I is ready for E2 reaction: The chlorine is in the axial position and the two alkyl groups are equatorial. (It is not possible for all three substituents to occupy the equatorial position; a "ring flip" would result in two axial substituent groups and one equatorial substituent group.) The E2 reaction of Compound I is therefore expected to proceed more rapidly.

The remaining question we need to answer is: Does the E2 reaction of Compound I lead to one alkene product, or is there a possibility of multiple products? The base can abstract either one of the two protons antiperiplanar to the chlorine:

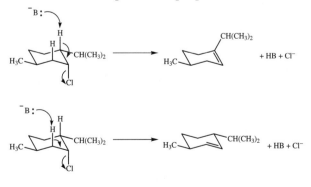

The reaction therefore leads to more than one product, and choice **B** is the correct answer.

## 6.  A

The chemistry of carbonyl compounds (ketones, aldehydes, carboxylic acids and their derivatives) is always an MCAT favorite. A thorough understanding of the principles behind the reactivity of these compounds and of the mechanisms of their common reactions is required. To answer this question, we need to have outside knowledge of the mechanism of ester hydrolysis, although the passage does describe the mechanism under both acidic and basic conditions for us. One of the key insights we need to gain is that every step of the acid-catalyzed hydrolysis of ester is a reversible equilibrium:

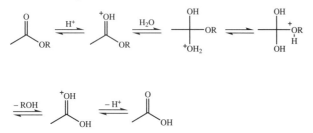

The reaction is completely reversible. Any individual ester molecule may go back and forth among the steps several times before forming the acid. Even then, if the product acid molecule encounters an R'OH molecule (an event of admittedly low probability since the solvent water molecules are much more plentiful), it may reform the ester.

In contrast, the base-promoted hydrolysis reaction does not yield the carboxylic acid, but the carboxylate anion, as described in the passage:

The reverse of the last deprotonation step is not expected to occur in basic conditions. In fact, when a base abstracts the proton from the carboxylic acid, it is irreversibly consumed and not recycled as a catalyst. (It is for this reason that purists refer to the reaction as "base-promoted" rather than "base-catalyzed.") Under basic conditions, then, the hydrolysis reaction is irreversible. Choice **A** is correct.

## 7.  B

Whenever an MCAT Organic Chemistry passage presents us with a complex, multistep reaction or synthesis scheme, we are likely to be asked to determine the outcome if one of the reagents used were isotopically labeled. This is one way the test makers can see if we can follow what goes on in a reaction step by step and formulate a mechanism for that reaction (or particular steps in a reaction).

In this question, we are asked to determine where the $O^{18}$ isotope ends up if the compound shown in the question stem undergoes enzyme-catalyzed hydrolysis. The compound shown is an ester. Figure 1 illustrates the hydrolysis of an amide catalyzed by a serine protease, but the passage tells us that the enzyme also catalyzes the hydrolysis of esters. If we compare the structure given in the question to the amide in Figure 1, we see that the isotopically labeled oxygen plays the role of the nitrogen atom. The R and R' groups correspond as follows:

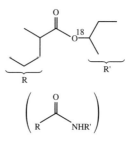

We are asked to determine where the isotopic label ends up. Again, by comparing the ester with the amide, we know that the answer can be found in Figure 1 by asking: What happens to the nitrogen atom of the amide? By examining the reaction, we know that the nitrogen atom is in the amine eliminated in Step 3. In other words, the C-N amide bond breaks, and the nitrogen-containing portion grabs a proton and leaves. If we apply this to the ester, we expect the C-O ester linkage to break, and the oxygen-containing portion to grab a proton and leave. What is the resulting molecule? An alcohol. More specifically, the oxygen will be incorporated into the following alcohol molecule:

$$\text{HO}^{18}\!\!-\!\!\big\langle$$

Choice **B** is therefore correct.

Choice **A** is incorrect. In order for the carboxylic acid molecule in the product to bear the isotopically labeled oxygen atom, the label should come from either the carbonyl oxygen of the ester, or the water molecule in Step 3. Choice **C** is incorrect, because no water molecule is generated during the reaction. Choice **D** is incorrect, because we can see that the serine residue keeps its oxygen atom throughout the reaction.

## 8.  C

This question demonstrates the importance of knowing the rules of nomenclature of organic compounds for the MCAT. We cannot answer the question correctly without knowing the structure of *N*-propylbutanamide, as shown in the following diagram:

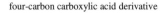

four-carbon carboxylic acid derivative

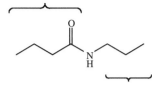

propyl group attached to N

If we compare this structure to the generic one shown in Figure 1, R and R' are both propyl groups. (R + carbonyl carbon = 4 carbons, hence <u>butan</u>amide.) In step 3, then, the amine that is formed and eliminated from the enzyme–substrate complex must have the formula $NH_2CH_2CH_2CH_3$. This is 1-propanamine. The R group ends up as part of a carboxylic acid molecule at the end of step 5. If R is a propyl group, the acid must therefore be butanoic acid. Hence, choice **C** is correct.

**9. C**

This is a very challenging question, because it calls for both sophisticated reasoning as well as an intimate knowledge of the principles of reactivity. In an earlier question, we concluded that ester hydrolysis is reversible in acidic, but irreversible in basic, conditions. One might expect the same to be true of amide hydrolysis. But according to the question stem here, this is not true: In fact, we are told, amide hydrolysis is irreversible in both acidic and basic conditions. The choices present us with some factors that may contribute to the explanation and we are asked to identify the one that is NOT expected to play a role. In this case it is best to evaluate each choice in turn.

Choice **A** states that the amine product becomes protonated at low pH. This statement is true because amines are weakly basic. In acidic (low pH) conditions, we expect the nitrogen to be protonated, forming a quaternary ammonium salt. Does this fact provide an explanation? Yes: In order for the hydrolysis reaction to be reversed (for the amide to reform), at some point an amine must act as a nucleophile and attack the carbonyl carbon of the acid, and subsequently displace a water molecule. This cannot happen if the nitrogen atom has no nucleophilic electron pair, which is the case at low pH. Choice **A** therefore DOES play a role in the irreversibility of the reaction and cannot be the correct answer.

Choice **B** states that at low pH, the nitrogen atom in the tetrahedral intermediate favors being protonated. This is also a true statement, as we know that the nitrogen atom is basic. Indeed, the protonation of the nitrogen is a crucial step in the hydrolysis of an amide, as it creates a good leaving group:

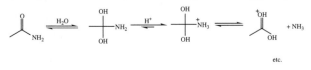

etc.

Protonation is more likely to occur at the nitrogen than it is at either oxygen atom, so the hydrolysis product forms more easily. Protonation of an oxygen would create a good water leaving group, whose departure would lead to the original amide. However, this is precisely what needs to occur if the hydrolysis is to be reversible. This is not expected to happen easily.

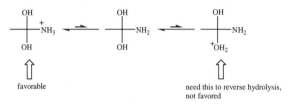

favorable

need this to reverse hydrolysis, not favored

Choice **B**, then, also helps explain why amide hydrolysis is not reversible in acidic conditions, and therefore cannot be the right choice.

Choice **C** states that at high pH, amide hydrolysis involves the elimination of the strongly basic $NH_2^-$ as leaving group. This is again a correct statement, as indicated in the passage, and as can be verified by envisioning the mechanism for amide hydrolysis in basic conditions. After the nucleophilic attack by hydroxide, the tetrahedral intermediate has the following structure:

Since the solution is basic, there is no proton source to protonate the nitrogen. In order for hydrolysis to proceed, the C–N bond must break, and this can only occur with $NH_2^-$ as the leaving group. Since it is strongly basic, it is not a good leaving group. (In fact, $NH_2^-$ abstracts a proton from a nearby molecule to form ammonia either concurrently with or immediately after elimination.) It is for this reason that harsh conditions are needed to carry out amide hydrolysis in base. Amides are considered "kinetically stable" in base.

This observation, however, does not help to explain why amide hydrolysis is irreversible. It simply tells us that it may be difficult to get the reaction going in the forward (hydrolysis) direction. Choice **C** is therefore the correct answer.

We can consider choice **D** for completeness. Choice **D** states that at high pH, the carboxylate ion does not possess a good leaving group. This is accurate. In base, the hydrolysis product is the carboxylate anion, just as in ester hydrolysis. For the same reason that ester hydrolysis is irreversible in base, this statement provides an explanation to the irreversibility of amide hydrolysis in base.

## 10.  B

An acyl group has the following structure:

An acyl-enzyme intermediate is therefore one in which the carbonyl carbon is bonded to the enzyme on the other end. Such a structure is formed in Step 2, where the –COR group is bonded to the enzyme at the serine 195 residue.

Step 1 leads to the formation of a tetrahedral intermediate. Step 3 involves the elimination of the amine. Step 4 actually breaks the acyl–enzyme complex to form another tetrahedral intermediate.

## 11.  D

An MCAT passage that presents an extraction sequence is usually accompanied by questions testing our understanding of the rationale behind specific steps. Often, how the acid-base properties of a compound affect its solubility is the key to the question. In Step 1, a weak base (bicarbonate ion, $HCO_3^-$) was added to the mixture. It will cause a relatively strong acid to deprotonate, converting it into its conjugate base. If the conjugate base is charged it will migrate into the aqueous layer where it preferentially dissolves, leaving the other nonacidic (or less acidic) organic compounds behind in the organic layer. This is the principle behind the separation. Among the four compounds shown, 2-methylbenzoic acid is the strongest acid and is expected to be the one extracted in Step 1. The bicarbonate ion causes it to deprotonate, and the carboxylate conjugate base dissolves in the aqueous layer. The HCl that was subsequently added reformed the acid. Before the addition of HCl, therefore, the predominant form of Compound A (which again we can conclude is 2-methylbenzoic acid) is the carboxylate ion, answer choice **A**.

The other choices either are not the conjugate base of a strong acid, or will not be extracted into the aqueous layer. Choice **A**, an amine salt, is the conjugate *acid* of an amine, not the conjugate base of something. Choice **B**, an amine, IS the conjugate base of a relatively strong acid, $R_3NH^+$. However, $R_3NH^+$, as a charged species, is already water-soluble. Addition of the bicarbonate would cause the formation of the *neutral* amine conjugate base. The neutral amine is expected to be less soluble in water than the conjugate acid, so it is not a likely method of extracting an amine. Choice **C** is the conjugate base of phenol, which is not as strong an acid as carboxylic acid. It will take the much more basic hydroxide ion in step 2 to deprotonate phenol.

## 12.  A

Pressure buildup within the funnel needs to be avoided, since it may cause the funnel to explode. This is something we need to watch out for whenever gas may be generated. This question is therefore essentially asking us to identify the step in the procedure that leads to the generation of gas. The only step in which a gas is created is Step 1, in which bicarbonate abstracts a proton from an acid:

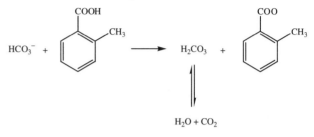

The carbonic acid $(H_2CO_3)$ formed establishes an equilibrium with carbon dioxide, which may escape from solution. (This results in the fizzing usually observed.) The generation of gas is the reason why we are usually instructed to shake the separatory funnel gently, and to vent often after each agitation.

## 13.  C

The MCAT expects students to be familiar with different techniques used to characterize compounds, and to be able to identify the technique that is most appropriate in a given situation. In this question we are asked how we could tell if the solution containing Compound C (the solution obtained after Step 4) also contains a fifth, unknown compound. In other words, we are looking for a technique that will tell us how many distinct components there are in the mixture. Thin-layer chromatography (TLC), choice **C**, is the appropriate technique: The number of components in the mixture will be revealed as the number of spots in the final chromatogram. (Different compounds will migrate up the plate at different rates based on their polarity and be assigned different $R_f$ values.)

Choice **A**, nuclear magnetic resonance, is a very useful technique in deducing the structure of a compound because it reveals the types of protons present in the molecule and how many of each proton type there are. However, if we supply a sample that actually contains two compounds, the spectrum will not inform us of this fact. This is also true of choices **B** and **D**, infrared (IR) spectroscopy and mass spectrometry. In particular, mass spectrometry causes the sample to break up into charged fragments, a step that essentially eliminates all information as to where the fragments may have come from.

## 14.  C

Benzylamine has the formula $C_6H_5CH_2NH_2$. Even if we could not identify the structure, we should at least be able to infer from its name the presence of an amine group, which is weakly basic. Its extraction can be accomplished by first adding an acid, then isolating the aqueous portion.

The addition of acid protonates the base, causing it to form the cationic conjugate acid $C_6H_5CH_2NH_3^+$. The cation dissolves in the aqueous layer because of the favorable solvation interactions by water molecules. The original neutral compound can be obtained by the introduction of another base which abstracts a proton from the conjugate acid. This is precisely what occurs in step 3. HCl protonates 4-methylaniline, which in its conjugate acid form will dissolve in the aqueous layer. Addition of NaOH causes the conjugate acid to deprotonate and yield the neutral aniline back. (Compound B is therefore 4-methylaniline.) Since benzylamine contains the same amine functional group, if it were present in the mixture it would also be extracted in the same step.

## 15.  D

To answer this question correctly we need to be able to do two things: Identify which proton type the compounds have in common, and then determine the chemical shift of this proton type. On the MCAT, students are expected to know the characteristic shifts of different proton types.

The only protons that all four compounds have in common are aryl protons: protons directly attached to an aromatic ring (this is the only type of proton that naphthalene possesses). Aromatic protons give proton-NMR signals with a chemical shift closest to that listed in choice **D**.

The chemical shift given in choice **A** is characteristic of methyl protons in saturated hydrocarbons. The chemical shift of choice **B** is characteristic of acetylenic protons ($-C\equiv C\text{-}\mathbf{H}$), alpha protons in ketones ($-\mathbf{CH}COR$), and benzylic protons ($Ar\text{-}\mathbf{CH}\text{-}$, e.g., the methyl protons on 2-methylbenzoic acid, 4-methylaniline, and *p*-cresol). The chemical shift of choice **C** is characteristic of vinylic protons ($=\mathbf{CH}R$).

## 16.  D

One of the skills tested on the MCAT is our ability to interpret the results of an experiment. This question asks us to determine what conclusions can be drawn about the structure of (+)-glucose given the fact that when oxidized by nitric acid, the resulting dicarboxylic acid is optically active. To arrive at the correct answer, we have to be able to visualize very concretely what happens to an aldohexose in the oxidation reaction.

First, we notice that all the compounds shown in Figure 1 are optically active. No plane of symmetry is possible since at one end of each molecule is an aldehyde group while at the other end is a primary alcohol group. However, we are told in the passage that nitric acid oxidation converts both these groups into the carboxyl group. Now that the two ends of the molecule are the same, there is a possibility of symmetry, and hence of optical inactivity. Those

aldohexoses in which the arrangement of –OH versus –H groups in the stereocenters is symmetric will be optically inactive after nitric acid oxidation.

We are told that after (+)-glucose has been oxidized by nitric acid oxidation, the resulting dicarboxylic acid is still optically active. That means that even with the two ends of the molecule now identical, there is still no plane of symmetry in the molecule. Hence, we can conclude that the arrangement of –OH versus –H groups in the stereocenters is not symmetric in (+)-glucose to begin with. We can eliminate from the eight structures any compound with such a symmetric arrangement from consideration. This is compound VII:

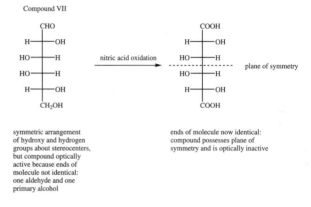

(Incidentally, we can also eliminate Compound I as a possible candidate for the structure of (+)-glucose from the same reasoning. The aldaric acid formed from either Compound I or Compound VII is a meso compound: It possesses stereocenters, but because a plane of symmetry exists for the molecule, it is optically inactive.)

The other compounds listed in the answer choices (Compounds IV, V, and VI), as well as Compounds II, III, and VIII, still remain as possibilities for glucose because they would all generate optically active aldaric acids upon nitric acid oxidation. For example, compound IV generates the following aldaric acid:

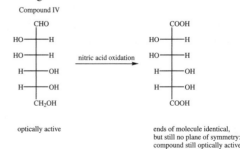

## 17.  C

This question tests us on our ability to apply our knowledge of stereochemistry to monosaccharides. D- and L-sugars of the same name are enantiomers—i.e., nonsuperimposable mirror images. Enantiomers differ in the configuration of every stereocenter. We can construct the enantiomer of L-gulose and match it with the compounds shown in Figure 1:

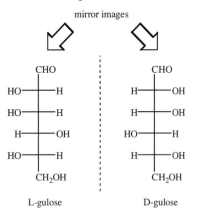

mirror images

L-gulose        D-gulose

We can see that the structure of D-gulose is identical to that of Compound V.

Among the wrong answer choices, notice that Compound IV differs from L-gulose in the configuration of the highest-numbered stereocenter only. This does not make it the enantiomer of L-gulose, because the configuration about every stereocenter has to be different in order for two compounds to be enantiomers. Instead, Compound IV and L-gulose are diastereomers. Indeed, Compounds III and VI (the other incorrect choices) are both diastereomers of L-gulose, of D-gulose, of Compound IV, and of each other.

## 18. D
Some fundamental knowledge of carbohydrate terminology is needed for the MCAT. A ketohexose is a six-carbon (hence *hex*) monosaccharide with a ketone (RCOR) rather than an aldehyde (RCHO) functionality (hence *keto*). In other words, the carbonyl carbon should be bonded to (non-hydrogen) alkyl groups on both sides. Only choice **D** satisfies both criteria.

Choice **A** is an aldohexose (six carbon atoms, but aldehyde functionality). Indeed, it is identical to Compound V in Figure 1, with the aldehyde group drawn explicitly. Choice **B** is a ketose, but only has five carbons. It is therefore a ketopentose. Choice **C** is also a ketose, but has seven carbons.

## 19. B
The passage indicates that the Kiliani–Fischer synthesis lengthens the carbon chain by one carbon at the aldehyde group, creating a new stereogenic center. In other words, the products are as follows:

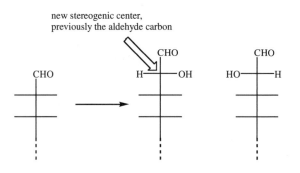

new stereogenic center, previously the aldehyde carbon

Notice that the rest of the molecule remains the same, so the two products are NOT enantiomers, but diastereomers that differ in the configuration of only one of the stereocenters (the newly created one).

We are told in the passage that when Fischer carried out the synthesis on an aldopentose, he obtained a mixture (+)-glucose and (+)-mannose. The two compounds must therefore differ only in the configuration about the first stereocenter (C2, the carbon atom immediately after the aldehyde group). This is true only of Compounds III and IV among the pairs given in the choices. In fact, we can conclude that (−)-arabinose must have the following structure:

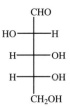

Choice **A**, Compounds II and III, differ in the configuration of C2 and C3. Choice **C**, Compounds V and VII, differ in the configuration of C3 only, not C2. Choice **D**, Compounds VI and VII, differ in the configuration of C2 and C3.

## 20. A
One of the properties of carbohydrates that we need to be aware of is the possibility of cyclization of some monosaccharides. In solution, aldohexoses tend to undergo cyclization to form a compound with a stable six-membered ring. This is accomplished by having the hydroxy group on the C5 atom attack the aldehyde carbon:

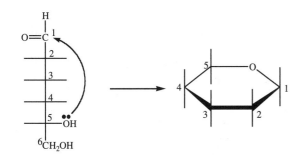

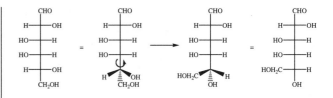

In this question, we are asked to identify the cyclic form of a compound whose linear structure is shown. To accomplish this task, it is of crucial importance to keep track of which carbon atom ends up where. One of the groups attached to C5 will be the –CH$_2$OH group. In other words, C6 is not part of the ring. In this question, we need to determine the orientation of the various –OH and –H groups, which is quite challenging. However, we can compare the relative configurations of the stereocenters in the linear versus the cyclic form. If we study Compound VII, we can see that C3 and C4 have their hydroxy groups pointing in the same direction, which is opposite to that of C2. In the cyclic structure, then, we look for the compound in which the hydroxy group on C2 points one way, while the hydroxy groups on C3 and C4 point the other way. This is choice **A**.

The "squiggly line" depicting the bond between C1 and its hydroxy group indicates that we are not interested in its orientation. We will get a mixture of both configurations at that stereocenter from the cyclization reaction. The two products are the α- and β-anomers.

Notice that this reasoning is adequate only because the answer choices do not ask us to choose between the following two compounds:

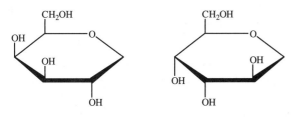

The structure on the left is choice **A**. The structure on the right (fortunately) does not appear among the answer choices. If it had, then we would have to determine how the orientation of the –CH$_2$OH group is related to the orientation of the hydroxy groups. This can be done by mentally rotating the C4-C5 bond in the linear molecule:

The –CH$_2$OH group therefore should point in the same direction as the hydroxy groups on C3 and C4, thus confirming that choice **A** is correct.

Choice **B** corresponds to the cyclic structure of Compound IV. Choice **C** corresponds to the cyclic form of Compound VI. Choice **D** is the cyclic form of Compound VIII.

### 21. B
This question tests whether we can apply the definition of a conjugate acid–base pair, but more importantly, it tests our knowledge of nomenclature of some nitrogen-containing compounds. If the product of Step 3 is the conjugate acid of something (whose identity we are trying to determine), then that "something" must be the conjugate base of the product of Step 3. The most acidic proton in the product of Step 3 is the one on the nitrogen atom. The question, then, is asking us to identify the name of the following functional group:

The compound contains an alkene functional group. One of the $sp^2$-hybridized carbon atoms is bonded to a nitrogen atom. This species is an enamine, so choice **B** is correct.

The structures of the incorrect answer choices are as follows:

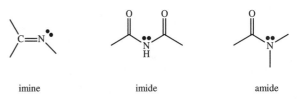

imine    imide    amide

### 22. D
This question takes us a little beyond the scope of the passage itself and asks us to determine what happens when the product of the reaction is subjected to certain reaction conditions (heat). MCAT questions do sometimes use a compound mentioned in the passage as a springboard for questions on aspects of organic chemistry not directly relevant to the passage itself. The final product of the reaction is a β-hydroxyketone: There is a hydroxy group bonded to the carbon atom that is beta to the carbonyl carbon. In other words, in addition to the carbonyl

functionality, it also acts as an alcohol. When heated, therefore, the compound, like many other alcohols, will undergo dehydration, a reaction in which a water molecule is eliminated. The generic alcohol dehydration is an acid-catalyzed reaction:

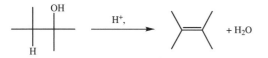

In this particular case, the driving force is the formation of a carbon–carbon pi bond that can be conjugated with the carbonyl pi bond. The double bond, therefore, has to be between the alpha and beta carbons.

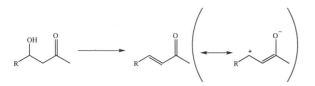

Choices **A** and **B** are incorrect, because heating alone is not sufficient to cause the compound to decompose into two carbonyl compounds. The products resemble those we might obtain from oxidative cleavage of alkenes, but the starting compound is not an alkene and the conditions for oxidative cleavage are not present. Choice **C** is incorrect, because the hydroxy group should no longer be a part of the molecule after dehydration.

### 23. D

This question asks us to deduce the conditions needed for Step 1 to proceed as indicated in the passage. It is a challenging question asking us to engage in relatively sophisticated reasoning based on the acid–base properties of the compounds involved. Step 1 involves the nucleophilic attack of the nitrogen in proline on the carbonyl carbon of acetone. The conditions must NOT be acidic. If they were, the nitrogen atom would be protonated and there would not be a lone pair of electrons available for nucleophilic attack. The medium must therefore be neutral or slightly basic to ensure that the nitrogen does not form a quaternary salt. However, immediately after the addition has taken place, we would obtain an alkoxide ion. The product of Step 1 as shown can only be accomplished by protonating the alkoxide in acidic conditions. This protonation step is necessary in order to get the dehydration in the next step to occur. In fact, further protonation (converting the hydroxy group into a water molecule) is necessary to create the leaving group. Choice **D** is therefore correct.

### 24. B

The MCAT may ask us to evaluate proposed hypotheses in light of information presented in the passage to test our critical thinking skills. This question is essentially asking us

to account for the enantioselectivity of the illustrated reaction. The stereogenic center in the β-hydroxyketone is created in Step 4 when the aldehyde adds to the proline-acetone complex. The transition state of Step 4 is shown in the passage. As mentioned in the passage, the transition state is a tricyclic complex, and one of the three rings is a six-membered ring involving the aldehyde. Notice that the R group is in the favored, equatorial position. In other words, the aldehyde adopts the more stable orientation relative to the complex, and it is this orientation preference that leads to the predominant creation of one enantiomer. In order to create the other enantiomer, the R and H will have to be swapped in the aldehyde. (i.e., the aldehyde will have to be rotated 180∞ about an axis going through the carbonyl bond.) That, however, will lead to higher strain in the transition state, as the R group will be in the axial position.

Choice **A** is incorrect, because we are not adding different halves of a molecule across the double bond, so the Markovnikov versus anti-Markovnikov designation is irrelevant. Choice **C** is incorrect. A general principle in organic synthesis is that we will never be able to create net optical activity using only optically inactive reagents. In other words, in order to create an enantiomer without its mirror image, there must be some chiral environment or reagents introduced at some point. If we started with a racemic mixture of proline, the final product would be a racemic mixture of the R and S isomers of the β-hydroxyketone. Choice **D** is incorrect, because the aldehyde is achiral. It does not have an enantiomer.

### 25. A

The MCAT expects students to identify the names of processes and transformations that occur in the course of a reaction. For this question, we are asked to determine which of the four processes does NOT occur. In other words, to eliminate an answer choice as incorrect, we should be able to see an example of it in the reaction.

The two carbonyl compounds involved in the reaction are a ketone and an aldehyde. Neither possesses a good leaving group. So no nucleophilic acyl substitution reaction is possible. The general scheme for a nucleophilic acyl substitution reaction is shown below:

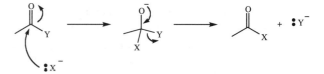

(The last step of the reaction is similar to the second step of a nucleophilic acyl substitution reaction under acidic conditions. The carbon–oxygen pi bond is formed as the proline acts as a leaving group and departs. However, the new carbonyl oxygen has never been part of a carbonyl compound. Instead, it comes from the water molecule that adds to the compound in Step 5, so the reaction is not a nucleophilic acyl substitution reaction.)

Choice **B** is incorrect, because it does occur in Step 1: The nitrogen acts as a nucleophile and attacks the carbonyl carbon. Choice **C** is incorrect, because addition to an alkene does occur in Step 4. The pi electrons of the C=C bond in the enamine are used to form the sigma bond to the aldehyde. Choice **D** is incorrect, because Steps 5 and 6 together constitute a hydrolysis reaction: A molecule is broken apart via the addition of a water molecule.

### 26. A

If we have very strong outside knowledge (possibly beyond the scope of what the MCAT requires), we can answer the question without any help from the passage. But the question can also be answered with an understanding and synthesis of different components of the passage.

Hydrogenation is mentioned in the first two tests described in the passage. It is imperative to pay close attention to the different results in the two cases. In the first test, we are told that hydrogenation of the unknown over Pd/C yielded stearic acid. From the condensed structural formula given for stearic acid, we should be able to tell that the alkyl portion of the acid is completely saturated—i.e., there are no carbon-carbon double or triple bonds. In Test 2, with the use of Lindlar's catalyst, only two molar equivalents of hydrogen were absorbed. In other words, only two pi bonds were saturated. The results of these two tests by themselves do not suggest any immediately obvious difference, and in fact they may have led to the exact same compound. The question to ask, then, is do the two tests actually yield the same compound? Is stearic acid obtained by saturating two pi bonds? To answer this we need to turn to the possible structures of the compounds given at the end of the passage. Both structures contain two carbon–carbon triple bonds and one carbon–carbon double bond. To convert the unknown into stearic acid requires the saturation of every carbon–carbon pi bond in the compound and would therefore require the absorption of five molar equivalents of hydrogen. (Recall that a triple bond contains two pi bonds and a double bond contains one pi bond.) Absorption of two molar equivalents of hydrogen (using Lindlar's catalyst) would still leave some pi bonds intact. What functionality do we have two of in the unknown? Triple bonds. It is therefore reasonable to assume that each triple bond is converted into a double bond, leaving a product containing three C=C bonds. Choice **A** is therefore correct. The situation is summarized for each of the two proposed structures in the diagram that follows:

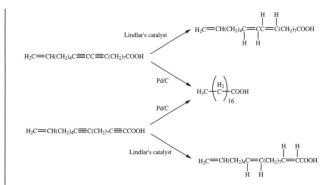

Choice **B** is not supported by evidence in the passage and can also be rejected because of its implausibility: Saturating a carbon–oxygen double bond (i.e., converting a carbonyl functionality into a hydroxy group) requires only one molar equivalent of hydrogen. Choice **C** is also unsupported and implausible: If we could determine the identity of the end product and if we knew the degree of unsaturation of the unknown, then there is no reason why quantitative measurement of hydrogen absorbed is not possible. Choice **D** is incorrect, because hydrogenation reactions are by definition reduction reactions.

### 27. A

In Test 3, the unknown is oxidized in $KMnO_4$. We are told that three of the products are dicarboxylic acids, and we are asked to determine the identity of the remaining product. We can examine the possible structures of the unknown (given at the end of the passage) and try to determine the effect of oxidation by $KMnO_4$. In general, $KMnO_4$ will cleave a carbon–carbon double and triple bond and convert each carbon on the end into a carboxylic acid functionality (after acid workup). (Under mild conditions use of $KMnO_4$ on an alkene may lead instead to the formation of diols—i.e., only the pi bond in the double bond will be broken. But the passage already indicates that carboxylic acids are formed.) If the unknown had the first of the two possible structures, the three dicarboxylic acids would have been obtained in the following manner:

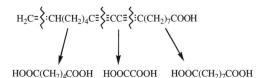

At this point we realize that the question can be rephrased as: What happens to the terminal methylene group upon oxidation? That product is the one species that is not a dicarboxylic acid. If our outside knowledge is strong, we can arrive at carbon dioxide as the correct answer immediately. But even if we are not aware of this, we may still have been able to eliminate the other choices. Our first intuition may be to treat the methylene group no differently: The carbon atom would become a carboxylic acid functional group:

$$H_2C = \Big\{ = \quad \xrightarrow{[O]} \quad \underset{HCOH}{\overset{O}{\parallel}}$$

or maybe even

$$\underset{HOCOH}{\overset{O}{\parallel}}$$

However, neither structure is among the answer choices.

We therefore have to resort to elimination. Choice **B** can be rejected because potassium permanganate cannot generate an extra carbon. The number of carbon atoms in each species is determined by the structure of the original compound (where the double and triple bonds occur). Choice **C** may be harder to reject, but we may surmise that if the reagent is capable of oxidizing all the other functionalities "all the way" to a carboxylic acid (with three C-O bonds), it is strange to halt the oxidation of the terminal methylene group at the alcohol stage. In other words, we would expect the species to be more oxidized. Choice **D** can be rejected because it is not an oxidation product but a reduction product. After we have tentatively rejected the other answer choices, we may be able to justify to ourselves why carbon dioxide is a reasonable choice. It is as oxidized as one can get (consistent with the production of dicarboxylic acids), and stoichiometrically it works:

$$H_2C = \Big\{ = \quad \xrightarrow{[O]} \quad CO_2 + H_2O$$

## 28.  D

The question asks us to identify the one piece of information that can be deduced based on Test 1 but that cannot be deduced based on Test 5. The results of Test 5 need not contradict the information, and indeed, they should not, since the tests are conducted on the same compound. So, the results of Test 5 should be unrelated to the property established by Test 1.

Test 1 indicates that upon hydrogenation, the unknown was converted into stearic acid, whose condensed structural formula is then given. Test 5 indicates that the unknown only has one –COOH group. The results of the two tests certainly do not contradict each other (and as mentioned above, they had better not!). In other words, the fact that the unknown yields stearic acid upon hydrogenation implies whatever is stated in the correct choice. However, the fact that it has one –COOH group does not in and of itself enable us to say that whatever is stated in the correct choice is true. What remains to be done now is to evaluate each answer choice in turn.

Choice **A** states that the unknown contains unsaturated carbon atoms. This is an incorrect choice because it is necessarily true given the result of Test 5: The carbonyl carbon of a carboxylic acid functional group is unsaturated. Choice **B** states that the unknown is not capable of *cis/trans* isomerism. *Cis/trans* isomerism can occur if the unknown contains a C=C bond, *and* if each carbon of the double bond is attached to two different groups. Test 1 tells us that the compound is unsaturated, but by itself it doesn't tell us if the compound contains C=C bonds (as opposed to the unsaturation arising solely from triple bonds), nor does it tell us what groups are attached to the double-bonded carbon atoms if they exist. Choice **B** is therefore not inferable from Test 1. Choice **C** states that the unknown contains an acidic hydrogen. This is inferable from *both* tests, so cannot be the correct choice. Choice **D**, by the process of elimination, must be correct. From the condensed structural formula of stearic acid, we can tell that the alkyl portion is straight-chained (seventeen carbons in a row followed by a –COOH group). The unknown must therefore also not be branched, since hydrogenation by itself does not rearrange the carbon skeleton. The fact that the unknown is unbranched is therefore inferable from Test 1. However, it is not inferable from Test 5, which has nothing to do with the alkyl portion. Just because it contains one –COOH group reveals nothing about what the alkyl portion might be like.

## 29.  C

The question asks us to determine the one property that will set stearic acid and the unknown apart. From the answer choices, we can tell that the property can be based on either IR spectrum, NMR spectrum, or boiling point. The correct answer must therefore apply to one of the two compounds. Incorrect answer choices will be true of both compounds or of neither compound.

What is needed from the passage is an awareness of the structural differences between stearic acid and the unknown. The unknown, unlike stearic acid, has carbon-carbon double and triple bonds. The distinguishing feature is therefore expected to hinge on the presence (or absence) of these unsaturated bonds. With this in mind, we can evaluate the answer choices. Choice **A** refers to a singlet in the proton NMR spectrum between 10 and 12 ppm. This chemical shift corresponds to the proton of a carboxylic acid group, which is present in both compounds. This feature therefore cannot be used to distinguish between the two. Choice **B** refers to a strong and broad IR absorption from 2500 to 3400 $cm^{-1}$. This band is characteristic of an O-H bond, which again is present on both compounds. So this too cannot be used to distinguish between them. Choice **C** refers to the absence of any IR stretches around 2200 $cm^{-1}$. This is where a C≡C bond is expected to absorb, so its absence would signify that the compound is stearic acid and not the unknown, which we know contains triple bonds. Choice **C** is therefore the correct answer. Finally, choice **D** can be rejected because both compounds, being carboxylic acids, will have higher boiling points than the corresponding alcohol. In fact, the alcohol listed in the answer choice has one fewer carbon atom, making its boiling point even lower.

**30. C**
Determining the isomeric relationship between two compounds is an MCAT favorite. Geometric isomers are isomers arising from the arrangement of groups around a double bond. While the structures do both contain a C=C bond, the fact that one carbon is attached to two hydrogen atoms (two identical groups) precludes the possibility of geometric isomers. So choice **A** is incorrect. Choice **B** is also incorrect, because diastereomers are either geometric isomers (rejected as a possibility) or stereoisomers with multiple chiral centers that are not enantiomers of each other. The structures proposed do not contain any chiral center, so they cannot be diastereomers. Choice **C** is correct: They differ in the connectivity of the atoms. In one case, the carboxyl group is attached to a chain of seven saturated carbon atoms; in the other case, the carboxyl group is directly bonded to an *sp*-hybridized carbon. Choice **D** is incorrect, because the two structures have the same molecular formula and are therefore isomers of each other.

**31. C**
Questions asking for the number of stereogenic centers in a compound are a perennial MCAT favorite. A stereogenic center, also referred to on the MCAT as a stereocenter or a chiral center, is (usually) a carbon atom bonded to four different groups. (Nitrogen and some other heteroatoms can also act as stereocenters if the arrangement of groups about the atom leads to distinct, nonsuperimposable mirror images.) The stereocenters of lovastatin, whose structure is shown in Equation 2, are labeled with an asterisk in the diagram below.

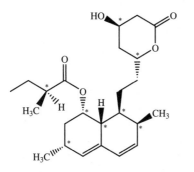

There are a total of eight stereocenters. Notice that we always need to keep in mind that hydrogen atoms needed to saturate the carbon atoms are not always indicated explicitly in chemical structures. However, if there are two such "implied hydrogens" attached to a carbon atom, that carbon atom cannot possibly be a stereocenter because it will not be bonded to four different groups. For this reason, the two carbon atoms labeled below are not stereocenters:

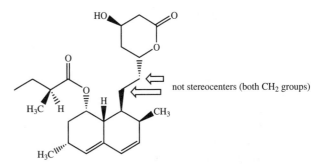

not stereocenters (both CH₂ groups)

Besides this issue of "implied hydrogen atoms," the other pitfall for questions like this arises in the case of a multicyclic compound. In the diagram below, the structure on the left has no stereocenters but the structure on the right has two stereocenters. Each of the atoms labeled with an asterisk is bonded to four distinct groups: the "bridge," a hydrogen atom, one half of the six-membered ring with the carbonyl group, and the other half of the six-membered ring without the carbonyl group. (In the structure on the left, the two halves of the six-membered ring are identical, so the four groups are not distinct.)

**32. A**
An MCAT Organic Chemistry passage that presents a new reaction may often be accompanied by questions in which we need to apply the reaction to a new set of reactants and determine the product(s). To answer this question, we need to first of all determine the structure of cyclopentadiene and then apply Equation 1 to the situation in which one molecule of cyclopentadiene acts as the diene while another molecule acts as the dienophile.

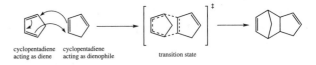

cyclopentadiene acting as diene    cyclopentadiene acting as dienophile      transition state

This is the structure shown in choice **A**. Even if we had not been able to visualize how the spatial relationships between the bonds evolve over the course of the reaction, we could have eliminated the other answer choices by some reasoning and by close examination of Equation 1. In Equation 1, we see that the diene and the dienophile join to form a six-membered ring, with a double bond in the position between the two double bonds in the original diene. Furthermore, we go from three double bonds (one from the dienophile and two from the diene) to one double bond in the product. In the case with two molecules of cyclopentadiene, however, we start off with an extra double bond: The dienophile itself contains two double bonds, one of which does not participate in the reaction. The number of double bonds in the product, then, is expected to be two. This enables us to eliminate choice **D**. Furthermore, we know that the second double bond in the product should not be part of the six-membered ring; i.e., the six-membered ring should only contain the one double bond that forms as a result of the reaction. Choice **B** can therefore be eliminated. Finally, choice **C** can be eliminated because the six-membered ring does not contain any double bond. The structure shown has both double bonds as part of a five-membered ring, which contradicts the reaction as illustrated in Equation 1.

### 33. C

In this question we are asked to determine where an isotopic label ends up after the reaction. This can be a very challenging question as the reaction, as illustrated in Equation 3, contains very little that can help us orient ourselves spatially to see how the two compounds join to form the bicyclic compound. However, we can keep track of certain functional groups. By examining where the $-OCH_3$, $-COCH_3$, and $-CH_3$ groups end up in the bicyclic compound, we can deduce how the molecule is "put together":

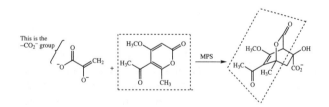

With the spatial relationships established, we can see that the radiolabeled oxygen in the question stem becomes the oxygen in the hydroxy group of the bicyclic compound. Choice **C** is therefore correct. The following diagram illustrates how the electrons are actually shifted around in the reaction.

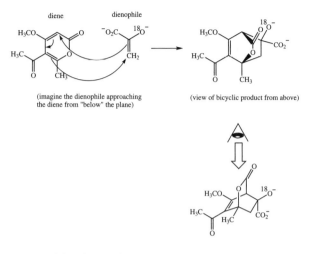

(imagine the dienophile approaching the diene from "below" the plane)

(view of bicyclic product from above)

Presumably the oxygen is protonated during an acid "workup" step to create the hydroxy group.

### 34. B

The question is essentially asking us to identify the one compound that will not participate in a Diels–Alder reaction. The choices are meant to act as analogs of the 2-pyrone shown in Equation 3. As the passage states, the Diels-Alder reaction involves the addition of an alkene (acting as a dienophile) to a conjugated diene. In addition, as can be deduced from examining the reaction shown in Equation 3, the 2-pyrone acts as the diene. In other words, the analogs must be conjugated dienes. A diene is conjugated if the pi electrons can be delocalized across the double bonds. In other words, we should be able to draw resonance structures for the compound in which the pi electrons are shifted around:

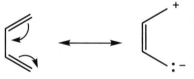

The compound shown in choice **B** is not a conjugated diene: The two carbon-carbon double bonds are separated by $sp^3$-hybridized atoms and the pi electrons are therefore not delocalized. It therefore cannot react with a dienophile to yield a Diels-Alder adduct.

### 35. D

The question is asking us to identify the process that will convert lovastatin as it appears in Equation 2 to the structure shown in the question stem. Focusing on the portion of the molecule that has undergone change, we are essentially asked to determine the name for the following transformation:

The original functionality is a (cyclic) ester, with the formula –COOR. The functionalities after the transformation are a carboxylic acid and an alcohol. The process is therefore one of ester hydrolysis.

Choices **A** and **B**, oxidation and reduction, are incorrect, because the number of carbon-oxygen bonds has not changed. Recall that oxidation of an organic compound implies forming more bonds between carbon and oxygen atoms (or between carbon and some other electronegative heteroatoms like nitrogen and chlorine), while the reduction of an organic compound implies forming more C–H bonds. The carbonyl carbon in the ester has three C–O bonds (one double and one single); the same is true in the carboxylic acid product. Choice **C**, ozonolysis, refers to the formation of carbonyl compounds by breaking a carbon-carbon double bond. The general ozonolysis scheme is as follows:

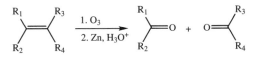

## Discrete Questions

### 36. B
The molecular formula of a compound indicates the number of atoms of each element in one molecule of the substance. The molecular formula for glucose, for example, is $C_6H_{12}O_6$. However, the molecular formula does not provide full information on the structure of the molecule or on what functional groups it contains. Drawing the structure out is not always feasible. Hence, organic chemists sometimes make use of condensed structural formulas to convey information on the structure. The MCAT expects test takers to be able to interpret condensed structural formulas.

The condensed structural formula given in the question corresponds to the following compound:

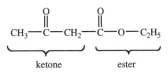

The compound therefore has both a ketone and an ester functionality. Since only ester appears as a choice, choice **B** is the correct answer.

Ethers, choice **A**, have the general formula ROR'. A condensed structural formula, for example, may look like $CH_3OCH_2CH_3$. The "$CH_3COCH_2$" in the formula in the question cannot indicate an ether linkage because the second carbon atom will not have a full octet. (The carbon–oxygen bonds in an ether are single bonds.) Choice **C**, acid anhydride, has the general formula RCOOCOR'. Choice **D**, carboxylic acid, has the general formula RCOOH.

### 37. A
Constitutional isomers (also referred to as structural isomers) are isomers that differ in the connectivity of the atoms. The carbon skeletons may have completely different appearances, and the molecules may have different functional groups. For example, one may be an ether while the other may be an alcohol. For this question, we know from the molecular formula (which contains only C's and H's) that the isomers are all going to be hydrocarbons, so the task is to come up with the different possibilities for the carbon skeleton. Notice that the carbon-to-hydrogen ratio indicates that the compounds are all saturated, noncyclic hydrocarbons. (A noncyclic alkane has the general formula $C_nH_{2n+2}$. A formula of $C_nH_{2n}$, for example, would indicate either a noncyclic alkene with one double bond or a cyclic alkane.)

The best way to tackle the question is to write down the different possible structures for $C_5H_{12}$:

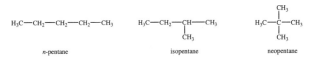

These three structures exhaust the possibilities for the formula $C_5H_{12}$. Any other structure that we can draw will turn out to be equivalent to one of these three possibilities, or will not be consistent with the formula. (Cyclopentane, for example, only has 10 hydrogen atoms.)

### 38. D
One of the things we are expected to do on the MCAT is to deduce something about the physical properties of a compound, especially relative to other analogous compounds. Physical properties refer to characteristics such as density, boiling point, melting point, solubility—properties that can be observed without having to subject the compound to any chemical reactions. Intermolecular attractions are a major factor in determining many physical properties, including boiling point. The stronger the attraction among the molecules, the higher the boiling point of the compound. Compounds capable of hydrogen bonding are generally expected to have higher boiling points than their non-hydrogen bonding counterparts, so carboxylic acids (choices **C** and **D**) are expected to have higher boiling points than ketones (choices **A** and **B**).

In fact, in the liquid state, carboxylic acid molecules form dimers held together by two hydrogen bonds instead of just one:

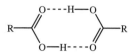

Within the same class of compounds, boiling point increases with molecular weight, since the compound with the higher molecular weight is generally larger and therefore engages in more dispersion interactions (another form of intermolecular attraction). Choice **D**, a carboxylic acid with eight carbon atoms, is therefore expected to have a higher boiling point than choice **C**, with seven carbon atoms.

**39. C**
Choice C is the correct answer for two reasons. Firstly, $(CH_3)_3COH$ will form a tertiary carbocation; $(CH_3)_3C^+$. Here, there are three alkyl groups which, by electron donation through sigma bonds, can stabilize the positive charge. Secondly, the polar protic solvent $H_2SO_4$ is used. This drives the formation of the carbocation, since it can stabilize the transition state that forms. (A) Distortion. No nucleophilic substitution reactions can occur in a nonpolar solvent. (B) Faulty Use of Detail. Choice B is wrong because even though $(CH_3CH_2)_3COH$ would form a tertiary carbocation, acetone is a polar aprotic solvent which would not be able to stabilize the transition state as effectively as a polar protic solvent. (D) Opposite. These conditions would be ideal for an $S_N2$ reaction, not $S_N1$.

**40. D**
A nitrogen atom with zero formal charge is basic by virtue of its lone pair of electrons, which can abstract a proton from an acid to form a quaternary ammonium salt. The more reactive the lone electron pair, the more basic the nitrogen atom. Conversely, the more stabilized the electron pair, the less basic the nitrogen atom. The nonbonding electron pair of each of the answer choices is shown explicitly below:

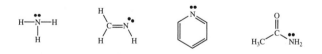

The amide in choice **D** has the least basic nitrogen atom, since the electron pair is resonance-stabilized:

Because the electron pair is delocalized, it is not as "eager" to form a bond to a proton. The lone pair on ammonia (choice **A**) and on the imine (choice **B**) cannot be resonance-stabilized. Nor can the electron pair in pyridine (choice **C**). The ring already has six pi electrons. The nonbonding electron pair resides in an $sp^2$-hybridized orbital that is in the same plane as the ring, so it is not delocalized.

**41. C**
The hydroxide ion is a strong nucleophile as well as a strong base, and dimethyl sulfoxide (DMSO) is a polar aprotic solvent. (An aprotic solvent is one that is incapable of participating in hydrogen bonds. Thus, water and alcohols are all protic solvents, but acetone and benzene are aprotic solvents.) The conditions are prime for a bimolecular reaction. The hydroxide ion attacks the alkyl halide, displacing the chloride group in a one-step (concerted) mechanism as follows:

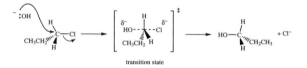

transition state

The reaction is an $S_N2$ reaction. It proceeds via a concerted mechanism: The attack of the hydroxide ion and the displacement of the leaving group occur in the same step, the one step that makes up the reaction. The rate law for a generic $S_N2$ reaction is rate = k[nucleophile][substrate]. In other words, the rate of the reaction is proportional to both the concentration of the nucleophile (in this case the hydroxide ion) and the concentration of the substrate (in this case 1-chloropropane). The statements in choices **B** and **D** are therefore both true and are not the correct answer.

Because the hydroxide ion is also a strong base, elimination (more specifically bimolecular elimination, E2) is a side reaction. The hydroxide ion acts as a base to abstract a proton from the carbon adjacent to the one bearing the halogen:

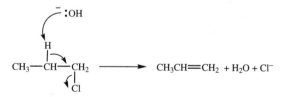

(The transition state is not shown.) An alkene is the product, and the statement in choice **A** is therefore true.

The statement in choice **C** is false. Less substituted alkyl halides participate in $S_N2$ reactions more rapidly because the carbon to be attacked is more accessible. 1-Chloropropane is a primary alkyl halide: The carbon atom bearing the chlorine is bonded to only one alkyl group, making it relatively easy for the hydroxide ion to approach it. 2-Chloropropane, however, is a secondary alkyl halide. The halogen-bearing carbon is more sterically hindered because it is bonded to two alkyl groups. The hydroxide ion finds it harder to attack the carbon, making the reaction slower. We therefore find that the reactivity of alkyl halides in $S_N2$ reactions decreases as follows: methyl > primary > secondary > tertiary.

**42. A**

Molecular bromine will add across a carbon-carbon double bond to form a dibromo compound:

The reaction leads to a loss of the characteristic reddish-brown color of bromine, and is used as the basis for a qualitative test for the presence of unsaturation. However, the carbonyl bond of a ketone does not participate in this reaction, so choice **A** is the only correct answer.

The bromination of an alkene is an example of a large class of reactions known as addition reactions. In an addition reaction, a double bond becomes saturated as sigma bonds to new groups are formed. Depending on the reaction conditions, the reaction can proceed through a variety of mechanisms and lead to many different types of products: alcohols, halohydrins, etc. The addition of a halogen (such as bromine), for example, proceeds via a cyclic intermediate:

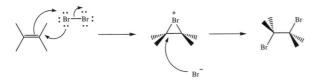

**43. D**

The main piece of information produced by mass spectroscopy, method I, is the molecular weight of the compounds involved. Since 2-hydroxymuconic semialdehyde contains two more oxygen atoms and one less hydrogen atom than does catechol, the mass spectrum of the two compounds would be clearly different. Moreover, the one showing the larger molecular weight would belong to the semialdehyde, and the one with the smaller molecular weight would belong to catechol. So the correct answer choice has to include method I, which means you can eliminate choice C.

Method II, NMR, or nuclear magnetic resonance spectroscopy, reveals the carbon skeleton of a compound. Specifically, it shows how many different, nonequivalent hydrogen atoms the compound has and how the carbon atoms they're attached to are connected. Catechol is an achiral molecule, so it has three sets of equivalent hydrogens and the compound should produce three different peaks. 2-hydroxymuconic semialdehyde is asymmetric and would produce a lot more different signals. Thus, even without getting into the specific structures of the two molecules and figuring out exactly what those peaks would look like, you'd be able to tell from looking at the spectrum that one was much simpler than the other. Method II also has to be in the correct answer, so you can eliminate choice A.

Finally, in Method III, infrared spectroscopy, the spectra will indicate the functional groups in each compound. The spectrum of 2-hydroxymuconic semialdehyde would have an aldehyde peak, whereas the spectrum of catechol would not. This means that the answer has to include choice III as well, making choice D correct.

**44. B**

The structure of 2-bromopropane is shown below. The molecule possesses two distinct proton types, labeled (a) and (b).

The protons from the two methyl groups are equivalent. There is therefore only one signal for the six protons. The signal is split by the proton labeled (b). The signal is therefore a doublet. Proton (b), in turn, is split by the six equivalent methyl protons. The signal is therefore a septet. For MCAT questions on NMR, it is important to master the concept of equivalent protons, and to be able to predict the splitting patterns that arise.

**45. A**

From an organic chemistry standpoint, one of the most interesting features of amino acids is their acid–base property. Every amino acid has a basic amino group and an acidic carboxyl group, as well as a side group that can potentially also be acidic or basic. An amino acid can therefore exist in several different protonation states depending on the pH of its environment. (An ability to interpret titration curves of amino acids is expected on the MCAT.)

In this question, the pH of the solution is higher than the pK value of every functionality of tyrosine, so each group acts as an acid toward the solvent. In other words, they all exist in the deprotonated, conjugate base form. The carboxyl group thus exists as the negatively charged carboxylate: $-COO^-$ instead of $-COOH$. The amino group exists as the neutral $-NH_2$ group instead of the $-NH_3^+$ group. The phenolic side chain exists as $-Ph-O^-$ instead of $-Ph-OH$. The structure of the amino acid at pH 11 is therefore as follows:

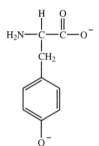

The net charge is therefore −2.

# CHAPTER 7

# Biology

When confronted with an MCAT Biology passage, many students try to apply the same strategies they used during their undergraduate years: They try to read for understanding and focus on details mentioned in the passage. In doing so they spend lots of time digesting the passage, which may result in running out of time before finishing the section. While reading for understanding and focusing on details may have worked for college courses, these strategies won't maximize your score on the MCAT. Since you have access to the passage at all times, you won't need to read for detail or understand everything about the passage to begin answering MCAT questions and earning points.

What can you do to manage your time most effectively and maximize your MCAT score? Read the passage only as needed and spend the majority of your time answering questions. Answering questions is what increases your score, not spending too much time reading passages.

## READING THE PASSAGE

### Passage Types

*Information* passages contain prose you might find in a textbook. They consist of paragraphs of text that are descriptive in nature. A passage may include a diagram or two related to the topic being discussed. For example, a typical information passage might discuss a particular disease, describe its symptoms, and include a pedigree illustrating its manner of inheritance. The majority of Biology passages on the MCAT are information passages.

*Experiment* passages describe one or more experiments and include a presentation of results. Since the results of the experiment or experiments are usually presented in table or graph form, these passages are often recognizable by the presence of tables and/or graphs. A diagram that illustrates an apparatus used in the experiment may also accompany the passage. For example, a typical experiment passage might present some background information about a topic, describe an experiment designed to investigate the topic, and use a table to present the results of the experiment.

*Persuasive argument* passages consist mainly of paragraphs of text that explain one (or more) different viewpoints or hypotheses. For example, a typical persuasive argument passage might present background information about a disease, and present two hypotheses about the cause of the disease. Here is an example of a persuasive argument passage:

The human auditory system has the remarkable capacity to distinguish sound frequencies that differ by as little as 3 Hz, with a dynamic range of detection from 20 Hz to 20 kHz. The mechanism that provides this ability lies in the inner part of the ear, in an organ named the cochlea.

The cochlea is a fluid-filled tubular structure that is coiled into the shape of a seashell. Traversing the tube is a flat, rigid membrane known as the basilar membrane, upon which sit ciliated "hair cells" that are capable of transmitting an electrical signal through the auditory nerve back to the brain. A stiff, gelatinous mass called the tectorial membrane overlies the hair cells.

A typical sound wave is conducted through the outer parts of the ear and induces minute vibrations at one end of the cochlea. These vibrations are then transmitted through the fluid inside and cause deflections in the basilar membrane proportional to the amplitude of the sound. Motion of the basilar membrane against the tectorial membrane causes the cilia on the hair cells to bend, mechanically triggering the opening of ion channels and causing the hair cells to "fire" like a neuron. Though this model accounts for the mechanism of sound detection, it does not explain how the frequency of a sound is encoded.

To date, two principles have been proposed governing the mechanism of sound frequency discrimination.

*The Place Principle*

The basilar membrane on which the hair cells sit vibrates differently along its length, with the base (the end facing the outer ear) the most sensitive to low-frequency sounds, and the apex (the opposite end) most sensitive to high-frequency sounds. According to the place principle, the brain can distinguish various frequencies based on the location of the hair cells that fire. Sounds of a specific frequency cause hair cells at a specific point along the basilar membrane to fire.

*The Volley Principle*

Neurons have the ability to fire in synchrony with a specific phase of a waveform, such that the frequency of neuronal firing will match the frequency of the sound vibration. This phenomenon is known as phase locking. According to the volley principle, sound frequency is simply encoded by the timing of the neuron's firing. Hence, a high-frequency sound will cause a rapid rate of firing, while a low-frequency sound will lead to a slow rate of firing.

Remember that your goal is to get through a passage as quickly as possible so that you can spend the majority of your time answering questions. Answering questions is what earns you points on the MCAT. Be careful not to spend so much time digesting a passage that you run out of time when answering questions. As previously mentioned, MCAT passages contain a lot of information and data; however, it is important for you to remember that this information will always be there for you to refer to, should you need it. When reading a Biology passage, you should perform two tasks: *map the passage* and *identify the topic.*

## Mapping the Passage

The key to being able to access the information you need is creating a passage map. A passage map is a breakdown of the main ideas and critical concepts in a passage, paragraph by paragraph. By spending time reading for main ideas rather than details, and noting where concepts are presented in the passage, you'll spend less time reading a passage while still having enough of a grasp of the passage to know where to go for information should you need it to answer a question.

As you read a passage, determine what kind of passage it is. Depending on the type of passage, your strategy when reading the passage will be different. Use your knowledge of what makes up a particular passage type to help you. For example, does the passage consist of paragraphs of prose that are textbook-like and descriptive in nature? These are characteristics of information passages.

If the passage is an information passage, skim each paragraph and write down the main idea of each paragraph on scratch paper. As you read each paragraph, ask yourself, "What is the main idea of this paragraph?" The objective is to not get stuck trying to understand every detail of the passage, but to note the main ideas and go to the questions.

Does the passage contain a presentation of one or more experiments and a discussion of experimental design and results? Does the passage contain graphs and/or tables that present the results of an experiment? These are characteristics of experiment passages. Read experiment passages with the goal of understanding the what and the why of the experiment. If there are tables or graphs, note what quantities are being measured and any general trends.

Does the passage consist mainly of paragraphs of text that explain different viewpoints or hypotheses? Does the passage contain headings such as "Hypothesis I," "Hypothesis II," or "Scientist I," "Scientist II"? These are characteristics of persuasive argument passages.

In persuasive argument passages, read the paragraphs that explain the hypotheses or arguments carefully and try to grasp the main points of each of the hypotheses or arguments being presented. Note the main points of each hypothesis or argument in the margin, or underline the relevant sentences in each paragraph.

## Identifying the Topic

After reading the passage, note the topic of the passage. The topic of the passage is related to the type of passage. Recall from chapter 3 the following useful tips:

The topic of an information passage usually has the following format:

> *The passage describes/discusses* (<u>phenomena</u>).

The topic of an experiment passage usually has the following format:

> *The passage is about an experiment, the purpose of which is to* (<u>purpose of experiment</u>).

The topic of a persuasive argument passage usually has the following format:

*The passage presents (<u>number</u>) hypotheses about (<u>phenomena</u>).*

Here is a sample information passage, mapped using the strategies described in the previous section.

> Melanocytes are cells containing melanosomes, which are the cellular organelles responsible for synthesizing melanin. Melanin is a skin, hair, and retinal pigment synthesized from the amino acid tyrosine via an enzymatic reaction pathway.

Background information about melanocytes, melanin.

> Albinism is a genetic disorder in which melanin synthesis is blocked. In most forms of human albinism, melanocytes appear to be normally distributed. Albinism occurs when a gene encoding an enzyme responsible for melanin production undergoes a mutation. As a result, individuals who suffer from albinism have extremely pale skin, white hair, and pinkish-colored eyes. They also experience vision problems because the eye's choroid, which is normally melanin-colored, is white. As a result, light entering the eye is reflected from, rather than absorbed into, the surface of the choroid and visual acuity is severely diminished. Albinos also run a greater risk for skin cancer, since the UV rays of the sun damage their unprotected skin cells.

Information about albinism: cause, symptoms.

> The frequency of the albino gene in the general population is 0.001, and is higher in many isolated populations, including the Amish and many Native American tribes. The pedigree in Figure 1 illustrates the pattern of inheritance for one form of human albinism.

Frequency of albino gene in general population and subpopulations

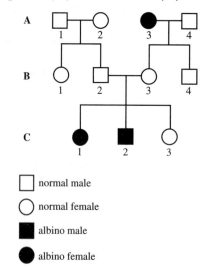

□ normal male

○ normal female

■ albino male

● albino female

**Figure 1**

Pattern of inheritance of one form of human albinism.

**Topic:** The passage describes/discusses albinism.

Next is an example of an experiment passage; again, pay close attention to the mapping:

> Researchers discovered that cooking meat with charcoal results in the formation of polynuclear aromatic hydrocarbons on the food. To test whether these compounds are carcinogens, the Ames test is used. The Ames test identifies compounds that are chemical mutagens, and since most chemical mutagens are carcinogens, this test is able to ascertain carcinogenic risk.

Background information. The Ames test identifies chemical mutagens. Use of the Ames test to determine if polynuclear aromatic hydrocarbons are carcingens.

> In the Ames test, a mutant bacterial strain of *Salmonella typhimurium* unable to grow in the absence of histidine is placed on agar plates containing minimal growth media. (Minimal growth media lacks histidine.) A filter paper disk with the suspected carcinogen and other compounds is placed in the center of the plates. The following four plates were used in this experiment.

Design of the experiment. A mutant bacterial strain is used that can't grow without histidine.

> Plate I: *Salmonella* alone
> Plate II: *Salmonella* + polynuclear aromatic hydrocarbons
> Plate III: *Salmonella* + polynuclear aromatic hydrocarbons + human liver preparation
> Plate IV: *Salmonella* + 2-aminoanthracene (a known carcinogen)

Plate I: bacteria alone
Plate II: bacteria + test compound
Plate III: bacteria + test compound + human liver preparation
Plate IV: bacteria + known carcinogen

> The plates were incubated at 37°C for 48 hours. Only bacteria that regain the ability to synthesize histidine through *back-mutation* will be able to survive on these plates. The results of the experiments are shown in Figure 1.

More details about the experiment. Only bacteria that regain the ability to synthesize histidine will grow.

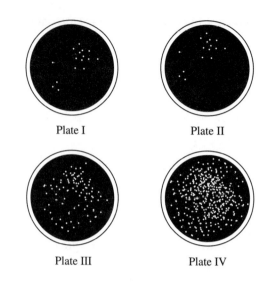

Plate I    Plate II

Plate III    Plate IV

**Figure 1**

Results of the experiment. Plates I and II show little growth, while Plates III and IV show extensive growth. Plate IV shows the most growth.

**Topic:** The passage is about an experiment, the purpose of which is to determine whether polynuclear aromatic hydrocarbons are carcinogens.

Here is the sample persuasive argument passage presented earlier, mapped using the strategies described in the previous section.

> The human auditory system has the remarkable capacity to distinguish sound frequencies that differ by as little as 3 Hz, with a dynamic range of detection from 20 Hz to 20 kHz. The mechanism that provides this ability lies in the inner part of the ear, in an organ named the cochlea.

Background on the sense of hearing.

> The cochlea is a fluid-filled tubular structure that is coiled into the shape of a seashell. Traversing the tube is a flat, rigid membrane known as the basilar membrane, upon which sits ciliated "hair cells" that are capable of transmitting an electrical signal through the auditory nerve back to the brain. A stiff, gelatinous mass called the tectorial membrane overlies the hair cells.

More background information.

> A typical sound wave is conducted through the outer parts of the ear and induces minute vibrations at one end of the cochlea. These vibrations are then transmitted through the fluid inside and cause deflections in the basilar membrane proportional to the amplitude of the sound. Motion of the basilar membrane against the tectorial membrane causes the cilia on the hair cells to bend, mechanically triggering the opening of ion channels and causing the hair cells to "fire" like a neuron. Though this model accounts for the mechanism of sound detection, it does not explain how the frequency of a sound is encoded.

How a sound wave is converted to an electrical signal to the brain.

> To date, two principles have been proposed governing the mechanism of sound frequency discrimination.

Two proposed principles regarding sound frequency discrimination.

> *The Place Principle*
>
> The basilar membrane on which the hair cells sit vibrates differently along its length, with the base (the end facing the outer ear) most sensitive to low-frequency sounds, and the apex (the opposite end) most sensitive to high-frequency sounds. Based on the place principle, the brain can distinguish various frequencies based on the location of the hair cells that fire. Sounds of a specific frequency cause hair cells at a specific point along the basilar membrane to fire.

The Place Principle: the location along the basilar membrane of the hair cells that fire encodes the frequency of the sound.

> *The Volley Principle*
>
> Neurons have the ability to fire in synchrony with a specific phase of a waveform, such that the frequency of neuronal firing will match the frequency of the sound vibration. This phenomenon is known as phase locking. According to the volley principle, sound frequency is simply encoded by the timing of the neuron's firing. Hence, a high-frequency sound will cause a rapid rate of firing, while a low-frequency sound will lead to a slow rate of firing.

The Volley Principle: The timing of neuronal firing encodes the frequency of the sound.

Passage type: Persuasive argument

**Topic:** The passage presents two hypotheses about sound frequency discrimination.

# HANDLING THE QUESTIONS

Recall the question types from chapter 3:

*Discrete questions.* These questions are not associated with any passage. They appear following a header such as "Questions 12–15 are NOT based on a descriptive passage." The Biological Sciences section contains 13 discrete questions spread throughout the section.

Here is an example of a discrete question:

> One form of hereditary diabetes is the result of an autoimmune disorder. The body produces antibodies that destroy its own insulin-producing cells. The most likely target of these antibodies are
>
> **A.** pancreas cells.
>
> **B.** spleen cells.
>
> **C.** adrenal cells.
>
> **D.** liver cells.

*Questions that require an understanding of the passage.* These questions ask you to evaluate the validity of a hypothesis or argument given a new piece of information, determine what evidence would support a hypothesis or argument, or compare and contrast the hypotheses or arguments with each other. To answer these questions, you need to understand the concepts presented in the passage. Another example of a question that requires an understanding of the passage is the data interpretation/analysis question. These questions require you to interpret data from a table or graph, or analyze an experiment.

Here is an example of a question that requires an understanding of the passage:

Which of the following best accounts for the visible colonies on Plate I?

A.  Random mutations resulted in *Salmonella* cells that regained the ability to synthesize histidine.

B.  The cells were able to grow because histidine is not an essential amino acid for *Salmonella*.

C.  In the absence of one amino acid, *Salmonella* substituted a similar amino acid in its place.

D.  Foreign chromosome fragments containing the normal genes for histidine biosynthesis were transformed into a few *Salmonella* cells.

This question asks you to provide an explanation for the results of an experiment.

*Questions where you need data from the passage.* These questions can be answered without conceptual knowledge from the passage; however, you may need to go back to a specific part of the passage to retrieve data from a table, for example.

Here is an example of a question where you need data from the passage:

According to Figure 1, at what $pO_2$ are half the $O_2$-binding sites on Hb available?

A.  20 mm Hg
B.  25 mm Hg
C.  85 mm Hg
D.  90 mm Hg

You need to look at a graph to determine the answer to this question.

*Questions that can stand alone from the passage.* These questions can be answered without conceptual knowledge or data from the passage.

Here is an example of a question that can stand alone from the passage:

Congenital defects in the skeletal structures of the limbs can be traced back to which of the following primary germ layer?

A. Mesoderm

B. Ectoderm

C. Endoderm

D. Notochord

This question can be answered without any information from the passage.

Certain question types appear more frequently with certain passage types. With an information passage, you will see more questions that can stand alone from the passage. With an experiment passage, you will see more questions where you need data from the passage. With persuasive argument passages, you will see more questions that require an understanding of the passage.

## Answering the Questions

When answering Biology questions, be sure to go through the steps laid out in chapter 3:

### Understand what you are being asked.

The first thing to do is read the entire question, including the answer choices. Reading the answer choices can help you focus your thoughts if the question stem by itself doesn't look particularly manageable. Using your reading comprehension skills, simplify the question to its bare essentials. Translate the question into your own words if necessary.

Here is a question that might appear with the passage about the experiment involving polynuclear aromatic hydrocarbons presented earlier:

Which of the following best accounts for the visible colonies on Plate I?

A. Random mutations resulted in *Salmonella* cells that regained the ability to synthesize histidine.

B. The cells were able to grow because histidine is not an essential amino acid for *Salmonella*.

C. In the absence of one amino acid, *Salmonella* substituted a similar amino acid in its place.

D. Foreign chromosome fragments containing the normal genes for histidine biosynthesis were transformed into a few *Salmonella* cells.

Simplify/translate the question: what is it asking?

Here you are asked to provide an explanation for the results of an experiment.

*Figure out where to go to get any information that you need.*

Do you have enough information to answer the question? Do you need information from the passage?

> Which of the following best accounts for the visible colonies on Plate I?
>
> A.  Random mutations resulted in *Salmonella* cells that regained the ability to synthesize histidine.
>
> B.  The cells were able to grow because histidine is not an essential amino acid for *Salmonella*.
>
> C.  In the absence of one amino acid, *Salmonella* substituted a similar amino acid in its place.
>
> D.  Foreign chromosome fragments containing the normal genes for histidine biosynthesis were transformed into a few *Salmonella* cells.

This question asks for an explanation for the results of the experiment. Can you answer this question without referring to the passage? If you need information from the passage, refer to your passage map.

From your map of the passage, you should be able to quickly locate any information that you may need. Here, you are asked about the growth on Plate I. From our earlier discussion of question types, this is a question that requires an understanding of the passage. If you don't remember the results, look back at the passage to refresh your memory, using your passage map as a guide.

Here is a question that might appear with a passage about pattern formation:

> Congenital defects in the skeletal structures of the limbs can be traced back to which of the following primary germ layer?
>
> A.  Mesoderm
>
> B.  Ectoderm
>
> C.  Endoderm
>
> D.  Notochord

This question can be answered without any information from the passage.

Although this question might appear with a passage regarding pattern formation, you are not required to know any information from the passage. Even if you have not seen the passage, there is enough information given in the question stem to allow you to answer this question.

*Integrating your science knowledge with any necessary passage research, determine the correct answer.*

Which of the following best accounts for the visible colonies on Plate I?

A. Random mutations resulted in *Salmonella* cells that regained the ability to synthesize histidine.

B. The cells were able to grow because histidine is not an essential amino acid for *Salmonella*.

C. In the absence of one amino acid, *Salmonella* substituted a similar amino acid in its place.

D. Foreign chromosome fragments containing the normal genes for histidine biosynthesis were transformed into a few *Salmonella* cells.

This question asks for an explanation for the results of the experiment. Using your passage map, you referred to the diagram presenting the results of the experiment and noted that Plate I showed relatively little growth compared with Plates III and IV. Try to formulate an explanation before going through the answer choices. If you are stuck, go through all of the answer choices and use your reasoning skills to eliminate wrong answer choices.

This is the step where you bring all the previous steps together with your science knowledge to determine the correct answer. Prior to arriving at this step, you need to understand what you are being asked and gather any information you may need from the passage. Once these tasks are accomplished, use your reasoning and/or calculation skills together with your science knowledge to arrive at the answer.

Try to formulate your own explanation before going through the answer choices. Plate I had *Salmonella* alone, with no additional chemicals or preparations. In the absence of other factors, random mutations will cause some strains of *Salmonella* to acquire the ability to make histidine. Thus Choice **A** is the correct answer.

Alternatively, go through all of the answer choices. Choice **A** sounds reasonable, since random mutation brings about genetic variability in a population. Choice **B** is inconsistent with information presented in the passage. In Paragraph 2, it is stated that the *Salmonella* strain used in the experiment is unable to grow in the absence of histidine. This means that for this strain, histidine is an essential amino acid. Choice **C** does not make sense, since from the passage, this strain of *Salmonella* is unable to grow in the absence of histidine. Choice **D** is not possible, since the plate contains *Salmonella* alone, and no other organisms from which genetic material could be transformed into the *Salmonella*.

The next few pages contain a list of Biology concepts and skills you should have in your MCAT arsenal before Test Day.

# IN PREPARING FOR THE MCAT, I SHOULD UNDERSTAND...

## 1. Molecular Biology

- Enzymes as biological catalysts
- Enzyme structure and function
- Competitive, noncompetitive, and feedback inhibition
- How enzymes are affected by changes in pH and temperature
- How a change in 3D structure affects an enzyme
- The difference between normal chromosomal inheritance and mitochondrial inheritance
- The basic structure of DNA and RNA
- How DNA is transcribed to RNA; regulation of transcription
- How RNA is translated to a polypeptide; regulation of transcription
- The structure and function of ribosomes
- Post-transcriptional modifications

## 2. Microbiology

- The basic structure of a bacterium
- Bacterial reproduction through binary fission
- How plasmids function in the transmission of bacterial genetic material
- The different processes by which bacteria can exchange genes: conjugation, transformation, and transduction
- The basic structure of a virus
- How bacteria and viruses differ
- The relative sizes of bacteria and viruses
- The general life cycle of a virus
- The mechanism of F plasmid transfer
- The characteristics of fungi: structural types, life history, and physiology

## 3. Generalized Eukaryotic Cell

- The functions of the major organelles
- The basic processes of cellular respiration and where they take place
- How the size of a typical eukaryotic cell compares to the size of a bacterium or virus
- Molarity and how a change in molarity affects a cell
- Structure and functions of the plasma membrane
- Osmosis, passive transport, active transport, endocytosis, exocytosis
- The structure and functions of the cytoskeleton
- Mitosis: where it falls in the cell cycle
- Mitosis: events that occur during each of the four phases
- The differences and similarities between mitosis and meiosis

## 4. Specialized Eukaryotic Cells and Tissues

- The basic structure of nerve and muscle cells
- How nerve cells and muscle cells are specialized for their unique functions
- Membrane potential, resting potential, action potential
- Saltatory conduction
- How calcium functions in the regulation of muscle contraction
- The characteristics of different types of muscle: striated, smooth, and cardiac
- The characteristics of cartilage

## 5. Nervous and Endocrine Systems

- The organization of the nervous system
- The difference between sensor and effector neurons
- How a nervous impulse is transmitted across the synapse
- The sympathetic and parasympathetic nervous systems ("fight or flight" versus "rest and digest")
- The structure of the ear
- The mechanism of hearing
- The structure of the eye
- The mechanism of vision
- The mechanism of taste
- The mechanism of smell
- How peptide hormones utilize second messengers
- The major endocrine glands, what hormones they produce, what organs the hormones act on, and what their effects are
- Negative and positive feedback
- The cellular mechanisms of hormone action
- Hormone transport
- Homeostasis
- How pairs of hormones function in feedback loops to maintain homeostasis
- How a reflex arc works

## 6. Circulatory, Lymphatic, and Immune Systems

- The functions of the circulatory system
- The role of the circulatory system in thermoregulation
- The structure and function of the heart and blood vessels
- The path of blood flow through the body
- Systolic and diastolic blood pressure
- The composition of blood
- The characteristics of red blood cells that make RBCs ideal for transporting oxygen
- The major organs and structures of the immune system
- How the body develops tolerance to "self" antigens

- The differences between the specific and nonspecific immune responses
- The roles of T and B lymphocytes in the immune response
- Where the cells of the immune system are produced and where they mature
- Antigens, antibodies, and antigen-antibody interaction
- The structures and functions of the lymphatic system

## 7.    Digestive and Excretory Systems

- The structures and functions of the digestive system
- Where each of the following is digested: protein, fat, carbohydrate
- What organs produce/store the various digestive enzymes, their substrates, and where they are secreted
- How the structure of the intestine enhances absorption of nutrients
- The structure and function of the kidney
- The structure and function of the nephron
- How urine is formed

## 8.    Muscle and Skeletal Systems

- What types of protein make up muscle fibers
- The functions of muscle
- The differences between voluntary and involuntary muscles
- How muscles contract, and the role of $Ca^{++}$ and ATP
- The functions of the skeletal system
- The structure of bone
- The role of bone as a calcium reservoir
- The structure and function of joints
- The role of cartilage, ligaments, and tendons

## 9.    Respiratory and Skin Systems

- The structures of the respiratory system
- The mechanics underlying ventilation
- Where gas exchange takes place in the lung
- The role of surfactant in gas exchange
- The role of the respiratory system in thermoregulation, protection against disease, and protection against particulate matter
- The basic anatomy of the skin
- How the skin helps regulate temperature
- The role of the skin as an excretory organ
- The role of the skin as a protective barrier

## 10. Reproductive System and Development

- The structures and functions of the male and female reproductive tracts
- The processes of spermatogenesis and oogenesis (similarities and differences)
- The structure and functions of the placenta
- Embryogenesis: fertilization, cleavage, blastulation, gastrulation, neurulation
- The major structures derived from the three germ layers: ectoderm, mesoderm, endoderm
- The mechanisms of development: cell specialization; determination; differentiation; induction

## 11. Genetics and Evolution

- The advantages of sexual reproduction over asexual reproduction
- How to use a Punnett square to solve basic genetics problems
- Meiosis: where it falls in the cell cycle
- Meiosis: events that occur during each of the phases
- The differences and similarities between mitosis and meiosis
- How meiosis and random mutation increase the genetic variability in a population
- How the Kingdom/Phylum/Class/Order/Family/Genus/Species classification system works
- The concept of "fitness" in evolutionary terms
- The conditions for Hardy–Weinberg equilibrium
- How to apply the Hardy–Weinberg equations to population genetics problems

# BIOLOGY PRACTICE SET

## Answer Sheet

1 Ⓐ Ⓑ Ⓒ Ⓓ
2 Ⓐ Ⓑ Ⓒ Ⓓ
3 Ⓐ Ⓑ Ⓒ Ⓓ
4 Ⓐ Ⓑ Ⓒ Ⓓ
5 Ⓐ Ⓑ Ⓒ Ⓓ

6 Ⓐ Ⓑ Ⓒ Ⓓ
7 Ⓐ Ⓑ Ⓒ Ⓓ
8 Ⓐ Ⓑ Ⓒ Ⓓ
9 Ⓐ Ⓑ Ⓒ Ⓓ
10 Ⓐ Ⓑ Ⓒ Ⓓ

11 Ⓐ Ⓑ Ⓒ Ⓓ
12 Ⓐ Ⓑ Ⓒ Ⓓ
13 Ⓐ Ⓑ Ⓒ Ⓓ
14 Ⓐ Ⓑ Ⓒ Ⓓ
15 Ⓐ Ⓑ Ⓒ Ⓓ

16 Ⓐ Ⓑ Ⓒ Ⓓ
17 Ⓐ Ⓑ Ⓒ Ⓓ
18 Ⓐ Ⓑ Ⓒ Ⓓ
19 Ⓐ Ⓑ Ⓒ Ⓓ
20 Ⓐ Ⓑ Ⓒ Ⓓ

21 Ⓐ Ⓑ Ⓒ Ⓓ
22 Ⓐ Ⓑ Ⓒ Ⓓ
23 Ⓐ Ⓑ Ⓒ Ⓓ
24 Ⓐ Ⓑ Ⓒ Ⓓ
25 Ⓐ Ⓑ Ⓒ Ⓓ

26 Ⓐ Ⓑ Ⓒ Ⓓ
27 Ⓐ Ⓑ Ⓒ Ⓓ
28 Ⓐ Ⓑ Ⓒ Ⓓ
29 Ⓐ Ⓑ Ⓒ Ⓓ
30 Ⓐ Ⓑ Ⓒ Ⓓ

31 Ⓐ Ⓑ Ⓒ Ⓓ
32 Ⓐ Ⓑ Ⓒ Ⓓ
33 Ⓐ Ⓑ Ⓒ Ⓓ
34 Ⓐ Ⓑ Ⓒ Ⓓ
35 Ⓐ Ⓑ Ⓒ Ⓓ

36 Ⓐ Ⓑ Ⓒ Ⓓ
37 Ⓐ Ⓑ Ⓒ Ⓓ
38 Ⓐ Ⓑ Ⓒ Ⓓ
39 Ⓐ Ⓑ Ⓒ Ⓓ
40 Ⓐ Ⓑ Ⓒ Ⓓ

41 Ⓐ Ⓑ Ⓒ Ⓓ
42 Ⓐ Ⓑ Ⓒ Ⓓ
43 Ⓐ Ⓑ Ⓒ Ⓓ
44 Ⓐ Ⓑ Ⓒ Ⓓ
45 Ⓐ Ⓑ Ⓒ Ⓓ

# BIOLOGY PRACTICE SET

## Time: 60 Minutes—45 Questions

DIRECTIONS: There are seven passages and ten discrete questions in this Biology test. Each passage is followed by five questions of above-average difficulty. After reading a passage, select the one best answer to each question. If you are not certain of an answer, eliminate the alternatives that you know to be incorrect and then select an answer from the remaining alternatives. (Note that although the passages and questions are test-like, this exercise is NOT meant to be an actual MCAT test section. For full-length MCAT practice, please see Kaplan *MCAT Practice Tests*).

## Passage I (Questions 1–5)

Endometriosis, a common cause of female sterility, is a condition in which endometrial tissue grows in locations outside the uterus, typically within the pelvic cavity. This abnormal endometrial tissue is nearly identical to that of the uterine endometrium, and is under the influence of the same ovarian hormones. Therefore, abnormal endometrial tissue periodically menstruates. This leads to an extensive accumulation of blood that causes the development of fibrous tissue (fibrosis) throughout the pelvis. Fibrosis can enshroud the ovaries as well as block the fallopian tubes.

There are three theories as to the cause of endometriosis. The first, known as the *regurgitation theory*, postulates that endometriosis is the result of backflow of menstrual tissue through the fallopian tubes. The second, the *metaplastic theory*, proposes that coelomic epithelium (the lining of the abdominal cavity) is transformed into abnormal endometrial tissue. The third theory, known as the *vascular or lymphatic dissemination theory*, suggests that endometrial glands are transported from the uterus to other locations by the circulatory or lymphatic systems.

Women suffering from endometriosis usually experience severe pelvic pain and painful menstruation. Treatment depends on the age and health of the patient, as well as her desire to have children. One possible treatment is the pharmacological suppression of ovarian hormone function to arrest the activity of the abnormal tissue. Another course of action is the surgical removal of as much of the abnormal tissue as possible.

1. The periodic bleeding of the nonuterine endometrial tissue is directly induced by which of the following hormonal changes?

   A. Increased secretion of FSH and LH
   B. Decreased secretion of FSH and LH
   C. Increased secretion of estrogen and progesterone
   D. Decreased secretion of estrogen and progesterone

2. Suppose that a woman with endometriosis takes estrogen and progesterone pills continuously to suppress ovarian hormone function. One event of the reproductive cycle that will nonetheless occur is

   A. secretion of gonadotropin-releasing hormone.
   B. implantation of the ovum.
   C. atrophy of the corpus luteum.
   D. thickening of the endometrium.

3. Endometrial tissue has been found in sites distant from the pelvic cavity, including the lungs and the nasal mucosa. Which of the theories is consistent with this information?

       I. Regurgitation theory
       II. Metaplastic theory
       III. Vascular or lymphatic dissemination theory

   A. I only
   B. III only
   C. I and III only
   D. II and III only

4. In 25–50% of cases of female infertility, endometriosis is diagnosed as the underlying cause. The most likely reason that a woman with endometriosis becomes infertile is that

    A. the ovum cannot enter the fallopian tubes.

    B. the zygote becomes implanted in abnormal endometrial tissue.

    C. ovarian hormone function is suppressed.

    D. ovulation cannot occur.

5. It is known that retrograde menstruation through the fallopian tubes is common even in healthy women. It can therefore be inferred that if the regurgitation theory is correct, then

    A. endometriosis is probably the result of differentiation of the coelomic epithelial lining.

    B. genetic, hormonal, or immunological factors are probably also involved in endometriosis.

    C. there must be a variety of conditions that cause irregular menstruation.

    D. endometriosis is a natural occurrence in the course of most women's reproductive lives.

## Passage II (Questions 6–10)

In the average adult, the small intestine absorbs around 7 liters of water per day. Most of the water is transported passively, driven by the osmotic gradient generated by sodium-potassium pumps in the capillary-side membrane of the epithelial cells. It has been suggested that water is also brought into the cell by secondary active transport, coupled to the transport of sodium and glucose into the epithelial cells by proteins in the lumenal membrane.

The osmotic movement of water has been understood for many years. Sodium pumps in the membrane adjacent to the capillaries transport sodium out of the cell into the interstitial fluid. This lowers the concentration of sodium within the cell and generates a high concentration of sodium in the interstitial fluid. Sodium is absorbed from the lumen of the small intestine, down its concentration gradient, in cotransport with glucose or amino acids. In concert with the movement of sodium from the lumen into the interstitial space, water moves by osmosis, through the cell and across the tight junctions between cells. Both water and sodium then diffuse into the capillary system of the villus. It is important to note that water can diffuse across the phospholipid bilayer directly. Although this movement of water is associated with the transport of sodium (and other solutes), it is not directly coupled with the activity of a membrane transport protein.

Passive osmosis can only occur from a hypotonic to a hypertonic environment. Thus, it does not describe the ability of the small intestine to absorb water when the contents of the small intestine have a higher osmolarity than the blood. It has been proposed that $Na^+$-glucose-water cotransport proteins exist. These membrane proteins move a water molecule into the cell with each sodium ion and glucose molecule it caries across the membrane. These proteins can transport water uphill (against the water concentration gradient) and provide an explanation for the observed absorption of water when the lumenal contents are hyperosmolar.

**GO ON TO THE NEXT PAGE.**

6. Assume that water is transported only by passive mechanisms. Which of the following best describes the effect of oubain, a $Na^+/K^+$ ATPase inhibitor, on the absorption of water in the small intestine?

A. Water will be absorbed only if the lumen is hypertonic to the blood.

B. Water will only be absorbed if the lumen is hypotonic to the blood.

C. Water will be absorbed if the lumen is hypertonic or isotonic to the blood.

D. Water will be absorbed if the lumen is hypotonic or isotonic to the blood.

7. A researcher observes no absorption of water from a hypertonic $Na^+$ solution in the lumen of a small-intestine tissue sample. Which of the following observations would support the claim that water is absorbed by secondary active transport, as described in the passage?

A. Addition of $Na^+$ to the lumen does not promote water absorption.

B. Dilution of the lumen solution promotes water absorption.

C. Addition of glucose to the lumen promotes water absorption.

D. Addition of $Na^+$ to the lumen promotes water absorption.

8. A single intestinal epithelial cell is exposed to an isotonic solution of salts, glucose, and amino acids. Which of the following would be a good means of monitoring the relative activity of the proposed water cotransporter?

A. Tracking the usage of ATP with radiolabeled phosphate

B. Measuring minute changes in cell volume over time

C. Observing the uptake of radiolabeled glucose

D. Measuring cell metabolic activity through purification of mitochondrial by-products

9. The large intestine uses the same passive absorption mechanism described in the passage to absorb the water which the small intestine was insufficiently efficient to absorb. Which of the following characteristics of the large intestine contributes to the greater efficiency of this mechanism in the large intestine than in the small intestine?

A. The endothelium of the large intestine has tighter tight junctions that block the leakage of sodium ion back into the lumen.

B. The large-intestine endothelium has more powerful $Na^+/K^+$ pumps that transport 5 $Na^+$ for each ATP hydrolyzed.

C. The greater surface area of the large-intestine endothelium facilitates more efficient absorption.

D. The greater length of the large intestine provides a longer exposure to the lumenal contents.

10. Which diagram best illustrates the co-transporter proposed in the last paragraph of the passage?

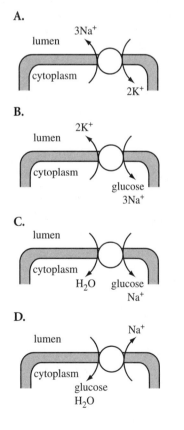

## Passage III (Questions 11–15)

Leber's hereditary optic neuropathy (LHON) is a neurodegenerative disease of the optic nerve that causes bilateral loss of central vision that eventually leads to blindness.

LHON is an unusual genetic disease in that it results from a mutation in the mitochondrial genome. The defect is a transition mutation where an adenine is erroneously substituted for a guanine.

A definitive diagnosis of LHON is made through analysis of a person's DNA. A sample of a patient's DNA is amplified via PCR technology and then analyzed for the gain or loss of restriction enzyme sites. Restriction enzymes are bacterial DNAases that recognize specific DNA sequences (about 6 nucleotides in length) and cleave the DNA at that site. The digested DNA is then run through gel electrophoresis to separate the DNA fragments according to size. Larger fragments cannot pass through the gel as freely as smaller fragments and so remain closer to the top of the gel.

A researcher analyzing a patient's DNA performs a restriction enzyme analysis using the restriction enzyme Acc I. The LHON mutation causes the loss of the Acc I restriction enzyme site. Lane 1 contains DNA size markers, lane 2 contains an undigested sample of the patient's DNA, lane 3 contains a normal DNA sample treated with Acc I, and lane 4 contains the patient's sample treated with the enzyme.

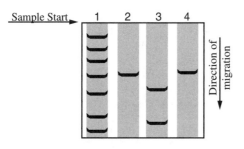

**Figure 1**

A sample that is suspected of having the LHON defect is confirmed by DNA sequencing. As evidenced from Figure 2, there is a loss of guanine and an addition of adenine at the expected location within the gene controlling the disease.

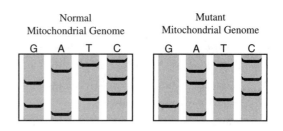

**Figure 2**

11. A transition mutation is

    **A.**  a point mutation in which a purine is substituted for a purine.

    **B.**  a point mutation in which a pyrimidine is substituted for a purine.

    **C.**  an insertion mutation in which a purine is substituted for a purine.

    **D.**  an insertion mutation in which a pyrimidine is substituted for a purine.

12. The patient whose DNA digest is shown in Figure 1

    **A.**  gained an Acc I site and has LHON.

    **B.**  gained an Acc I site and does not have LHON.

    **C.**  lost an Acc I site and has LHON.

    **D.**  lost an Acc I site and does not have LHON.

13. A researcher analyzing a sample of DNA performs a restriction enzyme analysis using the restriction enzyme Mae III. The LHON mutation causes a gain of a Mae III restriction enzyme site. Compared to normal DNA treated with this enzyme, the DNA from a patient with LHON treated with Mae III would be expected to

    **A.**  travel a shorter distance during gel electrophoresis.

    **B.**  travel a greater distance during gel electrophoresis.

    **C.**  travel the same distance during gel electrophoresis.

    **D.**  travel the same distance as it would if it were not treated with the Mae III enzyme.

**GO ON TO THE NEXT PAGE.**

14. Although LHON invariably leads to blindness, a patient with LHON retains normal pupillary responses to light. This suggests that

    **A.**  drops of epinephrine applied to the eye will cause pupil dilation.

    **B.**  the afferent nerve fibers are completely destroyed.

    **C.**  the sympathetic response of pupil contraction is intact.

    **D.**  the patient can regain vision.

15. Sperm that are to be used for artificial insemination are not checked for the genetically inheritable LHON because

    **A.**  restriction enzyme analysis is expensive and time-consuming.

    **B.**  sperm with defective mitochondria do not produce enough energy to reach the egg.

    **C.**  the acrosomal reaction cannot occur with sperm that have defective mitochondria.

    **D.**  when sperm and egg fuse, mitochondria do not enter the egg.

**GO ON TO THE NEXT PAGE.**

## Passage IV (Questions 16–20)

Humans have a remarkable ability to acclimatize to high altitudes up to 12,000 feet with little detrimental effect.

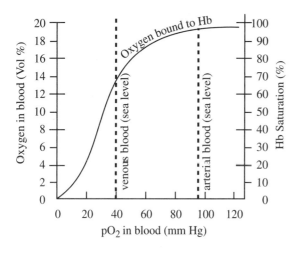

**Figure 1**

When a mountain climber ascends to 10,000 feet, the atmospheric $pO_2$ can decrease from 104 mm Hg (at sea level) to 60 mm Hg. Figure 1 shows that at 60 mm Hg, the hemoglobin is still around 90% saturated. At this altitude, when the hemoglobin releases oxygen to the tissues, the venous blood $pO_2$ falls to 35 mm Hg, only 5 mm Hg lower than its normal value. Hemoglobin's bonding characteristics are very effective at maintaining delivery of oxygen, but the body can actually alter its functioning in a number of ways to respond to low atmospheric $pO_2$.

Acclimatization to altitude occurs in a number of ways:

I.  The body immediately responds by increasing ventilation to around 65% above normal. This increase leads to the exhalation of $CO_2$ and an increase in blood pH which tends to inhibit the respiratory center and oppose the stimulatory effect of decreased $pO_2$. Over a period of 2–5 days, this inhibition declines and ventilation can increase up to five times normal.

II. After about 2 weeks at high altitude, the concentration of erythrocytes increases. Consequently, hemoglobin concentration in the blood increases as well.

III. At the time of exposure to low atmospheric pressure, the body increases cardiac output. The cardiac output falls back to normal after about 2 weeks. Over time, there is an increase in the capillarity of the tissues.

IV. In humans native to high altitudes, mitochondria and oxidative enzymes are more plentiful than in humans born at sea level. This cellular acclimatization allows more efficient oxygen utilization.

16. According to the graph in Figure 1, under normal conditions the body's tissues utilize approximately

    A.  75% of the oxygen bound to Hb.

    B.  75% of the oxygen transported in the blood (in solution and bound to Hb).

    C.  50% of the oxygen transported in the blood (in solution and bound to Hb).

    D.  25% of the oxygen bound to Hb.

17. A blood sample taken one week following exposure to high altitude would contain

    A.  a significantly higher concentration of erythrocytes.

    B.  a somewhat higher concentration of erythropoietin.

    C.  a much lower concentration of erythropoietin.

    D.  a significantly lower volume of oxygen (in solution and bound to hemoglobin).

18. According to the passage, two weeks after exposure to high altitude the cardiac output falls back to its normal level. This does not impair the delivery of oxygen to the tissues because

    A.  although the heart rate decreases, the stroke volume remains the same.

    B.  the respiratory rate will have increased to 65% of its normal value.

    C.  after two weeks, the concentration of hemoglobin in the blood has increased and thus oxygen transport is more efficient.

    D.  after two weeks, the number of mitochondria in the cells has increased, and thus oxygen transport is more efficient.

**GO ON TO THE NEXT PAGE.**

**19.** The acclimatizations described in the passage would alter the curve in Figure 1

  **A.**  by shifting it to the right.

  **B.**  by shifting it to the left.

  **C.**  by increasing the slope.

  **D.**  not at all.

**20.** At an altitude of 10,000 feet, blood in the pulmonary arteries has a $pO_2$ closest to

  **A.**  90 mm Hg.

  **B.**  60 mm Hg.

  **C.**  40 mm Hg.

  **D.**  35 mm Hg.

**GO ON TO THE NEXT PAGE.**

## Passage V (Questions 21–25)

Diseases that affect renal function can grouped according to two syndromes, the nephrotic and nephritic.

*Nephrotic Syndrome*

The nephrotic syndrome is caused by the release of an unknown chemical mediator from leukocytes, possibly from T cells, that damages glomerular capillary beds. Proteoglycans that electrostatically repel proteins from Bowman's capsule are damaged, allowing proteins (mostly albumin, the predominant protein in the blood) to leak into the nephron. Reabsorptive mechanisms are quickly overwhelmed, resulting in a sustained proteinuria that causes a severe drop in serum albumin levels resulting in decreased plasma osmotic pressure. This drop in osmotic pressure causes generalized swelling of the body, especially the extremities.

*Nephritic Syndrome*

The nephritic syndrome is the result of an unchecked inflammatory response. Circulating immune complexes deposit beneath the capillary epithelial cells of the glomeruli, attracting leukocytes that infiltrate and injure the cells by stimulating an inflammation reaction. The damage allows red blood cells to enter the nephron, but does not allow a significant amount of protein to escape. The blood loss induces hemodynamic changes that reduce the amount of blood reaching the kidneys, causing decreased urine production. The retention of water and release of renin result in severe hypertension.

To determine if a person has an abnormal amount of protein in their urine, a total protein assay is performed. A 24-hour urine sample is collected and the amount of light the sample absorbs is measured using a spectro-photometer. The protein concentration can then be determined using a calibrated curve, like the one shown below. The normal range for total protein urine concentration is 3.5–5.0 gm/dL.

| Patient | A | B | C | D |
|---|---|---|---|---|
| Absorption | 1.0 | 1.9 | 3.25 | 1.75 |

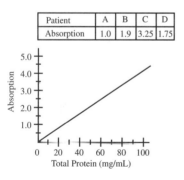

21. Which of the following is true for both the nephrotic and nephritic syndromes?

    A. Elevated protein in the urine

    B. Blood in the urine

    C. Hypertension

    D. Immune-mediated

22. Why is swelling part of the nephrotic syndrome?

    A. Injury to the nephron causes water retention.

    B. Fluid cannot be reabsorbed at the venule end of capillaries.

    C. The drop in osmotic pressure results in ADH release, resulting in water reabsorption and swelling.

    D. The drop in blood pressure stimulates the Starling response, which serves to increase interstitial fluid.

23. How can the release of renin cause hypertension?

    A. It stimulates an increases in salt and water reabsorption.

    B. It stimulates the release of ADH, resulting in water reabsorption.

    C. It stimulates the release of cortisone from the adrenal glands, resulting in salt and water reabsorption.

    D. It activates the sympathetic nervous system, causing vasoconstriction.

24. In a normal individual, all of the following are filtered through the glomerulus into Bowman's capsule EXCEPT

    I. sodium.

    II. urea.

    III. red blood cells.

    A. I only

    B. II only

    C. III only

    D. II and III only

**GO ON TO THE NEXT PAGE.**

**25.** Which of the following patients have proteinuria?

    **A.**   A

    **B.**   A and B

    **C.**   C

    **D.**   B and D

**GO ON TO THE NEXT PAGE.**

## Passage VI (Questions 26–30)

Antibody production is the result of a close interaction between two types of lymphocytes: B cells and helper T cells. When an animal is primed (injected) with an antigen, certain B cells synthesize antigen-specific antibodies, while other B cells and helper T cells become primed to that antigen. This is known as the *primary response*. When the animal is subsequently boosted (reinjected) with the antigen, the primed helper T cells stimulate the primed B cells to proliferate into antibody-secreting cells; this is known as the *secondary response*.

Injecting an animal with a foreign organic compound of low molecular weight—a *hapten*—fails to trigger antihapten antibody production unless the animal has been previously primed with a hapten-carrier complex. The *carrier* is a foreign protein to which the hapten has been chemically bound. When a rabbit is injected with a complex of ovalbumin (OA) and dinitrophenol (DNP), the helper T cells become primed to the carrier, OA, while the B cells become primed to the hapten, DNP. Boosting the rabbit with DNP–OA several weeks later results in substantial anti-DNP antibody production. This is known as the *carrier effect*.

The consequences of the carrier effect can be demonstrated by three simple experiments that utilize DNP, OA, and BSA (bovine serum albumin), another carrier.

*Experiment 1*

Rabbit 1 was primed with DNP–BSA and then boosted with DNP–BSA; Rabbit 2 was primed with DNP–OA and then boosted with DNP–OA.

*Experiment 2*

Rabbit 3 was primed with DNP–BSA and then boosted with DNP–OA; Rabbit 4 was primed with a mixture of DNP–BSA and free OA and then boosted with DPN–OA.

*Experiment 3*

Rabbit 5 was primed with DNP–BSA, Rabbit 6 was primed with free OA, and Rabbit 7 was irradiated, which rendered it incapable of immune response. B cells from Rabbit 5 and helper T cells from Rabbit 6 were transferred to Rabbit 7. Rabbit 7 was then boosted first with DNP–BSA and then with DNP–OA.

The rabbits' secondary responses were measured in terms of anti-DNP antibody production. The results are summarized in Tables 1 and 2.

**Table 1    Experiments 1 and 2**

| Rabbit | Primer | Booster | Anti-DNP antibody production |
|---|---|---|---|
| Rabbit 1 | DNP–BSA | DNP–BSA | Yes |
| Rabbit 2 | DNP–OA | DNP–OA | Yes |
| Rabbit 3 | DNP–BSA | DNP–OA | No |
| Rabbit 4 | DNP–BSA+ free OA | DNP–OA | Yes |

**Table 2    Experiment 3**

| Rabbit | Primer | Booster | Anti-DNP antibody production |
|---|---|---|---|
| Rabbit 5 | DNP–BSA | — | — |
| Rabbit 6 | free OA | — | — |
| Rabbit 7* | — | DNP–BSA | No |
| Rabbit 7* | — | DNP–OA | Yes |

*Rabbit 5 B cells + Rabbit 6 helper T cells

26. The results of Experiments 1 and 2 demonstrate that the secondary response

   A. is stronger when DNP is used as the carrier.
   B. is stronger when OA is used as the carrier.
   C. requires a lower dose of hapten-carrier complex than the primary response.
   D. requires priming and boosting with the same carrier.

27. Based on information in the passage, priming and boosting a rabbit with DNP-human albumin complex (DNP–HA) would most likely result in the production of

   A. anti-DNP–HA antibodies following the primer injection.
   B. anti-DNP–HA antibodies following the booster injection.
   C. anti-DNP antibodies following the primer injection.
   D. anti-DNP antibodies following the booster injection.

**GO ON TO THE NEXT PAGE.**

**28.** In Experiment 3, which of the following statements best accounts for the absence of a secondary response when Rabbit 7 was boosted with DNP–BSA?

   **A.** Rabbit 5 did not have helper T cells primed to BSA.

   **B.** Rabbit 7 did not have helper T cells primed to BSA.

   **C.** Rabbit 7 did not have B cells primed to DNP.

   **D.** The secondary response to DNP–OA prevented a secondary response to DNP–BSA.

**29.** In a modified version of Experiment 3, Rabbit 7 is primed with DNP–BSA following irradiation; the rest of the experiment remains unchanged. Would you expect anti-DNP antibody production when Rabbit 7 is boosted with DNP–BSA?

   **A.** No, because irradiation prevents Rabbit 7 from forming BSA-primed helper T cells, which are necessary for anti-DNP antibody production.

   **B.** No, because Rabbit 7 would now produce antibodies against the cells transferred from Rabbits 5 and 6.

   **C.** Yes, because Rabbit 7's own BSA-primed helper T cells would stimulate Rabbit 5's transferred B cells to produce the antibodies.

   **D.** Yes, because Rabbit 7's own DNP-primed B cells would stimulate Rabbit 5's transferred B cells to produce the antibodies.

**30.** The antibodies produced during a typical primary response are predominantly of the IgM class, while those produced during a typical secondary response are predominantly of the IgG class. Based on this information, which of the following statements is true?

   **A.** Rabbit 7 produced equal amounts of anti-DNP IgM and anti-DNP IgG after being boosted with DNP–OA.

   **B.** Rabbit 7 produced equal amounts of anti-DNP IgM and anti-DNP IgG after being boosted with DNP–BSA.

   **C.** Rabbit 4 produced anti-OA IgM after being primed with free OA and produced anti-OA IgG after being boosted with DNP–OA.

   **D.** Rabbit 4 produced both anti-OA IgM and anti-DNP IgM after being primed with DNP–BSA and free OA.

**GO ON TO THE NEXT PAGE.**

## Passage VII (Questions 31–35)

*Tat*, an HIV (human immunodeficiency virus) protein, plays a pivotal role in the emergence of infectious HIV from the latent state. *Tat* is secreted from HIV-positive cells and taken up by other cells. The *Tat* protein, which is encoded by two exons spliced together, is believed to be involved in the activation of T cells, which is a requirement for productive HIV infection.

*Tumor necrosis factor* (TNF), a cytokine, may be a target of *Tat*, since TNF is integral to T-cell function. (Cytokines are proteins produced by cells of the immune system.) TNF initiates and regulates the immune response by inducing the production of other cytokines. TNF also activates lymphocytes, and functions as a growth factor for several cell types, including helper T cells. The following experiment was designed to determine the effect of the *Tat* protein on host immune function, as measured by TNF gene expression.

Nonactivated T cells from HIV-negative donors were cultured for 24 hours in the following six separate media:

a. cells alone
b. 5 μg/mL of PHA—a mitogen
   (Both mitogens and antigens induce lymphocyte activation.)
$c_1$. 100 ng/mL of *Tat* peptide
$c_2$. 1 ng/mL of *Tat* peptide
$d_1$. 5 μg/mL of PHA and
      100 ng/mL of *Tat* peptide
$d_2$. 5 μg/mL of PHA and
      1 ng/mL of *Tat* peptide

mRNA from the T cells of all six media were then isolated and 1.25- and 2.5-μg samples were run on a gel to separate the mRNA by size. The mRNA was transferred to nitrocellulose paper and hybridized with a [32]P-labeled cDNA probe specific for human TNF. After exposure to film, the intensities of the bands were determined and the results are presented below in Table 1. The intensities are directly proportional to the amount of TNF gene expression.

**Table 1**

| Cell culture | Relative intensities of TNF gene expression in T-cells | | | |
| --- | --- | --- | --- | --- |
| | *Tat* peptide from Exon 1 | | *Tat* peptide from Exon 2 | |
| | 1.25 mg mRNA | 2.5 mg mRNA | 1.25 mg mRNA | 2.5 mg mRNA |
| a. cells alone | 33.70 | 62.00[3] | 34.07 | 69.14[3] |
| b. cells + PHA | 56.80 | 111.60[3] | 55.93 | 111.86[3] |
| $c_1$. cells + *Tat* (100 ng/mL) | 81.39[1] | 164.78[1,3] | 35.49 | 69.98 |
| $c_2$. cells + *Tat* (1 ng/mL) | 62.01[1] | 123.02[1,3] | 34.66 | 66.32 |
| $d_1$. cells + PHA + *Tat* (100 ng/mL) | 32.96[2] | 60.92[2,3] | 33.82[2] | 68.64[2,3] |
| $d_2$. cells + PHA + *Tat* (1 ng/mL) | 20.54[2] | 42.08[2,3] | 21.35[2] | 43.70[2,3] |

[1] Significantly different from Culture a

[2] Significantly different from Culture b

[3] Significantly different from 1.25-μg mRNA sample

**GO ON TO THE NEXT PAGE.**

31. Which of the following cell cultures served as controls for this experiment?

    I.   Culture a
    II.  Culture b
    III. Cultures $c_1$ and $c_2$
    IV.  Cultures $d_1$ and $d_2$

    A. I only
    B. III only
    C. I and II only
    D. I and IV only

32. According to Table 1, which sample resulted in the fewest TNF transcripts?

    A. 1.25 µg mRNA from Culture a, Exon 1
    B. 2.5 µg mRNA from Culture $c_1$, Exon 1
    C. 2.5 µg mRNA from Culture $c_1$, Exon 2
    D. 1.25 µg mRNA from Culture $d_2$, Exon 1

33. Based on the results of this experiment, which of the following statements best describes the effect that *Tat* peptide from Exon 1 has on HIV pathogenesis?

    A. Represses TNF gene expression in nonactivated T cells, thereby inhibiting the host immune response

    B. Stimulates TNF gene expression in non-activated T cells, thereby activating the cells and priming them for HIV infection

    C. Stimulates TNF gene expression in activated T cells, thereby enhancing the rate of cellular division by acting as a growth factor

    D. Does not affect TNF gene expression in nonactivated T cells, thereby inhibiting host immune response

34. Which of the following experimental results might be viewed as contrary to the trend observed in Cultures $c_1$ and $c_2$ with *Tat* peptide from Exon 1, where *Tat* caused an increase in TNF gene expression?

    A. Greater repression of TNF gene expression in Culture $d_2$ than in Culture $d_1$, due to *Tat* from Exon 1

    B. Greater repression of TNF gene expression in Culture $d_1$ than in Culture $d_2$, due to *Tat* from Exon 1

    C. Greater TNF gene expression in 2.5-µg mRNA samples than in 1.25 µg samples of the same culture

    D. Greater TNF gene expression in Culture b than in Culture a, due to *Tat* from Exon 1

35. The *Tat* protein found circulating in the blood of HIV-positive patients has a molecular weight of 16,000 daltons, but when the viral DNA containing the *Tat* gene is inserted into prokaryotic cells, the resulting protein has a molecular weight of 33,000 daltons. This difference most likely results because the protein synthesized in the prokaryote

    A. did not interact with human TNF.
    B. was translated from a longer mRNA transcript.
    C. underwent random mutations during its synthesis.
    D. was translated after exposure to PHA.

## Discrete Questions (Questions 36–45)

36. What is the approximate pH of the intermembrane space of a mitochondrion?

    A. 6
    B. 7
    C. 8
    D. 10

**GO ON TO THE NEXT PAGE.**

37. Which of the following would be expected to contain an abundant amount of smooth endoplasmic recticulum?

    A. Adrenal cortical cells

    B. Epithelial cells

    C. Endothelial cells

    D. Adipose cells

38. Which of the following intramolecular forces help stabilize the DNA double helix?

    I. Hydrogen bonding between complementary nitrogenous bases

    II. Electostatic attraction between adjacent phosphate groups

    III. Hydrogen bonding between adjacent ribose sugars

    A. I only

    B. I and II only

    C. I and III only

    D. I, II, and III

39. A scientist transplants embryonic cells from the arm bud of a fetal frog to the head. The cells continue to develop into an arm. The removed cells must have been

    A. totipotent.

    B. differentiated.

    C. mutant.

    D. determined.

40. The widespread use of antibacterial soaps has lead to a greater prevalence of resistant strains of bacteria. This is an example of

    A. stabilizing selection.

    B. directional selection.

    C. disruptive selection.

    D. speciation.

41. Osteoblasts secrete large quantities of alkaline phosphatase when they are actively depositing bone matrix. Insufficient dietary calcium would be indicated by

    A. increased concentration of alkaline phosphatase in the circulation.

    B. decreased concentration of alkaline phosphatase in the circulation.

    C. decreased concentration of osteoclasts in the circulation.

    D. increased concentration of $Ca^{++}$ in the circulation.

42. What is the mode of inheritance of the genetic disorder depicted in the following pedigree chart?

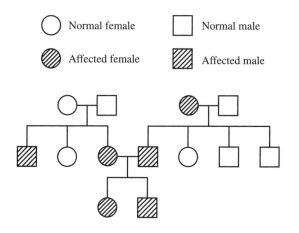

    A. Huntington's disease, an autosomal dominant disease

    B. Tay–Sachs disease, an autosomal recessive disease

    C. Retinitis pigmentosa, an X-linked dominant disease

    D. Duchenne muscular dystrophy, an X-linked recessive disease

**GO ON TO THE NEXT PAGE.**

**43.** A mature human sperm cell contains 23 chromosomes. How many chromosomes are present in the secondary spermatocytes arrested in metaphase of meiosis II?

    **A.** 23 (22 somatic plus either one X or one Y chromosome)

    **B.** 24 (23 somatic plus either one X or one Y chromosome)

    **C.** 46 (44 somatic plus either XY or XX chromosomes)

    **D.** 92 (88 somatic plus either two XY or two XX chromosomes)

**44.** The nucleus of a tadpole intestinal cell is removed and transplanted into a denucleated frog zygote. The zygote develops normally after the transplant. The experimental results suggest that

    **A.** cell differentiation is controlled by irreversibly repressing genes not needed by the cell.

    **B.** cell differentiation is controlled by selectively repressing genes not needed by the cell.

    **C.** the cytoplasm of the zygote contains all of the information needed for normal adult development in the form of RNA.

    **D.** the ribosomes found in the nucleus of the zygote are the same as those found in an adult frog.

**45.** A researcher sets up four test tubes, numbered I–IV. He adds type A blood to tube I, type B blood to tube II, type AB blood to tube III, and type O blood to tube IV. Red blood cells from a person with type A blood are added to each tube. Which of the following test tubes will contain precipitate?

    **A.** I only

    **B.** II only

    **C.** II and IV only

    **D.** II, III, and IV only

**STOP.** IF YOU FINISH BEFORE TIME HAS EXPIRED, CHECK YOUR WORK. YOU MAY GO BACK TO ANY QUESTION IN THIS PART ONLY.

**GO ON TO THE NEXT PAGE.**

# BIOLOGY PRACTICE SET

## Answer Key

**Passage I (Questions 1–5)**
1. D
2. D
3. B
4. A
5. B

**Passage II (Questions 6–10)**
6. B
7. C
8. B
9. A
10. C

**Passage III (Questions 11–15)**
11. A
12. C
13. B
14. A
15. D

**Passage IV (Questions 16–20)**
16. D
17. B
18. C
19. B
20. D

**Passage V (Questions 21–25)**
21. D
22. B
23. A
24. C
25. C

**Passage VI (Questions 26–30)**
26. D
27. D
28. B
29. A
30. C

**Passage VII (Questions 31–35)**
31. C
32. D
33. B
34. A
35. B

**Discrete Questions (Questions 36–45)**
36. A
37. A
38. A
39. D
40. B
41. B
42. B
43. A
44. B
45. C

# BIOLOGY PRACTICE SET

## Answers and Explanations

### Passage I (Questions 1–5)

**1. D**

Since the passage states that endometrial tissue outside the uterus is under the control of the same ovarian hormones that cause changes in the uterine endometrium, you can assume that the abnormal endometrial tissue will be sloughed off for the same reason that normal endometrium is sloughed off.

Menstruation occurs when there is a sudden reduction in the levels of secretion of the ovarian hormones estrogen and progesterone. This occurs approximately two weeks after ovulation. Progesterone, in particular, is essential for the maintenance of the endometrium; the drop in progesterone causes the endometrium to slough off, resulting in menstruation. A decrease in the secretion of progesterone and estrogen, therefore, is the hormonal change that induces the sloughing off of the endometrial tissue outside the uterus. Therefore, choice **C** is incorrect and choice **D** is correct. Follicle-stimulating hormone (FSH) and luteinizing hormone (LH) are gonadotropic hormones secreted by the anterior pituitary gland. FSH causes maturation of ovarian follicles in women, while LH stimulates ovulation and formation of the corpus luteum, which develops from the ruptured ovarian follicle. So choices **A** and **B** are incorrect.

For the MCAT, you should know the phases of the menstrual cycle, and also which hormones are in high concentrations in each phase. You should also be familiar with the effects of the hormones involved in the menstrual cycle.

**2. D**

Women who take birth control pills are taking estrogen and progesterone, but not continuously. At the appropriate time in their monthly cycle, the women either stop taking the pills, or take placebo pills instead. This allows menstruation to occur and a new cycle to begin. If they didn't stop taking hormone pills during part of their monthly cycle, the high level of progesterone would prevent the endometrium from ever breaking down and sloughing off. This is precisely why these hormones are used continuously to treat a patient with endometriosis: when estrogen and progesterone, in particular, are maintained at high levels, the abnormal endometrial tissue thickens but does not slough off and the bleeding is prevented. Remember, it is the secretion of progesterone and estrogen following ovulation that causes the thickening

of the endometrium in preparation for embryo implantation, and it is the decline in their secretion that causes menstruation. Thus, choice **D** is the correct answer.

Since progesterone also inhibits the secretion of gonadotropin-releasing hormone (GnRH), choice **A** is incorrect. Inhibiting GnRH in turn inhibits the secretion of LH and FSH, so the high level of progesterone in a woman being treated for endometriosis does not allow the reproductive cycle to begin again as it would in a normal female. The surge of LH that is essential in causing ovulation cannot occur either; therefore, there can be no "implantation of the ovum" (choice **B**) or "atrophy of the corpus luteum" (choice **C**).

**3. B**

Consider what each of the theories postulates as the source of the abnormal endometrial tissue. The regurgitation theory holds that the tissue comes from menstrual backflow through the fallopian tubes. Although this suffices as an explanation of the presence of endometrial tissue outside the uterus in the pelvic cavity, menstrual backflow could *not* possibly be the source of endometrial glands in the lungs or nasal mucosa. The same line of reasoning can be leveled at the metaplastic theory: If the source of abnormal tissue were the lining of the abdominal cavity, one certainly wouldn't expect to find endometrial tissue as far away as the nasal mucosa.

Having ruled out options I and II, we have one option, III, and one choice, **B**, remaining. The vascular or lymphatic dissemination theory, in contrast to the others, *does* provide a way to explain how endometrial tissue could be found so far away from the pelvic cavity; endometrial glands could be carried to the lungs, nose, or lymph nodes by the circulatory or lymphatic system. This makes choice **B** the correct answer.

This is an example of a question that requires an understanding of the passage. The passage presents several theories on endometriosis, and to answer this question, you should have an understanding of each of the theories presented. If you don't recall what each theory is about, use your map of the passage to help you locate the relevant parts of the passage.

**4. A**

When fibrous tissue covers the ovaries and blocks the fallopian tubes, an ovum expelled from a follicle during ovulation will not be able to enter one of the fallopian tubes. The ovum cannot come into contact with sperm, which means that fertilization cannot occur. This is why women suffering from endometriosis are often infertile. So, choice **B** is incorrect, and choice **A** is correct.

Ovarian hormone function, choice **C**, is not suppressed in a woman with endometriosis until she starts to undergo drug treatment, so this could not be the cause of her infertility. Inability to ovulate, choice **D**, is the most common cause of female sterility, but a woman with endometriosis can have normal ovulation and still be infertile. Thus, choices **C** and **D** are incorrect.

**5.  B**

You are asked to draw a conclusion based on two assumptions: (1) even normal women have regular menstrual backflow through the fallopian tubes and (2) the regurgitation theory is correct in that endometriosis is the result of menstrual backflow. If menstrual backflow through the fallopian tubes causes endometriosis, then why don't all women with menstrual backflow develop it? There must be something more involved; that is, there must be some factor or factors that make one woman prone to endometriosis and another woman resistant to it. The factor or factors contributing to susceptibility are likely to be genetic or hormonal or immunological, so choice **B** is correct.

None of the other choices provides an answer to the puzzle of why only certain women would develop endometriosis from menstrual backflow. Choice **A** has to do with the metaplastic theory, not the regurgitation theory, so it's incorrect. There is nothing in the question to indicate that there are a "variety of conditions that cause irregular menstruation" based on the two assumptions mentioned earlier, so choice **C** is incorrect. Endometriosis may be relatively common, but it does *not* develop in "most women," so choice **D** is incorrect. Again, choice **B** is the correct answer.

## Passage II (Questions 6–10)

**6.  B**

The passage describes the passive movement of water by osmotic pressures in the first paragraph. The $Na^+/K^+$ ATPase generates an osmotic gradient by effectively moving sodium from the lumen to the interstitial fluid and toward the circulation. This makes the lumenal content hypotonic relative to the blood and allows the flow of water from the lumen toward the blood by osmosis. If the $Na^+/K^+$ pump failed, sodium would not be moved and the concentration gradient would not be created. However, if the gradient already existed, water would still flow. Therefore, if the lumen is hypotonic to the blood, water will flow from the lumen to the blood by osmosis, answer choice **B**. Note that

if the lumen is isotonic, there will be no concentration gradient to drive the osmosis of water. If the lumen is hypertonic, water will actually flow from the blood toward the lumen by osmosis. This is what happens in cholera, a disease which makes endothelial bicarbonate pumps hyperactive, leading to oversecretion of bicarbonate ion into the lumen.

**7.  C**

The passage describes a cotransporter that actively transports $Na^+$, glucose, and water. If any of these is not present, we assume that the cotransporter will not function. Therefore, if the cotransporter exists, we do not expect water to be absorbed from a hypertonic $Na^+$ solution unless glucose is also present. If addition of glucose promotes water absorption, this supports the description of the cotransporter. Note that addition of glucose makes the solution *more* hypertonic, and so the water absorption can be explained only by active transport mechanisms (because passive transport would lead to movement of water from the tissue to the lumen).

The other answer choices do not support the claim that water is transported actively by the cotransporter. Addition of $Na^+$ to the lumen wouldn't promote passive or active transport. It does not imply the presence of the cotransporter. Choice **B** is incorrect, because water absorption is expected if the lumen is diluted and made hypotonic. Water would be absorbed by passive mechanisms even if the cotransporter were not present. This observation would not support the existence of the cotransporter. Choice **D** is incorrect, because addition of more $Na^+$ wouldn't promote absorption by the cotransporter described in the passage. Glucose is also needed.

**8.  B**

Before tackling the question, consider a single intestinal cell exposed to an isotonic solution on its lumenal side. $Na^+/K^+$ pumps on the capillary side will work to pump sodium out of the cell into the interstitial fluid (and capillaries), creating a concentration gradient for sodium. Sodium will flow down this gradient, from the lumen of the small intestine into the cell, coupled to the movement of glucose and water by the cotransport protein. Given these general conditions, consider the answer choices.

Choice **A** is incorrect, because ATP usage is not directly coupled to the activity of the cotransporter. Although ATP is used to generate the sodium gradient, this gradient is used by a number of the cell's systems besides the cotransporter. So an increase or decrease in ATP usage couldn't be directly correlated with an increase or decrease in cotransporter activity. Choice **B** is correct, because the flow of water directly affects the size of the cell. If the cell swells, this is a direct indication of the activity of the cotransporter. The Na$^+$-glucose-water cotransporter is the only means of moving water when no favorable concentration gradient exists. Choice **C** is incorrect, because it is possible that glucose is taken up by cotransporters that do not cotransport water. The passage describes two types of cotransport proteins—one that moves a Na$^+$ ion and a glucose molecule together, and another that moves a Na$^+$ ion, a glucose molecule, *and* a water molecule. So, tracking the movement of glucose will not isolate the activity of the water cotransporter. Choice **D** is incorrect, because the metabolic activity of the cell can be affected by many factors that are not associated with the water cotransporter.

**9. A**

The tighter tight junctions of the large intestine prevent the backflow of sodium from the interstitial fluid to the lumen and allow the large intestine to absorb water more efficiently. Recall that water is absorbed passively by moving water along with sodium. If sodium leaks back into the lumen, water will move with it. Also, note that the passage does not mention active cotransport of water in the large intestine.

Choice **B** is incorrect, because all sodium/potassium pumps in the body are the same. There are no "more powerful" sodium/potassium pumps. Choice **C** is incorrect, because the small intestine has a greater surface area, created by the villi and microvilli of the endothelium. Choice **D** is incorrect, because the small intestine is much longer than the large intestine.

**10. C**

The diagrams show a segment of the lumenal membrane of an endothelial cell. The passage describes a co-transporter that carries a Na$^+$, glucose, and water into the endothelial cell, as shown in choice **C**. Answer choice **A** shows the Na$^+$/K$^+$ pump. Not only is this not the cotransporter, it also only exists on the basolateral membrane of the small-intestine endothelial cells. Choice **D** is incorrect, because the movement of sodium down its concentration gradient, into the endothelial cell is what drives the transport of glucose and water (against their gradients).

## Passage III (Questions 11–15)

**11. A**

You do not need to know the definition of a transition mutation to answer this question correctly. In paragraph 2, the passage states that the LHON defect is a transition mutation in which an adenine is substituted for a guanine. When a mutation is limited to one nucleotide pair, it is called a point mutation. Choice **A** describes a point mutation involving purines, making it the correct choice. To remember which nucleotides are purines and which are pyrimidines, use the mnemonic "CUT the PY," which

should help you remember that **c**ytosine, **u**racil, and **t**hymine are the **py**rimidines.

Insertion mutations occur when one or more additional nucleotide pairs are placed within the genetic sequence. These insertions lead to frameshift mutations. Choices **C** and **D** are therefore incorrect, because nothing in the passage suggests that an insertion has occurred.

**12. C**

The fourth paragraph states that that the LHON mutation causes a loss of the Acc I restriction enzyme site. As a result, the DNA from an LHON patient will not be cleaved, and will remain as a large, intact piece. Being larger, it will not migrate though the gel as far as a cleaved DNA sample. Looking at lane 4 from Figure 1, the DNA did not migrate as far as the digested DNA sample from a normal patient in lane 3. This suggests that it was not cleaved, so the restriction site must have been lost. So at this point choices **A** and **B** can be ruled out, leaving **C** and **D** as possibilities. Since the passage states that a definitive diagnosis of LHON is made through DNA analysis, you can safely conclude that a patient with this mutation must have LHON, and thus choice **C** is correct. Choice **D** is incorrect, because there is no reason to believe that a patient can carry this mutation without having the disease.

**13. B**

This question is asking you to apply the concepts behind gel electrophoresis described in paragraph 3. The question stem states the LHON mutation causes a gain of a restriction enzyme site. Thus, the DNA will be cleaved into two pieces, whereas normal DNA will not be cleaved at all. The cleaved DNA pieces are smaller than the uncleaved DNA and so can travel further through the gel—choice **B**. The larger uncleaved DNA cannot pass through the pores of the gel easily and so gets "trapped" at the top of the gel.

**14. A**

The pupillary response to light is controlled by the autonomic nervous system. The autonomic nervous system is divided into the sympathetic nervous system (SNS) and parasympathetic nervous system (PNS). The SNS causes pupil dilation, and the PNS causes constriction. This eliminates answer choice **C**. The primary neurotransmitter involved in the SNS is epinephrine (adrenaline), and in the PNS the primary neurotransmitter is acetylcholine. If the pupillary response to light is intact, then the pupil will respond to both epinephrine (by dilating) and acetylcholine (by contracting). This confirms choice **A** as the correct answer.

Afferent nerves are responsible for delivering sensory input to the CNS. If the fibers were destroyed, as described in choice **B**, then the pupils would not be able to respond to light, and the CNS would have no way of "knowing" if light were present. Thus choice **B** is incorrect. Choice **D** is incorrect, since the question stem states that LHON always eventually leads to blindness. It is therefore impossible for patients to regain their vision.

### 15. D

This question asks you to draw on outside knowledge about reproduction, specifically about the formation of a zygote. When the sperm and egg fuse, the sperm contributes only its nucleus to the newly formed zygote, while all other cellular materials (including organelles such as mitochondria) come from the egg. The passage tells us that Leber's hereditary optic neuropathy is a mitochondrial genetic disease. As such, the disease can only be spread from a woman to her children. When a sperm and egg fuse, only the nucleus of the sperm enters the cytoplasm of the egg. So, if the sperm of a man with LHON has mitochondria with the genetic defect, there is no risk of the defective mitochondria entering the egg, and the disease will never be passed on to the next generation.

Choice **A** is incorrect; the cost of restriction enzyme analysis is beyond the scope of this passage. Choice **B** is also beyond the scope of the passage. The effect of the LHON mutation on sperm is never addressed. The only impact addressed in the passage that the mutation has on the body involved the optic nerve. Secondly, since the egg is being artificially inseminated, the sperm does not have to swim to the egg. Choice **C** is incorrect, because the acrosomal reaction involves the release of hydrolytic enzymes from the head of the sperm that digest the jelly coat of the egg. The reaction has nothing to do with mitochondria.

## Passage IV (Questions 16–20)

### 16. D

On the MCAT, pay special attention to charts and graphs. Note what is being measured, which is indicated by the column headers in a table or the labels of the axes of a graph. If a passage contains a table or graph, there will be questions that ask you to interpret the presented data in the table or graph. Here, the first thing to notice is that the graph in Figure 1 plots "pO$_2$ in the blood (mm Hg)" vs. "Hb Saturation (%)." From the graph you can see that the hemoglobin is about 97% saturated in the arteries and about 73% saturated in the veins. Thus, about 24% of the oxygen bonded to hemoglobin is taken up by the tissues, which is closest to answer choice **D**.

### 17. B

In order for the body to increase the concentration of Hb and erythrocytes in the blood two weeks after exposure, the signal to initiate this increase must come very soon after

exposure to a high altitude. That signal, the hormone erythropoietin, would be present in somewhat higher concentrations one week following exposure to high altitude.

Choice **A** is incorrect, because the increase in concentration of erythrocytes requires two weeks, as stated in the passage. Choice **C** is incorrect, because the concentration of erythropoietin will increase in order to increase the concentration of Hb and erythrocytes. Choice **D** is incorrect, because the passage indicates that the volume of oxygen in the blood will not change significantly (unless the climber is exposed to a very high altitude) even with large changes in atmospheric pO$_2$.

### 18. C

As the hemoglobin concentration increases, the cardiac output can decrease without a decrease in the oxygen delivery to the tissues. The passage states that hemoglobin concentration increases two weeks following exposure to high altitude. This is around the same time that cardiac output falls back to normal.

Choice **A** is incorrect, because the cardiac output is the product of the heart rate and the stroke volume. If the heart rate decreases and the stroke volume remains the same, the cardiac output will decrease. However, this does not explain the continued oxygen delivery to the tissues. Always be sure to answer the question that is being asked. Choice **B** is incorrect, because the respiratory rate is 65% immediately upon exposure to high altitude. By the end of two weeks, it can be as high as five times normal. Choice **D** is incorrect, because increased concentration in mitochondria only occurs in animals and people native to high altitudes. This adaptation does not increase oxygen transport.

### 19. B

This is a challenging question. First, consider which of the acclimatizations could possibly affect the hemoglobin/ oxygen dissociation curve in Figure 1. Let's consider the acclimatizations in order. First, the body responds by increasing ventilation. The passage states that the increase in ventilation "leads to increased exhalation of CO$_2$ and an increase in blood pH." Recall that the hemoglobin-oxygen dissociation curve shifts to the right with an increase in pCO$_2$ (decrease in blood pH) and shifts to the left with a decrease in pCO$_2$ (increase in blood pH). This is the Bohr effect, which allows hemoglobin to bind more oxygen in the lungs, where pCO$_2$ is low, and release more oxygen in the tissues, where pCO$_2$ is high. So increased exhalation will lead to a decreased pCO$_2$ throughout the circulation and an overall shift of the curve toward the left.

Next, examine the other acclimatizations. The concentration of erythrocytes increases after about two weeks. This would not affect the hemoglobin dissociation curve, but it would make more hemoglobin present in the blood to transport oxygen. The cardiac output also increases. This, too, would have no effect on the hemoglobin dissociation curve. Finally, the increase in mitochondria and enzymes in humans who are native to high altitudes would increase the efficiency of oxygen utilization but would not shift the hemoglobin curve.

**20.  D**

This question tests your ability to extract data from a graph and synthesize this information with information from the passage. The pulmonary arteries carry deoxygenated blood from the heart to the lungs. Therefore, the $pO_2$ in the pulmonary arteries is equal to the $pO_2$ in the systemic veins. The passage states that at 10,000 feet, "the venous blood $pO_2$ falls to 35 mm Hg." Therefore the pulmonary arteries have a $pO_2$ of around 35 mm Hg.

Choice **A** is the $pO_2$ of the systemic arteries at sea level. This is indicated in Figure 1: The dotted line that is labeled "arterial blood (sea level)" is at approximately 90 mm Hg. Choice **B** is the atmospheric $pO_2$ at around 10,000 ft. This information can be found in the first sentence after Figure 1, which states that at 10,000 feet, the atmospheric $pO_2$ can decrease "to 60 mm Hg." Choice **C** is the $pO_2$ in the venous systemic circulation at sea level. This is indicated in Figure 1: the dotted line that is labeled "venous blood (sea level)" is at approximately 40 mm Hg.

## Passage V (Questions 21–25)

**21.  D**

This question requires you to understand the basics of the nephrotic and nephritic syndromes. This is an example of a question that requires an understanding of the passage. The nephrotic and nephritic syndromes are the result of an abnormality in the immune system, specifically within leukocytes. The nephrotic syndrome is caused by a chemical presumably released from T-cells. The nephritic syndrome is caused by white blood cells that damage the glomeruli.

Choice **A** is incorrect, as elevated levels of protein in the urine is characteristic of the nephrotic syndrome only. Note in the description of the nephritic syndrome, the passage states that red blood cells enter the nephron but proteins do not. Blood in the urine, choice **B**, and hypertension, choice **C**, are part of the nephritic syndrome only. Hypertension is a result of the blood loss. In the nephrotic syndrome, only proteins escape into the urine.

**22.  B**

The answer to this question can be predicted before looking at the choices provided. At the end of the description of the nephrotic syndrome, the passage states

that low albumin levels cause a decrease in osmotic pressure, resulting in a derangement in Starling forces. Osmotic pressure is a measure of "water pulling power" that one given solution has relative to another. In blood, osmotic pressure is provided by plasma proteins, and the greater the osmotic pressure, the more water will be pulled into the bloodstream. The Starling hypothesis describes the movement of fluid through capillaries. According to the hypothesis, at the arteriole end of a capillary the hydrostatic pressure (provided by the pumping heart) is greater than the osmotic pressure, so fluids and nutrients are pushed out. At the venule end, the blood pressure has dropped, so the hydrostatic pressure is less than the osmotic pressure. As a result, water and dissolved metabolic waste products are pulled into the capillary. In the nephrotic syndrome, the low osmotic pressure bars water from being absorbed at the venule end of the capillary, causing swelling.

Choice **A** is incorrect, because the nephron itself is not injured. The damage occurs at the glomerular capillaries. A drop in osmotic pressure, described in choice **C**, would *prevent* ADH release. Osmoreceptors in the hypothalamus perceive the drop in osmotic pressure as too much water, and so ADH release would be inhibited in an attempt to correct the abnormality. Choice **D** is an incorrect answer choice, as there is no Starling response.

**23.  A**

This is an example of a question that can stand alone from the passage. This question asks you about the mechanism of action of renin. Renin can cause hypertension as the result of the actions of aldosterone. When released into the blood from juxtamedullary cells, renin converts the serum protein angiotensinogen into angiotensin I. A resident enzyme converts angiotensin I into angiotensin II, which, in addition to causing vasoconstriction, stimulates the release of the steroid aldosterone from the adrenal cortex. Aldosterone stimulates the kidney to reabsorb sodium, causing water to follow passively. The increase in blood volume increases blood pressure.

Renin has no effect on ADH release, so choice **B** is incorrect. As described above, renin stimulates aldosterone release, not cortisone, so choice **C** is incorrect. Renin does not stimulate the sympathetic nervous system, so choice **D** is incorrect. The vasoconstriction observed when renin is released is due to the action of angiotensin II.

**24.  C**

Glomerular filtrate has the nearly the same composition as plasma, except that it does not contain a significant amount of protein. In a normal individual, salts (including sodium), urea, sugars, and amino acids freely enter Bowman's capsule. Red blood cells are too large to be filtered through the glomerulus, and so, in a normal individual, they remain in the circulation rather than entering the nephron.

Imagine that the glomerulus is like a sieve or colander. Small molecules dissolved in the fluid will pass through the glomerulus (e.g., glucose, which is later reabsorbed), while large molecules such as proteins and blood cells will not. If blood cells or proteins are found in the urine, this indicates a problem at the level of the glomerulus.

**25.  C**

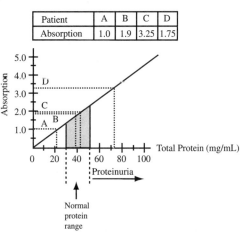

| Patient | A | B | C | D |
|---------|-----|-----|------|------|
| Absorption | 1.0 | 1.9 | 3.25 | 1.75 |

Using the absorption values and the graph, the urine protein concentrations of the patients can be determined. The normal range for total protein urine concentration is 3.5–5.0 gm/dL. Notice that the graph uses mg/mL for units, not gm/dL. The conversion of 5.0 gm/dL is as follows:

$$\frac{5.0 \text{ gm}}{1 \text{ dL}} \times \frac{1000 \text{ mg}}{1 \text{ gm}} \times \frac{10 \text{ dL}}{1 \text{ L}} \times \frac{1 \text{ L}}{1000 \text{ mL}} = \frac{50 \text{ mg}}{\text{mL}}$$

Converting the normal range to mg/mL yields 35–50 mg/mL. Patient C is the only one whose protein value is above normal.

## Passage VI (Questions 26–30)

**26.  D**

This question deals with the results of Experiments 1 and 2—either there *was* anti-DNP antibody production or there *wasn't*. Since anti-DNP antibody production is noted in Table 1 by a "Yes" or "No," there is no way for you to determine the strength of this response when BSA is used as the carrier relative to the response when OA is used as the carrier. Therefore, you can eliminate choices **A** and **B**. While it is true that the secondary response *does* require a lower dose of hapten-carrier complex than the primary response, this is a moot point in regard to the experiments. The results of the experiments do not illustrate this, since there is no data regarding quantities of hapten-carrier

complexes used in either priming or boosting. Thus choice **C** is also incorrect. You are left with choice **D**, which states that the results demonstrate that the secondary response requires priming and boosting with the same carrier. Rabbit 1 was primed and boosted with DNP–BSA and Rabbit 2 was primed and boosted with DNP–OA, and both rabbits produced anti-DNP antibody. Rabbit 3 was primed with DNP–BSA but boosted with DNP–OA and didn't produce any anti-DNP antibody. So far, this supports the claim of choice **D**. But what about Rabbit 4? Rabbit 4 was primed with both DNP–BSA and free OA, boosted with DNP–OA, and produced anti-DNP antibody. Why? Anti-DNP was produced because the DNP–BSA of the primer injection resulted in helper T cells primed to BSA and B cells primed to DNP, while the free OA of the primer resulted in helper T cells primed to OA. (The free OA also resulted in B cells that synthesized anti-OA antibodies and B cells primed to OA, but that's not relevant to the experimental design.) When Rabbit 4 was boosted with DNP–OA, the OA-primed helper T cells recognized the OA in DNP–OA and stimulated the DNP-primed B cells to proliferate into anti-DNP antibody-secreting cells. Remember, the passage tells you that it takes carrier-primed helper T cells and hapten-primed B cells to produce a secondary response to the hapten. Therefore, choice **D** is the correct answer.

**27.  D**

This is yet another question testing your understanding of the carrier effect as detailed in the passage and illustrated by the results of the experiments. Priming and boosting a rabbit with DNP–HA is no different from priming and boosting a rabbit with DNP–BSA or DNP–OA. Human albumin, HA, is a carrier just like BSA and OA; HA is a protein foreign to the rabbit's immune system. Therefore, priming the rabbit with DNP–HA results in DNP-primed B cells and HA-primed helper T cells, and when boosted with the same complex, these T cells will stimulate these B cells to produce anti-DNP antibodies. Hence, choice **D** is the right answer. Choices **A** and **B** are incorrect, because the B cells don't produce antibodies specific for the hapten-carrier complex as a unit. Choice **C** is incorrect, because the B cells are incapable of producing anti-hapten antibodies following the initial injection, because according to the passage, the hapten is too small to trigger antibody production. Again, choice **D** is the correct answer.

**28.  B**

To answer this question, you'll need to analyze Experiment 3. Rabbit 5 was primed with DNP–BSA, resulting in DNP-primed B cells and BSA-primed helper T cells. Rabbit 6 was primed with free OA, resulting in OA-primed B cells and OA-primed helper T cells. Rabbit 7 was irradiated, which rendered it incapable of mounting an immune response of its own, since radiation kills the lymphocytes. B cells from Rabbit 5, which are DNP-primed, and helper T cells from Rabbit 6, which are OA-primed, were transferred into Rabbit 7. When Rabbit 7 was boosted with DNP–BSA, anti-DNP antibody was *not* produced. Why? Because Rabbit 7 didn't have any BSA-primed helper T cells, and BSA-primed helper T cells would be needed to stimulate the DNP-primed B cells to proliferate into anti-DNP producing cells. If Rabbit 5's BSA-primed helper T cells had been transferred to Rabbit 7 in conjunction with its DNP-primed B cells, *then* a secondary response would have been elicited. When Rabbit 7 was boosted with DNP–OA, anti-DNP antibody was produced. Why? Because OA-primed helper T cells are needed to get anti-DNP producing B cells when OA is the carrier molecule used in the booster injection. Therefore, choice **B** is the correct answer. Choice **A** is incorrect not only because it's false, but also because you are concerned only with the cell types that were transferred to Rabbit 7. Choice **C** is incorrect, because the B cells transferred to Rabbit 7 from Rabbit 5 *were* DNP-primed. Rabbit 7 was boosted with DNP–BSA *prior* to being boosted with DNP–OA; so choice **D** is incorrect.

**29. A**

This question requires a bit of analysis and a complete understanding of the results of Experiment 3. In this question, Rabbit 7 is primed with DNP–BSA following irradiation; you are told that the rest of the experiment remains unchanged. In other words, B cells from DNP–BSA-primed Rabbit 5, along with helper T cells from OA-primed Rabbit 6, were transferred to Rabbit 7. Given this information, would you now expect Rabbit 7 to produce anti-DNP antibody when boosted with DNP–BSA? In the original version of Experiment 3, Rabbit 7 was unable to produce a secondary response when boosted with DNP–BSA because it lacked BSA-primed helper T cells. So you have to figure out if priming Rabbit 7 with DNP–BSA following irradiation would result in BSA-primed helper T cells. The answer is no. Irradiation prevents Rabbit 7 from mounting an immune response, thus preventing the production carrier-primed helper T cells and hapten-primed B cells. Rabbit 7 still has to rely on the powers of Rabbit 5's B cells and Rabbit 6's helper T cells to produce an immune response. Therefore, choice **A** is the correct answer. Choice **B** is incorrect, because an irradiated rabbit can't produce antibodies to the transferred cells. In fact, that's one of the reasons why Rabbit 7 was irradiated in the initial version of Experiment 3—so that Rabbit 7 wouldn't reject the donor cells from Rabbit 5 and Rabbit 6. Choices **C** and **D** are incorrect. Rabbit 7 doesn't have its own DNP-primed B cells and BSA-primed helper T cells to produce any anti-DNP antibody, so the "Yes" at the start of these choices eliminates them.

**30. C**

According to the question stem, IgM is the predominant class of antibody produced during a typical primary response, while IgG is the predominant class of antibody produced during a typical secondary response. The primary and secondary immune responses differ in other ways as well, such as the rate of antibody synthesis and the affinity of the antibody for the antigen, but you're not required to know any of this to answer the question. You should immediately rule out choices **A** and **B**, since the question stem states that a given immune response is predominated by either IgM or IgG; no response is ever 50-50 IgM to IgG. Furthermore, choice **B** is incorrect, because Rabbit 7 didn't produce any anti-DNP antibodies—IgM or IgG—after being boosted with DNP–BSA. It's not really made clear in either the passage or the question stem whether the anti-hapten antibody production elicited in the carrier effect is parallel to the antibody production of the primary response or the secondary response. However, it's not necessary to know this to know that choices **A** and **B** are incorrect. For choices **C** and **D**, we need to look at Rabbit 4, which was primed with both DNP–BSA and free OA and boosted with DNP–OA. This means that while its unclear whether Rabbit 4 produced anti-DNP IgM or IgG after being boosted with DNP–OA, it is clear that Rabbit 4 did *not* produce anti-DNP IgM after being primed. Anti-DNP is not produced before the booster injection, only after. Therefore, choice **D** is incorrect. So choice **C** must be the right answer. Priming Rabbit 4 with free OA results in the production of anti-OA IgM, since free OA is recognized by the rabbit's immune system upon first exposure. It's the hapten, not the carrier, which fails to trigger antibody production when injected alone. So when Rabbit 4 is boosted with DNP–OA, its OA-primed helper T cells stimulate its OA-primed B cells to proliferate into anti-OA IgG. Even though OA is complexed with a hapten, its presence still elicits anti-OA production. Therefore, you get more anti-OA antibodies produced following the booster injection, and this time around the predominant class of anti-OA antibodies synthesized is IgG. Therefore, choice **C** is correct.

## Passage VII (Questions 31–35)

**31. C**

This question is a Roman numeral question, which means that more than one item can be correct, so you need to identify all the correct items. After you have identified one correct item, you can eliminate any answer choices that don't contain that item.

You're asked to identify the control cultures used in this experiment. A control is a standard against which experimental observations may be evaluated, and as such, is identical in experimental procedure except for the *absence of the factor being studied*. Based on this definition, evaluate Roman numeral I, Culture a, which is the cells alone. This is a control, because unless you know the level of TNF present in nonactivated cells alone, you have no frame of reference to judge what effects the other compounds—PHA and *Tat*—are having on the cells. Therefore, Culture a must be a control. Since we have identified Roman numeral I as a correct choice, you can automatically eliminate choice **B**, Roman numeral III only. Since the whole point of the experiment is to determine what effect *Tat* has on host immune response, any culture containing *Tat* would not be a control. This means that Cultures c1, c2, d1, and d2 are not controls. So, in addition to eliminating Roman numeral III, you can eliminate IV as well; and so choice **D** must also be incorrect. Look at Roman numeral IV for a second—the two d cultures. PHA plus *Tat* is *not* a control because it shows the effect of the *Tat* peptide on activated cells. You know this because you're told that PHA activates cells. What about Roman numeral II, Culture b, which has the cells plus PHA? Since it's known that PHA induces T-cell activation, and that TNF is involved in T-cell activation, you would expect *higher* TNF levels when PHA is added to the cells than in Culture a. From Table 1, this is indeed true. In addition, Culture b serves as a control for the d cultures, which contain both PHA and *Tat*. There is no way to determine what effect *Tat* has on activated cells, which is what the cells of Culture b are, if you don't know what the level of TNF is in activated cells in the absence of *Tat*. So Roman numeral II is also a control. Because I and II are correct, choice **C** is the correct answer.

**32. D**

To answer this question, you need to interpret the data in Table 1. After looking at the table, ask yourself which of the four samples listed in the answer choices has the fewest TNF transcripts. How can you determine this from the table? Well, "TNF transcripts" refers to mRNA transcripts of the TNF gene isolated from the cultures. A radiolabeled probe specific for TNF was used to figure out the number of TNF transcripts. Although it's not possible to determine the absolute number of transcripts of TNF from the table, you can deduce the relative quantities. In other words, you can tell if, for a given sample size, Culture a has twice as many transcripts of TNF as does Culture b, for example. According to the passage, the intensities of the bands are directly proportional to TNF gene expression. This means that the lower the value in the table, the less TNF gene expression, and therefore the fewer TNF transcripts. So, to answer this question, look up the values for each answer choice and select the answer with the lowest number. According to the table, the values are: choice **A**, 33.70;

choice **B**, 164.78; choice **C**, 69.98; and choice **D**, 20.54. Since choice **D** has the lowest value, this means that there are the fewest number of TNF transcripts present in this culture. Therefore, choice **D** is the correct answer.

**33. B**

This question requires you to interpret the data in Table 1. By looking over the answer choices, you see that one of the distinguishing features is the concept of activated versus nonactivated cells. What does this mean? You're told that the experiment starts with nonactivated T cells from HIV-negative donors. So all the cells are initially nonactivated. However, according to the passage, PHA, which is the substance known as a mitogen, activates T cells. This means that Cultures a, c1, and c2 contain nonactivated cells, while Cultures b, d1, and d2 contain activated cells, since PHA is present in these cultures.

The next thing you have to do is determine whether TNF gene expression is repressed, stimulated, or unaffected by *Tat*. Repressed, or stimulated, or unaffected compared to what? Well, this is where the control cultures come into play: You need to compare the experimental cultures to the control cultures. The appropriate comparisons for this experiment are: Culture a is the control for Cultures c1 and c2, and Culture b is the control for Cultures d1 and d2. To determine the effect of *Tat* on nonactivated cells, Cultures c1 and c2 are compared to the control, Culture a. To determine the effect of *Tat* on activated cells, Cultures d1 and d2 are compared to the control, Culture b.

Next, see if you can discern any trends in the table. Remember that the values in the table are directly proportional to TNF gene expression. In the comparison of Cultures c1 and c2 to Culture a, you see that *Tat* from Exon 1 stimulates TNF gene expression in nonactivated cells, while *Tat* from Exon 2 does not. In the comparison of Cultures d1 and d2 to Culture b, you see that *Tat* from both Exon 1 and Exon 2 represses TNF gene expression in activated cells. Since the question only specifies *Tat* peptide from Exon 1, you can ignore any data about *Tat* from Exon 2.

With this information, see if you can eliminate any answer choices. Well, since *Tat does* affect TNF gene expression, choice **D** must be incorrect. In addition, you previously determined that *Tat* stimulates TNF gene expression in nonactivated cells. Therefore, choice **A** is incorrect. You also know that *Tat* represses TNF gene expression in activated cells. Based on this, you can rule out choice **C**. So, by the process of elimination, choice **B** is the correct answer. Notice that you only had to look at the first part of the answer choices to find the correct answer. The second half of the answer may have helped to identify the correct answer, but it wasn't needed.

**34. A**

Notice the trend in Cultures $c_1$ and $c_2$ treated with *Tat* from Exon 1—that is, the difference between the effect of 100 ng/mL of *Tat* from Exon 1 on nonactivated T cells versus the effect of 1 ng/mL of *Tat* from Exon 1 on nonactivated T cells. Looking at Table 1, you see that at either 1.25 g or 2.5 g of mRNA, there is *greater* TNF gene expression with 100 ng/mL of *Tat* than with 1 ng/mL of *Tat*. Therefore, it can be inferred that the *greater* the concentration of *Tat* from Exon 1 added to nonactivated cells, the *greater* the concentration of TNF mRNA. In other words, in nonactivated cells, the amount of TNF gene expression is *directly* proportional to the concentration of *Tat* from Exon 1.

To answer the question, find the most contrary, or opposite, trend. Since in nonactivated cells, the greater the *Tat* concentration the greater the TNF expression, you might have expected *Tat* to have the same effect on the activated cells of Cultures $d_1$ and $d_2$. However, if you look at the experimental results for the d cultures, the opposite occurs: In activated cells, the *greater* the *Tat* concentration the *less* TNF expression. In other words, there *is* greater repression of TNF gene expression at the *lower* concentration of *Tat* from Exon 1. This is contrary to the effect of the differing *Tat* concentrations on Cultures $c_1$ and $c_2$. Therefore, choice **A** is correct, and choice **B** is incorrect. While choices **C** and **D** are true—there is greater TNF expression in the larger mRNA sample sizes and in Culture b than in Culture a—neither is unexpected in light of the effect of *Tat* concentration on nonactivated cells. So choice **C** and choice **D** are both incorrect.

**35. B**

In the question stem you're told that the *Tat* protein found circulating in the blood of an HIV-positive patient has a molecular weight less than half that of the peptide synthesized from the *Tat* gene inserted in a prokaryotic cell. Why the difference in molecular weight? The key to this is found in the first paragraph of the passage: The *Tat* protein is encoded by two exons spliced together. The only way to get two exons spliced together is if the RNA that linked them together was excised. You don't have to know the specifics of HIV genetics to answer this question, but here is some background information. The two exons that code for *Tat* are separated by a sequence of DNA that codes for other viral protein products. When *Tat* needs to be synthesized, *all* of this DNA is transcribed: the two *Tat* exons plus the DNA that links them. However, since the desired protein product is *Tat*, the RNA coding for the other proteins is excised and the two *Tat* exons are spliced together. All of this occurs within the nucleus of the eukaryotic host cell; remember, you're dealing with a retrovirus, which must integrate into the host genome before the viral genes can be expressed. Therefore, the initial mRNA transcript is longer than the transcript from which *Tat* is translated.

Prokaryotes do not perform post-transcriptional modification. The initial mRNA transcript is directly translated. Prokaryotes are *incapable* of such processing. Remember, in prokaryotes, there is no nucleus to separate transcription from translation. Therefore, if the viral DNA that contains the two *Tat* exons was inserted into a prokaryote, the mRNA transcribed and translated by the cell would consist of the codons coding for several viral proteins, not just *Tat*. This means that the protein synthesized from this mRNA transcript will be much longer and much heavier than the protein synthesized in the HIV-positive patient. Therefore, this prokaryotic protein couldn't rightfully be referred to as *Tat*.

Now examine the answer choices. The molecular weight of the protein would not be influenced by interaction with TNF—there's no information in the passage that would lead you to believe this; so choice **A** is incorrect. Choice **B** basically sums up the differences between eukaryotic and prokaryotic protein synthesis, and is the correct answer. Random mutations during synthesis could have caused the protein to have the same, a greater, or a smaller molecular weight depending on the nature of the mutation. However, because mutations are a *random* event, it is highly unlikely that all of the prokaryotic DNA would undergo mutations that resulted in a peptide twice the size of its eukaryotic counterpart. This is *not* the most likely explanation, and so choice **C** is not the answer. As for choice **D**, nowhere in the question stem does it say that the prokaryotic cells were exposed to PHA. Furthermore, exposure to PHA does not affect *Tat* weight or the weight of any proteins. Therefore, choice **D** is incorrect.

## Discrete Questions (Questions 36–45)

**36. A**

The intermembrane space is the compartment between the outer and inner mitochondrial membranes. Protons are pumped from the matrix into the intermembrane space to create a proton motive force that is used to generate ATP during oxidative phosphorylation. Since the intermembrane space contains a high concentration of protons relative to the mitochondrial matrix (and cytoplasm), it will have an acidic pH. Only choice **A** contains a pH value in the acidic range ($< 7$).

**37. A**

To answer this question, you have to remember the function of the smooth endoplasmic reticulum (SER). The SER serves two major functions: detoxification and lipid synthesis. Cholesterol and phospholipids are the main lipids synthesized.

Adrenal cortical cells would be expected to contain an abundant amount of SER because they synthesize steroid hormones (glucocorticoids and mineralocorticoids). Cholesterol is the building block of steroid hormones, so adrenal cortical cells would require much SER in order to produce the corticoids necessary for homeostasis, answer choice **A**.

Epithelial cells and their cousins, endothelial cells, do not serve any capacity that involves the SER. These cells function primarily as a barrier. Adipose cells are the site of lipid storage, not synthesis. These cells also do not require an abundant amount of SER. An abundant amount of any organelle would take up precious storage space.

### 38. A

Statement I is a true statement, since the two nucleotide strands of DNA are held together by hydrogen bonds (two bonds between thymine and adenine, three between guanine and cytosine).

Statement II is false, because the phosphate groups that are part of the helical backbone are negatively charged. If anything, neighboring phosphate groups would repel one another, not attract.

Statement III is false, because the sugar that is part of the DNA helix consists of deoxyribose, not ribose.

Since Statement I is true, and statements II and III are false, choice **A** is the correct answer.

### 39. D

If cells are removed from one location in an embryo and placed into another location, and they continue to develop as if they were not moved, the fate of the cells must have already been established. Such a cell is called *determined*, in which its developmental fate has been set even if the cell's appearance and function have not yet achieved their final state.

A totipotent cell, choice **A**, is a cell that has the capability to develop into any cell type of that organism. Only the very early cells of development, and the germ cells, are totipotent. Choice **B** is incorrect, because the cells were not differentiated yet. A differentiated cell has completely matured into the cell type it will assume for the life of the organism. The cells in this experiment were removed while in the bud stage. The cells cannot be considered differentiated until they form an arm and all the associated structures. Choice **C** is incorrect, because the cells developed normally, and so cannot be considered mutant. If a cell experiences damage to its genome that results in a phenotype that differs from normal, then it is mutant.

### 40. B

Directional selection produces an adaptive change over time in response to some change in the environment. When bacteria are exposed to antibacterial soaps, only the resistant bacteria will survive, leading to a prevalence of resistant genes in the bacterial gene pool. This is identical to the directional selection that occurs when insects become resistant to a pesticide.

Choice **A** is incorrect, because a stabilizing selection maintains a uniform character by eliminating deviations. Choice **C** is incorrect, because a disruptive selection favors extremes over the intermediate phenotypes. Choice **D** is incorrect, because speciation is the evolution of a new species that can't interbreed with other species.

### 41. B

The question states that "osteoblasts secrete large quantities of alkaline phosphatase when they are actively depositing bone matrix." Thus, any condition that affects the activity of osteoblasts would affect the concentration of alkaline phosphatase in the circulation. Decreased dietary calcium intake would lead to a resorption of calcium from the bones. This is accomplished by osteoclasts, not osteoblasts. Therefore, there would be a decrease in osteoblast activity and a consequent decrease in alkaline phosphatase concentrations in the circulation.

Choice **C** is incorrect, because osteoclasts exist within the bones and are not generally found in the circulation. Note that decreased dietary calcium also leads to increased osteoclast activity in order to maintain the concentration of $Ca^{2+}$ in the circulation. Choice **D** is incorrect, because a decrease in dietary calcium tends to decrease $[Ca^{2+}]_{plasma}$ and would be compensated for by increased resorption of calcium from the bones.

### 42. B

There are several ways to determine the mode of inheritance of a disease represented in a pedigree chart. The most thorough method would be to go through each of the answer choices and see if the mode of inheritance is possible by ascribing the appropriate genotypes to each of the individuals. Before resorting to that, use your knowledge of genetics to eliminate answer choices. Below is a reproduction of the pedigree chart from the question, with each individual numbered and their genotypes listed.

First, notice in the $P_1$ generation that parents 1 and 2 do not have the disease, but some of their children do. Based on this, the disease cannot be dominant. If the disease were dominant, one or both of the parents must have the disease. You can therefore eliminate answer choices **A** and **C**. Next, notice that individual 7 is a female that has the disease, but her father does not. Based on this observation, the inheritance cannot be X-linked recessive. The steadfast rule is that for X-linked recessive traits, a female can express the trait only if her father expresses the trait. You can therefore eliminate choice **D**.

The above observations leave choice **B** as the correct answer.

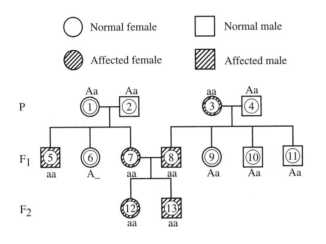

### 43. A

In meiosis I, the 46 chromosomes, each with two copies of the DNA, line up at the equator of the cell; and the paternal and maternal chromosomes segregate, leaving two cells with 23 chromosomes each. These cells will then begin to undergo meiosis II. In meiosis II, the sister chromatids (copies of the same DNA) divide and four cells with 23 chromosomes (only one copy) are created.

For the MCAT, you should understand the processes of mitosis and meiosis, and also know the similarities and differences between the two processes. You should know in what types of body cells each type of division takes place (somatic versus germ cells), differences in the end products (diploid versus haploid), and the number of divisions that take place.

### 44. B

The nucleus of a zygote contains all the genetic information needed by all future cells of an adult organism in the form of genes. As the zygote divides and differentiates, each cell maintains *all* of its genetic information, but it does not *express* all of these genes; that is, certain genes are selectively expressed, while others are repressed. Gene expression is selectively turned on or off, depending on the type of cell. This is very important, because even though a myocardial cell may contain the same genetic information as an osteoblast, you wouldn't want to have your myocardial cells making bone in the middle of your heart. When certain genes that are normally turned *off* are mistakenly turned *on*, cancer can develop.

In this question, there is an experiment where the nucleus of a tadpole intestinal cell is removed and transplanted into a denucleated frog zygote. The zygote develops normally after the nucleus transplant. The experimental results suggest that a differentiated nucleus contains the same genetic material as a zygote's nondifferentiated nucleus. The fact that the nucleus was originally in a differentiated cell also suggests that selective repression of DNA is possible. This conclusion is fairly straightforward since, if the salvaged nucleus lacked genetic material essential to a developing tadpole, the zygote would develop into, at best, a mass of intestinal cells. If certain genes were missing, the zygote would not be able to develop normally. These conclusions about the experimental results are best represented by choice **B**.

Examine the wrong choices to make sure choice **B** is the best answer. Choice **A** says that the results of the experiment suggest that cell differentiation is controlled by irreversibly shutting off genes not needed by that cell. In fact, the experiment proves that this is *not* true, and therefore choice **A** is incorrect. Shutting off genes must be reversible, otherwise this transplanted nucleus would *not* be able to direct the zygote to divide and develop into all of the different cell types found in a frog. Choice **C** suggests that the cytoplasm of the zygote contains all of the information needed for normal adult development in the form of RNA. This choice is incorrect, because the experiment did *not* specifically address this question. The results of the experiment do not support or contradict this claim. Although DNA is the known carrier of genetic information, if you wanted to test the RNA theory, you would perform a different experiment, such as seeing if a denucleated frog zygote develops normally. As for choice **D**, all eukaryotic ribosomes are the same and are found only in the cytoplasm of a cell, not the nucleus. Again, choice **B** is the correct answer.

### 45. C

This question tests your understanding of red blood cells, the antigens they express on their cell surfaces, and the types of antibody production these antigens elicit. There are four major blood groups: A, B, AB, and O. There are three alleles determining these four groups: Alleles A and B are codominant, while allele O is recessive. The A allele codes for the A antigen on the red blood cell surface, the B allele codes for the B antigen, and the O allele does not code for any antigen. So, a person with type A blood has the genotype AA or AO, a person with type B blood is either BB or BO, a person with type AB blood has the genotype AB, and a person with type O blood is OO. A person's blood serum does not contain antibodies to any of its own antigens, but does contain antibodies to the other blood antigens. This means that a person with type A blood will have antibodies to the B antigen in their blood serum, and a person with type B blood will have antibodies to the A antigen in their blood serum. A person with type AB blood would have neither anti-A nor anti-B antibodies, since his or her red blood cells have both antigens. People with type O blood, on the other hand, will have both anti-A and anti-B antibodies, since their red blood cells have neither the A nor B antigens.

The experiment in the question stem sets up four test tubes, numbered I through IV, with each test tube containing a different blood group. To each of these test tubes, type A red blood cells were added. To answer this question, you must determine which of these test tubes will form precipitate upon the addition of type A red blood cells. Precipitation occurs when the blood antigens react with their specific antibodies. Therefore, the test tubes containing blood serum with anti-A antibodies will form precipitate. The two blood types that will produce anti-A antibodies are type B and type O blood. Therefore, precipitate will form in test tube II, which contains type B blood, and test tube IV, which contains type O blood. Precipitate will not form in the other blood types because they do not contain the anti-A antibody. So the correct answer is choice **C**.

section three

# VERBAL REASONING

# CHAPTER 8

# Verbal Reasoning

The Verbal Reasoning section is perhaps the most familiar section of the MCAT, since it's similar to the reading comprehension sections of other standardized tests. The section is 60 minutes long and consists of 7 passages, with 5–7 questions per passage for a total of 40 multiple-choice questions. The passages are drawn from those natural sciences not included in the science portions of the test, and from the social sciences and humanities.

The science portions of the MCAT test your ability to work with the kind of information in which you have, or are expected to develop, expertise. The verbal sections test your reasoning abilities in working with material in which you are *not* expected to develop expertise.

The AAMC Verbal Reasoning question categories are:

### Comprehension
- Global: main idea, author's purpose
- Detail: answers stated expressly in the passage

### Evaluation
- Identify the function of a statement
- Describe the structure of the passage

### Deduction
- Inferences and Assumptions

### Application
- Apply ideas in the passage to new information

### Incorporation
- Apply new information to arguments made in the passage

## WHAT SKILLS ARE REWARDED IN VERBAL REASONING?

- The ability to stay "on point"—that is, to concentrate and not get distracted
- The ability to switch gears quickly from one passage and topic to the next
- The ability to recognize the overall purpose of a paragraph
- The ability to process large and small pieces of data and find a pattern within them
- Stamina

All of these have considerable applicability to medical school and your career as a physician.

## DO YOU NEED TO PREPARE FOR VERBAL REASONING?

Don't make the mistake of underestimating the challenge of the Verbal Reasoning section. The scoring gradient for Verbal Reasoning is very steep, and some medical schools add all your MCAT scores together for a composite score, so you can't afford to be cavalier.

We generally read for entertainment or information. MCAT Verbal Reasoning requires that you abandon standard reading habits and take on the role of a critical reader. To concentrate and glean meaning regardless of the nature of the text will mean working through your resistance to dry passages and overcoming anxiety or frustration. The more control you can muster, the quicker you can move through each passage, through the questions, and to a higher score.

## ESTABLISH AND ADHERE TO A SCHEDULE

If you're serious about improving your performance on MCAT Verbal Reasoning, start now to establish and follow a practice schedule. Verbal Reasoning requires that you internalize methods and strategies; there's nothing here that you can memorize at the last minute.

### Rough Calendar

Set up a timetable that works for you. Be realistic but demanding of yourself.

Set up a blank calendar for the period between now and Test Day, broken into months/weeks, or weeks/days, depending on how much time is left. Insert upcoming holidays (and allow yourself some time off). Then develop and build a proper study schedule. Here are some general principles:

- Assess the practice material available from AAMC and schedule that practice to develop your skills early and keep them strong.
- Keep working on small groups of passages until the day before your Test Day.
- Don't work on Verbal Reasoning for more than 120–150 minutes at a time.

On Test Day itself, plan to warm up your Verbal Reasoning skills with an old passage or two and its questions.

## Practice Tests and Passages

Time yourself on practice sets and tests, allowing 17 minutes for two passages (rather than timing each passage). Practice can establish a sense of pacing that will become second nature by Test Day.

Practice at the same time of day that you will be doing Verbal on Test Day. Verbal Reasoning is the second section and will be approximately 80 minutes after the start of your test.

Three things to be careful of:

- Don't be discouraged by the errors you make. Errors made in practice give you the opportunity to identify your strengths and weaknesses and to focus on modifying your habits.
- Don't wait too long to review explanations after taking a practice test.
- Don't do more than two passages at a time without taking a break; sensory overload will cause you to lose focus.

## Outside Reading

Select materials of the kinds that will appear in Verbal Reasoning but that you don't normally read. Take on at least one difficult outside-reading challenge per week. Sources of such outside reading include: *The Economist, Archaeology, Scientific American, The New York Times* op-ed pages, *Atlantic Monthly, Foreign Affairs, Modern Art, The New York Review of Books*—and see what literary and professional journals are available at your local library.

If possible, make two photocopies of the articles, one with the title and source hidden. Keep a log of your outside reading, and check it from time to time to ensure that you're keeping to your schedule and reading a good variety of disciplines. By continuing to read and analyze difficult pieces of prose you ensure that all of your skills will be sharp on Test Day.

Don't just read, read critically. One purpose of your outside reading is to increase your comfort and familiarity with the kinds of writing you'll find on the test, but the other is to practice all the Kaplan methods and strategies. Do the following things as you practice critical reading:

- Practice mapping paragraphs (as we'll discuss below).
- Ask yourself the author's purpose.
- Think about the standard Verbal Reasoning question types that can be asked based on material you've read.
- Notice your comfort levels and reading pace, and plan further reading to overcome problem areas.

# THE KAPLAN METHOD FOR VERBAL REASONING

The Kaplan Method for Verbal Reasoning is:

Step 1: Critically Read the Passage

Step 2: Interpret the Question Stem

Step 3: Review Your Map and Text

Step 4: Make a Prediction

Step 5: Read the Choices

We'll discuss each step briefly first, then examine each one in more detail with some of the strategies incorporated.

## Step 1: Critically Read the Passage

Reading and mapping Verbal Reasoning passages is different in important ways from the process used on science passages, principally because outside knowledge is irrelevant here, and the content is less important than the structure. To read passages critically means:

- Using Keywords to help you navigate the passage
- Capturing the gist by paraphrasing
- Identifying the topic, scope, and purpose of the passage
- Creating a map of the passage structure to locate details as required

The most important statements in any Verbal Reasoning passage are those in which conclusions (which we'll also call "opinions") are expressed. A passage may consist only of the author's opinion, or you may find two or more contrasted opinions. Sentences in which the *author's voice* is heard clue you in to the *author's purpose* in writing the passage. *Opinion sentences* shed light on the direction in which the text is moving—they provide a map that you can use to organize your thoughts about the text. And they direct your pacing—you should read opinions more carefully than supporting detail, and paraphrase them when you're done.

## Step 2: Interpret the Question Stem

Read the question stem to answer two questions:

First: Exactly what does the question ask?

Pay close attention: If you misread the question, all your other work will be wasted. Many standard "wrong answer choices" are based on common misreadings of the question (for example, they can be the opposite of what is asked). Some words (such as LEAST, EXCEPT, NOT, *strengthen*, or *weaken*) are called out for you, but you should note other essential terms that will help you find the answer. Many mistakes are made by losing sight of an essential element of the question.

Second: Do you expect to find the answer explicitly stated in the passage?

The stem may direct you to relevant text by line or paragraph number, or by direct quotes from the passage; or it may use names or other words that appear (sometimes repeatedly) in the text without any indication that they are quoted.

## Step 3: Review Your Map and Relevant Text

With the details of the question in mind, reground yourself in the passage—use the map you created by paraphrasing the passage to locate any relevant text. This step is easiest when the question refers to lines of text, a particular paragraph, or a specific argument. But some regrounding in the passage is helpful for every question type, even if it's only a review of the broad outlines of the passage and the author's scope and purpose. Even when you believe you remember the exact words in the passage that answer the question, you may find that you've overlooked a relevant detail.

## Step 4: Make a Prediction

Before you consult the answer choices, predict the content, or at least the broad outline, of the correct answer. Most often, this will require argument dissection skills that we'll discuss in detail below. Predicting your answer will speed up and focus your search among the choices and reduce your chances of being misled by a plausible wrong answer.

## Step 5: Read the Choices

Armed with your predictions and refreshed on the relevant text, you'll be ready to look for the right choice. Pay close attention to the wording of the answer choices—only one will be valid based on the passage. Read all the choices before selecting one—sometimes a wrong answer choice varies from the correct choice very subtly.

Before we start our in-depth analysis of the Kaplan strategies, let's try a practice passage with one of each of the AAMC question types. Critically read the passage below. Consider what the author is trying to say and how the ideas are communicated. Pause after each paragraph to paraphrase its ideas on scratch paper. On the following page are six questions; don't spend more than five or six minutes answering them.

Revisionist historians maintain that it was within the power of the United States, in the years during and immediately after the Second World War, to prevent the Cold War with the Soviet Union. Revisionists suggest that the prospect of impending conflict with the Soviets could have been avoided in several ways. The U.S. could have officially recognized the new Soviet sphere of influence in Eastern Europe instead of continuing to call for self-determination in those countries. A much-needed reconstruction loan could have helped the Soviets recover from the war. The Americans could have sought to assuage Soviet fears by giving up the U.S. monopoly of the atomic bomb and turning the weapons over to an international agency (with the stipulation that future nuclear powers do the same).

This criticism of the post-war American course of action fails to take into account the political realities in America at the time, and unfairly condemns the American policymakers who did consider each of these alternatives and found them to be unworkable. Recognition of a Soviet Eastern Europe was out of the question. Roosevelt had promised self-determination to the Eastern European countries, and the American people, having come to expect this, were furious when Stalin began to shape his spheres of influence in the region. The President was in particular acutely conscious of the millions of Polish-Americans who would be voting in the upcoming election.

Negotiations had indeed been conducted by the administration with the Soviets about a reconstruction loan, but the Congress refused to approve it unless the Soviets made enormous concessions tantamount to restructuring their system and withdrawing from Eastern Europe. This, of course, made Soviet rejection of the loan a foregone conclusion. As for giving up the bomb—the elected officials in Washington would have been in deep trouble with their constituents had that plan been carried out. Polls showed that 82 percent of the American people understood that other nations would develop bombs eventually, but that 85 percent thought that the U.S. should retain exclusive possession of the weapon. Policymakers have to abide by certain constraints in deciding what is acceptable and what is not. They, and not historians, are in the best position to perceive those constraints and make the decisions.

Revisionist historians tend to eschew this type of political explanation of America's supposed failure to reach a peaceful settlement with the Soviets in favor of an economic reading of events. They point to the fact that in the early post-war years American businessmen and government officials cooperated to expand American foreign trade vigorously and to exploit investment opportunities in many foreign countries. In order to sustain the lucrative expansion, revisionists assert, American policymakers were obliged to maintain an "Open Door" foreign policy, the object of which was to keep all potential trade opportunities open. Since the Soviets could jeopardize such opportunities in Eastern Europe and elsewhere, they had to be opposed. Hence, the Cold War. But if American policymakers were simply pawns in an economic game of expansionist capitalism, as the revisionists seem to think, why do the revisionists hold them responsible for not attempting to reach an accord with the Soviets? The policymakers, swept up by a tidal wave of capitalism, clearly had little control and little choice in the matter.

Even if American officials had been free and willing to make conciliatory gestures toward the Soviets, the Cold War would not have been prevented. Overtures of friendship would not have been reciprocated (as far as we can judge; information on the inner workings of the Kremlin during that time is scanty). Soviet expert George F. Kennan concluded that Russian hostility could not be dampened by any effort on the part of the United States. The political and ideological differences were too great, and the Soviets had too long a history of distrust of foreigners—exacerbated at the time by Stalin's rampant paranoia, which infected his government—to embark on a process of establishing trust and peace with the United States, though it was in their interest to do so.

1. The primary purpose of the passage is to

   A.  criticize historical figures.

   B.  refute an argument.

   C.  analyze an era.

   D.  reconcile opposing views.

2. The author refers to the Polish-Americans chiefly to illustrate that

   A.  the president had an excellent rapport with ethnic minorities.

   B.  immigrants had fled from Eastern European countries to escape communism.

   C.  giving up the idea of East European self-determination would have been costly in political terms.

   D.  the Poles could enjoy self-determination only in America.

3. A fundamental assumption underlying the author's argument in the second and third paragraphs is that

   A.  the American public was very well informed about the incipient Cold War situation.

   B.  none of the proposed alternatives would have had its intended effect.

   C.  the American public was overwhelmingly opposed to seeking peace with the Soviets.

   D.  the government could not have been expected to ignore public opinion.

4. The author would consider which of the following an example of the "certain constraints" (line 45) to which policymakers are subject?

   A.  The etiquette of international diplomacy

   B.  The danger of leaked information about atomic bombs

   C.  The views of the electorate

   D.  The potential reaction of the enemy

5. Which statement best summarizes the revisionist argument concerning the origin of the Cold War?

   A.  The Soviets were oblivious to the negative impact they had on the American economy.

   B.  The economic advantage of recognizing Soviet Europe outweighed the disadvantage of an angry public.

   C.  America could trade and invest with foreign countries only if it agreed to oppose the Soviet Union.

   D.  American economic interests abroad would have been threatened by any Soviet expansion.

6. Which of the following, based on the information in the passage, would most strengthen the author's judgment about the likelihood that the Cold War could have been averted?

   A.  Evidence that the author has no anti-communist bias

   B.  New documents giving a complete picture of the hostility of the Soviets to American conciliatory gestures

   C.  Support for the author's views by a noted authority

   D.  A demonstration of alternatives not suggested by the revisionists

Turn the page to read an example of what the passage looks like when mapped. How do your thoughts match the notes that follow the paragraphs? Following the passage map are the answers and explanations for the six questions. For each question you got right, could you have answered it more quickly? For each question you missed, why did you get it wrong? What can you fix about your approach to Verbal Reasoning questions so that you won't make the same mistake again?

## MAPPING THE PASSAGE

Revisionist historians maintain that it was within the power of the United States, in the years during and immediately after the Second World War, to prevent the Cold War with the Soviet Union. Revisionists suggest that the prospect of impending conflict with the Soviets could have been avoided in several ways. The U.S. could have officially recognized the new Soviet sphere of influence in Eastern Europe instead of continuing to call for self-determination in those countries. A much-needed reconstruction loan could have helped the Soviets recover from the war. The Americans could have sought to assuage Soviet fears by giving up the U.S. monopoly of the atomic bomb and turning the weapons over to an international agency (with the stipulation that future nuclear powers do the same).

This criticism of the post-war American course of action fails to take into account the political realities in America at the time, and unfairly condemns the American policymakers who did consider each of these alternatives and found them to be unworkable. Recognition of a Soviet Eastern Europe was out of the question. Roosevelt had promised self-determination to the Eastern European countries, and the American people, having come to expect this, were furious when Stalin began to shape his spheres of influence in the region. The President was in particular acutely conscious of the millions of Polish-Americans who would be voting in the upcoming election.

Negotiations had indeed been conducted by the administration with the Soviets about a reconstruction loan, but the Congress refused to approve it unless the Soviets made enormous concessions tantamount to restructuring their system and withdrawing from Eastern Europe. This, of course, made Soviet rejection of the loan a foregone conclusion. As for giving up the bomb—the elected officials in Washington would have been in deep trouble with their constituents had that plan been carried out. Polls showed that 82 percent of the American people understood that other nations would develop bombs eventually, but that 85 percent thought that the U.S. should retain exclusive possession of the weapon. Policymakers have to abide by certain constraints in deciding what is acceptable and what is not. They, and not historians, are in the best position to perceive those constraints and make the decisions.

Paragraph 1 explains the three things that, according to the Revisionists, could have been done to avoid the Cold War.

Argument #1

Argument #2

Argument #3

**Topic/Scope:** the Cold War, and why Revisionists are wrong

The author refutes these arguments; the American political atmosphere made these steps impossible.

Response to argument #1 above

Note strong judgmental and emotional words—it isn't necessary to catch each of them, but pick up on how they structure the argument.

Response to #2

Response to #3

More of the author's judgment

Revisionist historians tend to eschew this type of political explanation of America's supposed failure to reach a peaceful settlement with the Soviets in favor of an economic reading of events. They point to the fact that in the early post-war years American businessmen and government officials cooperated to expand American foreign trade vigorously and to exploit investment opportunities in many foreign countries. In order to sustain the lucrative expansion, revisionists assert, American policymakers were obliged to maintain an "Open Door" foreign policy, the object of which was to keep all potential trade opportunities open. Since the Soviets could jeopardize such opportunities in Eastern Europe and elsewhere, they had to be opposed. Hence, the Cold War. But if American policymakers were simply pawns in an economic game of expansionist capitalism, as the revisionists seem to think, why do the revisionists hold them responsible for not attempting to reach an accord with the Soviets? The policymakers, swept up by a tidal wave of capitalism, clearly had little control and little choice in the matter.

Even if American officials had been free and willing to make conciliatory gestures toward the Soviets, the Cold War would not have been prevented. Overtures of friendship would not have been reciprocated (as far as we can judge; information on the inner workings of the Kremlin during that time is scanty). Soviet expert George F. Kennan concluded that Russian hostility could not be dampened by any effort on the part of the United States. The political and ideological differences were too great, and the Soviets had too long a history of distrust of foreigners—exacerbated at the time by Stalin's rampant paranoia, which infected his government—to embark on a process of establishing trust and peace with the United States, though it was in their interest to do so.

Revisionists would claim the economic situation forced policymakers to oppose the Soviets.

If American officials were caught in an economic tide why blame them for not doing things differently?

There was no way the Cold War could have been avoided. Soviets were hostile, paranoid—a new argument.

The author of this passage has one overarching strategy and carries it out in a classic Verbal Reasoning passage structure: Set up the arguments of the revisionist historians and then refute that position throughout the rest of the passage. When a Verbal Reasoning passage begins with a "traditional" view, or a statement of what others believe, expect to see the author's subsequent opposition.

**1.   B**

When answer choices all start with verbs (as they frequently do in "purpose" and "main idea" questions), a vertical scan of the verbs can quickly reduce the number of answer choices you have to read in full. As we noted above, the author of this passage is primarily engaged in setting up and knocking down the arguments of the revisionists. This makes **B** correct and **D** wrong (the author is definitely not interested in reconciling his view with that of the revisionists). **A** is out because the author is defending historical figures—the policymakers—for what they did, not criticizing them. **C** is too neutral a choice for this passage; the author does engage in analysis of the era of the beginning of the Cold War, but his purpose is to do far more than just analyze events—he wants to rebut the revisionist theories. "Main idea" questions are rare on MCAT Verbal Reasoning, but knowing the main idea is helpful in answering Deduction questions and in eliminating wrong answer choices.

**2.   C**

For this Evaluation question, look at the second half of paragraph 2, where the author says Roosevelt could never have recognized a Soviet Eastern Europe, because the American people did not like the idea of the Soviets holding sway in that region. In particular, the president would have lost the votes of the Polish-Americans who, you can infer, did not want the Soviets controlling their "old country." **C** spells out this point. Each of the other choices misreads the sentence about the Polish-American voters.

**3.   D**

Deduction questions are the most common in Verbal Reasoning sections. To identify an assumption, identify the evidence and conclusion, and find the connection between them. In the second and third paragraphs, the author refutes the suggestions of the revisionists primarily by saying that the policymakers couldn't do what was necessary to avoid the Cold War because the American people were against it. The assumption the author makes is that the policymakers "could not have been expected to ignore public opinion," as stated in answer choice **D**. The author never says in the second and third paragraphs that none of the alternatives would work (**B**)—what he does say, in a later paragraph, is that if peace initiatives had not run aground due to American politics, then they would have run aground due to the Soviet climate. The author also does not say in the second and third paragraphs that the American public was "well informed" (**A**) or "overwhelmingly opposed to seeking peace" (**C**); all we know is that they opposed Soviet influence in Eastern Europe as well as the idea of giving up the atom bomb monopoly.

**4.   C**

This Application question is closely linked to the previous one. This is a common phenomenon in Verbal Reasoning, so if a question is difficult, answer the other questions for the passage before coming back to it. Here, the author refers to the "certain constraints" at the end of the third paragraph, in the midst of the discussion on the impact of public opinion on the policymakers. From context, then, you know that the constraints the author is talking about are the opinions of the people—in other words, "the views of the electorate," answer choice **C**. If you didn't put the sentence about "constraints" in context, any of the other choices might have looked appealing.

**5.   D**

This is a Detail question, merely asking that you paraphrase something stated in the passage. This question centers on paragraph 4, where the author explains the revisionists' view that American policymakers decided to oppose the Soviet Union because Soviet expansion could jeopardize United States trade and investment. Choice **D** captures this idea. The author says nothing about whether or not the Soviets knew about the negative impact they could have on the American economy, as stated in choice **A**. Choice **B** is out, because the Soviet Union was not recognized by the United States, so this could not possibly have had anything to do with the origin of the Cold War. Choice **C** is wrong, because there is no evidence in the paragraph to support it.

**6.   B**

Finally, an Incorporation question. The author's judgment is that the revisionists are wrong: The Cold War could not have been averted, due to American attitudes and Russian hostility. He does admit, however, that there isn't much information about what was going on in the Kremlin at the time, so he can't be totally sure of the latter argument. Choice **B** is therefore the correct answer. This argument would not be affected by evidence of the author's feelings against communism (choice **A**), or the contrary opinion of a "noted authority" (choice **C**), or the viability of other alternatives (choice **D**).

# SELF-EVALUATION

For students hoping only to "pass" a test, simply taking many practice tests will probably improve their score. But if you're already performing well and want to improve, constant self-evaluation is key. Make this a regular part of your preparation for Verbal Reasoning.

Instead of reviewing the explanations to questions completely, many students stop at seeing why one answer is correct. This is a costly mistake if you want to maximize your score. Learn all you can about your strengths and weaknesses between now and Test Day, then use that information to manage your test taking. Some people find they make certain mistakes consistently; others only find some tendency toward certain errors. In either case, you can reduce, or even eliminate, the problem if you recognize it.

After taking practice Verbal Reasoning test sections, be sure to review your work by creating 'Why I Missed It' sheets. First, list all of the questions you answered incorrectly in the first column of a sheet of scrap paper. Then, note the question type and why you missed the correct answer in subsequent columns. Finally, check which answers you got right. This will help you to identify any question type that you need to review and practice more, and will give you a better sense of when you can trust your instincts on questions of which you're unsure.

After practice sets or tests, consider the following questions:

**Time Management:** Did you spend too much time on any passage?

**Kaplan Methods and Strategies:** Did you use Kaplan's methods and strategies in the course of this practice session? These should be practiced until they're second-nature.

**Fatigue:** Did you start to make more mistakes later in the test? If so, you have to build your stamina methodically. Consider, too, taking minibreaks. Periodically put down your pencil, close your eyes and take deep breaths for 10–20 seconds, then go back to work.

**Why did you get questions wrong?** Get away from the sheer fact of getting a question wrong to learning to reconstruct why and how. The most common reasons for going wrong are:

*Misreading the passage:* That is, you misunderstood what the passage was saying, or went to the wrong part of the passage.

*Misreading the question:* Questions that are easy to misread are Reasoning questions, or the questions that employ the words LEAST/EXCEPT/NOT—perhaps you'll find you have a tendency to misread other types. Check the question one last time before settling on a final answer.

*Misreading the choices:* Quite common.

*Mismanaging time:* You ran out of time and became too pressed.

**Why did you reject the right answer?** When you pick a wrong answer, you reject the right one. Can you see any pattern in what you thought was wrong with the answer that turned out to be the correct one? Often the answer to this is one of the following:

*Nit-picked it.* Some students object to a preposition or adverb in the credited choice, rather than taking the choice in its totality. Don't fight the test. The right answers are rarely perfect.

*Misread it.* Hasty test takers are prey to this error. The best defense here is, of course, to read each choice as it's worded.

*Never read it.* Students often (out of panic, usually) go with the first choice that looks good. This is a bad habit based on false economy.

## Some Self-Evaluation Experiments

### Looking Ahead at the Questions

Some test takers feel more anchored as they read the passage if they've glanced at the questions first. As a rule, it won't save you time or effort to do so. Most of the questions require a general understanding of the passage. You need to read for meaning and for organization whether or not you've reviewed the questions. However, you may find that a very quick look to identify the subjects of the questions (and any line or paragraph references) helps you to focus on those areas as you read. Experiment with the possible benefits of looking at the questions before you read, and use this technique if it works for you.

One caveat, though: If you decide you can benefit from a preview of the questions, *don't look at the choices.* Some of you may know that the official test maker's word for wrong answers is "distractors"—they're designed to confuse and mislead, and you don't want information from the choices clouding your comprehension of the passage.

### Reading Speed

Finding your ideal reading pace is essential to maximizing your score in Verbal Reasoning. To do this, try reading a few passages differently. If you believe you tend to get bogged down in passages, try practicing the fastest skimming you can do and still glean the broad outline—the structure. If you believe you tend to skim too quickly, try forcing yourself to slow down; actually read each sentence and paraphrase each paragraph.

Then do the questions and see how your results compare with your usual reading speed. If you do about as well with the radically different speed, your best speed lies midway between the two. If you do significantly better at one extreme than at the other, your best speed lies closer to the former speed.

### Note-Taking Style

By Test Day you should have developed a note-taking style that works well for you. For some students that means copious notes, while others find that the less they note, the better. Your goal is to make as little notation as possible while still establishing and retaining a strong sense of the passage structure. Start with full paraphrases of the ideas in each passage—then strip your paraphrases down until you find a point at which your ability to respond to questions starts to drop, and return to the next higher level of "mapping."

The next couple of pages contain the self-evaluation form. Photocopy it and use it as often as possible as you work with full-length Verbal Reasoning sections.

# READING THE PASSAGE

Basically, the critical reading style appropriate for Verbal Reasoning passages means looking for the gist of each paragraph and the function of each part of the text. Don't judge the passages. You'll need to overcome the hurdle of reading material that doesn't interest you or expresses opinions contrary to your own. Don't try to memorize details. The majority of the Verbal Reasoning questions will focus on the author's purpose and the structure of arguments, and supporting details can be reviewed if needed.

To get an idea of what we mean: What is the gist and what is the function of the first sentence in the two following paragraphs?

> A well-educated electorate is essential to the survival of a democratic society. Since the only way to maintain a high standard of education throughout all levels of society is through an effectively maintained system of public education, our democratic society must devote significant resources to its public education system in order to assure its continued viability.

> A well-educated electorate is essential to the survival of a democratic society. In aristocracies and monarchies, decisions affecting the well-being of society are made by an elite group, while the great mass of people, having no influence on the outcome, can afford to ignore politics. In democracies, however, the ultimate governing authority rests with the people as a whole, who must be able to make informed decisions.

In the first paragraph, the first sentence is a building block—a supporting fact—for the author's conclusion that funds must be devoted to education. But in paragraph 2 the same sentence *is* the author's principal contention, developed and supported by the succeeding sentences: A counterexample and a comparison. Now let's look at some tools that help you to identify the structure and gist.

## Keywords

Keywords are words and phrases that identify purpose or structure. You probably respond to Keywords unconsciously already. Critical Reading involves *consciously* noting and interpreting them. This will save time and improve your comprehension. The common Keyword categories follow, in their order of importance. For each category, think of other words and phrases that convey the same type of information.

| Keywords | Purpose | Examples |
|---|---|---|
| **Contrast** | The author is shifting direction in order to take the reader to this real purpose for writing the passage. | But, however, although, nevertheless, alternatively, yet |
| **Emphasis** | Identify comparative importance or relevance. These include all superlatives (or comparatives when only two things are compared) | Above all, primarily, especially, particularly, indeed |
| **Conclusion** | Signal that the author is about to sum up someone's thesis (but a passage could contain several ideas, so conclusions could sum up a thesis other than the author's.) | Therefore, thus, so, consequently, [Toynbee] claims that |
| **Evidence** | The author is about to provide support for a point; that is, give you evidence for what the author has already said. | Because, for, since, the reason is that |
| **Continuation** | Announce that more of the same is about to appear | Also, furthermore, in addition, moreover, equally |
| **Illustration** | Signal an example is about to arrive | According to these experts, for historians, in the words of [Hannah Arendt] |
| **Sequence** | Identify a necessary order at work—by chronology, importance, or some other criterion | First, then, next, finally, recently |

When you spot a Keyword, be sure you see what ideas are joined or contrasted. Remember that the words here are just examples—you'll know a Keyword by the type of information it conveys. And the Keyword categories aren't mutually exclusive; Contrast, Emphasis, and Sequence clues add details about Conclusions and Evidence.

## Paraphrases

Each paragraph will explore a new aspect of the author's purpose, and one paragraph often provides strong clues about what to expect in the next. Paraphrase each important idea as you read, briefly and in your own words. Paraphrasing is putting the text into your own words, which assures that you aren't "glazing" and clarifies the major ideas in your mind. Consider this paragraph—how would you paraphrase its ideas?

> The challenge of building democracy-sustaining institutions is most acute in the countries of Eastern Europe now working their way out of "real socialism," but it is also a central issue for some noncommunist nations in Asia that have spent decades under various forms of authoritarian and dictatorial rule. True, these authoritarian and dictatorial governments have not achieved the degree of penetration of society attained in good part by the communist regimes of Eastern Europe. Neither have they had the propensity to destroy all elements of civil society or to reconstitute only those that served as instruments of the state and its ruling party. Nevertheless, they have been no more hospitable to the growth of many of the institutions and institutional complexes that are associated with

democratic political systems and market economies. They, too, confront a long agenda of institution building before they may be counted as fully formed and functioning democratic societies.

Paraphrase:

_____

_____

Your paraphrase doesn't have to be more than "for democs, different tasks face Europe and Asia."

What Keywords helped you? *Challenge* and *propensity to destroy* are Conclusion Keywords, and both *most* and *central* indicate Emphasis. *But*, *not*, *neither*, and *nevertheless* mark Contrasts. Any one of these words alone might not get your attention, but together they make the purpose of the paragraph clear.

## Topic, Scope, and Purpose

The author of every passage has a purpose that you can usually identify in the first few paragraphs. By the time you've finished the first third to half of the passage, you should have noted three elements:

**Topic**—the author's broad subject matter

**Scope**—the specific aspect of the topic that interests the author

**Purpose**—why the author has written the passage

All Verbal Reasoning passages can be described using one of the following five purposes (be alert for paraphrases of them in the questions):

Describe          Analyze          Compare          Advocate          Rebut

Two Helpful Statistics:

- In two-thirds of all Verbal Reasoning passages, the main idea is stated (or restated) in the last paragraph.
- In half of all Verbal Reasoning passages, the first sentence of a paragraph gives you its gist.

## Structure

The structure of a passage is its organizational framework: Where is a particular idea introduced? How does it relate to the previous idea? The author chooses a *structure* that imposes order on content to produce a persuasive, logical argument—to accomplish the author's *purpose*. So you'll find that certain structural patterns tend to emerge, based on which purpose the author wishes to pursue.

Unlike most other standardized admissions tests, MCAT Verbal Reasoning uses extracts from published sources for its passages—it doesn't have them written for the test. What's more, in selecting their excerpts, the test makers may lop off introductory and concluding material, or may even excerpt material from only one section of the "classic" formula—this is one reason Verbal Reasoning passages can be unlike the reading you're accustomed to. If you do see a classic pattern, use it—it will make your reading easier—but *don't assume* there'll be a classic pattern.

# HANDLING THE QUESTIONS

As we've seen, the AAMC question categories are:

| | |
|---|---|
| **Comprehension:** | Global—main idea, author's purpose |
| | Detail—answers stated expressly in the passage |
| **Deduction:** | Inferences and assumptions |
| **Evaluation:** | Identify the function of a statement or the structure of the passage |
| **Application:** | Apply ideas in the passage to new information |
| **Incorporation:** | Apply new information to arguments made in the passage |

A special note about another type of question you might see on the MCAT, the Roman Numeral question. All kinds of passages can and do contain Roman Numeral questions, and they can be detail, inference, logic, or application-based. Regardless of where and when Roman numeral questions appear, students often greet them with fear and dread. You may remember this question type from the SAT.

Why do so many examinees have trouble with this format? One reason, of course, is lack of familiarity. A second reason is lack of confidence; many people find it tough enough to handle questions where there's <u>one</u> right answer, let alone when there's the possibility of two or more. However, these questions can actually be among the most manageable. At the very least they are very amenable to educated guessing.

The Form: Typically three statements or phrases labeled I, II, and III; the answer choices are various combinations of those statements or phrases.

Tips:

- Scan the distribution of the choices before you begin.
- Deal with the Roman numeral statements in any way that makes sense to you—don't automatically start with Statement I.
- Eliminate choices strategically. The moment you decide whether a Roman numeral is "in" or "out," you automatically can discard one or more of the four answer choices, and instantly improve your guessing odds.

For all types, since the AAMC likes to vary its language, you'll have to watch for paraphrases, like assumption questions worded "what idea is implicit in the author's argument" or "in making this argument, the author relied on which of the following statements."

The skills you need to develop to answer Verbal Reasoning questions include:

- Paraphrasing the question to disclose its standard type
- Researching the passage using your map
- Predicting an answer
- Eliminating "pathological" wrong answer choices (see below)

## Argument Dissection

Critical reading takes you a long way toward scoring points on Verbal Reasoning, but most of the questions you'll face will require more than finding, paraphrasing, or categorizing the appropriate text; they'll require that you understand arguments. In Verbal Reasoning, an *argument* simply means

a *conclusion*, or *what* someone wants or believes, plus
its supporting *evidence*, the reasons *why.*

Don't be misled by the word *conclusion*—it can appear in the beginning, middle, or end of a passage or paragraph. The skills you'll need when a question calls for Argument Dissection include:

- Dissecting the structure of a written argument,
- Identifying the implied part of an argument, and
- Restating each argument in consistent, simplified form.

Answer Verbal Reasoning questions based on the passage—not based on outside knowledge. Remember, since outside information is not relevant in the Verbal Reasoning section, evaluating an argument will never require that you decide whether the evidence is true—just that you evaluate the structure of the argument itself.

Verbal Reasoning Arguments have four possible parts:

| Part | Function |
|------|----------|
| **Opinion** | stated conclusion |
| **Facts** | stated evidence |
| **Inference** | implied conclusion |
| **Assumption** | implied evidence |

Three of the components—conclusion, evidence, and assumption—are necessary for every argument, whereas inferences *can* be a part of the argument, but are not necessary for the argument to be complete. As used here, *Facts* and *Opinions* mean the parts of the argument that you find in the text, rather than the implied Inferences or Assumptions.

The st arguments are those with conclusions that *must* be true if the evidence is true. For example:

**Evidence:**          All Central High School volleyball players are over six feet tall, and Sally plays volleyball for Central High.

**Conclusion:**      Therefore, Sally is over six feet tall.

Don't allow your own biases to mislead you when answering Verbal Reasoning questions. An argument can be strong even if you reject its conclusion, or weak even if you believe its conclusion is true.

## The Stated Parts of Arguments

### Isolate Fact from Opinion Using Keywords

Read the following paragraph, then decide whether it's Fact, or Opinion, or a combination of the two:

> It is misleading to say that advances in communication have made it possible for people to be "better informed" about world events than was possible in the past. There's a limit to how much total information any person can absorb; so the only result of better communications is that whereas people used to know a great deal about the few places that concerned them directly, now they know very little about a great many places.

Fact _____     Opinion _____     Combination _____

The paragraph generally expresses an Opinion about the nature of information and people's capacity to absorb it, but the statement "There's a limit to how much total information any person can absorb" is given as Fact supporting the Opinion that follows it, which is introduced by the conclusion Keyword *so*—therefore, it's a combination. No Keyword labels the evidence, but the context distinguishes it—it's offered as an answer to the question "why should I believe the author's Opinion?" *Misleading* is a strong, judgmental word indicating the author's Opinion in the first sentence. In the second sentence, *only* is Emphasis, and *whereas...used to* and *now* indicate Contrast, which is reiterated in the details: "A great deal about a few places" contrasts with "very little about a great many places."

Note that, as in this case, you may find more than one conclusion in a single paragraph, not just the Opinion that represents the paragraph's principal argument. And often you'll have to dissect one of these subarguments rather than the principal argument.

Now try identifying the argument parts in this paragraph:

> While this may be the most commonly held belief, more enlightened scholars argue that these figures are actually Shinto religious images. They point out that Shinto artists often borrowed Buddhist iconography, so an image that resembles a lion cannot unequivocally be interpreted as a Buddhist piece. Furthermore, Shinto art characteristically displays a peculiar appreciation for the wood (reflecting the belief that a deity may reside in any natural object) and the artist who sculpted these statues carefully followed the natural direction of the wood grain in sculpting curls of the mane and the curves of the forelegs.

The first sentence is the conclusion. It's what the author wants you to believe. If the sentence said simply "other scholars argue" this could be evidence, citing one branch of scholarship on the topic. But the author describes these scholars as "more enlightened"—and that's the author's Opinion. The Keyword *While* prepares you for the second half of the sentence contrasting with the opening clause. Keywords *argue* and *actually* further identify the Opinion. You can see that it isn't necessary to recognize every Keyword, since they often reinforce each other throughout passages.

The second sentence is evidence identified by the Keywords *they point out that*—this is some of the supporting detail provided by the experts. Notice the subconclusion, introduced by *so*—the Opinion of this group of scholars, supported by the Fact that Shinto artists borrowed from Buddhist iconography.

The third sentence is more evidence—as the word *Furthermore* indicates.

### Isolate Fact from Opinion Using Context

Often we rely on the context to distinguish Fact from Opinion: Depending on the context, the same sentence can be either a conclusion or evidence. To prove this, identify the function of the italicized statement in the following argument:

> *My apartment is a mess.* My refrigerator is empty. I haven't done laundry in a month. I'm the world's worst housekeeper.

In this case, *My apartment is a mess* is evidence (together with a lot of laundry and an empty refrigerator) for the conclusion that this writer is a bad housekeeper. The first three sentences answer the question, "Why should I believe that this person a bad housekeeper?" You realize this, as you read, as soon as you get through the second sentence: The empty refrigerator doesn't relate to the messy apartment. Since these two statements don't fall into any relationship with each other, they must each relate to something else in the paragraph—each of them does relate to the concept of "housekeeper."

Now identify the function of the same statement in the next argument

> *My apartment is a mess.* The living room needs to be vacuumed. The sink is full of dishes. Dust completely fills the space under my bed.

What has changed? Here, the author concludes that the apartment is a mess based on the evidence in the next three sentences: The apartment has a dirty living room floor, a sink full of dishes, and dust—all aspects of the mess. Remember, the Opinion should answer the question, "what is the author's point?" The Facts should answer the question, "why should we believe the Opinion is true?"

### Restate the Argument

When you know what Facts support which Opinion, restate the argument in your own, simplified words:

> The author believes the Conclusion *because* of the Evidence.

This will give you a consistent form to work with, whatever the questions ask. With practice, this step will be automatic and instantaneous by Test Day—saving, not using, time.

Sorting the Opinion from the Facts, restate the argument made in the following paragraph:

> The "Robber Baron" industrialists of the late 19th and early 20th centuries are often portrayed as having no interest in the well-being of society as a whole in their ruthless pursuit of power and personal fortunes. Quite apart from the incidental benefits they provided to society through industrial development, this view ignores the philanthropic endeavors with which most of the Robber Barons were associated. Admittedly a good deal of their philanthropy took the form of bequests; still, these industrialists are responsible for many of our best museums and symphony halls, and the foundations they established continue to rank among the most important sources of charity to this day.

Argument: _____

You probably used different words, but the basic idea is: These industrialists were better than most people think *because* they developed industry *and* because they were very philanthropic.

Note that this argument is never affirmatively stated in the passage: It's expressed as a rebuttal of a common opinion, with the author's opinion apparent in the words *this view ignores. Quite apart from* indicates that the first part of the sentence—about the industrial benefits the Robber Barons provided—is in contrast to the more significant evidence—that their philanthropy is sufficient to redeem their reputations. *Admittedly* is another evidence Keyword; you *admit* facts that weaken or refute your conclusion. Although we discuss many of the Keywords present in our passages, remember that you shouldn't worry about catching every Keyword—they reinforce each other, and you only need to note enough to grasp the flow of the argument.

## The Unstated Parts of Arguments

### Assumptions

The process of deciphering what the author implies is deduction, and Deduction questions are the most common type on MCAT Verbal Reasoning. A Verbal Reasoning Assumption is unstated evidence—specifically, a connection between the Facts and Opinion that the author must believe is true in order to reach the stated conclusion. Read the following argument, and write the assumption on the line below.

> Sally plays volleyball for Central High School; therefore, Sally must be more than six feet tall (assuming that ...)

Assumption: _____

The Keyword *therefore* tells us that "Sally is more than six feet tall" is the conclusion, so "Sally plays volleyball..." is supporting evidence. But what's missing?

> All those who play volleyball for Central High are more than six feet tall.

This Assumption directly links the evidence to the conclusion, and it must be true if the conclusion follows from the stated evidence. Note that either Fact could have been left unstated in this argument. If you are told: "All volleyball players for Central High are more than six feet tall, therefore Sally must be more than six feet tall" then the author must be assuming that Sally plays volleyball for Central High.

Now identify the Opinion, Facts, and Assumption in a more subtle argument:

> The company president should allow the office to remain open late, instead of closing at 6:00; much more work would get done. . . .

Opinion: _____

Facts: _____

Assumption: _____

To find an argument's Assumption, focus on the differences between the terms of the evidence and conclusion. In this case, observe that the office doesn't do the work, employees do—so the missing connection between the number of hours the office is open and the amount of work that gets done is the behavior of the employees.

> Opinion: The office should be kept open late.
> Facts: More work would get done.
> Assumption: Employees will be productive for more hours if the office is open longer.

This Assumption directly links the evidence to the conclusion, and must be true if the conclusion follows from the stated evidence. The author's Opinion in this case is identified by the word *should*; the Facts contain no Keywords. Often either the Facts or the Opinion will have Keywords, but not both. So finding the Opinion may be, in part, by process of elimination from the Facts (or vice versa).

### Inferences

A Verbal Reasoning Inference is an implied part of an argument that must be true if the Facts are true. Consider the following:

> Sally plays volleyball for Central High School. All of Central High's volleyball players are more than six feet tall (therefore we can infer ...)

We can infer that Sally is over six feet tall. We are given Facts that necessarily add up to this conclusion. Note the difference between an Inference and an Assumption: The former is a conclusion supported by the given Facts, the latter is an unstated Fact necessary to support the stated Opinion. They aren't interchangeable parts. If you were told:

> Sally plays volleyball for Central High School *and* (rather than "therefore")
> Sally is more than six feet tall

you wouldn't be able to infer that "all volleyball players for Central High School are over six feet tall" as you did in the exercise on Assumptions; it's only a possibility. The information given doesn't support that statement as a conclusion.

Now try another familiar type of example. What is the Inference in this argument?

> Either you or I must clean this room, and I won't do it!

Conclusion: _____

Evidence: _____

> Conclusion: You have to clean the room.

> Evidence: Either you or I have to clean the room, and I won't.

This is another implicit conclusion—an Inference of a type that occurs commonly in conversation. Only evidence is stated in the argument. Note that, when there is no stated conclusion, there are not likely to be Keywords indicating the different roles played by the parts.

### The Denial Test

If you are uncertain about an Assumption or Inference answer choice, it may be easier to see what happens if that choice is *not* true. This is Kaplan's Denial Test. It's more time-consuming than predicting the correct answer, but it can be very powerful. Use it while you're practicing how to confirm your predictions; use it on the test when you can't predict.

Let's see how this would work with a simple argument:

> Sally plays volleyball for Central High School; therefore, Sally is more than
> six feet tall.

> Assumption: All Central High volleyball players are over six feet tall.

> Denial: *Not* all Central High volleyball players are over six feet tall.

We are no longer able to conclude that, without a doubt, Sally is over six feet tall as stated in the argument, so that assumption is necessary to the argument.

### Restate the Argument With Implied Parts

Restate arguments with implied parts in the same simplified form you use for arguments with only stated parts:

> The author believes the Opinion *because* of the Facts plus the Assumption.

> The Inference must be true *because* of the Facts and Opinions.

Practice by restating the argument in the following passage excerpt:

> ... It is a historical fact that only in conditions of profound societal instability are great works of literature produced. During the first century B.C., Rome experienced almost constant civil war accompanied by social upheaval. It wasn't until the ascension of Nerva to the throne in 96 A.D. that the situation stabilized. Throughout the second century A.D., Rome experienced a century of uninterrupted peace and stability.

Argument: _____

_____

The author left the conclusion unstated, but the facts left no room for doubt about it. A reasonable restatement might be:

> Great literature was created during the first centuries B.C. and A.D., but not during the second century A.D., *because* great literature requires social unrest *and* social unrest existed in the first centuries B.C. and A.D. but not the second century A.D.

# RECOGNIZING THE AUTHOR'S VOICE

On the MCAT, recognizing the author's voice is the most important part of any Verbal Reasoning passage, because so many questions ask about it in one way or another.

The author's voice reflects the author's opinion or purpose. When you break down the author's argument into its conclusion and evidence, the author's voice will provide the conclusion. And when you map the author's purpose on Test Day, you will essentially be making note of the author's voice.

The author's voice may be straightforward, subtle, or neutral; nevertheless, you'll always want to note it when it appears. If there are several opinions expressed in a passage, you'll want to be clear about which opinion belongs to the author of the passage and which opinions reflect ideas of others mentioned in the passage.

In the following paragraphs, underline the author's voice and restate it in your own words. If there are two opinions, focus on and rephrase that of the author.

1.  A scientific trial found that the administration of AZT (zidovudine) to HIV-positive women during pregnancy and delivery, and to their babies after birth, reduced the transmission of HIV to the infants by two-thirds, compared to a placebo. The validity of the study's result, however, is debatable. The design did not account for important variables: in particular, whether the amount of HIV in the subjects' bodies might have contributed to the difference in transmission rates.

Restate the author's opinion _____

_____

2. The position of the parfleche—an envelope-shaped rawhide container used by the Plains people for storing clothes, food, and personal items—held symbolic position in the lodge. It was stored beneath the bed of older women, not only because they were careful guardians, but also because they were closer to Grandmother Earth, from whose union with the lightning spirit the animals and plants of the middle worlds came to provide food and shelter. The symbolism of the parfleche, therefore, reflects the Cheyenne belief in a complementary worldview: the blending of the masculine spirit and the feminine physical matter.

Restate the author's opinion _____

_____

3. Early biologists tried to explain why, contrary to expectations, family size decreased after the Industrial Revolution, which ushered in a new prosperity. By drawing comparisons with the animal world, biologists suggested that animals that have many young tend to live in hostile, unpredictable environments. Since the odds against any offspring's survival are high, having many offspring increases the chance that at least one or two of them will survive. However, in more stable, affluent times, animals will have fewer children, since more of them are apt to survive. Critics of this theory argue instead that changes in social attitudes are adequate to explain this phenomenon.

Restate the author's opinion _____

_____

4. Containing invasive fish and animal species has become a focal point for environmentalists. However, scientific evidence is lacking about which containment measures work, and about how serious the threat posed by various invasive species actually is. Simply identifying an environmental threat does not mean we should automatically give it priority over other important issues. Instead, scientific data should be treated as just that—data that allow us to make informed and balanced policy decisions.

Restate the author's opinion _____

_____

5. In the fast new choreography of American compassion, explanation is twirled into excuse, and the spotlight's shine gives feeling a prominence that facts could only hope for. How we perceive something has become more important than its reality. We prefer to understand viewpoints rather than discern truths.

Restate the author's opinion _____

_____

### Discussion

1.   "The validity of the study's result, however, is debatable." The author's voice disagrees with the study's conclusions. The key here is the word "however." Contrast words may sometimes introduce the author's point of view. The rest of the passage will probably explain his objection and may also provide an alternative suggestion to the study.

2.   "The symbolism of the parfleche, therefore, reflects the Cheyenne belief in a complementary worldview: the blending of the masculine spirit and the feminine physical matter." The parfleche is important to the Cheyenne as a symbol of their beliefs. As noted by the word "therefore," the author is stating her conclusion about the parfleche. She is summing up, essentially saying that everything she wrote previously comes down to this one idea.

3.   "Early biologists tried to explain why, contrary to expectations, family size decreased after the Industrial Revolution, which ushered in a new prosperity." The author simply states that people tried to explain why families got smaller even though they had more resources and money. We have a neutral author here, since there is no particular point of view expressed— just a paradox. Note that when passages start with paradoxes or questions, the rest of the passage will give at least one explanation. You should actively read for the general idea behind the explanation, rather than the details.

4.   "However, scientific evidence is lacking about what containment measures work, and about how serious the threat posed by various invasive species actually is." Again we have the contrast word "however," indicating the author's point of view. This statement indicates that the author doesn't agree with previous ideas about how to control invasive species and how serious the problem is. The rest of the paragraph—the details, or evidence—will probably support his opinion.

5.   "How we perceive something has become more important than its reality. We prefer to understand viewpoints rather than discern truths." The author makes her opinion clear right up front. Specifically, she concludes that we are more interested in how we feel about things than in the facts about them. The rest of the passage will support this idea in the form of examples and details. Even though the details will be alluded to in questions, the author's point of view will be most important in getting the questions right.

## Attacking Tough Passages

### How many "tough" passages will you encounter on Test Day?

At least two, and at most three.

### Which passages are usually the "tough" ones?

Passages from subject areas that lend themselves to abstract language (e.g., social science and humanities) and passages from the world of philosophy or higher abstract thought.

### What makes these passages "tough"?

They present difficult ideas in a difficult framework. They tend to be abstract, dense, and rather dull. In fact, they tend to have few or no proper nouns, which makes establishing relationships very difficult.

### Take this example:

In deciding the characteristics of a legitimate state, what conception of humanity should we use? Hobbes was quite explicit on this point, making his case with what he considered to be the worst image of people. To find Nozick's opinion on the question, we again look to his discussion of Locke; and for Nozick, the position from which we justify the state is

Locke's state of nature. In Locke's state of nature, people have rights, and people generally respect one another's rights. Nozick accepts this, and proceeds to make his case without assuming any further responsibilities toward others. The resulting picture of humanity resembles a population of disinterested choosers, who need not have any concern for their fellows beyond respecting their basic rights.

Topic  _____

Scope  _____

Purpose  _____

### Discussion

**Topic:** the legitimate state

**Scope:** the conception of humanity that pertains to it

**Purpose:** to describe 3 different views: Hobbes—people are low, Locke—people are respectful, Nozick—people are self-centered and distant, indirectly respectful.

So you can see that by breaking down tough passages into discrete bits of information, you gain a better understanding of the author's purpose.

## Hints for Attacking Tough Passages

**Hint #1:** Make mental pictures.

Tough passages are often confusing since students are erroneously focusing on the prose, and not the ideas behind the prose. One excellent way to animate those ideas is to picture what is happening mentally. Let's take an example:

> Researchers have never directly observed the formation or existence of these super-heavy elements. The emission of hydrogen nuclei, presumably from the element's decay, is the only evidence that the experiments have succeeded.

### Discussion

For the "emission of hydrogen nuclei," picture sparks flying from a sort of core. That may keep you tuned into the fact that "these super-heavy elements"—whatever they are—actually exist, even though no one has seen them. You will now be ready to add or alter to this mental picture as more details pile on.

**Hint #2:** Pay the greatest attention to sentences in which the author clearly voices an opinion.

It's no surprise that the author's opinion is paramount on Test Day. This hint is just a reminder that when a passage is baffling or off-putting, you can get a handle on it simply by skipping past all the objective facts and highlighting the opinions instead. Look at the sample paragraph below:

> Marsupials are not known to exhibit protective behavior. Indeed, scientists have reported that frightened female kangaroos will drop their pouch-young as they flee, drawing a predator's attention to the less able

offspring while the adult escapes. This behavior, whether purposeful or accidental, instantaneously relieves the female marsupial of the mechanical difficulties of pregnancy with which her placental counterpart would be burdened, while marsupials can replace any lost young quickly. Thus, in the absence of any need for close maternal supervision, sacrificing their offspring in this manner may well have been favored in selection. Pointing to the absence of the "virtue" of maternal protectiveness in marsupials is an instance of how mistaken those theorists are who see similarities with humans as marks of evolutionary sophistication.

Summary _____

### Discussion

**Summary:** Some people use human standards to gauge just how evolved other animals are or have become. But, according to the author, they are wrong to do so, and this extended example is evidence of why. The keywords indicating this lies in the last sentence, "how mistaken those theorists are…"

**Hint #3:** Really "dumb it down."

Students (especially perfectionist pre-med students) mistakenly think that they are supposed to read like an expert in the given field of a passage, but that is not at all the case! When one is not an expert in that field, it's rational to expect to pick up only the bare bones of what is being said. This is especially true when you add the strict time limits on Test Day (only 8–9 minutes per passage)! Practice getting just the gist with the following example:

Social analysts of the 1950s sought to demonstrate how the increasing industrialization, urbanization, and bureaucratization of American society had, beginning in the early nineteenth century, altered the American psyche. Writers of the day like David Riesman and William H. Whyte argued that the achievement motive and the Protestant ethic of hard work had virtually died as Americans began to turn to communal togetherness. Riesman posited a transformation of the American character structure from inner direction (responding to a fixed internal code of morality) to other direction (responding to the demands of others in complex situations). Whyte believed that values themselves had changed, suggesting that the old value system of the Protestant ethic, defined as the drive for individual redemption, had been replaced by the social ethic whose basic tenet stressed the importance of the group, the many.

Bare-bones gist _____

### Discussion

**Bare-bones gist:** In the 1950s, some scholars thought that increasing industrialization, urbanization, and bureaucratization had changed American values; that Americans had turned from caring about themselves to caring about others.

You should worry about the other details, like Riesman and Whyte, when they appear in a question, not before.

**Hint #4:** Relate it to your world.

This is similar to the hint "make a mental picture," except that this requires you to conjure up a specific real-life example of the phenomenon described. If you can relate the ideas to "real life"— yours or somebody else's—you will be less intimidated by them and more able to answer questions about them. Be careful NOT to substitute your own ideas for the author's, though!

Try your hand at this hint in the passage excerpts below:

> The justification of political institutions is perhaps the fundamental question of political philosophy. For centuries, one of the leading theories in state justification has been contract theory. The general approach is as follows: citizens of a state enter into a contract with that state. The terms of that contract determine what is permissible. The state is justified insofar as it fulfills its responsibilities as defined in the contract. The state is also entitled to restrict the freedom of its citizens according to the terms of the contract. The key is consent: the contract is justified because we agreed to it.

Real-life example _____


> To apply extensionism, one starts with a set of individuals who are assumed to have moral value. Then these individuals are examined to determine what it is about them that entitles them to moral consideration. Having found that set of qualities X, any other thing that also has X also deserves moral consideration. That is, by virtue of having X, a thing may have moral consideration extended to it.

Real-life example _____


### Discussion

**Political Philosophy Example:** "citizens of a state enter into a contract with that state"— Income tax, or the rule of law as administered by police and judges.

**Extensionism Example:** "individuals who are assumed to have moral value"— The clergy, social crusaders), writers who point the moral truths of life for us in words and images.

**Hint #5:** Concentrate on the first and last sentence of each paragraph.

Over the years, Kaplan has found that in MCAT passages from the test maker (especially the denser and more abstract ones), the tougher prose is generally framed with more straightforward sentences at the beginning and at the end of the paragraph. The following paragraph illustrates this point really well:

> *Animal behavior was formerly thought to consist of simple responses, some of them innate and some of them learned, to incoming stimuli.* Complex behavior, if it was considered at all, was assumed to be the result of complex stimuli. However, a particular group of ethologists has established a new view of animal behavior. They have shown that the animal brain possesses certain specific competencies, that animals have an innate capacity for performing complex acts in response to simple stimuli. *The discovery that complex behavior patterns were inherited was a vitally important contribution to the study of evolution.*

### Discussion

The middle of the paragraph is essentially just filler, so reading just the first and last sentences can be a good way to save time if time is running low on Test Day.

**Hint #6:** There'll always be a few points there for the taking.

When students hit a tough passage, they tend to get discouraged and assume that because the passage is baffling them, the questions will as well. But remember that the passage is NOT an all-or-nothing scenario. All passages come equipped with a set of questions of varying difficulty levels, from easy questions that most students can handle to tough ones that few can.

So even when you think a passage is tough, you can still be confident that you will be able to answer a few of the questions correctly.

**Hint #7:** Use the answer choices to fill in content gaps.

If, even after all of the hints above, the main purpose of the passage is still elusive, you have one lifeline available to you: the answer choices! You can always work backward from them to help you reason out what must be true for that part of the passage.

**Hint #8:** Be confident!

A positive attitude can only help you on Test Day. Thanks to your preparations and your wise investment in Kaplan, you will be able to overcome any obstacles on the road to Verbal Reasoning success!

## Wrong-Answer Pathologies

Just like the questions, wrong answer choices are of several standard types. Knowing why a choice is wrong will increase your confidence in the correct choice when you find it. If you can't predict the answer or your prediction is vague, you can eliminate wrong choices to improve your chances of selecting the correct answer. The following are "pathological" choice types that Kaplan has found show up consistently in Verbal Reasoning; become familiar with them and you'll discard wrong choices quickly and confidently on Test Day.

> **Opposite:** States the opposite of what the question calls for or what's cited in the passage.
>
> **Outside the Scope:** Deals with material beyond the confines of the passage or the author's concern. (Note that since Topic is broader than scope, a choice can relate to the correct topic but still be outside the scope that the author takes up.)
>
> **Distortion:** Relates to a point in the passage, but confuses some aspect of it; the most common Distortions are too extreme or exaggerated.
>
> **FUD** (Faulty Use of Detail): Focuses on a detail from the wrong part of the passage or takes a relevant detail out of context. The most common FUD is a direct quote from the wrong part of the passage.

Some wrong-answer pathologies will naturally be more common with particular question types. For example, the most common wrong-answer pathologies on Detail questions are Distortion or FUD. You'll always find an Opposite answer choice on "strengthen" or "weaken" questions or LEAST/EXCEPT/NOT questions, since one of the most common mistakes made in Verbal Reasoning is to forget precisely what the question asks.

If you have to guess the answer to a question, answer the other questions for that passage first. To complete your list of "elimination strategies," here are a few other Kaplan tactics that are particularly useful when detailed prediction isn't possible or time is short:

If two answers are very close, one is probably right.

If two answers are opposites of each other, one is probably right.

In LEAST/EXCEPT/NOT questions, if the content of one answer seems different from the other three, it's probably right.

Extreme statements are most likely wrong.

# THINK LIKE A TEST MAKER

You've seen all the AAMC question categories. In their order of frequency, they are: Deduction, Evaluation, Application, Incorporation, Detail, and Global.

Detail and Global questions, of course, are relatively rare and can be drawn from any passage, and your critical reading will arm you to answer them.

But the other types can only be asked if appropriate material is present in the text. There are only a certain number of other questions that can be written for any particular passage—and their type is dictated by the passage itself. Although the AAMC likes to vary the wording of its questions to create the impression that each is unique, they actually translate into a fairly small number of standard questions:

| TYPE | BASIC FORMATS |
| --- | --- |
| **Deduction** | Inference: The author most likely would agree that . . .<br>Assumption: In arguing that . . . , the author implicitly relies on the idea that . . .<br>Definition-in-context: As used in the passage, the expression . . .<br>most likely means . . . |
| **Evaluation** | Structure: Which of the following best characterizes the author's claim that . . . ?<br>Function: The author most likely mentions . . . in order to: |
| **Application** | Hypotheticals: If . . . , the author would probably advise:<br>Analogies: Which of the following is most analogous to . . . ?<br>General statements: Which of the following general ideas is most consistent with . . . ?<br>Author identity: It reasonably can be inferred that the author of this passage is a: |
| **Incorporation** | Effect: Suppose . . . . What relevance would this information have to the passage?<br>Which of the following would most strengthen [or challenge] the argument . . . ?<br>Solution: Which of the following would the author consider a solution to [or explanation of] the problem of . . . ? |

Reading the Kaplan way means identifying the kinds of information that will appear in those Verbal Reasoning questions: The author's purpose, the expressed and implied Opinions, and the supporting evidence. If you also keep in mind the standard Verbal Reasoning question types, you can take this one step further—you'll start to "see" the questions to expect as you read the passage.

## Contrasts

Keeping the standard questions in mind, read the following passage excerpt. What questions do you see waiting to be asked in the text?

> Panspermia, the hypothesis that life on Earth originated in outer space, has had a number of supporters since the nineteenth century—some of them quite distinguished—but it has never won general acceptance among biologists. However, recent research has found possible support for panspermia. Most of the meteorites that strike the Earth originated in the lifeless wastes of the asteroid belt. A few, though, have been identified as fragments that were torn from the Moon and Mars by comets and asteroids, and eventually drifted to Earth. The Moon and Mars are lifeless, but there is reason to think that, billions of years ago, Mars was warmer and moister than it is now, and capable of supporting life. Indeed, Mars may have been more conducive to the development of life than Earth was at the time. It is feasible that life developed on Mars first, and was carried to Earth on space-borne debris.

This paragraph uses contrasts to structure its argument. The first sentence tells us the theory has some distinguished supporters, but not general acceptance. The next sentence says: However (but) new research provides some support for it. The rest of the paragraph details that new evidence. The questions you can expect will draw on your abilities to identify the number of different views presented, to see whether and how they are supported, and to determine which, if any, is endorsed by the author. There might be Inference or Evaluation questions such as

> The author mentions supporters of panspermia in lines 2–4 primarily in order to:

Here's another paragraph offering two views. What types of question are likely?

> There are, broadly, two opposed schools, echoing a conflict that has persisted down the centuries. One side believes that the mind's mental processes are somehow different from the physical stuff of the brain and body, a conviction widely referred to as "mind–body dualism." Opponents of dualism, determined to expel the "ghost in the machine," insist that there is only one sort of reality—material stuff. These "naturalists" maintain that the mind must be explained by explaining it away. Progress in understanding the mind depends on rejecting the idea of an inner self that governs our behavior and adopting a relentlessly reductionist approach to phenomena, reducing everything to its smallest, material, mechanical parts.

In this paragraph, the words *two opposed schools* and the other phrases in quotation marks help identify the different views presented. This is a likely candidate for Deduction or Evaluation questions, such as:

> According to the author, it can be inferred that the "mind–body dualists" would agree that

> Its opponents criticize dualism by claiming that it

> Which of the following best describes the structure of the passage above?

## Special Vocabulary

Technical terms or other specialized vocabulary might be tested by a Definition-in-context question or an Application question requiring that you determine what new information conforms to the meaning of the term:

> According to the author, which of the following would be an example of a "reductionist" explanation of a mental phenomenon?

### Experiments

Try another passage excerpt:

> REM (rapid eye movement) sleep, also called "paradoxical" sleep because of its neurologically aroused character, is best known as the sleep phase during which intense dreams occur in humans. Monitoring electrical activity in the brain indicates that, in contrast to the slow-wave patterns of dreamless sleep, REM sleep displays high-frequency, low-amplitude waves all but identical to those of wakefulness. It was thought until recently that PGO spikes (short-lived, high-amplitude electrical waves) occurred uniquely in REM sleep and spontaneously (without external stimulus). However when a laboratory worker accidentally struck a cage while a cat's slow-wave sleep was being traced, a PGO spike appeared almost instantly. Subsequent study indicated that both sound and touch produce PGO spikes in either REM or slow-wave sleep. PGO spikes seem to be general alerting responses occurring in several sleep phases.
>
> This finding prompted reevaluation of waves called eye-movement potentials (EMPs) that occur in the waking state. These were believed to depend on environmental levels of light, but in the EEG record they appeared identical to PGO spikes. Researchers seeking to test the validity of this idea eliminated environmental light from a cat's cage and then directed the odor of fish through the cage. They observed EMPs identical to PGO spikes. Sharp noises produced the same result.

A series of experiments provide fertile ground for questions about the reasons for new experiments (Incorporation or Application questions), analogous processes (an Application question), and the evaluation of results (Detail or Deduction questions). Possible questions include:

> Based on the information in the passage, fish odor was directed through a darkened cage in order to determine
>
> The author implies that EMPs were reevaluated because

### Implicit Statements

Wherever arguments are made, there may also be *implied* evidence or conclusions. You shouldn't spend time trying to identify these while you read—but the more you practice, the more often you'll find you can recognize the *presence* (though probably not the details) of implicit assumptions and inferences. Now consider this paragraph:

> In her 1929 classic *A Room of One's Own*, Virginia Woolf discusses the exclusion of women from English higher culture. To help explain the absence of female authors in the Elizabethan Age, she imagines what might have happened if William Shakespeare had a sister who possessed

all of her brother's genius. "Judith Shakespeare" is one of Woolf's most memorable fictional creations: Scorned by her family and by society at large for attempting to become a professional writer, she ends her days in squalor and misery. This picture influenced feminist thought for decades: If there are few great woman writers in the Western canon, it is because women were prevented from writing. Recent scholarship has shown how misleading this picture is. The oppression of women throughout history is real enough, but even in Shakespeare's England—undeniably a sexist society by modern standards—there were successful women authors.

The author strongly disagrees with Woolf's view, and offers proof for her position. Become alert for inconsistencies. Here, Judith Shakespeare is said to be "attempting to become a professional writer" and the existence of "successful woman authors" is given as proof that she could have become one—does "success" equate with "professional"? When you see the author's reasoning as well as her Opinion, look for Evaluation, Deduction, and Incorporation questions:

> In concluding that feminist thought was influenced by Woolf's writing, the author assumes

> Which of the following would be most useful in disputing the author's argument that successful women writers in Elizabethan England disprove Woolf's conclusion?

Now consider another:

> Although Dorothy Wordsworth was convinced that her journal entries were not literature, they were seamlessly incorporated by her brother William into some of his most famous poems, altered only by his use of the first-person pronoun, the "I." The important question concerning the relationship between Dorothy and William, however, is not whether William's borrowings constituted exploitation, but rather how the relationship contributed to Dorothy's inability to conceive of herself as a writer. Traditionally in literature, the authorial self, the "I," is identifiably masculine; the dominated "other" is feminine. In William's poems, the "other" is usually Nature, often personified as Dorothy. While these literary roles helped to sustain the close relationship between the two in real life, they also reinforced Dorothy's acceptance of the norms that defined her as "other." Thus, her access to authorial self-consciousness was blocked not just by the fact of her gender, but also by her accepted role in her brother's life and poetry.

When the author avoids stating a clearly implicit opinion, you can expect to find it in the questions:

> It can be inferred from the passage that the author believes which of the following about the quality of Dorothy Wordsworth's journal entries?

> It can be inferred from the passage that the author believes which of the following about the relationship between Dorothy Wordsworth and her brother?

You may also have noticed the unusual meaning of "self-consciousness" here—another question waiting to be asked. Now try another paragraph:

> In response to rapidly rising crime rates, legislators in Georgian England initiated a policy of imposing mandatory capital punishment for what to modern eyes is an astonishing range of crimes. Over 200 crimes were punishable by hanging: Not only murder and kidnapping, but also forgery, petty theft, and "posing as a gypsy." Yet, while the number of crimes punishable by death increased, and more and more criminals were brought to trial, the numbers of people who were actually hanged fell. Simple decency alone accounts for many of the instances in which the English chose not to apply their lethal laws. Judges could commute the death sentence for suitably penitent felons. Juries could undervalue stolen goods so as to bilk the prosecution. (Since the law demanded that anyone who stole 40 shillings or more must hang, hundreds of convictions were handed down every year for the theft of goods valued by the jury at 39 shillings.)

When something is stated as being done "in response" to something else (or any paraphrase of this language), the connection between the two is often assumed, leading to a Deduction question:

> In enacting capital punishment legislation, Georgians assumed that

### Lists and Categories

Lists are another frequent source of questions; there might be an Evaluation question about its function, or an Application question about items *not* mentioned by the author that also belong on the list. "Not only...but also" constructions suggest questions about the distinction between those categories—or perhaps about their similarities.

> The author mentions the crimes of forgery, petty theft, and posing as a gypsy in order to

Try a final paragraph:

> Sociologist Morton Marks's structural studies of several types of African American music show that the musical event is also a ritual event, defined here as a meaningful structure for social transition between cultures. Marks suggests that the abrupt switch from European to African performing rules in the middle of certain songs signals a transition from conventional "performance" to ritual. In Black American gospel music, for instance, "channel cues"—phrases like *going home* or *feeling the fire*—establish the ritual setting and introduce a trance event. Unlike the glossolalia ("speaking in tongues") common in some white churches, trance behavior in African American music takes place within the musical structure, and as such consists of elaborately patterned, linguistically meaningful statements. This transition to African modes, Marks contends, expresses a historical awareness of cultural distinctions between Africa and Europe.

Contrasts and categories established in the passage are frequently the basis for Verbal Reasoning questions:

> Which of the following might the author consider an example of a "channel cue"?

> The author contrasts the trance behavior in African American song rituals with glossolalia primarily to

As you can see, the elements Kaplan teaches you to look for as you read are the building blocks from which the questions are made. If you train yourself to read each passage critically—and be conscious of the standard questions—there will be few surprises in the questions at the end of each Verbal Reasoning passage.

# VERBAL REASONING PRACTICE SET

## Answer Sheet

| | | |
|---|---|---|
| 1 (A) (B) (C) (D) | 16 (A) (B) (C) (D) | 31 (A) (B) (C) (D) |
| 2 (A) (B) (C) (D) | 17 (A) (B) (C) (D) | 32 (A) (B) (C) (D) |
| 3 (A) (B) (C) (D) | 18 (A) (B) (C) (D) | 33 (A) (B) (C) (D) |
| 4 (A) (B) (C) (D) | 19 (A) (B) (C) (D) | 34 (A) (B) (C) (D) |
| 5 (A) (B) (C) (D) | 20 (A) (B) (C) (D) | 35 (A) (B) (C) (D) |
| | | |
| 6 (A) (B) (C) (D) | 21 (A) (B) (C) (D) | |
| 7 (A) (B) (C) (D) | 22 (A) (B) (C) (D) | |
| 8 (A) (B) (C) (D) | 23 (A) (B) (C) (D) | |
| 9 (A) (B) (C) (D) | 24 (A) (B) (C) (D) | |
| 10 (A) (B) (C) (D) | 25 (A) (B) (C) (D) | |
| | | |
| 11 (A) (B) (C) (D) | 26 (A) (B) (C) (D) | |
| 12 (A) (B) (C) (D) | 27 (A) (B) (C) (D) | |
| 13 (A) (B) (C) (D) | 28 (A) (B) (C) (D) | |
| 14 (A) (B) (C) (D) | 29 (A) (B) (C) (D) | |
| 15 (A) (B) (C) (D) | 30 (A) (B) (C) (D) | |

# VERBAL REASONING PRACTICE SET

## Time: 50 Minutes—35 Questions

DIRECTIONS: There are seven passages and 35 questions in this Verbal Reasoning test. Each passage is followed by five questions of above-average difficulty. After reading a passage, select the one best answer to each question. If you are not certain of an answer, eliminate the alternatives that you know to be incorrect and then select an answer from the remaining alternatives. (Note that although the passages and questions are test-like, this exercise is NOT meant to be an actual MCAT test section. For full-length MCAT practice, please see Kaplan *MCAT Practice Tests*).

## Passage I (Questions 1–5)

As Liebling showed us, there is no end to the supply of anecdotes about the failings of American journalism with which to trigger outrage or amusement. But pleasures and diversions aside, the problem is really one of approaching media coverage of public life more systematically. "Bias" is a word with many meanings. It suggests a single explanation—one of conscious, even willful preference—for a range of instances in which the message misinterprets or misconveys the reality. But few observers of, for example, the reporting of campaign finance would argue that conventional biases are operating here. There is no singling out of Democrats or Republicans, liberals or conservatives. All political action committees (PACs) and all campaign contributing and spending tend to be treated alike. Rather one has to look to more intrinsic and ingrained forms, to the "structural biases" of American newspapers and the "political assumptions" of their reporters, editors, and headline writers.

Structural biases are rooted in the very nature of journalism—in its professional norms, in marketplace imperatives, in the demands of communicating to an unsophisticated audience. Stories need identifiable actors, understandable activity, and elements of conflict, threat or menace. They cannot be long, and must avoid complexity. These define the "good" story. As for political assumptions, all observers bring a "cognitive map" to American politics. For some, it may be as simple as "all politicians are crooks"; for others, it involves an understanding of the distribution of power and influence in America.

The media bring a particular understanding to the ways of influence and decision making in government. Their understanding, moreover, colors the way they describe political reality. It also defines their responsibility in reporting that reality; contemporary reporters are in many ways the grandchildren of the Progressive muckrakers. Few aspects of American politics reinforce this Progressive worldview as effectively as the American way of campaign finance. Its cash is an easy measure of influence, and its PACs are perfect embodiments of vested, selfish interests. In assuming that public officials defer to contributors more easily than they do to their party, their own values, or their voting constituency, one has the perfect dramatic scenario for the triumph of wealthy special interests over the will of majorities and the public interest.

Systematic bias and political assumption, finally, meet in an analytical conundrum. A systematic bias dictates that newspapers print stories that will be read. But does the press publish the story because readers have been conditioned by newspapers to accept and believe such accounts, or does it publish the story because of its conviction that it represents political truth? Is there really any difference? Ultimately, the Progressive view of reality becomes a part of the imperatives of publishing a newspaper.

1. The author suggests that structural biases in American journalism result primarily from

   A. problems intrinsic to the publishing and marketing of newspapers.

   B. suppositions of journalists about the integrity of public officials.

   C. reporters' cynicism about the public's level of intelligence.

   D. growing competition among newspapers for a shrinking audience.

**GO ON TO THE NEXT PAGE.**

2. The author supports his contention that conventional political prejudices are not reflected in journalists' accounts of the finance activities of political parties with the observation that

    **A.** the press maintains an attitude of caution toward political misconduct.

    **B.** the public dislikes journalism that is colored by overt prejudice.

    **C.** political action committees are hotly opposed by most American journalists.

    **D.** journalists do not cite specific parties as exclusively blameworthy.

3. According to the passage, which of the following would indicate structural biases inherent in journalists' work?

    **A.** An article that adheres loyally to Progressivist dictates

    **B.** An article that successfully masks its biased opinions

    **C.** An article that is informed by political sophistication

    **D.** An article that is entertaining and easily comprehended

4. The author suggests in the passage that the American system of campaign finance

    **A.** is unjust and should be reformed.

    **B.** has exclusively served the interests of the wealthy.

    **C.** is an easy target for journalists.

    **D.** has been unfairly singled out for criticism by politicians.

5. Which of the following best describes the "analytical conundrum"?

    **A.** Newspapers promote Progressive ideas in which they do not believe.

    **B.** Since systematic bias and political assumptions have similar effects, it is difficult to differentiate their roles in journalistic publishing decisions.

    **C.** Systematic biases and political assumptions exert contradictory and conflicting pressures on newspaper publishers.

    **D.** Readers' preferences for dramatic news accounts reflecting Progressive ideas, rather than journalists' objective understanding of the political system, determine what is published.

**GO ON TO THE NEXT PAGE.**

## Passage II (Questions 6–10)

Any theory of spatial representation must assume a moving animal. In other words, when thinking about cognitive maps, we should first ask ourselves what information would most help a motile animal navigate. Here, I think we need to consider two classes of objects: Those that move and those that do not. When constructing spatial maps, animals will rely on stationary objects in their environments.

There are two reasons why animals are more likely to use objects in their environments and not themselves as a focal point on a map. First, if an animal used information generated by its own body movements, navigational errors would rapidly multiply, because small body movements would throw the system off. Second, an animal's location is only important relative to other objects, such as its nest or burrow. Thus, while an animal might make use of other regularities (e.g., angle of the sun, polarization of light, etc.), especially for large-scale migrations, they will also need to use landmarks to orient themselves or to recalibrate their position.

For example, one desert ant (*Cataglyphis fortis*) searches for food by making a winding path across the desert. Then, once it has found food, it makes a relatively straight path back to its nest. The ant makes use of a number of cues about the sun, and about its body movements, as it winds across the desert. In addition to these cues, which are sufficient to get the ant back to the general vicinity of its nest, the ant uses landmark cues to actually zero in on its nest. If one moves the landmarks to a new location, the ants will persist in going to this new location, even after they do not find their nest. There is evidence that bees use similar cues. While this skill is impressive, the ants do not seem to have a true map, however. They do not show transitivity. They might be able to get from A to B, and A to C, but they cannot get from B to C.

Other animals that store food use landmarks in order to find their food. In a series of experiments, many scientists have discovered that birds do not find their stores of food by following a regular pattern (e.g., first visit the tree with the knob, then the tree with the missing bark), by scent, or by seeing the food; instead, they use landmarks.

Since the location of one landmark is highly uninformative, animals will determine where they are relative to the configuration of a number of landmark objects. For example, some scientists tested rats in an eight-arm radial maze. By manipulating the position of cues, they discovered that the rats knew which arms they had visited by examining where they were relative to the configuration of landmarks outside the maze. Experiments with pigeons and black-capped chickadees produced similar results. In one experiment, black-capped chickadees were trained to find food in one of four feeders on a wall. After the animals learned the task, the researcher wanted to see what cues the birds used to find the food. So, he first changed the location of the feeder with the food; in a second manipulation, he changed the location within the array of the feeder with food; finally, in a third experiment, he changed the appearance of the feeders. He found that the chickadees usually returned to location of the feeder, then to the location within the array. This, and experiments with many other animals, support the idea that the identifying features of an object are of less importance than its absolute or relative location.

6. In theory, an animal should be able to get back to its original starting point by making, in reverse, all the movements it made to reach a given point. Based on information in the passage, why might this system not actually work?

   A. Since the animal would have to integrate all its body movements into a system of where it was, small body movements could throw its computations off.

   B. It is impossible to use this information since such information is not detailed enough.

   C. Body kinesthetic information is inherently subject to large errors from such sources as the sun.

   D. There is no evidence to suggest that kinesthetic maps could not actually work as well as other types of maps.

7. Based on information in the passage, one possible explanation for why animals might use a configuration of landmarks instead of a single landmark is that

   A. it is easier to remember where many objects are versus just one object.

   B. it is easier to identify many objects versus one object.

   C. it is less likely that the position of many objects would change than that the position of one object would change.

   D. it is less likely that the position of one object would change than that the position of many objects would change.

8. According to the author, what are the implications of the fact that all the animals discussed use similar cues when finding objects?

   A. There may be something about the brain that requires them to use similar cues.

   B. There may be something in the muscles that is common to all animals.

   C. It is probably random that animals use similar cues.

   D. It has not been shown that animals use similar cues.

9. According to the information in the passage, animals that use configuration cues are most likely to rely on which of their senses?

   A. Hearing, because sounds are usually specific to one location

   B. Sight, because this allows configurations to be detected at a distance

   C. Sight, because a single landmark object can provide all the information needed

   D. Touch, because this is the only sense that allows animals to identify objects unambiguously

10. If we discovered a previously unknown animal and we trained it to expect food in a particular place of our choice, what cues might it be expected to use to relocate the food, based on the information in the passage?

   A. There is no way to tell what cues it might use.

   B. It would probably use kinesthetic cues to find food.

   C. It would probably use properties of landmarks to find food.

   D. It would probably use configurations of landmarks to find food.

**GO ON TO THE NEXT PAGE.**

KAPLAN

## Passage III (Questions 11–15)

In order to discuss representation of women as a group rather than simply as individuals, we must consider whether women as a group have unique politically relevant characteristics, whether they have special interests to which a representative could or should respond. Can we argue that women as a group share particular social, economic, or political problems that do not closely match those of other groups, or that they share a particular viewpoint on the solution to political problems? If so, we can also argue that women share interests that may be represented.

Framing the working definition of "representable interests" in this fashion does not mean that the problems or issues are exclusively those of the specified interest group, any more than we can make the same argument about other types of groups more widely accepted as interest groups. The fact that there is a labor interest group, for example, reflects the existence of other groups such as the business establishment, consumers, and government, which in a larger sense share labor's concerns, but often have viewpoints on the nature of, or solutions to, the problems which conflict with those of labor. Nor does our working definition of an interest group mean that all of the potential members of that group are consciously allied, or that there is a clear and obvious answer to any given problem articulated by the entire group that differs substantially from answers articulated by others.

Research in various fields of social science provides evidence that women do have a distinct position and a shared set of problems that characterize a special interest. Many of these distinctions are located in the institution in which women and men are probably most often assumed to have common interests, the family. Much has been made of the "sharing" or "democratic" model of the modern family, but whatever democratization has taken place, it has not come close to erasing the division of labor and, indeed, stratification, by sex. Time-use studies show that women spend about the same amount of time on, and do the same proportion of, housework and child care now as women did at the turn of the century.

Furthermore, law and public policy continue to create and reinforce differences between women and men in property and contract matters, economic opportunity, protection from violence, control over fertility and child care, educational opportunities, and civic rights and obligations. The indicators generally used to describe differences in socioeconomic position also show that the politically relevant situations of women and men are different. Women in almost all countries have less education than men, and where they achieve equivalent levels of education, segregation by field, and therefore skills and market value, remains.

To say that women are in a different social position from that of men and therefore have interests to be represented is not, however, the same as saying that women are conscious of these differences, that they define themselves as having special interests requiring representation, or that men and women as groups now disagree on policy issues in which women might have a special interest. Studies of public opinion on the status and roles of women show relatively few significant differences between the sexes, and do not reveal women to be consistently more feminist than men.

11. With which of the following statements about the status of women would the author be LEAST likely to agree?

   A. In the modern family, housework and child care are more equitably divided than in the past.

   B. As groups, men and women do not necessarily disagree on issues of interest to women.

   C. Women have special interests to which representatives could respond.

   D. Women do not have full control over issues relating to their own fertility.

12. It can be most reasonably concluded that the author of this passage is

   A. a member of a women's rights group writing a list of proposals for legislators.

   B. a historian writing the introduction to book on history of women's suffrage.

   C. a professor writing an article on women's representation in a political science journal.

   D. a journalist writing a feature article on women's issues for a national newspaper.

**GO ON TO THE NEXT PAGE.**

13. Which of the following would the author most likely consider a necessary characteristic of a group having "representable interests"?

    A. The problems of the group are unique to its members.

    B. The group's proposed solutions to their problems differ radically from those proposed by other groups.

    C. Members of the group are not already represented as individuals.

    D. Members of the group tend to have similar opinions about the handling of particular political problems.

14. It can be inferred from the passage that which of the following statements is true of men and women as groups?

    A. In public opinion polls on women's issues, men's responses do not differ in a consistent way from those of women.

    B. Developments in recent years have given men more control over childcare issues.

    C. Women are becoming more aware of their differences with men than in the past.

    D. Men do not wish to recognize the special interests of women.

15. The author's discussion of interest groups in the second paragraph functions as

    A. a concession to arguments by opponents of the author's interpretation.

    B. an admission that the author's argument will ignore important aspects of the problem.

    C. a refinement of the author's working definition of an interest group.

    D. evidence for parallels between women's interest groups and other interest groups.

## Passage IV (Questions 16–20)

Remote karst islands off the southern coast of Chile contain some of the world's most inaccessible caves. A scattered and relatively rare geologic feature, karst forms when acidic groundwater and rainwater create tunnels, caverns, underground streams, and caves in limestone. Paleogeologists studied the region's geologic history by using plate tectonics to identify how these islands settled in their present positions.

Scientists dated the islands by examining the limestone found on Tarleton, an island in the group. The Tarleton limestone contains a fossil fauna rich in foraminifera, chiefly marine protozoans. Using these fossils, scientists determined that the limestone formed near the Equator in a tropical or subtropical environment during the late Carboniferous and early Permian geologic time periods, 315 to 240 million years ago. The foraminifera represent the carbonate cover deposited on submarine mountains or seamounts, most likely as a coral reef. Since the subpolar environment of these Chilean islands is inhospitable to marine animals of warmer seas, it would have been impossible for the limestone to have formed while the islands were at their present location.

Scientists know that during the Carboniferous period, Chile was not located in its present position, but at a latitude where coral reefs would not have formed. Continental drift and plate tectonics explain the movement of the Earth's crustal plates. Imagine the upper regions of the Earth as a conveyor belt. The lithosphere, about the top 60 miles or so of the mantle, moves over the athenosphere. The lithosphere contains all the continental and oceanic plates. As the plates collide against each other, one plate subducts beneath its neighbor. Mantle rocks rise to the surface while others are pushed down into the athenosphere. The Earth's internal heat keeps the rocks in the athenosphere in a partial liquid or plastic state, and the continental and oceanic plates ride on top of this layer. Earthquakes and volcanic eruptions take place on plate margins.

Paleogeologists reviewed the Earth's geography when the foraminifera were living. The Earth looked drastically different than it does today. Four hundred million years ago, the supercontinent Pangaea formed, becoming completely assembled in the early Permian (280 to 240 million years ago), the same period as the Tarleton limestone. The limestone, exotic to the

**GO ON TO THE NEXT PAGE.**

continental plate, was not always part of South America. The rocks were transported passively on top of one of the tectonic plates beneath what is now the Pacific Ocean. As the plate subducted under the edge of the South American plate in the Triassic or early Jurassic period (230 to 160 million years ago), the limestone accreted to the mainland. The faulted limestone is located along with sediments derived from the erosion of the approaching continent and small basaltic slices of the old Pacific ocean floor. The compressive tectonic processes recrystallized the limestone. Regional metamorphism and glacial periods also shaped the limestone. Strong winds and corrosive rains worked to form the karst landscape seen today. Limestone of similar origin has been found along the margins of the modern Pacific Ocean in Canada, Japan, and New Zealand, providing further evidence that as the ocean floor moved, it carried pieces of this near-equatorial reef all over the globe.

16. The author most likely describes the supercontinent Pangaea in order to support the scientific hypothesis that

    A. foraminifera mainly consist of marine protozoans.

    B. rocks from the athenosphere travel down to the lithosphere.

    C. plate tectonics explains the formation of karst.

    D. plate tectonics explains how rocks formed in one environment can be found in the opposite environment.

17. It can be inferred from the passage that by the Triassic period

    A. Pangaea was just assembling as a supercontinent.

    B. Pangaea had broken up.

    C. the Tarleton limestone was in the Tropics.

    D. the Tarleton limestone remained above the Equator.

18. According to the passage, plate tectonics explains how protozoans that formed near the Equator came to be found in rock deposits now located at latitudes not conducive to their growth. Which of the following would be LEAST consistent with the author's conclusions about how the limestone came to be off Chile's coast?

    A. Dating of the Chilean mainland to a different period than the Tarleton limestone

    B. Evidence that the assimilation of the supercontinent of Pangaea was a gradual process

    C. Evidence that the Chilean coast never experienced volcanic or earthquake activity

    D. The association of abundant sunshine with coral reef formation

19. It can be deduced from the passage that one of the contributions of the theory of plate tectonics to the understanding of paleogeology is

    A. an explanation for how marine protozoans form limestone.

    B. the ability for scientists to predict earthquakes and other seismic occurrences.

    C. an explanation for continental drift.

    D. the confirmation for the depths of different strata in the Earth's mantle.

20. Which of the following discoveries would most strengthen the author's argument that an equatorial coral reef was widely dispersed by plate tectonics?

    A. Madagascar and Chile are the same age.

    B. Madagascar was once part of India.

    C. Fossilized protozoans the same age as the fossil foraminfera on Tarleton Island were found on Madagascar.

    D. Fossils of the same chemical makeup as the Tarleton limestone can only be found off Chile's coast.

**GO ON TO THE NEXT PAGE.**

## Passage V (Questions 21–25)

Search for self-identity is one of the central themes of James Baldwin's fiction. Almost all his protagonists—from John in *Go Tell It on the Mountain* to Arthur in *Just Above My Head*—are involved in an agonizing quest for self. And self-knowledge and self-awareness, according to Baldwin, come only through suffering. Suffering, if endured creatively, leads to self-knowledge, which, in return, can offer the possibility of achieving a genuine sense of self. Hence, suffering has humanizing power and redemptive potential. If many of the black characters in Baldwin's fiction are presented as morally superior to most of the white characters—an aspect of his works that has annoyed many critics—it is *not* because those characters are black, but because their blackness inflicts additional suffering on them.

But self-discovery is never an entirely private battle; it can be achieved only in spiritual communion with others. Again, the bridge of suffering can enable one to define oneself through a compassionate understanding of the other. This idea of conquering the void of otherness through recognition and acceptance of another's humanity is examined in the novel *Just Above My Head*. The narrator, Hall, attempts to understand himself through gaining an understanding of his brother's anguished life. He gains that knowledge largely because he examines his brother's life with compassion and loving commitment. David in *Giovanni's Room*, on the other hand, fails to achieve a valid sense of self or span the chasm of otherness mostly because of two major flaws: First, he fails to forge his human identity through an acceptance of his sexuality and the suffering it entails; second, he lacks the capacity for communion with and commitment to another individual.

Self-discovery in Baldwin's fiction, however, is not always a result of private anguish and commitment to another individual; it is also dependent on identification of the self with group experience. Tradition, or heritage, is what one carries from the cultural past involuntarily; it is indispensable to achieving self-discovery. This idea of finding selfhood and strength through community is elaborately developed in Baldwin's poignant novel *If Beale Street Could Talk*. Here the family—symbolic of community—emerges as a source of enduring strength to the individual. The Rivers family is nurturing and protective. It is united in love and

commitment; therefore, it is able to offer stiff resistance to external oppression. The various members of the family as well as Fonny Hunt emerge as individualistic characters, but they are eager to unite communally to battle for justice. Baldwin's implication is clear: One ought to establish one's individual identity and find one's center within oneself, not in opposition to but in harmony with one's communal identity. And the individual, while strengthening the community, draws strength from it in return.

21. The author's primary purpose in the passage is to

   A. discuss the theme of self-discovery in James Baldwin's fiction.

   B. contrast the emphasis on individualism in Baldwin's early novels with the stress on community in his later works.

   C. illustrate the relationship between racial identity and self-awareness.

   D. argue that self-discovery cannot exist outside of a supportive community.

22. The author implies that, to Baldwin, all of the following contribute to a character's self-understanding EXCEPT

   A. a capacity to form close relationships.

   B. sympathy for the difficulties of others.

   C. endurance of personal hardship.

   D. a commitment to personal independence.

23. As it is used in the passage, the phrase "spiritual communion" (line 18) most nearly means

   A. involvement in religious worship.

   B. commitment to racial equality.

   C. an ability to endure suffering.

   D. sympathetic insight into others.

**GO ON TO THE NEXT PAGE.**

24. The author calls *If Beale Street Could Talk* "poignant" because it

    A. portrays the tension between the individual and the community.

    B. details the hardships that plague the black community.

    C. illustrates the need for a traditional family structure.

    D. presents a situation in which a united community overcomes hardship.

25. Implicit in the author's discussion of the relationship between self-discovery and group experience in the last paragraph is the idea that Baldwin

    A. is an advocate of social reform in the black community.

    B. presents the interrelation between individual and community as a theme common to all humankind.

    C. never abandons the belief that suffering is a necessary component of the search for self-discovery.

    D. believes self-discovery is attained by sacrificing part of the communal identity.

**GO ON TO THE NEXT PAGE.**

## Passage VI (Questions 26–30)

Mayan signs are by nature highly pictorial, often representing in considerable detail animals, people, body parts, and objects of daily life. The pictorial principle is taken to the extreme in inscriptions composed of "full-figure" glyphs, in which individual signs and numbers become animated and are shown interacting with one another. None of this should be taken to mean that the Maya had simple picture writing. On the contrary, the combination of consonant–vowel syllables and logographs enabled the scribes to write the words of their texts in detail.

Some of this flexibility comes from the availability of the two types of signs. For example, one very common honorific title in Mayan texts is ahaw, meaning "lord" or "noble." Ahaw may be written in logographic form as a head in profile, with the distinctive headband or scarf that marked the highest nobility in Mayan society. But it is also possible to write the word as a combination of three phonetic, syllabic signs: a-ha-wa. Likewise, the word pakal ("shield") can be indicated by a depiction of a shield or by the combination of syllabic elements pa-ka-la.

Because many Mayan signs remain undeciphered, it is not possible to state precisely the relative proportions of logographic and syllabic signs. The number of deciphered syllabic signs keeps growing, and today about half of the syllabic grid is filled. (The syllabic grid plots the consonants of the spoken Mayan language against its vowels and thus represents the totality of signs needed to write the language.) Half of the grid may seem a meager proportion, but it must be remembered that the discovery of the structure of the syllabic elements—Knorozov's main contribution—was made only a little more than 30 years ago. Furthermore, the consonant–vowel syllables that are already understood are the common ones. Many of the empty spaces in the syllabic grid remain so because they are linguistically rare; rare signs are more difficult to translate than common ones.

Nonetheless, the pace of phonetic decipherment is bound to increase in the coming years as more resources are trained on it. One aspect of Mayan writing that may complicate this progress is the fact that different signs can have the same value. Two signs that share a value are known as allographs. Such equivalences are common in Mayan texts, and in evaluating a particular phonetic interpretation of a syllable, it is very helpful to identify as many as possible of the variant forms. The process of recognizing allographs depends on the slow work of comparing many texts in order to find variant spellings of the same word.

26. The passage suggests that the Maya were able to write detailed texts primarily because

   A. the Maya depicted animals, people, and body parts in their logographs.

   B. one sign was used to express two concepts in the Mayan language.

   C. Mayan texts were composed of both syllabic and logographic signs.

   D. allographs, signs that share a value, are common in Mayan texts.

27. The author implies which of the following about the ratio of logographic to syllabic signs in Mayan writing?

   A. Its practical value has failed to attract serious attention.

   B. A meaningful ratio may never be established.

   C. More work must be done before the ratio can be determined.

   D. It can be calculated by using a small but representative number of signs.

28. The author discusses the words *ahaw* and *pakal* in order to

   A. estimate the number of meanings that some common Mayan words may possess.

   B. compare the flexibility of Mayan logographs to that of consonant–vowel syllables.

   C. illustrate the difficulty of understanding detailed Mayan texts.

   D. demonstrate that Mayan words may appear in both logographic and syllabic form.

**GO ON TO THE NEXT PAGE.**

29. The author mentions that the structure of syllabic elements was discovered "only a little more than 30 years ago" in order to suggest that

    A. scholarly standards are more exacting today than they were 30 years ago.

    B. filling in the syllabic grid is more time-consuming than phonetic decipherment.

    C. the grid will probably be completed sometime during the next 30 years.

    D. the half-completed grid should not be considered an unimpressive accomplishment.

30. It can be inferred from the author's discussion of allographs that

    A. Mayan scribes often disagreed about the correct spelling of words.

    B. the grammatical structure of the Mayan language is irregular.

    C. the rate of phonetic decipherment is determined in part by the rate at which the allographs are identified.

    D. the value of each allograph is unique.

**GO ON TO THE NEXT PAGE.**

## Passage VII (Questions 31–35)

It is to be regretted that a portion of our community should be practically in slavery, but to propose to solve the problem by enslaving the entire community is childish. Every man must be left quite free to choose his own work. No form of compulsion must be exercised over him. If there is, his work will not be good for him, will not be good in itself, and will not be good for others. And by work I simply mean activity of any kind.

I hardly think that any Socialist, nowadays, would seriously propose that an inspector should call every morning at each house to see that each citizen rose up and did manual labour for eight hours. Humanity has got beyond that stage, and reserves such a form of life for the people whom, in a very arbitrary manner, it chooses to call criminals. But I confess that many of the socialistic views that I have come across seem to me to be tainted with ideas of authority, if not of actual compulsion. Of course, authority and compulsion are out of the question. All association must be quite voluntary. It is only in voluntary associations that man is fine.

But it may be asked how Individualism, which is now more or less dependent on the existence of private property for its development, will benefit by the abolition of such private property. The answer is very simple. It is true that, under existing conditions, a few men who have had private means of their own, such as Byron, Shelley, Browning, Victor Hugo, Baudelaire, and others, have been able to realize their personality, more or less completely. Not one of these men ever did a single day's work for hire. They were relieved from poverty. They had an immense advantage. The question is whether it would be for the good of Individualism that such an advantage should be taken away. Let us suppose that it is taken away. What happens then to Individualism? How will it benefit?

It will benefit in this way. Under the new conditions Individualism will be far freer, far finer, and far more intensified than it is now. I am not talking of the great imaginatively realized Individualism of such poets as I have mentioned, but of the great actual Individualism latent and potential in mankind generally. For the recognition of private property has really harmed Individualism, and obscured it, by confusing a man with what he possesses. It has led

Individualism entirely astray. It has made gain, not growth, its aim, so that man thought that the important thing was to have, and did not know that the important thing is to be. The true perfection of man lies, not in what man has, but in what man is.

31. In the first two paragraphs, the author is primarily concerned with

    A. rejecting the enforcement of Socialist policy by governmental coercion.

    B. advocating membership in voluntary organizations.

    C. refuting arguments in favor of the eight-hour workday.

    D. proposing reforms in the treatment of criminals.

32. The author most likely mentions Byron, Shelley, Browning, Hugo, and Baudelaire in order to

    A. give examples of the harmful effect of money on Individualism and art.

    B. call attention to the rarity of artistic genius.

    C. define what is meant by the phrase "realize their personality."

    D. stress the importance of financial independence.

33. Which of the following would the author be most likely to consider an example of "enslaving the entire community"?

    I. South Africa under apartheid, where rights of citizenship were denied to the black majority, and granted in full only to the white minority

    II. Cambodia under the Khmer Rouge, where the urban population was forcibly deported to the countryside to perform agricultural labor

    III. Sweden under the Social Democrats, where all citizens pay high taxes to support extensive social programs

    A. I only

    B. II only

    C. I and II only

    D. II and III only

**GO ON TO THE NEXT PAGE.**

34. As used in the second paragraph of the passage, the words "the people whom, in a very arbitrary manner, it chooses to call criminals" imply which of the following?

   A. All actions should be permitted.

   B. Notions of justice are open to question.

   C. No one would commit crimes in a Socialist society.

   D. Criminals are better suited for mandatory labor than other people.

35. Suppose that Baudelaire was actually not wealthy, and often had to work to earn money. What relevance would this information have to the passage?

   A. It would refute the author's claim that artists require independent wealth to create.

   B. It would refute the author's claim that poets are people who can realize their own personality.

   C. It would strengthen the author's claim that the acquisition of wealth leads Individualism astray.

   D. The central thesis of the passage would remain equally valid.

---

**STOP.** IF YOU FINISH BEFORE TIME HAS EXPIRED, CHECK YOUR WORK. YOU MAY GO BACK TO ANY QUESTION IN THIS PART ONLY.

---

# VERBAL REASONING PRACTICE SET

## Answer Key

**Passage I (Questions 1–5)**

1. A
2. D
3. D
4. C
5. B

**Passage II (Questions 6–10)**

6. A
7. C
8. A
9. B
10. D

**Passage III (Questions 11–15)**

11. A
12. C
13. D
14. A
15. C

**Passage IV (Questions 16–20)**

16. D
17. B
18. C
19. C
20. C

**Passage V (Questions 21–25)**

21. A
22. D
23. D
24. D
25. B

**Passage VI (Questions 26–30)**

26. C
27. C
28. D
29. D
30. C

**Passage VII (Questions 31–35)**

31. A
32. D
33. B
34. B
35. D

# VERBAL REASONING PRACTICE SET

## Answers and Explanations

### Passage I (Questions 1–5)

**Topic and Scope:** The nature of biases inherent in journalism

**Paragraph structure:** After the introduction in paragraph 1 of the two principal types of bias in journalism, paragraph 2 tells us what the author means by these two factors. Paragraph 3 describes how the author discerns the two factors at work in a specific situation, reporting on campaign financing.

**Handling this passage:** Paragraph 1 is a classic Verbal Reasoning introductory paragraph. The author first offers the idea of willful bias as an explanation for the character of reporting. But it's not safe to say, "I've got the main idea" and skip to the next paragraph. Notice further on the "But few observers…" and "Rather one has to look at…." This switch (common in Verbal Reasoning passages) announces that willful bias is not the main idea. There are two other factors—structural biases and political assumptions—that account for the character of reporting. Always keep alert for Keywords signaling contrasts, agreements, disagreements, and emphasis to help identify the gist of the passage and the author's attitudes.

Note too that the passage begins by referring to Liebling (and his anecdotes that trigger "outrage or amusement"). Don't worry about who Liebling is—it's unlikely there would be a question about him, and if there is, you'll simply look back at this sentence. Verbal Reasoning passages often start in the middle of something, with unclear references—don't let them throw you.

**Think like a test maker:** When an author identifies two factors as important, the questions are sure to test whether you've understood the differences and relationships between them. Paragraphs 2 and 3 will be key to these questions: What are the factors, why do they exist, how do they influence journalism? The last paragraph makes a complicated summation that fortunately turns up in only one question.

**1.    A**

Critical reading takes you a long way toward scoring points on Verbal Reasoning, but *most* of the questions you'll face will require more than finding, paraphrasing, or categorizing the appropriate text; they'll require that you understand arguments. Deduction questions are the most frequently encountered type in Verbal Reasoning—they ask you to identify unstated elements of the argument: Inferences, assumptions, definitions-in-context, or text clarification. (Note that, in Verbal Reasoning question stems, "suggest" usually means Inference, although occasionally it merely requires a paraphrase from the passage.)

This question asks about the *why* of structural bias. The answer comes from the first part of paragraph 2; structural biases are "rooted in the very nature of journalism," and involve "marketplace imperatives" and the "unsophisticated audience"—the "problems intrinsic to the publishing and marketing of newspapers" cited in choice **A**. Choice **B** describes political assumptions, not structural biases. Choice **C** is Faulty Use of Detail (FUD)—it picks up an attitude in the passage (that the public is unsophisticated and easily bored) and attributes it to cynical reporters. In the passage, this is attributed to the institution of journalism itself (which includes editors and other newspaper people), and to the author. If anything, it's one of the factors more fully summed up in choice **A**. Choice **D** is another FUD—it misapplies the "marketplace imperatives"; we're told nothing about competition for a smaller audience, and this is only one factor among several.

**2.    D**

The third step in the Kaplan Method for Verbal Reasoning (the first step after critically reading the passage) is to know what the question asks. This one makes it difficult (as many Verbal Reasoning questions do) by its wordiness. Untangle and annotate the question first. According to the question stem, this author believes journalists *don't* take the traditional sides when discussing campaign financing. The question asks how that belief is supported. Evaluation questions—which require analysis of either how the argument is built or the role of a particular statement—are the second most common in Verbal Reasoning.

The question stem paraphrases the second half of paragraph 1: "few observers…would argue that conventional biases are operating here." The author then says that to journalists all PACs are alike. That idea appears in choice **D**. Choice **B** is Opposite: This author sees in most journalists, and in the public, at least some degree of political cynicism; he wouldn't ascribe idealistic beliefs to either group. Choices **A** and **C** match the author's attitudes much better. But "hot opposition"—choice **C**—is too strong to describe how journalists regard PACs (extreme answer choices are the most common type of Distortion); and choice **A** has this author, rather than political reporting or the public, automatically associating campaign finance with political misconduct.

**3.    D**

Remember that answering one question may provide help in answering another, and the work you did on one makes the next easier. So skip difficult questions until you've answered the others for the passage. This is an Application question, the third most common in Verbal Reasoning. Application questions require that you apply ideas in the passage to new information supplied in the question stem or the answer choices.

It is easiest (and therefore most common) for the test makers to create wrong-answer choices based on the four standard "pathologies"—Opposite, FUD (Faulty Use of Detail), Distortion, or Outside the Scope.

This is another "structural bias" question, this time dealing with the *how* of it: How does this phenomenon influence the work of a journalist? Back to the beginning of paragraph 2, where stories are described as filled with character and plot while remaining short and uncomplicated. Choice **C** is Opposite—according to this author, journalism regards the public as unable to appreciate sophisticated analysis. The reference to Progressivism in choice **A** is appealing but FUD; Progressivism is discussed as part of political assumption, not structural bias. Choice **B** is a Distortion that refers to the type of bias discussed—and dismissed—in the beginning of paragraph 1.

**4.    C**

Annotate the question stem as you read. Some words (such as LEAST, EXCEPT, NOT, *strengthen*, or *weaken*) are "pre-annotated" for you, but you should take mental note of other essential terms that will help you find the answer—here you might make note of *author suggests* and *campaign finance*. Many mistakes are made by losing sight of an essential element of the question.

This topic keeps cropping up in the questions because it's a perfect illustration of the author's point: Structural bias and political assumptions rule journalism. It's easy for a journalist to make a simple, dramatic story about campaign financing, because people are ready to believe the rich are selfish and politicians mercenary. Phrases in the passage such as *an easy measure of influence* and *the perfect dramatic scenario* in paragraph 3 justify the phrase *easy target* in choice **C**. Choices **A** and **B** are FUDs that mix up these attitudes. They describe what such journalism could suggest, what readers may believe, *not* what the author thinks. Choice **D** is Opposite; it contradicts the passage since there's not even a hint of "criticism by politicians."

**5.    B**

At last a question that deals with paragraph 4. If you had trouble puzzling through the "conundrum" (a difficult or unsolvable problem), keep in mind that the entire passage

dealt with *two* types of influence on journalism, and so does this last paragraph.

Note the "is it because of X, or is it because of Y" structure of the paragraph; there are *two* possible reasons. The author is asking: does systematic bias, the factor that conditions people "to accept and believe such accounts," influence journalism more? Or do political assumptions, the factor that makes journalists believe they're reporting the political truth, influence journalism more? Rhetorical questions are always likely sources of questions, since they require that you convert the question into its implied Opinion.

The answer is in the last two sentences: There's really hardly any difference, because both have the same effect. In other words, "it is difficult to differentiate their roles," as stated in choice **B**. Choice **A** is FUD; it's right about the newspapers promoting Progressive ideas, but wrong about the lack of belief—the last sentence makes it clear that at least the newspapers don't disbelieve the Progressive view. Choice **C** is Opposite: The whole point in paragraph 4 is that the two factors push in the same direction. Choice **D** poses the very question posed by the author but then gives the wrong answer—and note the words *objective understanding*, the opposite of political assumption.

# Passage II (Questions 6–10)

**Topic and Scope:** Mechanisms by which animals locate objects in their environment

**Paragraph structure:** The first paragraph introduces the subject of animals mapping their environment. The second discusses reasons why animals use objects, rather than their own body movements, to map their environment. The third paragraph describes one example, a desert ant. The fourth paragraph describes the example of birds who store food and locate it using "landmarks." The final paragraph discusses the relevance of the "configuration" of such landmarks.

**Handling this passage:** Although it starts out contrasting two categories in paragraph 1, this passage quickly dismisses one of the two right away in paragraph 2. The rest of the passage is devoted to further analysis of the only remaining category. Be ready for such changes in direction in Verbal Reasoning passages. Two or three passages will deal with the history or ethics of science, or with sciences that do not appear in the science sections of the MCAT. No outside knowledge will be relevant in answering the questions.

**Think like a test maker:** When the passage is rich in detail, note the location of details but don't try to memorize them, and don't worry if not all the details are immediately comprehensible. Some test takers think that if a passage is about poetry, then they have to read with all of the interest, vocabulary, and background of a literary critic. If it's about geology, they think that they have to read like a geologist. But that's just not so!

**6. A**

This Application question requires that you consider the effect of information in the passage on a hypothetical method mentioned in the question stem. With the details of the question in mind, reground yourself in the passage—review your map and any relevant text. This step is easiest when the question refers to specific lines of text or a specific argument. But some regrounding in the passage is helpful for every question type, even if it's only a review of the broad outlines of the passage and the author's scope and purpose.

The author clearly states in the second paragraph that navigational errors would multiply rapidly in any kinesthetic system because small variations in the animal's movements would throw the system off; this supports choice **A**. There is sufficient information in the passage to answer the question, which rules out choice **B**. There is no evidence to support choice **C**—it is Outside the Scope. Choice **D** is Opposite; it's contradicted by other information in the second paragraph.

**7. C**

Incorporation questions ask about the effect of the new information on the passage. This fairly unusual type of Incorporation question requires you to consider what events in the answer choices might be used to explain an outcome described in the passage. As often happens in Verbal Reasoning, you are presented with two sets of answer–choice pairs, one based on "likelihood" and the other on "ease"—so determining which of these factors is relevant will cut in half the number of choices you have to read fully.

There is no reason to suspect that it is easier to remember many objects than to remember one object, and common sense suggests that the reverse is probably true; this contradicts choices **A** and **B**. Also, common sense suggests (and nothing in the passage opposes this) that one object could more easily be moved than several objects could, contradicting choice **D**. Choice **C** is the correct answer.

**8. A**

Even when the answer is not stated in the passage and the question draws on the author's overall purpose, before you consult the answer choices you should predict the content, or at least the broad outline, of the correct answer. Predicting your answer will speed up and focus your search among the choices and reduce your chances of being misled by a plausible wrong answer. Where does this

author draw conclusions about the "implications" of the data discussed?

If in every instance an animal operates similarly, it is reasonable to assume that something about animals requires them to act that way. This would eliminate choice **C**. Choice **D** is Opposite; it's contradicted by information in the passage. There is no reason given in the passage to think that the muscles, themselves, perform any computations, so choice **B** is out. Choice **A** is the best choice.

**9. B**

Where are "configuration" cues discussed in the passage? What kind of information can we expect to find in the correct answer choice? As an elimination strategy (in case you should have to guess), if two answer choices are similar, as **B** and **C** are here—or if two answers are opposite to each other—one of them is likely to be the correct answer.

Configuration cues are discussed in the last paragraph. Choice **B** is the best answer because it takes into account the fact that animals are using these cues from a distance—an implied Fact. Don't be confused by the language at the end of the preceding paragraph that says the birds don't find their food "by seeing the food…they use landmarks." This doesn't imply that sight is not involved with landmarks, only that the food itself isn't visible. Choice **C** is Opposite: It's directly contradicted by information in the first sentence of this paragraph. There is no evidence for choice **A** or **D**; they are Outside the Scope.

**10. D**

An Application question is essentially a Deduction question with new information added. This one asks that you identify a parallel between the answer choices and some detail or argument in the passage. Review the relevant passage text and identify the broad outlines, the essential elements, of the text. Predict the general structure of the correct choice.

If we find that every example of something operates similarly, then it is reasonable to assume that a newly found example will operate in the same way. This would eliminate choice **A**. So, we would assume that this animal will find food similarly to the way other animals do, by a configuration of landmarks, choice **D**.

# Passage III (Questions 11–15)

**Topic and Scope:** Whether women should be represented as a group politically

**Paragraph structure:** This passage has a very straightforward outline: Paragraphs 1–2 present the author's definition of an interest group; paragraphs 3–5 give evidence that women fit this definition. Paragraph 5 qualifies the conclusion slightly.

**Handling this passage:** Always take a moment after reading the passage to define for yourself its "main idea"—most of the questions will deal with in one way or another. Here, it's that women have "representable interests" as defined in paragraph 2. This idea is presented in the first paragraph, then repeated in paragraph 3 and again in paragraph 5 (with the qualification that women may not define themselves as such). Three or more passages come from such Social Science areas as psychology, anthropology, history, or sociology. The two most common wrong answer pathologies in these passages are FUD and Outside the Scope.

**Think like a test maker:** Expect two or three difficult abstract Verbal Reasoning passages on your MCAT—don't try to understand everything in them, and do make your paraphrases very broad. Capture the structure alone, if the ideas are unclear to you.

**11.  A**

Deduction questions ask you to identify unstated Facts or Opinions based on the information in the passage—in this case to put yourself into the mind of the author and infer what he would believe based on what he says.

This Deduction question is asking you to identify the choice that the author would *not* agree with, so you should plan to eliminate three choices the author *would* agree with, or about which we have no basis to infer the author's opinion—so the wrong answer choices will be Opposite or Outside the Scope.

In the third paragraph, the author states that the current model of the modern family has not erased the division of labor within the family and modern woman spends about the same amount of time on housework as her turn-of-the-century counterpart. Choice **A** contradicts this and is therefore a statement with which the author would disagree. Choice **B** is a paraphrase of the last sentence of the passage. Choice **C** deals with the "big idea" in the passage: Women do have representable interests; thus **C** is a statement with which the author would *agree*. Choice **D** can be inferred from the first sentence of paragraph 4.

**12.  C**

Application questions ask you to apply ideas in the passage to new information. In questions about the probable occupation of an author, the answer choices often specify both an occupation and a source for the passage: The first speaks to the tone of the passage, the second to the style. You don't actually have enough information to infer these answer choices, but you *can* ask yourself which choice is

likely to demonstrate the qualities you identified in the passage.

This excerpt deals with the issue on a theoretical level and in a scholarly manner. This style would seem to best fit an article that would appear in a journal of political science, and "women's representation" restates the topic, so choice **C** is the correct answer. Choice **A** can be ruled out immediately—nowhere does this passage propose any practical solutions to women's problems. Choice **B** doesn't work because the author doesn't deal with suffrage at all. Choice **D** isn't likely because the passage doesn't present this issue in a "newsy" way; it's theoretical.

**13.  D**

All of the answer choices for this question can be easily checked by referring back to paragraphs 1 and 2, where the author presents and qualifies the criteria needed for a group to have representable interests.

**Think like a test maker:** Whenever a definition is at the core of the author's purpose in the passage, there will definitely be questions relating to it—either a "Definition-in-context" or an Application question (or both).

The author presents two of these criteria toward the end of paragraph 1, and choice **D**, which accurately rephrases the second of these, is the best answer. Choices **A** and **B** are specifically rejected in paragraph 2; aside from this, their emphatic language (*unique, radically*) doesn't match the author's carefully qualified manner. So, these choices are Opposite choices in terms of content and Distortions in terms of tone. Choice **C** is a Distortion of the first sentence, which simply distinguishes between individual and group representation without implying that group members can't be represented as individuals.

**14.  A**

Another Deduction question—the correct answer will stay closely aligned with the tone and content of the passage text. If you are uncertain about an Assumption or Inference answer choice, it may be easier to see what happens if that choice is not true. This is Kaplan's **Denial Test**. It's more time consuming than predicting the correct answer, but it can be very powerful. Use it while you're practicing to confirm your predictions; use it on the test when you can't predict.

The author compares the relative status of men and women in paragraphs 3–5. Choice **A** can be inferred from the last sentence: If women are not more feminist than men in polls, then men's answers are not consistently different from women's. Choice **B** makes an unwarranted inference, a Distortion. The author states in paragraph 4 that there are differences between women and men in control over child care, but the exact nature of this difference is never stated, and it's an ongoing problem, not one that developed "in recent years." As for choice **C**, nowhere does the author imply that women are now more aware of their differences from men. In fact, the final paragraph says many women may be unaware of differences or may not regard them as important. Choice **D** is incorrect, because the author never implies that men as a group willfully ignore the special interests of women.

**15.   C**

Many questions will require a general knowledge of the passage as well as of the specific text referred to—that's why it's important to read and grasp the broad terms of the passage before trying the questions. Here, the function of the discussion at issue relates to both the first and second paragraphs. Common wrong-answer pathologies on Evaluation questions are Distortions and FUDs.

The function of each statement made in the passage is one of the things you should be thinking about as you read it critically. Use Keywords and context to determine whether a statement is Fact or Opinion: Is the author providing more support? Expanding on previous examples or themes? Outlining a further consequence of the argument? That should give you a head start when you encounter these questions.

In paragraph 1, the author outlines the broad criteria that determine whether women as a group have representable interests. In paragraph 2 the author excludes certain possible interpretations of these criteria, in a way that pinpoints exactly what he means. Choice **C** best describes this: Refinement of the definition. The other answer choices can be eliminated by looking at the way they begin. Paragraph 2 does not contain any "evidence" by any stretch of the imagination (choice **D**), nor does it contain a concession (choice **A**) or an admission (choice **B**).

# Passage IV (Questions 16–20)

**Topic and Scope:** The paleogeology of southern Chilean islands, in particular, the formation and relocation of a group of limestone islands

**Paragraph structure:** The first paragraph defines and explains the present terrain of the islands. The second paragraph explains how and when the limestone formed. The third paragraph explains how the theory of the plate tectonics can be applied to the formation of these islands. The fourth describes the supercontinent Pangaea and discusses how the islands came to be in their present locations. The passage concludes by giving information about other parts of the world where similar islands can be found.

**Handling this passage:** This is an unusual Natural Sciences passage; you expect to find all this vivid description in humanities passages. But use the elaborate imagery when it's there—visualize what the passage describes and it will be easier to remember. Many passages follow the classic essay pattern: Introduction, thesis, counter-thesis, synthesis, conclusion—and when that structure is used, just reading the first few lines and last few lines of the passage can "summarize" its main idea for you. In this case, that procedure would suggest that the entire passage is about the formation of karst islands. In fact, the bulk of the passage is about how those islands were relocated—plate tectonics. The AAMC selects excerpts to present a variety of structures, and simple approaches may not work.

**Think like a test maker:** As you read, keep in mind the types of questions used in Verbal Reasoning; there are only a certain number of questions that can be written for any particular passage—and their type is dictated by the passage itself. Annotate the passage as you read; when terms are defined or processes described, you can anticipate questions involving their details. Note, too, that the first paragraph of this passage might mislead you as to its overall purpose; it's relevant, but doesn't establish the author's main idea, which is first raised in paragraph 2.

**16.   D**

This Evaluation question requires that you determine why the author discusses Pangaea. To evaluate an argument, identify the relevant Opinion, its support, and any assumption made to connect them. Note that the question stem gives you half of the answer—the discussion at issue serves as support for a hypothesis presented in the passage.

Paragraph 4 describes Pangaea and explains how the Earth looked when the Tarleton limestone formed. Choice **A** is FUD, based on a detail found in paragraph 2. Pangaea has nothing to do with foraminfera formation. Choice **B** is not directly related to Pangaea—it is also inaccurate. Rocks would travel from the lithosphere down to the athenosphere, so eliminate choice **B**. Choice **C** is wrong. Paragraph 1 explains karst formation, which has nothing to do with Pangaea. Choice **D** restates the idea that limestone that formed in the tropics is now found in a subpolar environment.

**17.   B**

The fourth step in the Kaplan Method is to review any relevant text and your map. What does this passage say about the Triassic period, and where? Your prediction of the correct answer choice may be very detailed or only a general sense of what the answer should look like or contain.

Paragraph 4 tells you that during the Triassic and early Jurassic periods (lasting from 230 to 160 million years ago), the Tarleton limestone accreted to the South American tectonic plate. Pangaea must have broken apart for this accretion to occur. Choice **B** is correct. You can eliminate choice **A**, since Pangaea assembled much earlier than the Triassic period, in the early Permian. Choices **C** and **D** are incorrect, since you are told that during the Triassic, the limestone was colliding with the South American plate and therefore could not be located either in the Tropics or above the Equator.

**18. C**

The most common Incorporation question types will ask you either to strengthen or to weaken an argument, or to identify the effect of new information on an argument. As with all Verbal Reasoning questions, the AAMC will vary the wording of Incorporation questions—you'll see synonyms for *strengthen*, such as *support*, or *bolster*, and synonyms for *weaken*, such as *challenge*, *inconsistent*, or *compromise*. Pay close attention: If you misread the question, all your other work will be wasted.

You'll always see an Opposite wrong answer choice on a *strengthen/weaken* question—one of the most common errors is to misread or lose sight of the question.

Choice **A** would support the author's conclusion found in paragraph 4 that the Tarleton limestone was formed separately from the Chilean mainland. Choice **B** is irrelevant to the conclusions in the passage. Whether or not the process that formed Pangaea was gradual, Pangaea still formed. Choice **C** would refute the author's conclusions. Paragraph 3 explains that volcanic and earthquake activity is evidence of plate tectonics, and plate tectonics is necessary to explain how the limestone moved position. Choice **D** is Outside the Scope of the passage and would neither strengthen nor weaken the author's conclusions.

**19. C**

To answer this question, you have to apply what the passage says about plate tectonics to how paleogeologists determined the origin of these Chilean islands. Armed with your prediction and refreshed on the relevant text, you'll be ready to look for the right choice. Pay close attention to the wording of the answer choices—only one will be valid based on the passage. Read all the choices before selecting one—sometimes a wrong answer choice varies from the correct choice very subtly.

Choice **A** is FUD. The formation of limestone does not apply to plate tectonics. While choice **B** makes logical sense since the passage talks about these geologic events resulting from moving plates, the question asks how plate tectonics relates to paleogeology and this answer doesn't address the question. It is Outside the Scope of the passage. Choice **C** is

correct. Continental drift is explained by plate tectonics. Choice **D** is another FUD.

**20. C**

Don't try to prove or disprove the argument in a *strengthen/weaken* question; just locate the choice that makes it more or less likely to be true. The correct choice may reinforce or undercut one or more of the Facts in the passage or an underlying assumption.

This question asks you to analyze how the author can tell that an equatorial reef has been dispersed. Choice **C** supports the idea that a coral reef was dispersed by plate tectonics. Choice **A** is a Distortion. The age of the Chilean mainland has nothing to do with the dispersal of an equatorial reef. Choice **B** is Outside the Scope of the passage. Choice **D** is Opposite: It would weaken and not strengthen the argument.

## Passage V (Questions 21–25)

**Topic and Scope:** Analysis of the theme of self-discovery in James Baldwin's novels

**Paragraph structure:** The first paragraph discusses the role of suffering in the search for self-identity; Baldwin's characters realize their identity by undergoing some sort of personal ordeal. Paragraphs 2 and 3 expand this theme by discussing how self-discovery also involves understanding other people as individuals (paragraph 2) and communities (paragraph 3).

**Handling this passage:** Three or more passages will deal with such Humanities topics as art, music, or literature—often in their historical context. Some students find the dry, academic passage, which is often on a topic that's of little interest to them, the most difficult to read. This is in large part because they read them rarely, and find the conventions and vocabulary strange. Be sure to include in your practice reading material of the types that you don't usually read.

**Think like a test maker:** As you read, ask yourself what each sentence and each paragraph is adding—how it relates to what came before it. The test maker selected these excerpts with the Verbal Reasoning question types in mind.

**21. A**

If you are reading critically and mapping the passage, you already have a prediction for this question type. Just take a moment to be sure your answer covers the entire passage.

The first sentence of the first paragraph sums up the big idea of this passage: That the search for self-discovery is a central theme in James Baldwin's fiction. Choice **A** captures this idea, and reflects the author's descriptive tone. Choice **B** is incorrect, because it suggests a *contrast* between the themes of individualism and community, whereas the author states at the beginning of paragraph 3 that *both* are important aspects of the theme of self-discovery. Also, no mention is made of contrasts between Baldwin's early and later work. Choice **C** is FUD—the relationship between racial identity and self-awareness is mentioned at the end of the first paragraph as one aspect of self-discovery. Although the author discusses the relationship between self-discovery and group experience in the third paragraph, she does not "argue" that self-discovery *cannot* take place outside a supportive community, as choice **D** suggests.

**22. D**

Although the answer choices seem to contain the bulk of the information in this question, refresh your grasp of the author's major opinions.

LEAST/EXCEPT/NOT questions can be confusing because of their focus on the negative—and the test makers depend on the Opposite answer choice misleading many test takers. Take advantage of the built-in annotation by confirming the answer choice you've selected against the capitalized word.

Choice **D** is the one factor which does *not* contribute to Baldwin's portrayal of self-discovery outlined in the passage. A "commitment to personal independence" contradicts paragraph 2, which says that self-discovery involves an understanding relationship with others; a commitment to *personal* independence would seem to exclude such relationships. Since paragraph 2 stresses compassionate understanding of others as a necessary part of self-discovery, choices **A** and **B** are both true, and therefore neither is the correct answer. Choice **C** is Opposite, because the author suggests in paragraph 1 that suffering or personal hardship is integral to self-discovery.

**23. D**

A "definition-in-context" is either an Inference or an Assumption; either you are given all the Facts necessary to infer the definition; or the definition is an assumed Fact, without which the conclusion is invalid.

The question asks about the phrase's meaning in the context of the passage. Be careful not to rely on your understanding of a phrase from its common usage (that will be one of the wrong answer choices, and Outside the Scope of the passage).

Look for the answer to this inference question in paragraph 2, where the phrase "spiritual communion" is found. In the sentence that follows, the author talks about compassionate understanding of others, so the phrase "spiritual communion" seems to suggest a metaphor for gaining insight into others

through the spirit of compassion, as opposed to seeking understanding alone. Choice **D**, "sympathetic insight into others," best expresses this thought, and is the correct answer. Choice **A** can be rejected, because the author never discusses religious worship as a theme in Baldwin's fiction—this is an Outside the Scope trap for those who look for the common usage meanings of the words. Choice **B** is incorrect, because racial issues are neither specifically mentioned nor implied in the context of the discussion of "spiritual communion with others" in paragraph 2. An ability to endure suffering, choice **C**, is mentioned as an aspect of self-discovery in paragraph 1, where the author never mentions relationships with others.

**24. D**

Here you are *not* asked what *poignant* means, but what Facts make the word appropriate in this context. But the same method applies; use the immediate context surrounding the phrase or word in question to answer this question about why the author finds the novel "poignant."

*Beale Street* is mentioned in paragraph 3, as providing an example of a family that finds "selfhood and strength through community." Choice **D** captures this; the novel's poignancy lies in its portrayal of a united community overcoming hardship. Choice **A** is Opposite; it contradicts the novel's theme of the individual uniting with the community to fight adversity successfully. Choice **B** is Outside the Scope; the author never addresses any hardships specific to the Black community. Choice **C** is FUD or Outside the Scope—the author mentions the family's support for the individual, but we don't know whether the Rivers family is traditionally structured or not, so *Beale Street* could hardly illustrate a need for *traditional* family structure.

**25. B**

An "idea" that is "implicit" is an AAMC paraphrase for an Assumption. A Verbal Reasoning Assumption is unstated evidence—specifically, a connection between the Facts and Opinion that the author *must* believe is true in order to reach the stated conclusion. Focus on the differences between the terms of the evidence and the terms of the conclusion. The Assumption directly links the evidence to the conclusion, and *must* be true if the conclusion follows from the stated evidence.

Since the last paragraph focuses on the interrelationship between the individual and the community, choice **B** provides the most reasonable assumption. Choice **A**, on the other hand, raises the issue of social reform in the black community, a topic which the author never discusses—it's Outside the Scope. Choice **C** is a Distortion and Outside the Scope of the paragraph; it overemphasizes suffering, which the author describes as only one aspect of the process of self-discovery, and it sharply digresses from the third paragraph's discussion of community experience. Choice **D** is Opposite; it contradicts the main idea of the passage in suggesting that self-discovery and community identity are incompatible; the very end of the third paragraph says that this isn't the case.

## Passage VI (Questions 26–30)

**Topic and Scope:** Mayan writing; specifically, deciphering Mayan signs

**Paragraph structure:** Paragraph 1 introduces the two types of Mayan writing—logographic and syllabic—which allowed their texts to communicate detail. In paragraph 2 the author expands on the flexibility of Mayan writing, showing how certain words can be expressed either logographically or syllabically. In paragraph 3 the focus shifts to the current state of research into Mayan signs. Paragraph 4 expresses confidence that the pace of phonetic decipherment will increase in the future despite one factor that may make the process more difficult.

**Handling this passage:** This fairly dense passage is highly structured. The key to handling a passage like this is keeping track of the progression of the paragraphs.

**Think like a test maker:** When you see terms defined, like "ahaw" and "pakal" in paragraph 2, you can be sure that at least one question will focus on those terms. Note the author's optimism about the future of phonetic decipherment of Mayan texts, which is hinted at in paragraph 3 and expanded upon in paragraph 4. Note in paragraph 4 that the author mentions a potential obstacle to the phonetic decipherment—at least one question will test your understanding of what the obstacle is and how it can be overcome.

**26. C**
Deduction questions ask you to identify implied elements of the argument—what must be true based on the information in the passage. Never answer on a hunch—research the relevant text from the passage before moving to the answer choices.

The author discusses what enabled the Maya to write "detailed texts" in paragraph 1. If you've kept track of the paragraph structure, locating it should be easy. In this case, the author notes that "the combination of consonant-vowel symbols and logographs" is what allowed the Maya to include a lot of detail in their texts, so choice **C** is correct. Choice **A** is FUD; it mentions logographs but doesn't consider syllabic signs. Choice **B** is a Distortion of the idea that one concept can be expressed by more than two signs in Mayan; the author never suggests that one sign can

express two subjects. Also, choice **B** refers to text from the wrong paragraph—paragraph 2, which details how logographic and syllabic signs contributed to flexibility. Choice **D** is a correct statement but FUD, since the author's discussion of allographs in paragraph 4 is irrelevant to the writing of detailed texts described in paragraph 1.

**27. C**
Another Deduction question. Mine the question stem for clues as to where the relevant details are discussed in the passage. When inferences or new information constitute the answer choices, always review the relevant opinions before reading the choices. Wrong answer choices will include statements by the wrong party in the passage, or statements on a different point, which it would be easy to confuse with the correct choice without this "regrounding" on the relevant point.

In this case, the word *ratio* in the question stem should point you to paragraph 3's reference to "relative proportions." In that paragraph, the author notes that the relative proportions of logographic to syllabic signs can't be stated because many Mayan signs remain undeciphered. The author implies that more work must be done before this ratio becomes clear. Choice **C** states this clearly. Choice **A** is Outside the Scope; the author never discusses the failure of any theory to attract attention. Choice **B** is a Distortion; the author's predictions for increasing decipherment would seem to imply that the ratio may eventually be established. Similarly, choice **D** is wrong because the author never suggests solving the problem using a "small but representative number of signs."

**28. D**
The key to this type of Evaluation question is to consider the context in which the relevant detail appears in the passage: what are the Facts, and what are the Opinions? Remember that, the easier the question stem seems, the trickier the wrong answer choices might be.

The words *ahaw* and *pakal* are discussed in paragraph 2, which describes the flexibility of Mayan by showing that both words can be written in logographic and syllabic form, so choice **D** is correct. Choice **A** is a Distortion; the author's example shows the different forms in which a word can be expressed, not how many different meanings it can have. Choice **B** is another Distortion; logographic signs are not more flexible than syllabic ones—both types, taken together, create flexibility. Choice **C** refers to the difficulty of understanding Mayan texts, discussed in paragraph 4, making it FUD.

**29. D**
For this Evaluation question, remember to consider the context in which the detail at issue was presented. Watch out for choices that distort the author's ideas.

The line reference points us to paragraph 3, which focuses on the current state of the decipherment of Mayan. The recent date of discovery of the syllabic structure is there to suggest that the half-completed grid should not be considered unimpressive, as choice **D** states. Choice **A** is Outside the Scope: There is nothing to suggest that standards today are more exacting. Choice **B** misinterprets the comparison between the time it would take to fill in the syllabic grid and phonetic decipherment. Paragraphs 3 and 4 say that filling in the grid depends on the rate of phonetic decipherment; so both processes are time-consuming. You can eliminate choice **C**, because you can't infer that the half-completed grid will take another 30 years to fill.

**30.    C**

The correct answer to a Deduction question will not stray far from the passage. Remember to eliminate choices that distort the passage text or seem to come from left field.

The author discusses allographs in paragraph 4; the process of identifying them may complicate, and slow down, the process of phonetic decipherment, although the author believes that the rate of phonetic decipherment will increase in the future, choice **C**. Choice **A** is Distortion of the last line of the passage. The fact that variant spellings exist for the same word hardly means that scribes couldn't agree on correct spellings. Choice **B** is incorrect, because variation in spelling doesn't imply irregular grammar. Choice **D** is a Distortion; the author suggests in the last paragraph not that each allograph is unique, but that each allograph consists of two signs which have the same value.

## Passage VII (Questions 31–35)

**Topic and Scope:** The author's argument against private property

**Paragraph structure:** The first paragraph argues against any form of compulsion in determining what work men do. The second argues that Socialism is tainted with "authority," which the author considers related to "compulsion." The third paragraph describes the current connection between Individualism (which the author sees as a goal) and private property (which frees those who have it from any compulsion to work). The fourth paragraph expresses the author's view that Individualism for all mankind (rather than for a few persons) will benefit from eliminating private property.

**Handling this passage:** This is a very formal, even old-fashioned writing style—a type that can be encountered in MCAT Verbal Reasoning. Be sure that you read some material from older works, as well as contemporary writers, in your preparations. The politics of this passage

are also unpopular today, but don't let your differences of opinion (or your agreement) with the author distract you from the quality and nature of the arguments made.

**Think like a test maker:** When two people, ideas, or theories are presented within the first paragraph of a passage, ask yourself why the author chose to include more than one viewpoint—to support one over the other, to claim that both are valid or invalid, or to reconcile them? Establish the purpose of the comparison and the rest of the passage should fall into place. In this case, the author establishes his ironic tone immediately by contrasting the idea of the enslavement of the few with the idea of enslavement of everyone. Once you get past the dated prose, this is actually a very simply structured argument. This author's Keywords include his verbs (*regretted* and *must be left quite free* and *tainted*), adjectives (*childish* and *arbitrary* and *fine*), adverbs (*I hardly think* and *seriously*) and all other word choices. With so many Opinions offered, you know you'll find questions asking the differences between them.

**31.    A**

There are five common purposes in Verbal Reasoning passages. Whenever a question calls for the author's purpose or intent, you can predict an answer based on synonyms of *to describe, to analyze, to compare, to advocate, or to rebut*. And remember that a vertical scan of the verbs can reduce the number of choices you have to read in full.

Pick up on the author's tone as well as his stated Opinions. Two of the four answer choices here offer positive purposes (*advocating* and *proposing*) while two offer negative purposes (*rejecting* and *refuting*). The number of choices you have to read in full can be cut in half immediately.

The words *primarily concerned* require that you identify the author's overall purpose in the cited paragraphs. This may not be explicitly stated. In the first two paragraphs, the author rejects "slavery," "compulsion," and "authority," which support choice **A**. Choice **B** is a Distortion: "Voluntary organizations" are not advocated by the author. He says only that whatever "associations" men have should be voluntary. Choice **C** is Opposite; the author ironically refers to a scenario in which each citizen "did manual labor for eight hours" as something not even the authoritarian Socialists would want. While the author refers to our handling of "criminals" as done "in a very arbitrary manner," he does not discuss any reform proposals here—choice **D** is Outside the Scope.

**32.    D**

This Evaluation question asks you to identify the function of a detail in the passage—you should identify where it is located in the passage and consider its context. Whenever you see a list in a passage, you can expect a question about its function—the longer the list, the greater the likelihood that question will appear.

These five poets are mentioned in the third paragraph as examples of "men who have had private means of their own," who have the "immense advantage" of being "relieved from poverty." In fact, the entire paragraph is there to demonstrate the current benefits of private property—so choice **A** is Opposite and choice **B** is Outside the Scope. Choice **C** is also Outside the Scope, because the author never discusses what he means by this phrase.

## 33. B

This Application question asks that you identify a parallel between the answer choice and some detail or argument in the passage. Review the relevant passage text and identify the broad outlines, the essential elements, of the text. Predict the general structure of the "analogous" choice. Roman numeral questions require you to consider each of three options before you can determine the correct answer choice. Consider the numeral that appears in the greatest number of answer choices first.

Where does the author refer to "enslaving the entire community"? Does he mean this literally, or is some specialized meaning assigned? As we've noted, this author is speaking simply and literally. Item II matches his intent: The example of Cambodia describes a situation in which everyone is forced to work. In South Africa most people (the black majority) were enslaved—figuratively, if not literally—but some people (the white minority) were not. Sweden is an example in which no one is enslaved: People simply pay taxes, which is Outside the Scope of the author's argument.

## 34. B

Note that in eliminating answer choice **D** for question 31, you started the review process for this question—another example of one question helping with another.

Choices **A** and **C** are rather extravagant statements that the author does not make in the passage. (And your answer should be based only on information in the passage. If you feel, personally, that someone who questions our system of criminal justice is likely to be an anarchist, you have to keep that opinion from influencing your choice.) Choice **D** is a Distortion; the author's point is that only when we've determined someone is a criminal do we feel justified in using "compulsion" in connection with him—not that the criminal is in any way suited for such labor.

## 35. D

Hypotheticals in question stems may be lengthy and confusing; *before reading their details*, identify what the question asks—will you be looking for an analogy in the passage, or assessing the effect of the new information on the author's argument?

You don't have to know anything about Baudelaire; just refer back to where he is mentioned. The argument there, simply stated, is that some people have been able to "realize" themselves fully because they were freed from any compulsion to work by their private property. Baudelaire is one of five poets mentioned in support of that conclusion. What is the effect if the statement proves untrue with respect to him? There are only four supporting examples instead of five—the logic of the argument is unaffected.

Choices **A** and **B** attribute opinions to the author that he never expresses. The author does make the claim that choice **C** says he does, but the information in the question stem does not strengthen it—It's FUD. This information does not affect the validity of the author's other supporting examples, so the validity of the main argument is not affected.

# Getting Prepared for Medical School

When you have aced the MCAT and gotten accepted to medical school, don't forget the hard work and dedication that led to your success. After all, you will need it to get through medical school, pass the USMLE, and get into the residency program of your choice!

The next step in your journey will be four years of medical school, filled with new experiences every step of the way. Intensive coursework, your first exposure to real patients, and USMLE exams are just some of the challenges you will face. Don't let this unnerve you—you've got Kaplan Medical on your side to help you succeed every step of the way. Kaplan Medical offers the most realistic, complete, up-to-date, and effective medical school content review and USMLE prep through live lectures, video lectures, books, and online products.

Here are some useful tips from the Kaplan Medical staff.

## Should I Join a Note-Taking Coop?

Note-taking coops have pros and cons. They fill the gaps if you have to miss a lecture due to illness or an unexpected emergency, but notes may be distributed long after the lecture, which means you'll have little time to study material that is presented just before exams.

## How Can I Study for My Classes and the USMLE?

USMLE review materials such as Kaplan's MedEssentials are great condensed versions of the most important principles and concepts that your faculty will expect you to master. Using review material now and personalizing it with your highlightings and marginalia means that they'll be familiar and super useful when you begin preparing for Step 1. Go to your favorite bookstore or **kaptest.com/store** to get your copy before you head back into the classroom.

## Establish a Study Space

Pick an area on campus or in your house that you visit only when it's time to buckle down and study for class or the USMLE. Used regularly for just this purpose, that space will actually help you focus and get down to business each time you visit it.

## Preview for Upcoming Lecture Topics

USMLE review books can help create a mental framework so that you'll get more out of hearing your class lectures.

## Prep Your Life So It Doesn't Get in the Way of School

Be sure to settle in before classes begin so the process won't intrude on needed study time. Here are some tasks that you should plan to complete before your first day of classes:

- Scout out grocery stores, ATMs, gas stations, laundry/dry cleaning stores convenient to your school and housing.
- Establish banking, utilities, internet, and/or other services that you'll need.
- Finalize housing arrangements and set up your living space.
- Reach out to students ahead of you for advice.
- Reach out to classmates to form study partners.
- Begin building a support network.
- Understand your school's curriculum design:
  Traditional (by subject)
  Organ System or Problem-based
  Mix of both

Congratulations on your successes so far, and good luck with medical school! For more information on **Kaplan Medical** products and services, go to **kaplanmedical.com**